A CENTURY OF DISHONOR

A CENTURY OF DISHONOR

A SKETCH

OF THE UNITED STATES GOVERNMENT'S DEALINGS

WITH SOME OF THE INDIAN TRIBES

Helen Jackson

INDIAN HEAD BOOKS

New York

This edition published by Indian Head Books,
a division of Barnes & Noble, Inc.

1994 Indian Head Books

ISBN 1-56619-167-X *casebound*
ISBN 1-56619-809-7 *paperback*

Printed and bound in the United States of America

MC 9 8 7 6 5 4
MP 9 8 7 6 5 4 3 2 1

CONTENTS.

CONTENTS.

CHAPTER IX.

CHAPTER X.

APPENDIX.

PREFACE.

I HAVE been requested to write a preface to this sad story of
"A Century of Dishonor." I cannot refuse the request of one
whose woman's heart has pleaded so eloquently for the poor Red
men. The materials for her book have been taken from official
documents. The sad revelation of broken faith, of violated treaties, and of inhuman deeds of violence will bring a flush of shame
to the cheeks of those who love their country. They will wonder
how our rulers have dared to so trifle with justice, and provoke
the anger of God. Many of the stories will be new to the reader.
The Indian owns no telegraph, employs no press reporter, and his
side of the story is unknown to the people.

Nations, like individuals, reap exactly what they sow; they
who sow robbery reap robbery. The seed-sowing of iniquity replies in a harvest of blood. The American people have accepted
as truth the teaching that the Indians were a degraded, brutal
race of savages, whom it was the will of God should perish at
the approach of civilization. If they do not say with our Puri-
tan fathers that these are the Hittites who are to be driven out
before the saints of the Lord, they do accept the teaching that
manifest destiny will drive the Indians from the earth. The inexorable has no tears or pity at the cries of anguish of the doom-
ed race. Ahab never speaks kindly of Naboth, whom he has
robbed of his vineyard. It soothes conscience to cast mud on the
character of the one whom we have wronged.

The people have laid the causes of Indian wars at the door of
the Indian trader, the people on the border, the Indian agents,
the army, and the Department of the Interior. None of these are
responsible for the Indian wars, which have cost the United States
five hundred millions of dollars and tens of thousands of valuable lives. In the olden time the Indian trader was the Indian's
friend. The relation was one of mutual dependence. If the
trader oppressed the Indian he was in danger of losing his debt;

if the Indian refused to pay his debts, the trader must leave the country. The factors and agents of the old fur companies tell us that their goods were as safe in the unguarded trading-post as in the civilized village. The pioneer settlers have had too much at stake to excite an Indian massacre, which would overwhelm their loved ones in ruin. The army are not responsible for Indian wars; they are "men under authority," who go where they are sent. The men who represent the honor of the nation have a tradition that lying is a disgrace, and that theft forfeits character. General Crook expressed the feeling of the army when he replied to a friend who said, "It is hard to go on such a campaign." "Yes, it is hard; but, sir, the hardest thing is to go and fight those whom you know are in the right." The Indian Bureau is often unable to fulfil the treaties, because Congress has failed to make the appropriations. If its agents are not men of the highest character, it is largely due to the fact that we send a man to execute this difficult trust at a remote agency, and expect him to support himself and family on $1500 a year. The Indian Bureau represents a system which is a blunder and a crime.

The Indian is the only human being within our territory who has no individual right in the soil. He is not amenable to or protected by law. The executive, the legislative, and judicial departments of the Government recognize that he has a possessory right in the soil; but his title is merged in the tribe—the man has no standing before the law. A Chinese or a Hottentot would have, but the native American is left pitiably helpless. This system grew out of our relations at the first settlement of the country. The isolated settlements along the Atlantic coast could not ask the Indians, who outnumbered them ten to one, to accept the position of wards. No wise policy was adopted, with altered circumstances, to train the Indians for citizenship. Treaties were made of the same binding force of the constitution; but these treaties were unfilled. It may be doubted whether one single treaty has ever been fulfilled as it would have been if it had been made with a foreign power. The treaty has been made as between two independent sovereigns. Sometimes each party has been ignorant of the wishes of the other; for the heads of both parties to the treaty have been on the interpreter's shoulders, and he was the owned creature of corrupt men, who desired to use the Indians as a key to unlock the nation's treasury. Pledges, solemnly made, have been shamelessly violated. The Indian has had no redress but war. In these wars ten white men were killed to one Indian, and the Indians who were killed have cost the Government a hundred thousand dollars each. Then came a new treaty, more violated faith, another war, until we have not a hundred miles between the Atlantic and Pacific which has not been the scene of an Indian massacre.

All this while Canada has had no Indian wars. Our Government has expended for the Indians a hundred dollars to their one. They recognize, as we do, that the Indian has a possessory right to the soil. They purchase this right, as we do, by treaty; but their treaties are made with *the Indian subjects* of Her Majesty. They set apart a *permanent* reservation for them; they seldom remove Indians; they select agents of high character, who receive their appointments for life; they make fewer promises, but they fulfil them; they give the Indians Christian missions, which have the hearty support of Christian people, and all their efforts are toward self-help and civilization. An incident will illustrate the two systems. The officer of the United States Army who was sent to receive Alaska from the Russian Government stopped in British Columbia. Governor Douglas had heard that an Indian had been murdered by another Indian. He visited the Indian tribe; he explained to them that the murdered man was a subject of Her Majesty; he demanded the culprit. The murderer was surrendered, was tried, was found guilty, and was hanged. On reaching Alaska the officer happened to enter the Greek church, and saw on the altar a beautiful copy of the Gospels in a costly binding studded with jewels. He called upon the Greek bishop, and said, "Your Grace, I called to say you had better remove that copy of the Gospels from the church, for it may be stolen." The bishop replied, "Why should I remove it? It was the gift of the mother of the emperor, and has lain on the altar seventy years." The officer blushed, and said, "There is no law in the Indian country, and I was afraid it might be stolen." The bishop said, "The book is in God's house, and it is His book, and I shall not take it away." The book remained. The country became ours, and the next day the Gospel was stolen.

Our Indian wars are needless and wicked. The North American Indian is the noblest type of a heathen man on the earth. He recognizes a Great Spirit; he believes in immortality; he has a quick intellect; he is a clear thinker; he is brave and fearless, and, until betrayed, he is true to his plighted faith; he has a passionate love for his children, and counts it joy to die for his people. Our most terrible wars have been with the noblest types of the Indians, and with men who had been the white man's friend. Nicolet said the Sioux were the finest type of wild men he had ever seen. Old traders say that it used to be the boast of the Sioux that they had never taken the life of a white man. Lewis and Clarke, Governor Stevens, and Colonel Steptoe bore testimony to the devoted friendship of the Nez Percés for the white man. Colonel Boone, Colonel Bent, General Harney, and others speak in the highest praise of the Cheyennes. The Navahoes were a semi-civilized people.

Our best friends have suffered more deeply from our neglect and violated faith than our most bitter foes. Peaceable Indians often say, "You leave us to suffer; if we killed your people, then you would take care of us."

Our Indian wars have not come wholly from violated faith. In time of peace it has been our policy to establish "almshouses" to train and educate savage paupers. We have purchased paint, beads, scalping-knives, to deck warriors, and have fed them in idleness at the agency. Around this agency and along the border were gathered influences to degrade the savage, and sink him to a depth his fathers had never known. It has only needed a real or a fancied wrong to have this pauperized savagery break out in deeds of blood. Under President Grant a new departure was taken. The peace policy was little more than a name. No change was made in the Indian system; no rights of property were given; no laws were.passed to protect the Indians. The President did take the nomination of Indian agents from politicians, who had made the office a reward for political service. He gave the nomination of Indian agents to the executive committees of the missionary societies of the different churches. Where these Christian bodies established schools and missions, and the Government cast its influence on the side of labor, it was a success. More has been done to civilize the Indians in the past twelve years than in any period of our history. The Indian Ring has fought the new policy at every step; and yet, notwithstanding our Indian wars, our violated treaties, and our wretched system, thousands of Indians, who were poor, degraded savages, are now living as Christian, civilized men. There was a time when it seemed impossible to secure the attention of the Government to any wrongs done to the Indians: it is not so to-day. The Government does listen to the friends of the Indians, and many of the grosser forms of robbery are stopped. No permanent reform can be secured until the heart of the people is touched. In 1862

I visited Washington, to lay before the Administration the causes which had desolated our fair State with the blood of those slain by Indian massacre. After pleading in vain, and finding no redress, Secretary Stanton said to a friend, "What does the Bishop want? If he came here to tell us that our Indian system is a sink of iniquity, tell him we all know it. Tell him the United States never cures a wrong until the people demand it; and when the hearts of the people are reached the Indian will be saved." In this book the reader will find the sad story of a century—no, not the whole story, but the fragmentary story of isolated tribes. The author will have her reward if it shall aid in securing justice to a noble and a wronged race. Even with the sad experiences of the past we have not learned justice. The Cherokees and other tribes received the Indian Territory as a compensation and atonement for one of the darkest crimes ever committed by a Christian nation. That territory was conveyed to them by legislation as strong as the wit of statesmen could devise. The fathers who conveyed this territory to the Cherokees are dead. Greedy eyes covet the land. The plans are laid to wrest it from its rightful owners. If this great iniquity is consummated, these Indians declare that all hope in our justice will die out of their hearts, and that they will defend their country with their lives.

The work of reform is a difficult one; it will cost us time, effort, and money; it will demand the best thoughts of the best men in the country. We shall have to regain the confidence of our Indian wards by honest dealing and the fulfilment of our promises. Now the name of a white man is to the Indians a synonyme for "liar." Red Cloud recently paid a visit to the Black Hills, and was hospitably entertained by his white friends. In bidding them good-bye he expressed the hope that, if they did not meet again on earth, they might meet beyond the grave "in a land where white men ceased to be liars."

Dark as the history is, there is a brighter side. No missions to the heathen have been more blessed than those among the Indians. Thousands, who were once wild, painted savages, finding their greatest joy in deeds of war, are now the disciples of the Prince of Peace. There are Indian churches with Indian congregations, in which Indian clergy are telling the story of God's love in Jesus Christ our Saviour. Where once was only heard the medicine-drum and the song of the scalp-dance, there is now the bell calling Christians to prayer, and songs of praise and words of prayer go up to heaven. The Christian home, though only a log-cabin, has taken the place of the wigwam; and the poor, de-graded Indian woman has been changed to the Christian wife and mother.   With justice, personal rights, and the protection of law, the Gospel will do for our Red brothers what it has done for other races—give to them homes, manhood and freedom.

H. B. WHIPPLE, *Bishop of Minnesota.*

NEW YORK, *November 11th,* 1880.

INTRODUCTION.

THE present number of Indians in the United States does not exceed three hundred thousand, but is possibly as large now as when the Europeans began the settlement of the North American continent. Different tribes then existing have dwindled, and some have become extinct; but there is reason to believe that the vast territory now occupied by the United States, if not then a howling wilderness, was largely an unpeopled solitude. The roaming wild men who met the new discoverers were, however, numerous enough to make the Indian problem at the outset a serious one, while neither its gravity nor its difficulty yet shows signs of diminution.

The difficulty is not because the Indians are wild and savage men, for such men have in the past history of the human race been subdued and civilized in unnumbered instances, while the changes which in our time have been wrought among the cannibals of the South Sea and the barbarians of South Africa, and among the wildest and most savage of the North American Indians themselves, show abundantly that the agencies of civilization ready to our hand are neither wanting nor weak.

The great difficulty with the Indian problem is not with the Indian, but with the Government and people of the United States. Instead of a liberal and far-sighted policy looking to the education and civilization and possible citizenship of the Indian tribes, we have suffered these people to remain as savages, for whose future we have had no adequate care, and to the consideration of whose present state the Government has only been moved when pressed by some present danger. We have encroached upon their means of subsistence without furnishing them any proper return; we have shut them up on reservations often notoriously unfit for them, or, if fit, we have not hesitated to drive them off for our profit, without regard to theirs; we have treated them sometimes as foreign nations, with whom we have had treaties; sometimes as wards, who are entitled to no voice in the management of their affairs; and sometimes as subjects, from whom we have required obedience, but to whom we have recognized no obligations. That the Government of the United States, which has often plighted its faith to the Indian, and has broken it as often, and, while punishing him for his crimes, has given him no status in the courts except as a criminal, has been sadly derelict in its duty toward him, and has reaped the whirlwind only because it has sown the wind, is set forth in no exaggerated terms in the following pages, and ought to be acknowledged with shame by every American citizen.

It will be admitted now on every hand that the only solution of the Indian problem involves the entire change of these people from a savage to a civilized life. They are not likely to be exterminated. Unless we ourselves withdraw from all contact with them, and leave them to roam untrammeled over their wilds, or until the power of a Christian civilization shall make them consciously one with us, they will not cease to vex us.

But how shall they become civilized? Civilization is in a most important sense a gift rather than an acquisition. Men do not gain it for themselves, except as stimulated thereto by some incitement from above themselves. The savage does not labor for the gratifications of civilized life, since he does not desire these. His labors and his desires are both dependent upon some spiritual gift, which, having kindled him, quickens his desires and calls forth his toil. Unless he has some help from without, some light and life from above to illumine and inspire him, the savage remains a savage, and without this all the blandishments of the civilization with which he might be brought into contact could no more win him into a better state than could all the light and warmth of the sun woo a desert into a fruitful field. When English missionaries went to the Indians in Canada, they took with them skilled laborers who should teach the Indians how to labor, and who, by providing them at first with comfortable houses, and clothing, and food, should awaken their desires and evoke their efforts to perpetuate and increase these comforts. But the Indian would not work, and preferred his wigwam, and skins, and raw flesh, and filth to the cleanliness and conveniences of a civilized home; and it was only as Christian influences taught him his inner need, and how this could be supplied, that he was led to wish and work for the improvement of his outer condition and habits of life. The same is true everywhere. Civilization does not reproduce itself. It must first be kindled, and can then only be kept alive by a power genuinely Christian.

But it is idle to attempt to carry Christian influences to any one unless we are Christian. The first step, therefore, toward the desired transformation of the Indian is a transformed treatment of him by ourselves. In sober earnest, our Government needs, first of all, to be Christian, and to treat the Indian question as Christian principles require. This means at the outset that we should be honest, and not talk about maintaining our rights until we are willing to fulfil our obligations. It means that we should be kind, and quite as eager to give the Indian what is ours as to get what is his. It means that we should be wise, and patient, and persevering, abandoning all makeshifts and temporary expedients, and setting it before us as our fixed aim to act toward him as a brother, until he shall act as a brother toward us. There is no use to attempt to teach Christian duty to him in words till he has first seen it exemplified in our own deeds.

The true Christian principle of self-forgetful honesty and kindness, clearly and continuously exhibited, is the first requisite of true statesmanship in the treatment of the Indian question. This would not require, however, the immediate entrance of the Indian upon all the privileges of citizenship and self-direction. Christianized though he might be, he would need for a longer or shorter time guardianship like a child. A wise care for his own interests could not be expected of him at the outset, and the Government should care for him with wise forethought. Obedience to the law should be required of him, and the protection of the law afforded him. The jurisdiction of the courts and the presence of the Government should be felt in the Indian Territory and upon every Indian reservation as powerfully as in the most enlightened portions of the land. The court should go as early as the school, if not before, and is itself an educational agency of incalculable importance.

When the Indian, through wise and Christian treatment, becomes invested with all the rights and duties of citizenship, his special tribal relations will become extinct. This will not be easily nor rapidly done; but all our policy should be shaped toward the gradual loosening of the tribal bond, and the gradual absorption of the Indian families among the masses of our people. This would involve the bringing to an end of the whole system of Indian reservations, and would forbid the continued isolation of the Indian Territory. It is not wise statesmanship to create impassable barriers between any parts of our country or any portions of our people.

Very difficult questions demanding very careful treatment arise in reference to just this point. Certain Indian tribes now own certain Indian reservations and the Indian Territory, and this right of property ought to be most sacredly guarded. But it does not, therefore, follow that these Indians, in their present state, ought to control the present use of this property. They may need a long training before they are wise enough to manage rightfully what is nevertheless rightfully their own. This training, to which their property might fairly contribute means, should assiduously be given in established schools with required attendance.

If the results thus indicated shall gradually come to pass, the property now owned by the tribes should be ultimately divided and held in severalty by the individual members of the tribes. Such a division should not be immediately made, and, when made, it should be with great care and faithfulness; but the Indian himself should, as soon as may be, feel both the incentives and the restraints which an individual ownership of property is fitted to excite, and the Government, which is his guardian, having educated him for this ownership, should endow him with it. But until the Indian becomes as able as is the average white man to manage his property for himself, the Government should manage it for him, no matter whether he be willing or unwilling to have this done.

A difficulty arises in the cases—of which there are many—where treaties have been made by the Government of the United States with different Indian tribes, wherein the two parties have agreed to certain definitely named stipulations. Such treaties have proceeded upon the false view—false in principle, and equally false in fact—that an Indian tribe, roaming in the wilderness and living by hunting and plunder, is a nation. In order to be a nation, there must be a people with a code of laws which they practise, and a government which they maintain. No vague sense of some unwritten law, to which human nature, in its lowest stages, doubtless feels some obligation, and no regulations instinctively adopted for common defence, which the rudest people herded together will always follow, are enough to constitute a nation. These Indian tribes are not a nation, and nothing either in their history or their condition could properly invest them with a treaty-making power.

And yet when exigencies have seemed to require, we have treated them as nations, and have pledged our own national faith in solemn covenant with them. It were the baldest truism to say that this faith and covenant should be fulfilled. Of course it should be fulfilled. It is to our own unspeakable disgrace that we have so often failed therein. But it becomes us wisely and honestly to inquire whether the spirit of these agreements might not be falsified by their letter, and whether, in order to give the Indian his real rights, it may not be necessary to set aside prerogatives to which he might technically and formally lay claim. If the Indian Territory and the Indian reservations have been given to certain tribes as their possession forever, the sacredness of this guarantee should not shut our eyes to the sacredness also of the real interests of the people in whose behalf the guarantee was given. We ought not to lose the substance in our efforts to retain the shadow; we ought not to insist upon the *summum jus*, when this would become the *summa injuria*.

Of course the utmost caution is needed in the application of such a principle. To admit that a treaty with the Indians may be set aside without the consent of the Indians themselves, is to open the door again to the same frauds and falsehoods which have so darkly branded a " Century of Dishonor." But our great trouble has been that we have sought to exact justice from the Indian while exhibiting no justice to him; and when we shall manifest that all our procedure toward him is in truth and uprightness, we need have no fear but that both his conscience and his judgment will in the end approve.

JULIUS H. SEELYE.

AMHERST COLLEGE, *December* 10, 1880.

AUTHOR'S NOTE.

ALL the quotations in this book, where the name of the authority is not cited, are from Official Reports of the War Department or the Department of the Interior.

The book gives, as its title indicates, only a sketch, and not a history.

To write in full the history of any one of these Indian communities, of its forced migrations, wars, and miseries, would fill a volume by itself.

The history of the missionary labors of the different churches among the Indians would make another volume. It is the one bright spot on the dark record.

All this I have been forced to leave untouched, in strict adherence to my object, which has been simply to show our causes for national shame in the matter of our treatment of the Indians. It is a shame which the American nation ought not to lie under, for the American people, as a people, are not at heart unjust.

If there be one thing which they believe in more than any other, and mean that every man on this continent shall have, it is "fair play." And as soon as they fairly understand how cruelly it has been denied to the Indian, they will rise up and demand it for him.

H. H.

A CENTURY OF DISHONOR.

CHAPTER I.

THE question of the honorableness of the United States' dealings with the Indians turns largely on a much disputed and little understood point. What was the nature of the Indians' right to the country in which they were living when the continent of North America was discovered? Between the theory of some sentimentalists that the Indians were the real owners of the soil, and the theory of some politicians that they had no right of ownership whatever in it, there are innumerable grades and confusions of opinion. The only authority on the point must be the view and usage as accepted by the great discovering Powers at the time of discovery, and afterward in their disposition of the lands discovered.

Fortunately, an honest examination of these points leaves no doubt on the matter.

England, France, Spain, little Portugal—all quarrelling fiercely, and fighting with each other for the biggest share in the new continent—each claiming "sovereignty of the soil" by right of priority of discovery — all recognized the Indians' "right of occupancy" as a right; a right alienable in but two ways, either by purchase or by conquest.

All their discussions as to boundaries, from 1603 down to

1776, recognized this right and this principle. They reiterated, firstly, that discoverers had the right of sovereignty—a right in so far absolute that the discoverer was empowered by it not only to take possession of, but to grant, sell, and convey lands still occupied by Indians—and that for any nation to attempt to take possession of, grant, sell, or convey any such Indian-occupied lands while said lands were claimed by other nations under the right of discovery, was an infringement of rights, and just occasion of war; secondly, that all this granting, selling, conveying was to be understood to be "subject to the Indians' right of occupancy," which remained to be extinguished either through further purchase or through conquest by the grantee or purchaser.

Peters, in his preface to the seventh volume of the "United States Statutes at Large," says, "The history of America, from its discovery to the present day, proves the universal recognition of these principles."

Each discovering Power might regulate the relations between herself and the Indians; but as to the existence of the Indians' "right of occupancy," there was absolute unanimity among them. That there should have been unanimity regarding any one thing between them, is remarkable. It is impossible for us to realize what a sudden invitation to greed and discord lay in this fair, beautiful, unclaimed continent—eight millions of square miles of land—more than twice the size of all Europe itself. What a lure to-day would such another new continent prove! The fighting over it would be as fierce now as the fighting was then, and the "right of occupancy" of the natives would stand small chance of such unanimous recognition as the four Great Powers then justly gave it.

Of the fairness of holding that ultimate sovereignty belonged to the civilized discoverer, as against the savage barbarian, there is no manner nor ground of doubt. To question this is feeble sentimentalism. But to affirm and uphold this is not in any wise to overlook the lesser right which remained; as good, of its kind, and to its extent, as was the greater right to which, in the just nature of things, it was bound to give way.

It being clear, then, that the Indians' "right of occupancy" was a right recognized by all the great discovering Powers, acted upon by them in all their dispositions of lands here discovered, it remains next to inquire whether the United States Government, on taking its place among the nations, also recognized or accepted this Indian "right of occupancy" as an actual right. Upon this point, also, there is no doubt.

"By the treaty which concluded the War of our Revolution, Great Britain relinquished all claims not only to the government, but to the proprietary and territorial rights of the United States whose boundaries were fixed in the second Article. By this treaty the powers of the government and the right to soil which had previously been in Great Britain passed definitely to these States. We had before taken possession of them by declaring independence, but neither the declaration of independence nor the treaty confirming it could give us more than that which we before possessed, or to which Great Britain was before entitled. It has never been doubted that either the United States or the several States had a clear title to all the lands within the boundary-lines described in the treaty, subject only to the Indian right of occupancy, and that the exclusive right to extinguish that right was vested in that government which might constitutionally exercise it."*

"Subject to the Indian right of occupancy." It is noticeable how perpetually this phrase reappears. In their desire to define, assert, and enforce the greater right, the "right of sovereignty," the makers, interpreters, and recorders of law did not realize, probably, how clearly and equally they were defin-

---

* Peters, United States Statutes at Large, vol. vii.

ing, asserting, and enforcing the lesser right, the "right of occupancy."

Probably they did not so much as dream that a time would come when even this lesser right — this least of all rights, it would seem, which could be claimed by, or conceded to, an aboriginal inhabitant of a country, however savage—would be practically denied to our Indians. But if they had foreseen such a time, they could hardly have left more explicit testimony to meet the exigency.

"The United States have unequivocally acceded to that great and broad rule by which its civilized inhabitants now hold this country. They hold and assert in themselves the title by which it was acquired. They maintain, as all others have maintained, that discovery gave an exclusive right to extinguish the Indian title of occupancy, either by purchase or conquest, and gave also a right to such a degree of sovereignty as the circumstances of the people would allow them to exercise.

"The power now possessed by the United States to grant lands resided, while we were colonies, in the Crown or its grantees. The validity of the titles given by either has never been questioned in our courts. It has been exercised uniformly over territories in possession of the Indians. The existence of this power must negative the existence of any right which may conflict with and control it. An absolute title to lands cannot exist at the same time in different persons or in different governments. An absolute must be an exclusive title, or at least a title which excludes all others not compatible with it. All our institutions recognize the absolute title of the Crown, subject only to the Indian right of occupancy, and recognize the absolute title of the Crown to extinguish the right. This is incompatible with an absolute and complete title in the Indians."*

---

* Peters.

Certainly. But it is also "incompatible with an absolute and perfect title" in the white man! Here again, in their desire to define and enforce the greater right, by making it so clear that it included the lesser one, they equally define and enforce the lesser right as a thing to be included. The word "subject" is a strong participle when it is used legally. Provisions are made in wills, "subject to" a widow's right of dower, for instance, and the provisions cannot be carried out without the consent of the person to whom they are thus declared to be "subject." A title which is pronounced to be "subject to" anything or anybody cannot be said to be absolute till that subjection is removed.

There have been some definitions and limitations by high legal authority of the methods in which this Indian "right of occupancy" might be extinguished even by conquest.

"The title by conquest is acquired and maintained by force. The conqueror prescribes its limits. Humanity, however, acting on public opinion, has established as a general rule that the conquered shall not be wantonly oppressed, and that their condition shall remain as eligible as is compatible with the objects of the conquest. Usually they are incorporated with the victorious nation, and become subjects or citizens of the government with which they are connected. * * * When this incorporation is practicable. humanity demands, and a wise policy requires, that the rights of the conquered to property should remain unimpaired; that the new subjects should be governed as equitably as the old. * * * When the conquest is complete, and the conquered inhabitants can be blended with the conquerors, or safely governed as a distinct people, public opinion, which not even the conqueror can disregard, imposes these restraints upon him, and he cannot neglect them without injury to his fame, and hazard to his power."*

---

* Peters, United States Statutes at Large, vol. vii.

In the sadly famous case of the removal of the Cherokee tribe from Georgia, it is recorded as the opinion of our Supreme Court that "the Indians are acknowledged to have an unquestionable, and heretofore unquestioned, right to the lands they occupy until that right shall be extinguished by a voluntary cession to the Government." * * * "The Indian nations have always been considered as distinct independent political communities, retaining their original natural rights as the undisputed possessors of the soil, from time immemorial, with the single exception of that imposed by irresistible power, which excluded them from intercourse with any other European potentate than the first discoverer of the coast of the particular region claimed; and this was a restriction which those European potentates imposed on themselves as well as on the Indians. The very term 'nation,' so generally applied to them, means 'a people distinct from others.' The Constitution, by declaring treaties already made, as well as those to be made, to be the supreme law of the land, has adopted and sanctioned the previous treaties with the Indian nations, and consequently admits their rank among those powers who are capable of making treaties. The words 'treaty' and 'nation' are words of our own language, selected in our diplomatic and legislative proceedings by ourselves, having each a definite and well understood meaning. We have applied them to Indians as we have applied them to other nations of the earth. They are applied to all in the same sense."*

In another decision of the Supreme Court we find still greater emphasis put upon the Indian right of occupancy, by stating it as a right, the observance of which was stipulated for in treaties between the United States and other nations.

"When the United States acquired and took possession of the Floridas, the treaties which had been made with the Indian

---

* Worcester *vs.* State of Georgia, 6 Peters, 515.

tribes before the acquisition of the territory by Spain and Great Britain remained in force over all the ceded territory, as the law which regulated the relations with all the Indians who were parties to them, and were binding on the United States by the obligation they had assumed by the Louisiana treaty as a supreme law of the land.

"The treaties with Spain and England before the acquisition of Florida by the United States, which guaranteed to the Seminole Indians their lands, according to the right of property with which they possessed them, were adopted by the United States, who thus became the protectors of all the rights they (the Indians) had previously enjoyed, or could of right enjoy, under Great Britain or Spain, as individuals or nations, by any treaty to which the United States thus became parties in 1803. * * *

"The Indian right to the lands as property was not merely of possession; that of alienation was concomitant; both were equally secured, protected, and guaranteed by Great Britain and Spain, subject only to ratification and confirmation by the license, charter, or deed from the government representing the king." * * *

The laws made it necessary, when the Indians sold their lands, to have the deeds presented to the governor for confirmation. The sales by the Indians transferred the kind of right which they possessed; the ratification of the sale by the governor must be regarded as a relinquishment of the title of the Crown to the purchaser, and no instance is known of refusal of permission to sell, or of the rejection of an Indian sale.*

"The colonial charters, a great portion of the individual grants by the proprietary and royal governments, and a still greater portion by the States of the Union after the Revolu-

---

* United States *vs.* Clark, 9 Peters, 168.

tion, were made for lands within the Indian hunting-grounds. North Carolina and Virginia, to a great extent, paid their officers and soldiers of the Revolutionary War by such grants, and extinguished the arrears due the army by similar means. It was one of the great resources which sustained the war, not only by those States but by other States. The ultimate fee, encumbered with the right of occupancy, was in the Crown previous to the Revolution, and in the States afterward, and subject to grant. This right of occupancy was protected by the political power, and respected by the courts until extinguished." * * * "So the Supreme Court and the State courts have uniformly held."*

President Adams, in his Message of 1828, thus describes the policy of the United States toward the Indians at that time:

"At the establishment of the Federal Government the principle was adopted of considering them as foreign and independent powers, and also as proprietors of lands. As independent powers, we negotiated with them by treaties; as proprietors, we purchased of them all the land which we could prevail on them to sell; as brethren of the human race, rude and ignorant, we endeavored to bring them to the knowledge of religion and letters."

Kent says: "The European nations which, respectively, established colonies in America, assumed the ultimate dominion to be in themselves, and claimed the exclusive right to grant a title to the soil, subject only to the Indian right of occupancy. The natives were admitted to be the rightful occupants of the soil, with a *legal* as well as just claim to retain possession of it, and to use it according to their own discretion, though not to dispose of the soil at their own will, except to the government claiming the right of pre-emption." * * * "The United States adopted the same principle; and their exclusive right to

---

* Clark *vs.* Smith, 13 Peters.

extinguish the Indian title by purchase or conquest, and to grant the soil and exercise such a degree of sovereignty as circumstances required, has never been judicially questioned."

Kent also says, after giving the Supreme Court decision in the case of Johnson *vs.* M'Intosh : "The same court has since been repeatedly called upon to discuss and decide great questions concerning Indian rights and title, and the subject has of late become exceedingly grave and momentous, affecting the faith and the character, if not the tranquillity and safety, of the Government of the United States."

In Gardner's "Institutes of International Law" the respective rights to land of the Indians and the whites are thus summed up : "In our Union the aborigines had only a possessory title, and in the original thirteen States each owned in fee, *subject to the Indian right,* all ungranted lands within their respective limits ; and beyond the States the residue of the ungranted lands were vested in fee in the United States, *subject to the Indian possessory* right, to the extent of the national limits."

Dr. Walker, in his "American Law," makes a still briefer summary : "The American doctrine on the subject of Indian title is briefly this : The Indians have no fee in the lands they occupy. The fee is in the Government. They cannot, of course, aliene them either to nations or individuals, the exclusive right of pre-emption being in the Government. Yet they have a qualified right of occupancy which can only be *extinguished by treaty, and upon fair compensation;* until which they are entitled to be protected in their possession."

"Abbott's Digest," one of the very latest authorities, reiterates the same principle : "The right of occupancy has been recognized in countless ways, among others by many decisions of courts and opinions of attorney-generals."

It being thus established that the Indian's "right of occupancy" in his lands was a right recognized by all the Great

Powers discovering this continent, and accepted by them as a right necessary to be extinguished either by purchase or conquest, and that the United States, as a nation, has also from the beginning recognized, accepted, and acted upon this theory, it is next in order to inquire whether the United States has dealt honorably or dishonorably by the Indians in this matter of their recognized "right of occupancy."

In regard to the actions of individuals there is rarely much room for discussion whether they be honorable or dishonorable, the standard of honor in men's conduct being, among the civilized, uniform, well understood, and undisputed. Stealing, for instance, is everywhere held to be dishonorable, as well as impolitic; lying, also, in all its forms; breaking of promises and betrayals of trust are scorned even among the most ignorant people. But when it comes to the discussion of the acts of nations, there seems to be less clearness of conception, less uniformity of standard of right and wrong, honor and dishonor. It is necessary, therefore, in charging a government or nation with dishonorable conduct, to show that its moral standard ought in nowise to differ from the moral standard of an individual; that what is cowardly, cruel, base in a man, is cowardly, cruel, base in a government or nation. To do this, it is only needful to look into the history of the accepted "Law of Nations," from the days of the Emperor Justinian until now.

The Roman jurisconsults employed as synonymous, says Wheaton, "the two expressions, 'jus gentium,' that law which is found among all the known nations of the earth, and 'jus naturale,' founded on the general nature of mankind; nevertheless, of these two forms of the same idea, the first ought to be considered as predominant, since it as well as the 'jus civile' was a positive law, the origin and development of which must be sought for in history."

Nations being simply, as Vattel defines them, "societies of

men united together," it is plain that, if there be such a thing as the "law of nature," which men as individuals are bound to obey, that law is also obligatory on the "societies" made up of men thus "united."

Hobbes divides the law of nature into that of man and that of States, saying, "The maxims of each of these laws are precisely the same; but as States, once established, assume personal properties, that which is termed the natural law when we speak of the duties of individuals is called the law of nations when applied to whole nations or States." The Emperor Justinian said, "The law of nations is common to the whole human race."

Grotius draws the distinction between the law of nature and the law of nations thus: "When several persons at different times and in various places maintain the same thing as certain, such coincidence of sentiment must be attributed to some general cause. Now, in the questions before us, that cause must necessarily be one or the other of these two—either a just consequence drawn from natural principles, or a universal consent; the former discovers to us the law of nature, and the latter the law of nations."

Vattel defines the "necessary law of nations" to be the "application of the law of nature to nations." He says: "It is 'necessary,' because nations are absolutely bound to observe it. This law contains the precepts prescribed by the law of nature to States, on whom that law is not less obligatory than on individuals; since States are composed of men, their resolutions are taken by men, and the law of nations is binding on all men, under whatever relation they act. This is the law which Grotius, and those who follow him, call the Internal Law of Nations, on account of its being obligatory on nations in the point of conscience."

Vattel says again: "Nations being composed of men naturally free and independent, and who before the establishment of civil societies lived together in the state of nature, nations or sovereign States are to be considered as so many free persons living together in the state of nature."

And again: "Since men are naturally equal, and a perfect equality prevails in their right and obligations as equally proceeding from nature, nations composed of men, and considered as so many free persons living together in the state of nature, are naturally equal, and inherit from nature the same obligations and rights. Power or weakness does not in this respect produce any difference. A dwarf is as much a man as a giant; a small republic no less a sovereign State than the most powerful kingdom."

In these two last sentences is touched the key-note of the true law of nations, as well as of the true law for individuals—justice. There is among some of the later writers on jurisprudence a certain fashion of condescending speech in their quotations from Vattel. As years have gone on, and States have grown more powerful, and their relations more complicated by reason of selfishness and riches, less and less has been said about the law of nature as a component and unalterable part of the law of nations. Fine subtleties of definition, of limitation have been attempted. Hundreds of pages are full of apparently learned discriminations between the parts of that law which are based on the law of nature and the parts which are based on the consent and usage of nations. But the two cannot be separated. No amount of legality of phrase can do away with the inalienable truth underlying it. Wheaton and President Woolsey to-day say, in effect, the same thing which Grotius said in 1615, and Vattel in 1758.

Says Wheaton: "International law, as understood among civilized nations, may be defined as consisting of those rules of conduct which reason deduces as consonant to justice from the nature of the society existing among independent nations."

President Woolsey says: "International law, in a wide and

abstract sense, would embrace those rules of intercourse between nations which are deduced from their rights and moral claims; or, in other words, it is the expression of the jural and moral relations of States to one another.

"If international law were not made up of rules for which reasons could be given satisfactory to man's intellectual and moral nature, if it were not built on principles of right, it would be even less of a science than is the code which governs the actions of polite society."

It is evident, therefore, that the one fundamental right, of which the "law of nations" is at once the expression and the guardian, is the right of every nation to just treatment from other nations, the right of even the smallest republic equally with "the most powerful kingdom." Just as the one fundamental right, of which civil law is the expression and guardian, is the right of each individual to just treatment from every other individual: a right indefeasible, inalienable, in nowise lessened by weakness or strengthened by power—as majestic in the person of "the dwarf" as in that of "the giant."

Of justice, Vattel says: "Justice is the basis of all society, the sure bond of all commerce. * * *

"All nations are under a strict obligation to cultivate justice toward each other, to observe it scrupulously and carefully, to abstain from anything that may violate it. * * *

"The right of refusing to submit to injustice, of resisting injustice by force if necessary, is part of the law of nature, and as such recognized by the law of nations.

"In vain would Nature give us a right to refuse submitting to injustice, in vain would she oblige others to be just in their dealings with us, if we could not lawfully make use of force when they refused to discharge this duty. The just would lie at the mercy of avarice and injustice, and all their rights would soon become useless. From the foregoing right arise, as two distinct branches, first, the right of a just defence, which belongs to every nation, or the right of making war against whoever attacks her and her rights; and this is the foundation of defensive war. Secondly, the right to obtain justice by force, if we cannot obtain it otherwise, or to pursue our right by force of arms. This is the foundation of offensive war."

Justice is pledged by men to each other by means of promises or contracts; what promises and contracts are between men, treaties are between nations.

President Woolsey says: "A contract is one of the highest acts of human free-will: it is the will binding itself in regard to the future, and surrendering its right to change a certain expressed intention, so that it becomes, morally and jurally, a wrong to act otherwise.

"National contracts are even more solemn and sacred than private ones, on account of the great interests involved; of the deliberateness with which the obligations are assumed; of the permanence and generality of the obligations, measured by the national life, and including thousands of particular cases; and of each nation's calling, under God, to be a teacher of right to all, within and without its borders."

Vattel says: "It is a settled point in natural law that he who has made a promise to any one has conferred upon him a real right to require the thing promised; and, consequently, that the breach of a perfect promise is a violation of another person's right, and as evidently an act of injustice as it would be to rob a man of his property. * * *

"There would no longer be any security, no longer any commerce between mankind, if they did not think themselves obliged to keep faith with each other, and to perform their promises."

It is evident that the whole weight of the recognized and accepted law of nations is thrown on the side of justice between nation and nation, and is the recognized and accepted standard of the obligation involved in compacts between nation and nation.

We must look, then, among the accepted declarations of the law of nations for the just and incontrovertible measure of the shame of breaking national compacts, and of the wickedness of the nations that dare to do it.

We shall go back to the earliest days of the world, and find no dissent from, no qualification of the verdict of the infamy of such acts. Livy says of leagues: "Leagues are such agreements as are made by the command of the supreme power, and whereby the whole nation is made liable to the wrath of God if they infringe it."

Grotius opens his "Admonition," in conclusion of the third book of his famous "Rights of War and Peace," as follows: "'For it is by faith,' saith Cicero, 'that not commonwealths only, but that grand society of nations is maintained.' 'Take away this,' saith Aristotle, 'and all human commerce fails.' It is, therefore, an execrable thing to break faith on which so many lives depend. 'It is,' saith Seneca, 'the best ornament wherewith God hath beautified the rational soul; the strongest support of human society, which ought so much the more inviolably to be kept by sovereign princes by how much they may sin with greater license and impunity than other men. Wherefore take away faith, and men are more fierce and cruel than savage beasts, whose rage all men do horribly dread. Justice, indeed, in all other of her parts hath something that is obscure; but that whereunto we engage our faith is of itself clear and evident; yea, and to this very end do men pawn their faith, that in their negotiations one with another all doubts may be taken away, and every scruple removed. How much more, then, doth it concern kings to keep their faith inviolate, as well for conscience' sake as in regard to their honor and reputation, wherein consists the authority of a kingdom.'"

Vattel says: "Treaties are no better than empty words, if nations do not consider them as respectable engagements, as rules which are to be inviolably observed by sovereigns, and held sacred throughout the whole earth.

"The faith of treaties—that firm and sincere resolution, that invariable constancy in fulfilling our engagements, of which we make profession in a treaty—is therefore to be held sacred and inviolable between the nations of the earth, whose safety and repose it secures; and if mankind be not wilfully deficient in their duty to themselves, infamy must ever be the portion of him who violates his faith. * * *

"He who violates his treaties, violates at the same time the law of nations, for he disregards the faith of treaties, that faith which the law of nations declares sacred; and, so far as dependent on him, he renders it vain and ineffectual. Doubly guilty, he does an injury to his ally, and he does an injury to all nations, and inflicts a wound on the great society of mankind. * * *

"On the observance and execution of treaties," said a respectable sovereign, "depends all the security which princes and States have with respect to each other, and no dependence could henceforward be placed in future conventions if the existing ones were not to be observed."

It is sometimes said, by those seeking to defend, or at least palliate, the United States Government's repeated disregard of its treaties with the Indians, that no Congress can be held responsible for the acts of the Congress preceding it, or can bind the Congress following it; or, in other words, that each Congress may, if it chooses, undo all that has been done by previous Congresses. However true this may be of some legislative acts, it is clearly not true, according to the principles of international law, of treaties.

On this point Vattel says: "Since public treaties, even those of a personal nature, concluded by a king, or by another sovereign who is invested with sufficient power, are treaties of State, and obligatory on the whole nation, real treaties, which were intended to subsist independently of the person who has concluded them, are undoubtedly binding on his successors; and the obligation which such treaties impose on the State passes successively to all her rulers as soon as they assume the public authority. The case is the same with respect to the rights acquired by those treaties. They are acquired for the State, and successively pass to her conductors."

Von Martens says: "Treaties, properly so called, are either personal or real. They are personal when their continuation in force depends on the person of the sovereign or his family, with whom they have been contracted. They are real when their duration depends on the State, independently of the person who contracts. Consequently, all treaties between republics must be real. All treaties made for a time specified or forever are real. * * *

"This division is of the greatest importance, because real treaties never cease to be obligatory, except in cases where all treaties become invalid. Every successor to the sovereignty, in virtue of whatever title he may succeed, is obliged to observe them without their being renewed at his accession."

Wheaton says: "They (treaties) continue to bind the State, whatever intervening changes may take place in its internal constitution or in the persons of its rulers. The State continues the same, notwithstanding such change, and consequently the treaty relating to national objects remains in force so long as the nation exists as an independent State."

There is no disagreement among authorities on this point. It is also said by some, seeking to defend or palliate the United States Government's continuous violations of its treaties with the Indians, that the practice of all nations has been and is to abrogate a treaty whenever it saw good reason for doing so. This is true; but the treaties have been done away with in one of two ways, either by a mutual and peaceful agreement to that effect between the parties who had made it—the treaty being considered in force until the consent of both parties to its abrogation had been given—or by a distinct avowal on the part of one nation of its intention no longer to abide by it, and to take, therefore, its chances of being made war upon in consequence. Neither of these courses has been pursued by the United States Government in its treaty-breaking with the Indians.

Vattel says, on the dissolution of treaties: "Treaties may be dissolved by mutual consent at the free-will of the contracting powers."

Grotius says: "If either party violate the League, the other party is freed; because each Article of the League hath the form and virtue of a condition."

Kent says: "The violation of any one article of a treaty is a violation of the whole treaty. * * *

"It is a principle of universal jurisprudence that a compact cannot be rescinded by one party only, if the other party does not consent to rescind it, and does no act to destroy it. * * *

"To recommence a war by breach of the articles of peace, is deemed much more odious than to provoke a war by some new demand or aggression; for the latter is simply injustice, but in the former case the party is guilty both of perfidy and injustice."

It is also said, with unanswerable irrelevancy, by some who seek to defend or palliate the United States Government's continuous violation of its treaties with the Indians, that it was, in the first place, absurd to make treaties with them at all, to consider them in any sense as treaty-making powers or nations. The logic of this assertion, made as a justification for the breaking of several hundred treaties, concluded at different times during the last hundred years, and broken as fast as concluded, seems almost equal to that of the celebrated defence in the case of the kettle, which was cracked when it was lent, whole when returned, and, in fact, was never borrowed at all. It would be a waste of words to reason with minds that can see in this position any shelter for the United States Government against the accusation of perfidy in its treaty relations with the Indians.

The statement is undoubtedly a true one, that the Indians, having been placed in the anomalous position as tribes, of "domestic dependent nations," and as individuals, in the still more anomalous position of adult "wards," have not legally possessed the treaty-making power. Our right to put them, or to consider them to be in those anomalous positions, might be successfully disputed; but they, helpless, having accepted such positions, did, no doubt, thereby lose their right to be treated with as nations. Nevertheless, that is neither here nor there now : as soon as our Government was established, it proceeded to treat with them as nations by name and designation, and with precisely the same forms and ratifications that it used in treating with other nations; and it continued to treat with them as nations by name and designation, and with continually increasing solemnity of asseveration of good intent and good faith, for nearly a century. The robbery, the cruelty which were done under the cloak of this hundred years of treaty-making and treaty-breaking, are greater than can be told. Neither mountains nor deserts stayed them; it took two seas to set their bounds.

In 1871, Congress, either ashamed of making treaties only to break them, or grudging the time, money, and paper it wasted, passed an act to the effect that no Indian tribe should hereafter be considered as a foreign nation with whom the United States might contract by treaty. There seems to have been at the time, in the minds of the men who passed this act, a certain shadowy sense of some obligation being involved in treaties; for they added to the act a proviso that it should not be construed as invalidating any treaties already made. But this sense of obligation must have been as short-lived as shadowy, and could have had no element of shame in it, since they forthwith proceeded, unabashed, to negotiate still more treaties with Indians, and break them; for instance, the so-called "Brunot Treaty" with the Ute Indians in Colorado, and one with the Crow Indians in Montana—both made in the summer of 1873. They were called at the time "conventions" or "agreements," and not "treaties;" but the difference is only in name.

They stated, in a succession of numbered articles, promises of payment of moneys, and surrenders and cessions of land, by both parties; were to be ratified by Congress before taking effect; and were understood by the Indians agreeing to them to be as binding as if they had been called treaties. The fact that no man's sense of justice openly revolted against such subterfuges, under the name of agreements, is only to be explained by the deterioration of the sense of honor in the nation. In the days of Grotius there were men who failed to see dishonor in a trick if profit came of it, and of such he wrote in words whose truth might sting to-day as, no doubt, it stung then :

"Whereas there are many that think it superfluous to require that justice from a free people or their governors which they exact daily from private men, the ground of this error is this: because these men respect nothing in the law but the profit that ariseth from it, which in private persons, being single and unable to defend themselves, is plain and evident; but for great cities, that seem to have within themselves all things necessary for their own well-being, it doth not so plainly appear that they have any need of that virtue called justice which respects strangers."

These extracts from unquestioned authorities on international law prove that we may hold nations to standards of justice and good faith as we hold men; that the standards are the same in each case; and that a nation that steals and lies and breaks promises, will no more be respected or unpunished than a man who steals and lies and breaks promises. It is possible to go still farther than this, and to show that a nation habitually guilty of such conduct might properly be dealt with therefor by other nations, by nations in nowise suffering on account of her bad faith, except as all nations suffer when the interests of human society are injured.

"The interest of human society," says Vattel, "would authorize all the other nations to form a confederacy, in order to humble and chastise the delinquent." * * * When a nation "regards no right as sacred, the safety of the human race requires that she should be repressed. To form and support an unjust pretension is not only doing an injury to the party whose interests are affected by that pretension; but to despise justice in general is doing an injury to all nations."

The history of the United States Government's repeated violations of faith with the Indians thus convicts us, as a nation, not only of having outraged the principles of justice, which are the basis of international law; and of having laid ourselves open to the accusation of both cruelty and perfidy; but of having made ourselves liable to all punishments which follow upon such sins—to arbitrary punishment at the hands of any civilized nation who might see fit to call us to account, and to that more certain natural punishment which, sooner or later, as surely comes from evil-doing as harvests come from sown seed.

To prove all this it is only necessary to study the history of any one of the Indian tribes. I propose to give in the following chapters merely outline sketches of the history of a few of them, not entering more into details than is necessary to show the repeated broken faith of the United States Government toward them. A full history of the wrongs they have suffered at the hands of the authorities, military and civil, and also of the citizens of this country, it would take years to write and volumes to hold.

There is but one hope of righting this wrong. It lies in appeal to the heart and the conscience of the American people. What the people demand, Congress will do. It has been—to our shame be it spoken—at the demand of part of the people that all these wrongs have been committed, these treaties broken, these robberies done, by the Government.

So long as there remains on our frontier one square mile of land occupied by a weak and helpless owner, there will be a strong and unscrupulous frontiersman ready to seize it, and a weak and unscrupulous politician, who can be hired for a vote or for money, to back him.

The only thing that can stay this is a mighty outspoken sentiment and purpose of the great body of the people. Right sentiment and right purpose in a Senator here and there, and a Representative here and there, are little more than straws which make momentary eddies, but do not obstruct the tide. The precedents of a century's unhindered and profitable robbery have mounted up into a very Gibraltar of defence and shelter to those who care for nothing but safety and gain. That such precedents should be held, and openly avowed as standards, is only one more infamy added to the list. Were such logic employed in the case of an individual man, how quick would all men see its enormity. Suppose that a man had had the misfortune to be born into a family whose name had been blackened by generations of criminals; that his father, his grandfather, and his great-grandfather before them had lived in prisons, and died on scaffolds, should that man say in his soul, "Go to! What is the use? I also will commit robbery and murder, and get the same gain by it which my family must have done?" Or shall he say in his soul, "God help me! I will do what may be within the power of one man, and the compass of one generation, to atone for the wickedness, and to make clean the name of my dishonored house!"

What an opportunity for the Congress of 1880 to cover itself with a lustre of glory, as the first to cut short our nation's record of cruelties and perjuries! the first to attempt to redeem the name of the United States from the stain of a century of dishonor!

CHAPTER II.

WHEN Hendrik Hudson anchored his ship, the *Half Moon*, off New York Island in 1609, the Delawares stood in great numbers on the shore to receive him, exclaiming, in their innocence, " Behold ! the gods have come to visit us !"

More than a hundred years later, the traditions of this event were still current in the tribe.   The aged Moravian missionary, Heckewelder, writing in 1818, says :

" I at one time, in April, 1787, was astonished when I heard one of their orators, a great chief of the Delawares, Pachgants-chilias by name, go over this ground, recapitulating the most extraordinary events which had before happened, and concluding in these words: ' I admit that there are good white men, but they bear no proportion to the bad; the bad must be the strongest, for they rule.   They do what they please.   They enslave those who are not of their color, although created by the same Great Spirit who created them.   They would make slaves of us if they could; but as they cannot do it, they kill us.   There is no faith to be placed in their words.   They are not like the Indians, who are only enemies while at war, and are friends in peace.   They will say to an Indian, " My friend; my brother !"   They will take him by the hand, and, at the same moment, destroy him.   And so you ' (he was addressing himself to the Christian Indians at Gnadenbütten, Pennsylvania) ' will also be treated by them before long.   Remember that this day I have warned you to beware of such friends as these. I know the Long-knives. They are not to be trusted.'"

The original name of the Delawares was Lenni Lenape, or "original people." They were also called by the Western tribes Wapenachki, "people at the rising of the sun." When the name "Delawares" was given to them by the whites, they at first resented it; but being told that they, and also one of their rivers, were thus named after a great English brave—Lord De la Warre—they were much pleased, and willingly took the name. Their lands stretched from the Hudson River to the Potomac. They were a noble-spirited but gentle people; much under the control of the arrogant and all-powerful Iroquois, who had put upon them the degradation of being called "women," and being forced to make war or give up land at the pleasure of their masters.

During William Penn's humane administration of the affairs of Pennsylvania, the Delawares were his most devoted friends. They called him Mignon, or Elder Brother.

"From his first arrival in their country," says Heckewelder, "a friendship was formed between them, which was to last as long as the sun should shine, and the rivers flow with water. That friendship would undoubtedly have continued to the end of time, had their good brother always remained among them."

In the French and Indian war of 1755 many of them fought on the side of the French against the English; and in the beginning of our Revolutionary war the majority of them sided with the English against us.

Most of the memorable Indian massacres which happened during this period were the result of either French or English influence. Neither nation was high-minded enough to scorn availing herself of savage allies to do bloody work which she would not have dared to risk national reputation by doing herself. This fact is too much overlooked in the habitual esti-

mates of the barbarous ferocity of the Indian character as
shown by those early massacres.*

The United States' first treaty with the Delawares was made
in 1778, at Fort Pitt. The parties to it were said to be "the
United States and the Delaware Nation." It stipulates that there
shall be peace, and that the troops of the United States may pass
"through the country of the Delaware Nation," upon paying the
full value of any supplies they may use. It further says that,
"Whereas the enemies of the United States have endeavored
by every artifice to possess the Indians with an opinion that
it is our design to extirpate them, and take possession of their
country; to obviate such false suggestions, the United States
guarantee to said nation of Delawares, and their heirs, all their
territorial rights in the fullest and most ample manner as
bounded by former treaties."

The treaty also provides that, "should it for the future be
found conducive for the mutual interest of both parties to invite any other tribes who have been friends to the interests of
the United States to join the present confederation and form
a State, whereof the Delaware Nation shall be the head," it
shall be done; and the Delawares shall be entitled to send a
representative to Congress.†

The Delawares agreed to send all the warriors they could
spare to fight for us, and that there should be peace and perpetual friendship.

At this time the rest of the Ohio tribes, most of the New
York tribes, and a large part of the Delawares were in arms on
the British side. When the war of the Revolution was concluded, they were all forced to make peace as best they could
with us; and in our first treaty we provided for the reinstating
in the Delaware Nation of the chiefs and headmen who had

---

* See Appendix, Art. X.

† It is superfluous to say that these provisions were never carried out.

made that old alliance with us; they having lost caste in their tribe for having fought on our side.

"It is agreed," says the final Article of the treaty, "that the Delaware chiefs, Kelelamand, or Lieut.-colonel Henry, Henque Pushees, or the Big Cat, and Wicocalind, or Captain White Eyes, who took up the hatchet for the United States, and their families, shall be received into the Delaware Nation in the same situation and rank as before the war, and enjoy their due portions of the lands given to the Wyandotte and Delaware nations in this treaty, as fully as if they had not taken part with America, or as any other person or persons in the said nations."

This Captain White Eyes had adhered to our cause in spite of great opposition from the hostile part of the tribe. At one time he was threatened with a violent death if he should dare to say one word for the American cause; but by spirited harangues he succeeded in keeping the enthusiasm of his own party centred around himself, and finally carrying them over to the side of the United States. Some of his speeches are on record, and are worthy to be remembered:

"If you will go out in this war," he said to them at one time, when the band were inclined to join the British, "you shall not go without me. I have taken peace measures, it is true, with the view of saving my tribe from destruction; but if you think me in the wrong, if you give more credit to runaway vagabonds than to your own friends—to a man, to a warrior, to a Delaware—if you insist on fighting the Americans—go! and I will go with you. And I will not go like the bear-hunter, who sets his dogs on the animal to be beaten about with his paws, while he keeps himself at a safe distance. No; I will lead you on; I will place myself in the front; I will fall with the first of you! You can do as you choose; but as for me, I will not survive my nation. I will not live to bewail the miserable destruction of a brave people, who deserved, as you do, a better fate."

Were there many speeches made by commanders to their troops in those revolutionary days with which these words do not compare favorably?

This treaty, by which our faithful ally, Wicocalind, was reinstated in his tribal rank, was made at Fort M'Intosh in 1785. The Wyandottes, Chippewas, and Ottawas, as well as the Delawares, joined in it. They acknowledged themselves and all their tribes to be "under the protection of the United States, and of no other sovereign whatsoever." The United States Government reserved "the post of Detroit" and an outlying district around it; also, the post at Michilimackinac, with a surrounding district of twelve miles square, and some other reserves for trading-posts.

The Indians' lands were comprised within lines partly indicated by the Cuyahoga, Big Miami, and Ohio rivers and their branches; it fronted on Lake Erie; and if "any citizen of the United States," or "any other person not an Indian," attempted "to settle on any of the lands allotted to the Delaware and Wyandotte nations in this treaty"—the fifth Article of the treaty said—"the Indians may punish him as they please."

Michigan, Ohio, Indiana, Pennsylvania, all are largely made up of the lands which were by this first treaty given to the Indians.

Five years later, by another treaty at Fort Harmar, the provisions of this treaty were reiterated, the boundaries somewhat changed and more accurately defined. The privilege of hunting on all the lands reserved to the United States was promised to the Indians "without hinderance or molestation, so long as they behaved themselves peaceably;" and "that nothing may interrupt the peace and harmony now established between the United States and the aforesaid nations," it was promised in one of the articles that white men committing offences or murders on Indians should be punished in the same way as Indians committing such offences.

The year before this treaty Congress had resolved that "the sum of $20,000, in addition to the $14,000 already appropriated, be appropriated for defraying the expenses of the treaties which have been ordered, or which may be ordered to be held, in the present year, with the several Indian tribes in the Northern Department; and for extinguishing the Indian claims, the whole of the said $20,000, together with $6000 of the said $14,000, to be applied solely to the purpose of extinguishing Indian claims to the lands they have already ceded to the United States by obtaining regular conveyances for the same, and for extending a purchase beyond the limits hitherto fixed by treaty."

Here is one of the earliest records of the principle and method on which the United States Government first began its dealings with Indians. "Regular conveyances," "extinguishing claims" by "extending purchase." These are all the strictest of legal terms, and admit of no double interpretations.

The Indians had been much dissatisfied ever since the first treaties were made. They claimed that they had been made by a few only, representing a part of the tribe; and, in 1786, they had held a great council on the banks of the Detroit River, and sent a message to Congress, of which the following extracts will show the spirit.

They said: "It is now more than three years since peace was made between the King of Great Britain and you; but we, the Indians, were disappointed, finding ourselves not included in that peace according to our expectations, for we thought that its conclusion would have promoted a friendship between the United States and the Indians, and that we might enjoy that happiness that formerly subsisted between us and our Elder Brethren. We have received two very agreeable messages from the Thirteen United States. We also received a message from the king, whose war we were engaged in, de-

siring us to remain quiet, which we accordingly complied with.
During this time of tranquillity we were deliberating the best
method we could to form a lasting reconciliation with the Thirteen United States. * * * We are still of the same opinion
as to the means which may tend to reconcile us to each other;
and we are sorry to find, although we had the best thoughts
in our minds during the before-mentioned period, mischief has
nevertheless happened between you and us.   We are still anxious of putting our plan of accommodation into execution, and
we shall briefly inform you of the means that seem most probable to us of effecting a firm and lasting peace and reconciliation, the first step toward which should, in our opinion, be
that all treaties carried on with the United States on our parts
should be with the general will of the whole confederacy, and
carried on in the most open manner, without any restraint on
either side; and especially as landed matters are often the subject of our councils with you—a matter of the greatest importance and of general concern to us—in this case we hold it
indisputably necessary that any cession of our lands should be
made in the most public manner, and by the united voice of
the confederacy, holding all partial treaties as void and of no
effect. * * * We say, let us meet half-way, and let us pursue such steps as become upright and honest men.   We beg
that you will prevent your surveyors and other people from
coming upon our side of the Ohio River."

These are touching words, when we remember that only
the year before the United States had expressly told these Indians that if any white citizens attempted to settle on their
lands they might "punish them as they pleased."

"We have told you before we wished to pursue just steps,
and we are determined they shall appear just and reasonable in
the eyes of the world.   This is the determination of all the
chiefs of our confederacy now assembled here, notwithstanding
the accidents that have happened in our villages, even when in

council, where several innocent chiefs were killed when absolutely engaged in promoting a peace with you, the Thirteen United States."

The next year the President instructed the governor of the territory northwest of the Ohio to "examine carefully into the real temper of the Indian tribes" in his department, and says: "The treaties which have been made may be examined, but must not be departed from, unless a change of boundary beneficial to the United States can be obtained." He says also: "You will not neglect any opportunity that may offer of extinguishing the Indian rights to the westward, *as far as the Mississippi.*"

Beyond that river even the wildest dream of greed did not at that time look.

The President adds, moreover: "You may stipulate that any white persons going over the said boundaries without a license from the proper officers of the United States may be treated in such manner as the Indians may see fit."

I have not yet seen, in any accounts of the Indian hostilities on the North-western frontier during this period, any reference to those repeated permissions given by the United States to the Indians, to defend their lands as they saw fit. Probably the greater number of the pioneer settlers were as ignorant of these provisions in Indian treaties as are the greater number of American citizens to-day, who are honestly unaware—and being unaware, are therefore incredulous—that the Indians had either provocation or right to kill intruders on their lands.

At this time separate treaties were made with the Six Nations, and the governor says that these treaties were made separately because of the jealousy and hostility existing between them and the Delawares, Wyandottes, etc., which he is "not willing to lessen," because it weakens their power. "Indeed," he frankly adds, "it would not be very difficult, if circumstances required it, to set them at deadly variance."

Thus early in our history was the ingenious plan evolved of first maddening the Indians into war, and then falling upon them with exterminating punishment. The gentleman who has left on the official records of his country his claim to the first suggestion and recommendation of this method is "Arthur St. Clair, governor of the territory of the United States northwest of the Ohio River, and commissioner plenipotentiary of the United States of America for removing all causes of controversy, regulating trade, and settling boundaries with the Indian nations in the Northern Department."

Under all these conditions, it is not a matter of wonder that the frontier was a scene of perpetual devastation and bloodshed ; and that, year by year, there grew stronger in the minds of the whites a terror and hatred of Indians; and in the minds of the Indians a stronger and stronger distrust and hatred of the whites.

The Delawares were, through the earlier part of these troubled times, friendly. In 1791 we find the Secretary of War recommending the commissioners sent to treat with the hostile Miamis and Wabash Indians to stop by the way with the friendly Delawares, and take some of their leading chiefs with them as allies. He says, "these tribes are our friends," and, as far as is known, "the treaties have been well observed by them."

But in 1792 we find them mentioned among the hostile tribes to whom was sent a message from the United States Government, containing the following extraordinary paragraphs :

"Brethren: The President of the United States entertains the opinion that the war which exists is an error and mistake on your parts. That you believe the United States want to deprive you of your lands, and drive you out of the country. *Be assured that this is not so ;* on the contrary, that we should be greatly gratified with the opportunity of imparting to you all the blessings of civilized life; of teaching you to cultivate the earth, and raise corn; to raise oxen, sheep, and other domestic animals; to build comfortable houses; and to educate your children so as ever to dwell upon the land.

"Consult, therefore, upon the great object of peace; call in your parties, and enjoin a cessation of all further depredations; and as many of the principal chiefs as shall choose repair to Philadelphia, the seat of the Great Government, and there make a peace founded on the principles of justice and humanity. *Remember that no additional lands will be required of you, or any other tribe, to those that have been ceded by former treaties.*"

It was in this same year, also, that General Putnam said to them, in a speech at Post Vincennes: "The United States don't mean to wrong you out of your lands. They don't want to take away your lands by force. They want to do you justice." And the venerable missionary, Heckewelder, who had journeyed all the way from Bethlehem, Pennsylvania, to try to help bring about peace, said to them, "The great chief who has spoken to you is a good man. He loves you, and will always speak the truth to you. I wish you to listen to his words, and do as he desires you."

In 1793 a great council was held, to which came the chiefs and headmen of the Delawares, and of twelve other tribes, to meet commissioners of the United States, for one last effort to settle the vexed boundary question. The records of this council are profoundly touching. The Indians reiterated over and over the provisions of the old treaties which had established the Ohio River as one of their boundaries. Their words were not the words of ignorant barbarians, clumsily and doggedly holding to a point; they were the words of clear-headed, statesman-like rulers, insisting on the rights of their nations. As the days went on, and it became more and more clear that the United States commissioners would not agree to the establishment of the boundary for which the Indians contended, the speeches of the chiefs grow sadder and sadder. Finally, in desperation, as a last hope, they propose to the commissioners that all the money which the United States offers to pay to them for their lands shall be given to the white settlers to induce them to move away. They say:

"Money to us is of no value, and to most of us unknown; and as no consideration whatever can induce us to sell the lands on which we get sustenance for our women and children, we hope we may be allowed to point out a mode by which your settlers may be easily removed, and peace thereby obtained.

"We know that these settlers are poor, or they would never have ventured to live in a country which has been in continual trouble ever since they crossed the Ohio. Divide, therefore, this large sum of money which you have offered us among these people; give to each, also, a proportion of what you say you would give to us annually, over and above this very large sum of money, and we are persuaded they would most readily accept of it in lieu of the lands you sold them. If you add, also, the great sums you must expend in raising and paying armies with a view to force us to yield you our country, you will certainly have more than sufficient for the purpose of repaying these settlers for all their labor and their improvements.

"You have talked to us about concessions. It appears strange that you should expect any from us, who have only been defending our just rights against your invasions. We want peace. Restore to us our country, and we shall be enemies no longer.

" * * * We desire you to consider, brothers, that our only demand is the peaceable possession of a small part of our once great country. Look back and review the lands from whence we have been driven to this spot. We can retreat no farther, because the country behind hardly affords food for its present inhabitants, and we have therefore resolved to leave our bones in this small space to which we are now confined."

The commissioners replied that to make the Ohio River the boundary was now impossible; that they sincerely regretted that peace could not be made; but, "knowing the upright and liberal views of the United States," they trust that "impartial judges will not attribute the continuance of the war to them."

Notice was sent to the governor that the Indians "refused to make peace;" and General Anthony Wayne, a few weeks later, wrote to the Secretary of War, "The safety of the Western frontiers, the reputation of the legion, the dignity and interest of the nation—all forbid a retrograde manoeuvre, or giving up one inch of ground we now possess, till the enemy are compelled to sue for peace."

The history of the campaigns that followed is to be found in many volumes treating of the pioneer life of Ohio and other North-western States. One letter of General Wayne's to the Secretary of War, in August, 1794, contains a paragraph which is interesting, as showing the habits and method of life of the people whom we at this time, by force of arms, drove out from their homes—homes which we had only a few years before solemnly guaranteed to them, even giving them permission to punish any white intruders there as they saw fit. By a feint of approaching Grand Glaize through the Miami villages, General Wayne surprised the settlement, and the Indians, being warned by a deserter, had barely time to flee for their lives. What General Wayne had intended to do may be inferred from this sentence in his letter: "I have good grounds to conclude that the defection of this villain prevented the enemy from receiving a fatal blow at this place when least expected."

However, he consoles himself by the fact that he has "gained possession of the grand emporium of the hostile Indians of the West without loss of blood. The very extensive and highly cultivated fields and gardens show the work of many hands. The margins of those beautiful rivers—the Miamis, of the Lake, and Au Glaize—appear like one continued village for a number of miles, both above and below this place; nor have I ever before beheld such immense fields of corn in any part of America, from Canada to Florida."

All these villages were burnt, and all these cornfields destroyed; the Indians were followed up and defeated in a sharp fight. The British agents did their best to keep them hostile, and no inconsiderable aid was furnished to them from Canada. But after a winter of suffering and hunger, and great vacillations of purpose, they finally decided to yield to the inevitable, and in the summer of 1795 they are to be found once more assembled in council, for the purpose of making a treaty; once more to be told by the representatives of the United States Government that "the heart of General Washington, the Great Chief of America, wishes for nothing so much as peace and brotherly love;" that "such is the justice and liberality of the United States," that they will now a third time pay for lands; and that they are "acting the part of a tender father to them and their children in thus providing for them not only at present, but forever."

Eleven hundred and thirty Indians (eleven tribes, besides the Delawares, being represented) were parties to this treaty. By this treaty nearly two-thirds of the present State of Ohio were ceded to the United States; and, in consideration of these "cessions and relinquishments, and to manifest the liberality of the United States as the great means of rendering this peace strong and perpetual," the United States relinquished all claims "to all other Indian lands northward of the River Ohio, eastward of the Mississippi, and westward and southward of the Great Lakes and the waters uniting them, according to the boundary line agreed upon by the United States and the King of Great Britain, in the treaty of peace made between them in the year 1783," with the exception of four tracts of land. But it was stated to the Indians that these reservations were not made "to annoy or impose the smallest degree of restraint on them in the quiet enjoyment and full possession of their lands," but simply to "connect the settlements of the people of the United States," and "to prove convenient and advantageous to the different tribes of Indians residing and hunting in their vicinity."

The fifth Article of the treaty is: "To prevent any misunderstanding about the Indian lands now relinquished by the United States, it is explicitly declared that the meaning of that relinquishment is this: that the Indian tribes who have a right to those lands are quietly to enjoy them—hunting, planting, and dwelling thereon *so long as they please* without any molestation from the United States; but when those tribes, or any of them, shall be disposed to sell their lands, or any part of them, they are to be sold only to the United States; and until such sale the United States will protect all the said Indian tribes in the quiet enjoyment of their lands against all citizens of the United States, and against all other white persons who intrude on the same."

The sixth Article reiterates the old pledge, proved by the last three years to be so worthless—that, "If any citizen of the United States, or any other white person or persons, shall presume to settle upon the lands now relinquished by the United States, such citizen or other person shall be out of the protection of the United States; and the Indian tribe on whose land the settlement may be made may drive off the settler, or punish him in such manner as they shall think fit."

The seventh Article gives the Indians the liberty "to hunt within the territory and lands which they have now ceded to the United States, without hinderance or molestation, so long as they demean themselves peaceably."

The United States agreed to pay to the Indians twenty

thousand dollars' worth of goods at once; and " henceforward, every year, forever, useful goods to the value of nine thousand five hundred dollars." Peace was declared to be " established" and " perpetual."

General Wayne told the Indians that they might believe him, for he had never, " in a public capacity, told a lie;" and one of the Indians said, with much more dignity, " The Great Spirit above hears us, and I trust we shall not endeavor to deceive each other."

In 1813, by a treaty at Vincennes, the bounds of the reservation of the Post of St. Vincennes were defined, and the Indians, " as a mark of their regard and attachment to the United States, relinquished to the United States the great salt spring on the Saline Creek."

In less than a year we made still another treaty with them for the extinguishment of their title to a tract of land between the Ohio and the Wabash rivers (which they sold to us for a ten years' annuity of three hundred dollars, which was to be " exclusively appropriated to ameliorating their condition and promoting their civilization "); and in one year more still another treaty, in which a still further cession of land was made for a permanent annuity of one thousand dollars.

In August of this year General Harrison writes to the Secretary of War that there are great dissensions between the Delawares and Miamis in regard to some of the ceded lands, the Miamis claiming that they had never consented to give them up. General Harrison observes the most exact neutrality in this matter, but says, " A knowledge of the value of land is fast gaining ground among the Indians," and negotiations are becoming in consequence much more difficult. In the course of this controversy, " one of the chiefs has said that he knew a great part of the land was worth six dollars an acre."

It is only ten years since one of the chiefs of these same tribes had said, " Money is to us of no value." However, they must be yet very far from having reached any true estimate of real values, as General Harrison adds: "From the best calculation I have been able to make, the tract now ceded contains at least two millions of acres, and embraces some of the finest lands in the Western country."

Cheap at one thousand dollars a year!—even with the negro man thrown in, which General Harrison tells the Secretary he has ordered Captain Wells to purchase, and present to the chief, The Turtle, and to draw on the United States Treasury for the amount paid for him.

Four years later (1809) General Harrison is instructed by the President "to take advantage of the most favorable moment for extinguishing the Indian title to the lands lying east of the Wabash, and adjoining south;" and the title was extinguished by the treaty of Fort Wayne—a little more money paid, and a great deal of land given up.

In 1814 we made a treaty, simply of peace and friendship, with the Delawares and several other tribes: they agreeing to fight faithfully on our side against the English, and we agreeing to "confirm and establish all the boundaries" as they had existed before the war.

In 1817 it was deemed advisable to make an effort to "extinguish the Indian title to all the lands claimed by them within the limits of the State of Ohio. Two commissioners were appointed, with great discretionary powers; and a treaty was concluded early in the autumn, by which there was ceded to the United States nearly all the land to which the Indians had claim in Ohio, a part of Indiana, and a part of Michigan. This treaty was said by the Secretary of War to be "the most important of any hitherto made with the Indians." "The extent of the cession far exceeded" his most sanguine expectations, and he had the honesty to admit that "there can be no real or well-founded objection to the amount of the compensation given for it, except that it is not an adequate one."

The commissioners who negotiated the treaty were apprehensive that they would be accused of having made too liberal terms with the Indians, and in their report to the department they enumerate apologetically the reasons which made it impossible for them to get the land cheaper. Mr. Cass says of the terms: "Under any circumstances, they will fall infinitely short of the pecuniary and political value of the country obtained."

The Indians, parties to this treaty, surrendered by it almost the last of their hunting-grounds, and would soon be driven to depending wholly upon the cultivation of the soil.

In 1818 the Delawares again ceded land to the United States—ceded all to which they laid claim in the State of Indiana—and the United States promised to provide for them "a country to reside in on the west side of the Mississippi," and "to guarantee to them the peaceable possession" of the same. They were to have four thousand dollars a year in addition to all the sums promised by previous treaties, and they were to be allowed to remain three years longer by sufferance in their present homes. The Government also agreed to pay them for their improvements on their lands, to give them a hundred and twenty horses, and a "sufficient number of pirogues to aid in transporting them to the west side of the Mississippi;" also provisions for the journey.

In 1829 a supplementary Article was added to this treaty. The United States Government began to show traces of compunction and pity. The Article says, "Whereas the Delaware Nation are now willing to remove," it is agreed upon that the country in the fork of the Kansas and Missouri rivers, selected for their home, "shall be conveyed and forever secured by the United States to the said Delaware Nation, as their permanent residence ; and the United States hereby pledges the faith of the Government to guarantee to the said Delaware Nation, forever, the quiet and peaceable and undisturbed enjoyment of the same against the claims and assaults of all and every other people whatever."

An additional permanent annuity of one thousand dollars is promised; forty horses, "and the use of six wagons and ox-teams to assist in removing heavy articles," provisions for the journey, and one year's subsistence after they reach their new home; also the erection of a grist and saw mill within two years.

In 1833 the Secretary of War congratulated the country on the fact that "the country north of the Ohio, east of the Mississippi, including the States of Ohio, Indiana, Illinois, and the Territory of Michigan as far as the Fox and Wisconsin rivers," has been practically "cleared of the embarrassments of Indian relations," as there are not more than five thousand Indians, all told, left in this whole region.

The Commissioner of Indian Affairs in the same year says that it is "grateful to notice" how much the Indians' condition is "ameliorated under the policy of removal." He says that they, "protected by the strong arm of the Government, and dwelling on lands *distinctly* and permanently established as their own, enjoying a delightful climate and a fertile soil, turn their attention to the cultivation of the earth, and abandon the chase for the surer supply of domestic animals."

This commissioner apparently does not remember, perhaps never read, the records of the great fields of corn which the Delawares had on the Miami River in 1795, and how they returned twice that summer and replanted them, after General Wayne had cut down and burnt the young crops. They had "turned their attention to the cultivation of the soil" forty years ago, and that was what came of it. We shall see how much better worth while it may be for them to plant corn in their new "permanent home," than it was in their last one.

The printed records of Indian Affairs for the first forty years of this century are meagre and unsatisfactory. Had the practice prevailed then, as at the present time, of printing full annual reports for the different tribes, it would be possible to know much which is now forever locked up in the traditions and the memories of the Indians themselves. For ten years after the making of this last quoted treaty, there is little official mention of the Delawares by name, beyond the mention in the fiscal reports of the sums paid to them as annuities and for education. In 1833 the commissioner says, "The agent for the Delawares and Shawnees states that he was shown cloth that was spun and wove, and shirts and other clothing made by the Indian girls."

In 1838 the Delawares are reported as cultivating one thousand five hundred acres of land in grain and vegetables, and raising a great many hogs, cattle, and horses. "They are a brave, enterprising people," and "at peace with all neighboring Indians."

Parties of them frequently make excursions into the Rocky Mountains after beaver, and return with a rich reward, sometimes as much as one thousand dollars to an individual; but their money is soon spent, chiefly for ardent spirits. The agent says: "The only hinderance now in the way of the Delawares, Shawnees, and Kickapoos is ardent spirits. * * * These whiskey traffickers, who seem void of all conscience, rob and murder many of these Indians; I say rob—they will get them drunk, and then take their horses, guns, or blankets off their backs, regardless of how quick they may freeze to death; I say they murder—if not directly, indirectly, they furnish the weapon—they make them drunk, and, when drunk, they kill their fellow-beings. Some freeze to death when drunk; several drunken Indians have been drowned in the Missouri River this season, aiming to cross when drunk."

In 1844 the chiefs of the Delawares met together, and prepared a remarkable document, which was forwarded to the Secretary of War. In this paper they requested that all the school funds to which they were entitled by treaty provisions might be paid to the Indian Manual Labor School near the Fort Leavenworth Agency; might be pledged to that school for ten years to come, and that they might therefor be guaranteed the education and subsistence of Delaware children, not exceeding fifty at any one time. It came out, in course of this negotiation, that two thousand dollars were due them on arrearages of their school fund.

The Secretary acceded to this request, but imposed five conditions upon it, of which the fourth seems worth chronicling, as an indication of the helplessness of the Delawares in the matter of the disposition of their own money: "The interest to be paid annually when it may suit the Treasury; and this ratification to be subject to withdrawal, and the agreement itself to rescission, and to be annulled at the pleasure of the Department."

In 1845 the Delawares "raise a sufficiency to subsist on. The women do a large portion of the work on the farms. In many families, however, the women do not work on the farm. They raise corn, pumpkins, beans, pease, cabbages, potatoes, and many kinds of garden vegetables. Some few raise wheat and oats. They have lately had built, out of their own means, a good saw and grist mill, with two run of stones, one for corn and the other for wheat. There is a constant stream, called the Stranger, in their country that affords excellent water privileges. On this stream their mills are built."

At this time they are waiting with much anxiety to see if their "Great Father" will punish the Sioux, who have at two different times attacked them, and murdered in all some thirty men. "They say they do not wish to offend and disobey their Great Father, and before they attempt to revenge themselves they will wait and see if their Great Father will compel the Sioux to make reparation."

In 1848 "almost every family is well supplied with farming-stock; and they have raised abundance of corn, some wheat, potatoes, oats, and garden vegetables; have made butter and cheese; and raised fruit, etc., etc.   They dwell in good log-cabins, and some have extremely neat houses, well furnished. They have their outhouses, stables, well-fenced lots, and some have good barns."   There are seventy scholars in one school alone that are taught by the Friends; and the teacher reports: "It is truly astonishing to see the rapidity with which they acquire knowledge.   The boys work on the farm part of the time, and soon learn how to do what they are set at.   The girls spend a part of their time in doing housework, sewing, etc.   Many of them do the sewing of their own, and some of the clothes of the other children."

In 1853 the Delawares are recorded as being "among the most remarkable of our colonized tribes.   By their intrepidity and varied enterprise they are distinguished in a high degree. Besides being industrious farmers and herdsmen, they hunt and trade all over the interior of the continent, carrying their traffic beyond the Great Salt Lake, and exposing themselves to a thousand perils."

Their agent gives, in his report for this year, a graphic account of an incident such as has only too often occurred on our frontier.   "A small party of Delawares, consisting of a man, his squaw, and a lad about eighteen years of age, recent-ly returning from the mountains, with the avails and profits of a successful hunt and traffic, after they had commenced their journey homeward the second day the man sickened and died. Before he died he directed his squaw and the young man to hasten home with their horses and mules—thirteen in number —their money (four hundred and forty-five dollars), besides many other articles of value.   After a few days' travel, near some of the forts on the Arkansas, they were overtaken by four white men, deserters from the United States Army—three on foot, and one riding a mule.   The squaw and young man loaned each of the men on foot a horse or mule to ride, and furnished them with provisions. They all travelled on friendly together for some six or seven days, till they arrived at Cottonwood Creek, thirty-five or forty miles west of Council Grove. One evening, while resting, the young man was killed by these men; and the squaw was also supposed by these wretches to be dead, having had her throat cut badly and her head fractured. The two were then dragged off in the grass, supposed to be dead. The men gathered the mules, horses, money, guns, blankets—all that they supposed of value—and made for Jackson County, Missouri, where they disposed of the stock as best they could, and three of them took steamer for St. Louis. The squaw, on the day after, resuscitated; and soon discovering that her companion had been killed, and everything they possessed had disappeared, she, in her feeble and dangerous condition, took the road to Council Grove. The fifth day, she says, she was overtaken by a Kaw Indian, and brought into Council Grove, where the traders had every attention paid her, and sent a runner to the Delaware traders and myself, and we soon succeeded in capturing one of the men in Liberty, Clay County, Missouri, where he confessed the whole tragedy — the murder, robbing, etc. The three others had left for St. Louis. A telegraphic despatch to St. Louis, however, had the desired effect, and the three men were taken and brought back to Liberty, where, on trial before two justices of the peace, they were committed for trial in the District Court of the United States for the State of Missouri. As feeble as the squaw was, I was under the necessity of having her taken to Liberty as a witness. She readily recognized and pointed out in a large crowd of persons three of the prisoners. I have caused four of the recovered mules and horses to be turned over to the unfortunate squaw. I expect to recover two or three more; the balance, I am of opinion, will never be obtained."

In the report of the Indian Commissioner for this year there is also a paragraph which should not be omitted from this sketch: "The present seems to be an appropriate occasion for calling the attention of Congress to certain treaty stipulations with various Indian tribes which the Government, for a number of years, has failed to execute. In consideration of the cession of their lands to the United States"—by some nine tribes of the Mississippi and Missouri regions, among whom were the Delawares—"it was stipulated on the part of the Government that certain sums should be paid to said tribes, amounting in the aggregate to $2,396,600, and that the same should be invested in safe and profitable stocks, yielding an interest of not less than five per cent. per annum.

"Owing, however, to the embarrassed condition of the Treasury, it was deemed advisable by Congress, in lieu of making the investments, to appropriate from year to year a sum equal to the annual interest at five per cent. on the several amounts required to be invested. On this amount the Government has already paid from its treasury $1,742,240 — a sum which is now equal to two-thirds of the principal, and will in a few years be equal to the whole, if the practice of appropriating the interest be continued. As there is no limitation to the period of these payments, such a policy indefinitely continued would prove a most costly one to the Government. At the end of every twenty years it will have paid from the public treasury by way of interest the full amount of the stipulated investments. * * * The public finances are in a prosperous condition. Instead of fiscal embarrassment, there is now a redundancy of money, and one of the vexed questions of the day is, What shall be done with the surplus in the Treasury? Considering the premises, it seems to be quite clear that so much thereof as may be necessary for the purpose should be promptly applied to the fulfilment of our treaty obligations."

In 1854 the influx of white settlers into Kansas was so great, it became evident that the Indian reservations there could not be kept intact; and the Delawares made a large cession of their lands back to the United States, to be restored to the public domain. For this they were to receive ten thousand dollars. The sixth Article of this treaty provided for the giving of annuities to their chiefs. " The Delawares feel now, as heretofore, grateful to their old chiefs for their long and faithful services. In former treaties, when their means were scanty, they provided by small life annuities for the wants of the chiefs, some of whom are now receiving them. These chiefs are poor, and the Delawares believe it their duty to keep them from want in their old age." The sum of ten thousand dollars, therefore, was to be paid to their five chiefs—two hundred and fifty dollars a year each.

Article second provided that the President should cause the land now reserved for their permanent home to be surveyed at any time when they desired it, in the same manner as the ceded country was being surveyed for the white settlers.

In the following year their agent writes thus of the results which have followed the opening of this large tract to white settlers : " The Indians have experienced enough to shake their confidence in the laws which govern the white race. The irruptions of intruders on their trust lands, their bloody dissensions among themselves, outbreaks of party, etc., must necessarily, to these unsophisticated people, have presented our system of government in an unfavorable light.

" Numerous wrongs have been perpetrated on many parts of the reserve ; the white men have wasted their most valuable timber with an unsparing hand ; the trust lands have been greatly injured in consequence of the settlements made thereon. The Indians have complained, but to no purpose. I have found it useless to threaten legal proceedings.* * * The Government is bound in good faith to protect this people. * * *

The agricultural portion of this tribe have done well this season; abundant crops of corn promise them a supply of food for the ensuing year."

The simple-minded trustingness of these people is astonishing. Even now they assent to an Article in this treaty which says that, as the means arising from the sale of all this land they had given up would be more than they could use, the remainder should be "from time to time invested by the President of the United States in safe and profitable stocks; the principal to remain unimpaired, and the interest to be applied annually for the civilization, education, and religious culture of the Delaware people, and such other objects of a beneficial character as in his judgment are proper and necessary." Another Article stipulates that, if any of the Delawares are worthless or idle, the President can withhold their share of the moneys.

Article fifteenth says, gravely, "The primary object of this instrument being to advance the interests and welfare of the Delaware people, it is agreed that, if it prove insufficient to effect these ends from causes which cannot now be foreseen, Congress may hereafter make such farther provision, by law not inconsistent herewith, as experience may prove to be necessary to promote the interests, peace, and happiness of the Delaware people."

In 1860 the United States made its next treaty with the Delawares, in which they consented to give the Leavenworth, Pawnee, and Western Railroad Company right of way and certain lands in their reserve. In 1861 another treaty, in which, as the railway company had not paid, and was not able to pay, the $286,742 which it had promised to pay the Delawares, the President authorized the Commissioners of Indian Affairs to take the bonds of said railroad for that amount, and a mortgage on one hundred thousand acres of the land which the Indians had sold to the railway company.

There was another very curious bit of legislation in regard to the Delawares this year, viz., an Act of Congress authorizing the Secretary of the Treasury to enter on his books $423,990 26 to the credit of the Delawares; being the amount of bonds which the United States had invested for the Delawares in State bonds of Missouri, Tennessee, and North Carolina, and which had been stolen while in the custody of Jacob Thompson, late Secretary of the Interior, in whose department they had been deposited for safe-keeping. (At the same time there were stolen $66,735 belonging to the Iowas, and $169,686 75 belonging to the confederated bands of Kaskaskias, Peorias, Piankeshaws, and Keas.)

In this year the Commissioner of Indian Affairs visited the Delawares, and reported them well advanced in civilization, in possession of comfortable dwellings and farms, with personal property averaging one thousand dollars to an individual. Many of them were traders, and travelled even to the boundaries of California.

In 1862 two regiments of Delawares and Osages enlisted as soldiers in an expedition to the Indian Territory, under Colonel Weer, who says of them: "The Indian soldiers have far exceeded the most sanguine expectations. They bore the brunt of the fighting done by the expedition, and, had they been properly sustained, would have effectually ended the sway of the rebels in the Indian Territory."

There was during this year a terrible condition of affairs in Kansas and the Indian Territory. The Indians were largely on the side of the rebels; yet, as the Indian Commissioner said in his report for this year—a paragraph which is certainly a species of Irish bull—" While the rebelling of a large portion of most of the tribes abrogates treaty obligations, and places them at our mercy, the very important fact should not be forgotten that the Government first wholly failed to keep its treaty stipulations with them in protecting them." " By withdrawing all

the troops from the forts in the Indian Territory," it left them
"at the mercy of the rebels."   That is, we first broke the treaty;
and then their subsequent failure to observe it "placed them at
our mercy !"

"It is," he says, "a well-known fact that in many instances
self-preservation compelled them to make the best terms they
could with the rebels; and that this is the case has been proved
by a large number of them joining our army as soon as a sufficient force had penetrated their country to make it safe for
them to do so."

The Delawares enlisted, in 1862, one hundred and seventy
men in the Union army, and this out of a population of only
two hundred males between the ages of eighteen and forty-five.
There was probably no instance in the whole country of such
a ratio of volunteers as this.   They were reported as being in
the army "tractable, sober, watchful, and obedient to the com-
mands of their superiors."   They officered their own companies, and the use of spirituous liquors was strictly prohibited
among them—a fact the more remarkable, as drunkenness was
one of their chief vices at home.

Already, however, the "interests" of the white settlers in
Kansas were beginning to be clearly in opposition to the interests of the Indians.   "Circumscribed as they are, and closely
surrounded by white settlements, I can see nothing in the future
for them but destruction," says the commissioner.   "I think it
is for the interest of the Indians that they be removed to some
other locality as soon as possible."

"Several of them have from fifty to one hundred acres of
land in cultivation, with comfortable dwellings, barns, and out-
houses. * * * All the families are domiciled in houses. * * *
Their crops of corn will yield largely.   Nearly every family
will have a sufficiency for their own consumption, and many of
the larger farmers a surplus. * * * There are but few Delaware
children of the age of twelve or fourteen that cannot read."

Here is a community of a thousand people, larger than many of the farming villages in New England, for instance, "the average of personal property amounting to one thousand dollars;" all living in their own houses, cultivating from fifty to one hundred acres of land, nearly all the children in schools, and yet it is for their "interest to be moved!" The last sentence of the following paragraph tells the story:

"When peace is restored to our country, a removal of all the Indians in Kansas will certainly be advantageous to them as well as to the State."

In 1863 their agent writes: "Since the question of the removal of the Indians from Kansas has been agitated, improvements have been much retarded among the Delawares and other Indians in Kansas.

"I think they are sufficiently prepared to make new treaties with the Government, * * * having in view settlement in the Southern country of those who elect to emigrate, compensation for the homes they relinquish, and a permission to remain in their present homes for all who are opposed to leaving Kansas."

At this time, "one-half the adult population are in the volunteer service of the United States. They make the best of soldiers, and are highly valued by their officers. * * * No State in the Union has furnished so many men for our armies, from the same ratio of population, as has the Delaware tribe. * * * The tribe has 3900 acres of land under cultivation, in corn, wheat, oats, and potatoes." (And yet one-half the adult men are away!)

In this year the Delawares, being "sufficiently prepared" to make new treaties looking to their removal out of the way of the white settlers in Kansas, petitioned the United States Government to permit them to take eight hundred dollars of their annuity funds to pay the expense of sending a delegation of their chiefs to the Rocky Mountains, to see if they could find

there a country which would answer for their new home.   The
commissioner advises that they should not be allowed to go
there, but to the Indian Territory, of which he says, "The
geographical situation is such that its occupation by lawless
whites can be more easily prevented than any other portion
of the country."   "By common consent, this appears to be recognized as the Indian country, and I have strong hopes that it
will eventually prove for them a prosperous and happy home."

In 1864 their agent writes that the greater part of the personal property owned by the Delawares is in stock, "which is
constantly being preyed upon by the whites, until it has become so reduced that it is difficult to obtain a good animal in
the nation."   He says he is unable, for the want of proper information, to determine what amount they had at the beginning of the year, but believes, from observation, "that it has
undergone a depletion to the extent of twenty thousand dollars in the past year."

What a picture of a distressed community!   The men away
at war, old men, women, and children working the farms, and
twenty thousand dollars of stock stolen from them in one
year!

In 1865 a large proportion of those who had enlisted in the
United States Army were mustered out, and returned home.
The agent says: "It affords me great pleasure to chronicle the
continued loyalty of this tribe during the past four years; and,
as events tend westward, they evince every disposition to aid
the Government by contributing their knowledge of the country to the officers of the army, and rendering such services
thereto as they are qualified to perform."

They "have distinguished themselves in many instances in
the conflicts on the borders;" nevertheless, in this same year,
these discharged soldiers were prohibited by the Government
from carrying revolvers.   When the commissioner instructed
the agent to disarm them, the agent very properly replied,

stating the difficulties in the case: "Firstly, what disposition
is to be made of weapons taken forcibly from these Indians?
Secondly, many of these Indians are intelligent, only using
weapons when any well-disposed white person would have
done so; and if one class is disarmed, all must be;" on which
the commissioner so modified his order as to say that "peaceably disposed Indians" might keep the usual weapons used by
them in hunting; but whenever they visited agencies or towns
they must deliver up all weapons to the agent, who would receipt for them, and return them "at proper times." This order is to be enforced, if possible, by an "appeal to their better
judgment."

There are no records of the practical working of this order.
Very possibly it fell at once, by its own weight, into the already large category of dead-letter laws in regard to Indians.
It is impossible to imagine an Indian who had served four
years as an officer in the army (for the Delawares officered
their own companies) submitting to be disarmed by an agent
on any day when he might need to go to Atchison on business.
Probably even that "appeal to his better judgment" which
the commissioner recommends, would only draw from him a
very forcible statement to the effect that any man who went
about in Kansas at that time unarmed was a fool.

In 1866 the Indian Commissioner reports that "the State
of Kansas is fast being filled by an energetic population who
appreciate good land; and as the Indian reservations were selected as being the best in the State, but *one result can be expected to follow.*

"Most of the Indians are anxious to move to the Indian
country south of Kansas, where white settlers cannot interfere
with them.

"Intermingled as the Kansas reservations are with the public lands, and surrounded in most cases by white settlers who
too often act on the principle that an Indian has no rights

that a white man is bound to respect, they are injured and annoyed in many ways. Their stock are stolen, their fences broken down, their timber destroyed, their young men plied with whiskey, their women debauched; so that, while the un-civilized are kept in a worse than savage state, having the crimes of civilization forced upon them, those farther advanced, and disposed to honest industry, are discouraged beyond en-durance."

In spite of all this the Delawares raised, in 1866, 72,000 bushels of grain, 13,000 bushels of potatoes, and owned 5000 head of cattle.

In July of this year a treaty was made with them, providing for the removal to the Indian Territory of all who should not decide to become citizens of Kansas, and the sale of their lands. The superintendent of the Fort Leavenworth Agency writes at this time: "The running of the Union Pacific Rail-road through the Delawares' diminished reserve has been a source of grievous annoyance and damage to the Delawares, as has also an organization styled the Delaware Lumber Com-pany. Out of these two companies grew much complaint and investigation, resulting in the appointment of a special agent to sell to the railroad the timber required for the construction of the road, and no more. The Delaware Lumber Company being thus restricted" (*i. e.*, being prevented from helping themselves to the Indians' timber), immediately "gave up their business, and stopped their mills," but not before they had damaged the Indians' property to the amount of twenty-eight thousand dollars.

Twenty thousand dollars' worth of stock and twenty-eight thousand dollars' worth of timber having been stolen in two years from this little village of farmers, no wonder they are "sufficiently prepared to move." Other causes have conspired also to render them in haste to be gone. The perpetual expec-tation of being obliged to remove had unsettled the whole community, and made them indifferent to effort and improvement. The return of their young men from the war had also had a demoralizing effect. Drunken frays were not uncommon, in which deadly weapons were used, spite of the Department's regulations for disarming all Indians.

In July of this year the Delaware chiefs, distressed by this state of affairs, drew up for their nation a code of laws which compare favorably with the laws of so-called civilized States.*

In 1867 the Delawares are said to be "very impatient to be gone from their reserve, in order to build houses this autumn for winter use, and to be fencing fields for the ensuing year at their new reserve." The annuities due them in April of this year have not been paid till autumn, and this has delayed their movements. Many of the young men are still away, acting as scouts and guides in the army. In the course of this year and the next the whole tribe moved by detachments to their new home. "Those who removed during the winter went to work in a laudable manner, and made their improvements—many building comfortable houses and raising respectable crops" the first season. They are said to be now in a fair way to be better off than ever before. They have "given up their tribal organization and become Cherokee citizens. They report that they are well pleased with their new homes; and, being separated from the many temptations by which they were surrounded in their old reservation, are learning to appreciate the many benefits to be derived from leading a temperate, industrious, and consequently a prosperous and happy life."

In 1869 it is said that, "as soon as the final arrangement relative to their funds is perfected, they will lose their nationality and become identified with the Cherokees."

In 1870 we find nearly all the Delawares in Indian Territory; but it seems that, owing to a carelessly surveyed boundary, some

---

* See Appendix, Art. 8.

three hundred of them had settled down on lands which were outside the Cherokee Reservation, and had been assigned by the Government to the Osages. This unfortunate three hundred, therefore, are removed again; this time to the lands of the Peorias, where they ask permission to establish themselves. But in the mean time, as they had made previous arrangements with the Cherokees, and all their funds had been transferred to the Cherokee Nation, it is thought to be "very unfortunate that they should be thus obliged to seek a new home;" and it is said to be "quite desirable that the parties in interest should reconcile their unsettled affairs to mutual advantage."

We are too much inclined to read these records carelessly, without trying to picture to ourselves the condition of affairs which they represent. It has come to be such an accepted thing in the history and fate of the Indian that he is to be always pushed on, always in advance of what is called the march of civilization, that to the average mind statements of these repeated removals come with no startling force, and suggest no vivid picture of details, only a sort of reassertion of an abstract general principle. But pausing to consider for a moment what such statements actually mean and involve; imagining such processes applied to some particular town or village that we happen to be intimately acquainted with, we can soon come to a new realization of the full bearing and import of them; such uprooting, such perplexity, such loss, such confusion and uncertainty, inflicted once on any community of white people anywhere in our land, would be considered quite enough to destroy its energies and blight its prospects for years. It may very well be questioned whether any of our small communities would have recovered from such successive shocks, changes, and forced migrations, as soon and as well as have many of these Indian tribes. It is very certain that they would not have submitted to them as patiently.

After this we find in the Official Reports no distinctive mention of the Delawares by name, except of a few who had been for some time living in the Indian Territory, and were not included in the treaty provisions at the time of the removal from Kansas. This little handful—eighty-one in number—is all that now remain to bear the name of that strong and friendly people to whom, a little more than one hundred years ago, we promised that they should be our brothers forever, and be entitled to a representation in our Congress.

This band of Delawares is associated with six other dwindled remnants of tribes — the Caddoes, Ionies, Wichitas, Towaconies, Wacoes, Keechies, and Comanches—on the Wichita Agency, in Indian Territory.

They are all reported as being "peaceable, well disposed," and "actively engaged in agricultural pursuits."

Of the Delawares it is said, in 1878, that they were not able to cultivate so much land as they had intended to during that year, " on account of loss of stock by horse-thieves."

Even here, it seems, in that "Indian country south of Kansas, where" (as they were told) "white settlers could not interfere with them," enemies lie in wait for them, as of old, to rob and destroy ; even here the Government is, as before, unable to protect them ; and in all probability, the tragedies of 1866 and 1867 will before long be re-enacted with still sadder results.

CHAPTER III.

THE CHEYENNES.

OUR first treaty with the Cheyennes was made in 1825, at the mouth of the Teton River. It was merely a treaty of amity and friendship, and acknowledgment on the part of the Cheyennes of the "supremacy" of the United States. Two years before this, President Monroe reported the "Chayenes" to be "a tribe of three thousand two hundred and fifty souls, dwelling and hunting on a river of the same name, a western tributary of the Missouri, a little above the Great Bend." Ten years later, Catlin, the famous painter of Indians, met a "Shienne" chief and squaw among the Sioux, and painted their portraits. He says, "The Shiennes are a small tribe of about three thousand in number, living neighbors to the Sioux on the west of them, between the Black Hills and the Rocky Mountains. There is no finer race of men than these in North America, and none superior in stature, except the Osages: scarcely a man in the tribe full grown who is less than six feet in height." They are "the richest in horses of any tribe on the continent; living where the greatest herds of wild horses are grazing on the prairies, which they catch in great numbers, and sell to the Sioux, Mandans, and other tribes, as well as to the fur-traders.

"These people are the most desperate set of warriors and horsemen, having carried on almost unceasing wars with the Pawnees and Blackfeet. The chief was clothed in a handsome dress of deer-skins, very neatly garnished with broad bands of porcupine-quill work down the sleeves of his shirt and leggings. The woman was comely, and beautifully dressed. Her dress of the mountain - sheepskin tastefully ornamented with quills and beads, and her hair plaited in large braids that hung down on her breast."

In 1837 the agent for the "Sioux, Cheyennes, and Poncas" reports that "all these Indians live exclusively by the chase;" and that seems to be the sum and substance of his information about them. He adds, also, that these remote wandering tribes have a great fear of the border tribes, and wish to avoid them. In 1838 the Cheyennes are reported as carrying on trade at a post on the Arkansas River near the Santa Fe road, but still depending on the chase.

In 1842 they are spoken of as a "wandering tribe on the Platte;" and in the same year, Mr. D. D. Mitchell, Supt. of Indian Affairs, with his head-quarters at St. Louis, writes: "Generations will pass away before this territory" [the territory in which the wild tribes of the Upper Mississippi were then wandering] "becomes much more circumscribed; for if we draw a line running north and south, so as to cross the Missouri about the mouth of the Vermilion River, we shall designate the limits beyond which civilized men are never likely to settle. At this point the Creator seems to have said to the tides of emigration that are annually rolling toward the West, 'Thus far shalt thou go, and no farther.' At all events, if they go beyond this, they will never stop on the east side of the Rocky Mountains. The utter destitution of timber, the sterility of sandy soil, together with the coldness and dryness of the climate, furnish obstacles which not even Yankee enterprise is likely to overcome. A beneficent Creator seems to have intended this dreary region as an asylum for the Indians, when the force of circumstances shall have driven them from the last acre of the fertile soil which they once possessed. Here no inducements are offered to the ever-restless Saxon breed to erect their huts. * * * The time may arrive when the whole of the Western Indians will be

forced to seek a resting-place in this Great American Desert;
and this, in all probability, will form a new era in the history
of this singular and ill-fated race. They will remain a wandering, half civilized, though happy people. 'Their flocks and
herds will cover a thousand hills,' and will furnish beef and
mutton for a portion of the dense population of whites that
will swarm in the more fertile sections of the great valley of
the Mississippi."

This line, recommended by Mr. Mitchell, runs just east of
Dakota, through the extreme eastern portion of Nebraska, a lit-
tle to the east of the middle of Kansas, through the middle of
Indian Territory and Texas, to the Gulf of Mexico. Montana,
Idaho, Colorado, and New Mexico, all lie west of it.

The records of the War Department for 1846 contain an interesting account of a visit made to all the wild tribes of the
Upper Missouri Agency—the Yankton Sioux, the Arrikarees,
Mandans, Assinaboines, Arapahoes, Cheyennes, and others. In
reply to the agent's remonstrances with one of the Sioux chiefs
in regard to their perpetual warring with each other, the chief
" was very laconic and decided, remarking 'that if their great-
grandfather desired them to cease to war with their enemies,
why did he not send each of them a petticoat, and make squaws
of them at once?'" This same chief refused to allow the boys
of his tribe to go to the Choctaw schools, saying, "They would
return, as the few did who went to St. Louis, drunkards, or die
on the way."

The Cheyennes and other Indians living on the Platte complained bitterly of the passage of the emigrants through their
country. They said they ought to be compensated for the
right of way, and that the emigrants should be restricted by
law and the presence of a military force from burning the
grass, and from unnecessary destruction of game. They were
systematically plundered and demoralized by traders. Whiskey
was to be had without difficulty; sugar and coffee were sold

at one dollar a pound; ten-cent calico at one dollar a yard; corn at seventy-five cents a gallon, and higher.

In 1847 a law was passed by Congress forbidding the introduction of whiskey into the Indian country, and even the partial enforcement of this law had a most happy effect. Foremost among those to acknowledge the benefits of it were the traders themselves, who said that the Indians' demand for substantial articles of trade was augmented two hundred per cent.: "They enjoy much better health, look much better, and are better people. * * * You now rarely ever hear of a murder committed, whereas when whiskey was plenty in that country murder was a daily occurrence." These Indians themselves were said to be "opposed to the introduction of ardent spirits into their country; * * * but, like almost all. other Indians, will use it if you give it to them, and when under its influence are dangerous and troublesome." There were at this time nearly forty-six thousand of these Upper Missouri Indians. Five bands of them—"the Sioux, Cheyennes, Gros Ventres, Mandans, and Poncas"—were "excellent Indians, devotedly attached to the white man," living "in peace and friendship with our Government," and "entitled to the special favor and good opinion of the Department for their uniform good conduct and pacific relations."

In 1848 it was estimated from the returns made by traders that the trade of this agency amounted to $400,000. Among the items were 25,000 buffalo tongues. In consequence of this prosperity on the part of the Indians, there was a partial cessation of hostilities on the whites; but it was still a perilous journey to cross the plains, and in 1849 the necessity for making some sort of treaty stipulations with all these wild tribes begins to be forced emphatically upon the attention of the United States Government. A safe highway across the continent must be opened. It is a noticeable thing, however, that, even as late as this in the history of our diplomatic relations with the Indian, his right to a certain control as well as occupancy of the soil was instinctively recognized.   The Secretary of the Interior, in his report for 1849, says: "The wild tribes of Indians who have their hunting-grounds in the great prairie through which our emigrants to California pass, have, during the year, been more than usually pacific.   They have suffered our people to pass through their country with little interruption, though they travelled in great numbers, and consumed on their route much grass and game.   For these the Indians expect compensation, and their claim is just."

The Secretary, therefore, concurs in the recommendation of the Commissioner of Indian Affairs that treaties be negotiated with these tribes, stipulating for the right of way through their country, and the use of grass and game, paying them therefor small annuities in useful articles of merchandise, and agricultural implements, and instruction.   "The right of way"— "through their country."   A great deal is conceded, covered, and conveyed by such phrases as these.   If they mean anything, they mean all that the Indians ever claimed.

The Indians were supposed to be influenced to this peaceableness and good-will more by a hope of rewards and gifts than by a wholesome fear of the power of the Government; and it was proposed to take a delegation of chiefs to Washington, "in order that they may acquire some knowledge of our greatness and strength, which will make a salutary impression on them, and through them on their brethren," and "will tend to influence them to continue peaceful relations."

It begins to dawn upon the Government's perception that peace is cheaper as well as kinder than war.   "We never can whip them into friendship," says one of the superintendents of the Upper Missouri Agency.   A treaty "can do no harm, and the expense would be less than that of a six months' war. * * * Justice as well as policy requires that we should make some remuneration for the damages these Indians sustain in consequence of the destruction of their game, timber, etc., by the whites passing through their country."

"Their game, timber," "their country," again. The perpetual recurrence of this possessive pronoun, and of such phrases as these in all that the Government has said about the Indians, and in all that it has said to them, is very significant.

In 1850 the Indian Commission writes that "it is much to be regretted that no appropriation was made at the last session of Congress for negotiating treaties with the wild tribes of the plains. These Indians have long held undisputed possession of this extensive region; and, regarding it as their own, they consider themselves entitled to compensation not only for the right of way through their territory, but for the great and injurious destruction of game, grass, and timber committed by our troops and emigrants."

The bill providing for the negotiation of these treaties was passed unanimously by the Senate, but "the unhappy difficulties existing on the subject of slavery" delayed it in the House until it was too late to be carried into effect.

All the tribes had been informed of this pending bill, and were looking forward to it with great interest and anxiety. In 1849 they had all expressed themselves as "very anxious to be instructed in agriculture and the civilized arts." Already the buffalo herds were thinning and disappearing. From time immemorial the buffalo had furnished them food, clothing, and shelter; with its disappearance, starvation stared them in the face, and they knew it. There can be no doubt that at this time all the wild tribes of the Upper Missouri region — the Sioux, Cheyennes, Arapahoes — were ready and anxious to establish friendly relations with the United States Government, and to enter into some arrangement by which some means of future subsistence, and some certainty of lands enough to live on, could be secured to them. Meantime they hunted with greater diligence than ever; and in this one year alone had sold to the fur-traders within the limits of one agency $330,000 worth of buffalo-robes, and "furs, peltries, and miscellaneous goods to the amount of $60,000. What they thus receive for their furs, robes, etc., would be ample for their support," says Hatton, "were it not that they have to give such exorbitant prices for what they purchase from the whites."

In the winter and spring of 1850 all these tribes were visited by an agent of the Government. He reported them as "friendly disposed," but very impatient to come to some understanding about the right of way. "This is what the Indians want, and what they are anxious about; having been told long since, and so often repeated by travellers passing (who care little about the consequences of promises so they slip through safely and unmolested themselves), that their 'Great Father' would soon reward them liberally for the right of way, the destruction of timber, game, etc., as well as for any kindness shown Americans passing through their country."

In the summer of 1851 this much desired treaty was made. Seven of the prairie and mountain tribes gathered in great force at Fort Laramie. The report of this council contains some interesting and noticeable points.

"We were eighteen days encamped together, during which time the Indians conducted themselves in a manner that excited the admiration and surprise of every one. The different tribes, although hereditary enemies, interchanged daily visits, both in their individual and national capacities; smoked and feasted together; exchanged presents; adopted each other's children, according to their own customs; and did all that was held sacred or solemn in the eyes of these Indians to prove the sincerity of their peaceful and friendly intentions, both among themselves and with the citizens of the United States lawfully residing among them or passing through the country."

By this treaty the Indians formally conceded to the United States the right to establish roads, military or otherwise, throughout the Indian country, "so far as they claim or exercise ownership over it."

They agreed "to maintain peaceful relations among themselves, and to abstain from all depredations upon whites passing through their country, and to make restitution for any damages or loss that a white man shall sustain by the acts of their people."

For all the damages which they had suffered up to that time in consequence of the passing of the whites through their country, they accepted the presents then received as payment in full.

An annuity of $50,000 a year for fifty years to come was promised to them. This was the price of the "right of way."

"Fifty thousand dollars for a limited period of years is a small amount to be distributed among at least fifty thousand Indians, especially when we consider that we have taken away, or are rapidly taking away from them all means of support," says one of the makers of this treaty. There would probably be no dissent from this opinion. A dollar a year, even assured to one for fifty years, seems hardly an adequate compensation for the surrender of all other "means of support."

The report continues: "Viewing the treaty in all its provisions, I am clearly of opinion that it is the best that could have been made for both parties. I am, moreover, of the opinion that it will be observed and carried out in as good faith on the part of the Indians as it will on the part of the United States and the white people thereof. There was an earnest solemnity and a deep conviction of the necessity of adopting some such measures evident in the conduct and manners of the Indians throughout the whole council. On leaving for their respective homes, and bidding each other adieu, they gave the strongest possible evidence of their friendly intentions for the future, and the mutual confidence and good faith which they had in each other. Invitations were freely given and as freely accepted by each of the tribes to interchange visits, talk, and smoke together like brothers, upon ground where they had never before met except for the purpose of scalping each other. This, to my mind, was conclusive evidence of the sincerity of the Indians, and nothing but bad management or some untoward misfortune ever can break it."

The Secretary of the Interior, in his report for this year, speaks with satisfaction of the treaties negotiated with Indians during the year, and says : " It cannot be denied that most of the depredations committed by the Indians on our frontiers are the offspring of dire necessity. The advance of our population compels them to relinquish their fertile lands, and seek refuge in sterile regions which furnish neither corn nor game : impelled by hunger, they seize the horses, mules, and cattle of the pioneers, to relieve their wants and satisfy the cravings of nature. They are immediately pursued, and, when overtaken, severely punished. This creates a feeling of revenge on their part, which seeks its gratification in outrages on the persons and property of peaceable inhabitants. The whole country then becomes excited, and a desolating war, attended with a vast sacrifice of blood and treasure, ensues. This, it is believed, is a true history of the origin of most of our Indian hostilities.

"All history admonishes us of the difficulty of civilizing a wandering race who live mainly upon game. To tame a savage you must tie him down to the soil. You must make him understand the value of property, and the benefits of its separate ownership. You must appeal to those selfish principles implanted by Divine Providence in the nature of man for the wisest purposes, and make them minister to civilization and refinement. You must encourage the appropriation of lands by individuals; attach them to their homes by the ties of interest; teach them the uses of agriculture and the arts of peace ; * * * and they should be taught to look forward to the day when they may be elevated to the dignity of American citizenship.

"By means like these we shall soon reap our reward in the

suppression of Indian depredations; in·the diminution of the expenses of the Department of War; in a valuable addition to our productive population; in the increase of our agriculture and commerce; and in the proud consciousness that we have removed from our national escutcheon the stain left on it by our acknowledged injustice to the Indian race."

We find the Cheyennes, therefore, in 1851, pledged to peace and good-will toward their Indian neighbors, and to the white emigrants pouring through their country. For this conceded right of way they are to have a dollar a year apiece, in "goods and animals;" and it is supposed that they will be able to eke out this support by hunting buffaloes, which are still not extinct.

In 1852 the Commissioner of Indian Affairs writes: "Notwithstanding the mountain and prairie Indians continue to suffer from the vast number of emigrants who pass through their country, destroying their means of support, and scattering disease and death among them, yet those who were parties to the treaty concluded at Fort Laramie, in the fall of 1851, have been true to their obligations, and have remained at peace among themselves and with the whites."

And the superintendent writes: "Congress made a very liberal appropriation of $100,000 to make a treaty with the prairie and mountain tribes. A very satisfactory treaty was made with them last fall at Fort Laramie, the conditions of which, on their part, have been faithfully observed—no depredations having been committed during the past season by any of the tribes parties to the Fort Laramie treaty. The Senate amended the treaty, substituting *fifteen* instead of *fifty* years as the period for which they were to have received an annual supply of goods, animals, etc., at the discretion of the President. This modification of the treaty I think very proper, as the condition of these wandering hordes will be entirely changed during the next fifteen years. The treaty, however, should have been sent back to the Indians for the purpose of obtaining their sanction to the modification, as was done in the case of the Sioux treaty negotiated by Commissioners Ramsey and Lea. It is hoped this oversight will be corrected as early as practicable next spring, otherwise the large amounts already expended will have been uselessly wasted, and the Indians far more dissatisfied than ever."

To comment on the bad faith of this action on the part of Congress would be a waste of words; but its impolicy is so glaring that one's astonishment cannot keep silent—its impolicy and also its incredible niggardliness. A dollar apiece a year, "in goods, animals," etc., those Indians had been promised that they should have for fifty years. It must have been patent to the meanest intellect that this was little to pay each year to any one man from whom we were taking away, as the commissioner said, "his means of support." But, unluckily for the Indians, there were fifty thousand of them. It entered into some thrifty Congressman's head to multiply fifty by fifty, and the aggregate terrified everybody. This was much more likely to have been the cause of the amendment than the cause assigned by the superintendent, viz., the probable change of localities of all the "wandering hordes" in the next fifteen years. No doubt it would be troublesome to the last degree to distribute fifty thousand dollars, " in goods, animals," etc., to fifty thousand Indians wandering over the entire Upper Missouri region; but no more troublesome, surely, in the sixteenth year than in the fifteenth. The sophistry is too transparent; it does not in the least gloss over the fact that, within the first year after the making of our first treaty of any moment with these tribes—while they to a man, the whole fifty thousand of them, kept their faith with us—we broke ours with them in the meanest of ways—robbing them of more than two-thirds of the money we had promised to pay.

All the tribes "promptly" assented to this amendment, however; so says the Annual Report of the Indian Commissioner for 1853; and adds that, with a single exception, they have maintained friendly relations among themselves, and "manifested an increasing confidence in and kindness toward the whites."

Some of them have begun to raise corn, beans, pumpkins, etc., but depend chiefly on the hunt for their support. But the agent who was sent to distribute to them their annuities, and to secure their assent to the amendment to the treaty, reports: "The Cheyennes and the Arapahoes, and many of the Sioux, are actually in a starving state. They are in abject want of food half the year, and their reliance for that scanty supply, in the rapid decrease of the buffalo, is fast disappearing. The travel upon the roads drives them off, or else confines them to a narrow path during the period of emigration, and the different tribes are forced to contend with hostile nations in seeking support for their villages. Their women are pinched with want, and their children constantly crying with hunger. Their arms, moreover, are unfitted to the pursuit of smaller game, and thus the lapse of a few years presents only the prospect of a gradual famine." And in spite of such suffering, these Indians commit no depredations, and show increasing confidence in and kindness toward the whites.

This agent, who has passed many years among the Indians, speaks with great feeling of the sad prospect staring them in the face. He says: "But one course remains which promises any permanent relief to them, or any lasting benefit to the country in which they dwell; that is, simply to make such modifications in the 'intercourse' laws as will invite the residence of traders among them, and open the whole Indian Territory for settlement. Trade is the only civilizer of the Indian. It has been the precursor of all civilization heretofore, and it will be of all hereafter. It teaches the Indian the value of other things besides the spoils of the chase, and offers to him other pursuits and excitements than those of war. All obstructions to its freedom, therefore, only operate injuriously. * * * The Indians would soon lose their nomadic character, and forget the relations of tribes. * * * And this, while it would avoid the cruel necessity of our present policy—to wit, extinction — would make them an element in the population, and sharer in the prosperity of the country." He says of the "system of removals, and congregating tribes in small parcels of territory," that it has "eventuated injuriously on those who have been subjected to it. It is the legalized murder of a whole nation. It is expensive, vicious, and inhuman, and producing these consequences, and these alone. The custom, being judged by its fruits, should not be persisted in."

It is in the face of such statements, such protests as these, that the United States Government has gone steadily on with its policy, so called, in regard to the treatment of the Indian.

In 1854 the report from the Upper Missouri region is still of peace and fidelity on the part of all the Indians who joined in the Fort Laramie treaty. "Not a single instance of murder, robbery, or other depredation has been committed by them, either on the neighboring tribes parties to the treaty or on whites. This is the more remarkable, as before the treaty they were foremost in the van of thieves and robbers—always at war, pillaging whoever they met, and annoying their own traders in their own forts."

In the summer of this year the Cheyennes began to be dissatisfied and impertinent. At a gathering of the northern band at Fort Laramie, one of the chiefs demanded that the travel over the Platte road should be stopped. He also, if the interpreter was to be relied on, said that next year the Government must send them out one thousand white women for wives. The Southern Cheyennes had given up to their agent some Mexican prisoners whom they had taken in the spring, and this act, it was supposed, had seemed to the northern band a needless interference on the part of the United States. Moreover, it was a matter constantly open to the observation of all friendly Indians that the hostiles, who were continually plundering and attacking emigrant trains, made, on the whole, more profit out of war than they made out of peace. On the North Platte road during this year the Pawnees alone had stolen several thousands of dollars' worth of goods; and, in addition to this, there was the pressure of public sentiment—a thing which is as powerful among Indians as among whites. It was popular to be on the war-path: the whites were invaders; it was brave and creditable to slay them. Taking all these things into account, it was only to be wondered at that these Cheyennes, Arapahoes, and Sioux kept to the provisions of their treaty at all. Nevertheless, the Cheyennes, Arapahoes, and some bands of the Sioux continued peaceable and friendly; and in 1855 they begged to be supplied with a farmer to teach them how to farm; also with a blacksmith. Their agent strongly recommends that this be done, saying that there is not "in the whole Indian country a more favorable location for a farm for grazing stock and game than the South Platte. In a very short period of time the Arapahoes and Cheyennes would become fixed and settled, and a part of each tribe—the old women and men—would become agriculturists; rude, it is true, yet sufficiently skilful to raise corn, potatoes, and beans, and dwell in cabins or fixed habitations."

In the summer of 1856 the Cheyennes were, by a disastrous accident, forced into the position of hostiles. A small war-band went out to attack the Pawnees; they were in camp near the North Platte road: as the mail-wagon was passing, two of the Cheyennes ran toward it to beg tobacco. The mail-carrier, terrified, fired on them, and the Indians fired back, wounding him; the chiefs rushed out, stopped the firing, explained the matter, and then severely flogged the Indians who had returned the mail-carrier's fire. But the mischief had been done.

The mail-carrier reported his having been fired at by a Cheyenne Indian, and the next day troops from Fort Kearny attacked the Indians and killed six of the war-party. The rest refused to fight, and ran away, leaving their camp and all it contained. The war-party, thoroughly exasperated, attacked an emigrant train, killed two men and a child, and took one woman captive. The next day they killed her, because she could not ride on horseback and keep up with them. Within a short time two more small war-parties had left the band, attacked trains, and killed two men, two women, and a child. The chiefs at first could not restrain them, but in September they sent a delegation to the agency to ask their agent's assistance and advice. They said that the war-party was now completely under their control, and they wished to know what they could do. They implored the Great Father not to be angry with them, "for they could not control the war-party when they saw their friends killed by soldiers after they had thrown down their bows and arrows and begged for life."

In October the agent reported that the Cheyennes were "perfectly quiet and peaceable, and entirely within control, and obedient to authority." The chiefs had organized a sort of police, whose duty was to kill any war-parties that might attempt to leave the camp.

Through the winter the Cheyennes remained in the south and south-eastern parts of the agency, and strictly observed the conditions which their agent had imposed upon them. In the following August, however, a military force under General Sumner was sent out "to demand from the tribe the perpetrators of their late outrages on the whites, and ample security for their good conduct." The Cheyennes were reported by General Sumner as showing no disposition to yield to these demands; he therefore attacked them, burnt their village to the ground, and destroyed their winter supplies—some fifteen or twenty thousand pounds of buffalo meat.

Of how they lived, and where, during the winter following this fight, there is little record. In the next year's reports the Cheyennes are said to be very anxious for a new treaty, which will assign to them a country in which they can dwell safely. "They said they had learned a lesson last summer in their fight with General Sumner—that it was useless to contend with the white man, who would soon with his villages occupy the whole prairie. They wanted peace; and as the buffalo—their principal dependence for food and clothing (which even now they were compelled to seek many miles from home, where their natural enemies, the Pawnee and Osage, roamed), would soon disappear entirely, they hoped their Great Father, the white chief at Washington, would listen to them, and give them a home where they might be provided for and protected against the encroachments of their white brothers, until at least they had been taught to cultivate the soil and other arts of civilized life. They have often desired ploughs and hoes, and to be taught their use."

The next year's records show the Government itself aware that some measures must be taken to provide for these troublesome wild tribes of the prairie: almost more perplexing in time of peace than in time of war is the problem of the disposition to be made of them. Agents and superintendents alike are pressing on the Government's attention the facts and the bearing of the rapid settling of the Indian lands by the whites; the precariousness of peaceful relations; the dangers of Indian wars. The Indians themselves are deeply anxious and disturbed.

"They have heard that all of the Indian tribes to the eastward of them have ceded their lands to the United States, except small reservations; and hence, by an Indian's reasoning, in a few years these tribes will emigrate farther west, and, as a matter of necessity, occupy the hunting-grounds of the wild tribes."

When the agent of the Upper Platte Agency tried to reason on this subject with one of the Sioux chiefs, the chief said: " When I was a young man, and I am not yet fifty, I travelled with my people through the country of the Sac and Fox tribe, to the great water Minne Toukah (Mississippi), where I saw corn growing, but no white people; continuing eastward, we came to the Rock River valley, and saw the Winnebagoes, but no white people. We then came to the Fox River valley, and thence to the Great Lake (Lake Michigan), where we found a few white people in the Pottawattomie country. Thence we returned to the Sioux country at the Great Falls of Irara (St. Anthony), and had a feast of green corn with our relations, who resided there. Afterward we visited the pipe-clay quarry in the country of the Yankton Sioux, and made a feast to the ' Great Medicine,' and danced the ' sun dance,' and then returned to our hunting-grounds on the prairie. And now our Father tells us the white man will never settle on our lands, and kill our game; but see! the whites cover all of those lands I have just described, and also the lands of the Poncas, Omahas, and Pawnees. On the South Platte the white people are finding gold, and the Cheyennes and Arapahoes have no longer any hunting-grounds. Our country has become very small, and before our children are grown up we shall have no game."

In the autumn of this year (1859) an agent was sent to hold a council with the Cheyennes and Arapahoes, and tell them of the wish of the Government that they should " assume a fixed residence, and occupy themselves in agriculture. This they at once received with favor, and declared with great unanimity to be acceptable to them. They expected and asked that the Department shall supply them with what is necessary to establish themselves permanently. * * * Both these tribes had scrupulously maintained peaceful relations with the whites, and with other Indian tribes, notwithstanding the many causes of irritation growing out of the occupation of the gold region, and the emigration to it through their hunting-grounds, which are no longer reliable as a certain source of food to them."

It was estimated that during the summer of 1859 over sixty thousand emigrants crossed these plains in their central belt. The trains of vehicles and cattle were frequent and valuable in proportion; and post lines and private expresses were in constant motion.

In 1860 a commissioner was sent out to hold a council with the Cheyennes and Arapahoes at Bent's Fort, on the Upper Arkansas, and make a treaty with them. The Arapahoes were fully represented; but there were present only two prominent chiefs of the Cheyennes — Black Kettle and White Antelope. (White Antelope was one of the chiefs brutally murdered five years later in the Chivington massacre in Colorado.) As it was impossible for the rest of the Cheyennes to reach the Fort in less than twenty days, and the commissioner could not wait so long, Black Kettle and White Antelope wished it to be distinctly understood that they pledged only themselves and their own bands.

The commissioner says: " I informed them as to the object of my visit, and gave them to understand that their Great Father had heard with delight of their peaceful disposition, although they were almost in the midst of the hostile tribes. They expressed great pleasure on learning that their Great Father had heard of their good conduct, and requested me to say, in return, that they intended in every respect to conform to the wishes of the Government. I then presented to them a diagram of the country assigned them, by their treaty of 1851, as their hunting-grounds, which they seemed to understand perfectly, and were enabled without difficulty to give each initial point. In fact, they exhibited a degree of intelligence seldom to be found among tribes where no effort has been made to civilize them. I stated to them that it was the intention of their Great Father to reduce the area of their present reservation, and that they should settle down and betake themselves to agriculture, and eventually abandon the chase as a means of support. They informed me that such was their wish; and that they had been aware for some time that they would be compelled to do so: that game was growing more scarce every year, and that they had also noticed the approach of whites, and felt that they must soon, in a great measure, conform to their habits. * * * It has not fallen to my lot to visit any Indians who seem more disposed to yield to the wishes of the Government than the Cheyennes and Arapahoes. Notwithstanding they are fully aware of the rich mines discovered in their country, they are disposed to yield up their claims without any reluctance. They certainly deserve the fostering hand of the Government, and should be liberally encouraged in their new sphere of life."

This treaty was concluded in February of the next year, at Fort Wise. The chiefs of the Cheyennes and Arapahoes there "ceded and relinquished" all the lands to which they had any claim, "wherever situated," except a certain tract whose boundaries were defined. The land relinquished included lands in Kansas and Nebraska, and all of that part of Colorado which is north of the Arkansas, and east of the Rocky Mountains.

The Cheyennes and Arapahoes, in "consideration of their kind treatment by the citizens of Denver and the adjoining towns," "respectfully requested," in the eleventh Article of this treaty, that the United States would permit the proprietors of these towns to enter their lands at the minimum price of one dollar and twenty-five cents an acre. This Article was struck out by the Senate, and the Indians consented to the amendment; but the proof of their good-will and gratitude remained on record, nevertheless.

The desire of the Government to make farmers of these Indians was reiterated in this treaty, and evidenced by pledges of purchase of stock, agricultural implements, etc.; mills, also, and mechanic shops they were to have, and an annuity of $30,000 a year for fifteen years. There was this clause, however, in an article of the treaty, "Their annuities may, at the discretion of the President of the United States, be discontinued entirely should said Indians fail to make reasonable and satisfactory efforts to improve and advance their condition; in which case such other provision shall be made for them as the President and Congress may judge to be suitable or proper." Could there be a more complete signing away than this of all benefits provided for by the treaty?

Lands were to be assigned to them "in severalty," and certificates were to be issued by the Commissioner of Indian Affairs, specifying the names of individuals; and that the "said tracts were set apart for the exclusive use and benefit of the assignees and their heirs." Each Indian was to have forty acres of land, "to include in every case, as far as practicable, a reasonable portion of timber and water."

The tenth Article of the treaty provided that the annuities now paid to the Arapahoes and Cheyennes should be continued to them until the stipulations of such treaties or articles of agreement should be fulfilled; and the seventh Article provided that the President, with the assent of Congress, should have power to modify or change any "of the provisions of former treaties" "in such manner and to whatever extent" he might judge it to be necessary and expedient for their best interests.

Could a community of people be delivered up more completely bound and at the mercy of a government? Some of the bands of the Cheyennes who were not represented at this council were much dissatisfied with the treaty, as evidently they had great reason to be. And as time went on, all the bands became dissatisfied. Two years later we find that, instead of their being settled on those farms "in severalty," the survey of their lands has been just completed, and that "a contract will soon be made for the construction of a ditch for the purpose of irrigating their arable land." "It is to be hoped," the Superintendent of the Colorado Agency writes, that "when suitable preparations for their subsistence by agriculture and grazing are made, these tribes will gradually cease their roaming, and become permanently settled." It would seem highly probable that under those conditions the half-starved creatures would be only too glad to cease to roam. It is now ten years since they were reported to be in a condition of miserable starvation every winter, trying to raise a little corn here and there, and begging to have a farmer and a blacksmith sent out to them. They are now divided and subdivided into small bands, hunting the buffalo wherever they can find him, and going in small parties because there are no longer large herds of buffaloes to be found anywhere. The Governor of Colorado says, in his report for 1863, that "these extensive subdivisions of the tribes caused great difficulty in ascertaining the really guilty parties in the commission of offences." Depredations and hostilities are being frequently committed, but it is manifestly unjust to hold the whole tribe responsible for the acts of a few.

Things grew rapidly worse in Colorado. Those "preparations for their subsistence by agriculture and grazing"—which it took so much room to tell in the treaty—not having been made; the farmer, and the blacksmith, and the grist-mill not having arrived; the contract not having been even let for the irrigating-ditch, without which no man can raise any crops in Colorado, not even on arable lands—many of the Cheyennes and Arapahoes took to a system of pilfering reprisals from emigrant trains, and in the fights resulting from this effort to steal they committed many terrible murders. All the tribes on the plains were more or less engaged in these outrages; and it was evident, before midsummer of 1864, that the Government must interfere with a strong hand to protect the emigrants and

Western settlers—to protect them from the consequences of its own bad faith with the Indians. The Governor of Colorado called for military aid, and for authority to make a campaign against the Indians, which was given him. But as there was no doubt that many of the Indians were still peaceable and loyal, and he desired to avoid every possibility of their sharing in the punishment of the guilty, he issued a proclamation in June, requesting all who were friendly to come to places which he designated, where they were to be assured of safety and protection. This proclamation was sent to all the Indians of the plains. In consequence of it, several bands of friendly Arapahoes and Cheyennes came to Fort Lyon, and were there received by the officer in charge, rationed, and assured of safety. Here there occurred, on the 29th of November, one of the foulest massacres which the world has seen. This camp of friendly Indians was surprised at daybreak, and men, women, and children were butchered in cold blood. Most of those who escaped fled to the north, and, joining other bands of the tribe, proceeded at once to take most fearful, and, it must be said, natural revenge. A terrible war followed. Some of them confederated with the Sioux, and waged relentless war on all the emigrant routes across the plains. These hostilities were bitter in proportion to the bitterness of resentment felt by the refugees from this massacre. "It will be long before faith in the honor and humanity of the whites can be re-established in the minds of these barbarians," says an official report, "and the last Indian who escaped from the brutal scene at Sand Creek will probably have died before its effects will have disappeared."*

In October of the next year some of the bands, having first had their safety assured by an old and tried friend, I. H. Leavenworth, Indian Agent for the Upper Arkansas, gathered to-

* See Appendix, Arts. I. and XI.

gether to hold a council with United States Commissioners on the Little Arkansas. The commissioners were empowered by the President to restore to the survivors of the Sand Creek massacre full value for all the property then destroyed; "to make reparation," so far as possible. To each woman who had lost a husband there they gave one hundred and sixty acres of land; to each child who had lost a parent, the same. Probably even an Indian woman would consider one hundred and sixty acres of land a poor equivalent for a murdered husband; but the offers were accepted in good part by the tribe, and there is nothing in all the history of this patient race more pathetic than the calm and reasonable language employed by some of these Cheyenne and Arapahoe chiefs at this council. Said Black Kettle, the chief over whose lodge the American flag, with a white flag tied below, was floating at the time of the massacre, " I once thought that I was the only man that persevered to be the friend of the white man; but since they have come and cleaned out our lodges, horses, and everything else, it is hard for me to believe white men any more. * * * All my friends, the Indians that are holding back, they are afraid to come in; are afraid that they will be betrayed as I have been. I am not afraid of white men, but come and take you by the hand." Elsewhere, Black Kettle spoke of Colonel Chivington's troops as "that fool - band of soldiers that cleared out our lodges, and killed our women and children. This is hard on us." With a magnanimity and common - sense which white men would have done well to imitate in their judgments of the Indians, he recognized that it would be absurd, as well as unjust, to hold all white men in distrust on account of the acts of that "fool-band of soldiers."*

---

* Gen. Harney, on being asked by Bishop Whipple if Black Kettle were a hostile Indian, replied, laying his hand on his heart, " I have worn this uniform fifty-five years. He was as true a friend of the white man as I am."

By the terms of this treaty, a new reservation was to be set apart for the Cheyennes and Arapahoes; hostile acts on either side were to be settled by arbitration; no whites were to be allowed on the reservation; a large tract of country was to be "relinquished" by the Indians, but they were "expressly permitted to reside upon and range at pleasure throughout the unsettled portions of that part of the country they claim as originally theirs." The United States reserved the right to build roads and establish forts in the reservation, and pledged itself to pay "annually, for the period of forty years," certain sums of money to each person in the tribe: twenty dollars a head till they were settled on their reservation; after that, forty dollars a head. To this end an accurate annual census of the Indians was promised at the time of the annuity payment in the spring.

The Indians went away from this council full of hope and satisfaction. Their oldest friends, Colonel Bent and Kit Carson, were among the commissioners, and they felt that at last they had a treaty they could trust. Their old reservation in Colorado (to which they probably could never have been induced to return) was restored to the public domain of that territory, and they hoped in their new home for greater safety and peace. The Apaches, who had heretofore been allied with the Kiowas and Comanches, were now allied with them, and to have the benefits of the new treaty. A small portion of the tribe—chiefly young men of a turbulent nature—still held aloof, and refused to come under the treaty provisions. One riotous band, called the Dog Soldiers, were especially refractory; but, before the end of the next year, they also decided to go southward and join the rest of the tribe on the new reservation. Occasional hostilities took place in the course of the winter, one of which it is worth while to relate, the incident is so typical a one.

On the 21st of February a son of one Mr. Boggs was killed and scalped by a party of four Cheyenne Indians about six miles east of Fort Dodge, on the Arkansas River. On investigation, it appeared that Mr. Boggs had gone to the Indian camp without any authority, and had there traded off eleven one-dollar bills for ten-dollar bills. The Indian on whom this trick had been played found Mr. Boggs out, went to him, and demanded reparation; and, in the altercation and fight which ensued, Mr. Boggs's son was killed. This story is given in the official report of Lieutenant-colonel Gordon, U.S.A., and Colonel Gordon adds, "I think this case needs no further comment."

The Cheyennes did not long remain at peace; in the summer the Senate had added to this last treaty an amendment requiring their new reservation to. be entirely "outside the State of Kansas, and not within any Indian territory, except on consent of the tribes interested." As the reservation had been partly in Kansas, and partly on the lands of the Cherokees, this amendment left them literally without any home whatever. Under these circumstances, the young men of the tribe soon began to join again with other hostile Indians in committing depredations and hostilities along the great mail-routes on the plains. Again they were visited with summary and apparently deserved vengeance by the United States troops, and in the summer of 1867 a Cheyenne village numbering three hundred lodges was burnt by United States soldiers under General Hancock. Fortunately the women and children had all fled on the first news of the approach of the army. Soon after this another council was held with them, and once more the precarious peace was confirmed by treaty; but was almost immediately broken again in consequence of the failure of the Government to comply with the treaty provisions. That some members of these tribes had also failed to keep to the treaty provisions is undoubtedly true, but by far the greater part of them were loyal and peaceable. "The substantial cause of this war," however, was acknowledged by the Indian Bureau itself to be "the fact that the Department, for want of appropriations, was compelled to stop their supplies, and to permit them to recur to the chase for subsistence."

In 1868 "the country bounded east by the State of Arkansas, south by Texas, north by Kansas, and west by the hundredth meridian of longitude, was set apart for the exclusive use of the Cheyennes, Arapahoes, Kiowas, and Comanches, and such other bands as might be located there by proper authority;" and the whole was declared to constitute "a military district," under command of Major-general Hazen, U.S.A. In October of the same year Major Wynkoop, who had been the faithful friend of the Cheyennes and Arapahoes ever since the days of Sand Creek, published his last protest in their behalf, in a letter to the Commissioner of Indian Affairs. He says that the failure of the Government to fulfil treaty provisions in the matter of supplies forced them to resort to hunting again; and then the refusal of the Government to give them the arms and ammunition promised in the treaty, left them without any means of securing the game; hence the depredations. The chiefs had promised to deliver up the guilty ones to Major Wynkoop, "but before sufficient time had elapsed for them to fulfil their promises the troops were in the field, and the Indians in flight. * * * Even after the majority of the Cheyennes had been forced to take the war-path, in consequence of the bad acts of some of their nation, several bands of the Cheyennes, and the whole Arapahoe tribe, could have been kept at peace had proper action been taken at the time; but now all the Indians of the Upper Arkansas are engaged in the struggle."*

In 1869 many Arapahoes and Cheyennes had made their way to Montana, and were living with the Gros Ventres; most of those who remained at the south were quiet, and seemed to be disposed to observe the provisions of the treaty, but were earnestly imploring to be moved farther to the north, where they might hunt buffalo.

* On October 27th of this year Black Kettle and his entire band were killed by Gen. Custer's command at Antelope Hills, on the Wichita River.

In 1870, under the care of an agent of the Society of Friends, the improvement of the Southern Cheyennes was remarkable. Buildings were put up, land was broken and planted, and the agent reports that, "with proper care on the part of the Government," there will not be any "serious trouble" with the tribe, although there are still some "restless spirits" among them.

In 1872 the Cheyennes and Arapahoes are reported as "allied to the Government in the maintenance of peace on the border. Very strong inducements have been made by the raiding bands of Kiowas, at critical times in the past two years, to join them in hostile alliance in raids against the whites; but all such appeals have been rejected, and, as a tribe, they have remained loyal and peaceful."

Thirty lodges of the Northern Cheyennes returned this year and joined their tribe, but many of them were still roaming among the Northern Sioux. In 1874 there were said to be over three thousand of these Northern Cheyennes and Arapahoes at the Red Cloud Agency. The Government refused any longer to permit them to stay there; and, after repeated protests, and expressions of unwillingness to move, they at last consented to go to the Indian Territory. But their removal was deferred, on account of the unsettled state of the Southern Cheyennes. Early in the spring troubles had broken out among them, in consequence of a raid of horse-thieves on their reservation. The chief, Little Robe, lost forty-three head of valuable ponies. These ponies were offered for sale in Dodge City, Kansas, where Little Robe's son, with a small band of young men, made an unsuccessful effort to reclaim them. Failing in this, the band, on their way back, stole the first stock they came to; were pursued by the Kansas farmers, the stock recaptured, and Little Robe's son badly wounded. This was sufficient to bring on a general war against white men in the whole region; and the history of the next few months was a history of murders and outrages by Cheyennes, Kiowas, Osages, and Comanches. Sixty lodges of the Cheyennes took refuge under the protection of the United States troops at the agency, and the old problem returned again, how to punish the guilty without harming the innocent. A vigorous military campaign was carried on under General Miles against the hostiles until, in the spring of 1875, the main body surrendered. Wretched, half starved, more than half naked, without lodges, ponies—a more pitiable sight was never seen than this band of Indians. It was inconceivable how they had so long held out; nothing but a well-nigh indomitable pride and inextinguishable hatred of the whites and sense of wrongs could have supported them. It was decided that thirty-three of the most desperate ones should be sent as prisoners to St. Augustine, Florida; but before the selection was completed a general stampede among the surrendered braves took place, resulting in the final escape of some four hundred. They held their ground from two P. M. until dark against three companies of cavalry and two Gatlin guns, and, "under cover of an extremely dark and stormy night, escaped, leaving only three dead on the field." It is impossible not to admire such bravery as this. The Report of the Indian Bureau for 1875 says of the condition of affairs at this agency at this time: "The friendly Cheyennes have had their loyalty put to the severest test by comparing their own condition with that of the full-fed and warmly-housed captives of the War Department. Notwithstanding all privations, they have been unswerving in their friendship, and ever ready to assist the agent in maintaining order, and compelling the Northern Cheyennes who have visited the agency to submit to a count." In consequence of the hostilities, they were obliged to remain close to the agency in camp—a hardship that could hardly be endured, and resulted in serious suffering. Their rations were not enough to subsist them, and yet, being cut off from hunting, they were entirely dependent on them. And even these inadequate rations did not arrive when they were due. Their agent writes, in 1875: "On last year's flour contract not a single pound was received until the fourteenth day of First Month, 1875, when six months of cold weather and many privations had passed, notwithstanding the many protestations and urgent appeals from the agent."

The now thoroughly subjugated Cheyennes went to work with a will. In one short year they are reported as so anxious to cultivate the ground that, when they could not secure the use of a plough or hoe, they used "axes, sticks of wood, and their hands, in preparing the ground, planting and cultivating their garden spots."

The Northern Cheyennes are still on the Red Cloud Agency, and are reported as restless and troublesome.

In 1877 they were all removed to the Cheyenne and Arapahoe Agency, in Indian Territory. The Reports of the Department say that they asked to be taken there. The winter of 1866 and the summer of 1867 were seasons of great activity and interest at this agency. In the autumn they went off on a grand buffalo hunt, accompanied by a small detail of troops from Fort Reno. Early in the winter white horse-thieves began to make raids on their ponies, and stole so many that many of the Indians were obliged to depend on their friends' ponies to help them return home. Two hundred and sixty in all were stolen—carried, as usual, to Dodge City and sold. A few were recovered; but the loss to the Indians was estimated at two thousand nine hundred dollars. "Such losses are very discouraging to the Indians," writes their agent, and are "but a repetition of the old story that brought on the war of 1874."

In midsummer of this year the "Cheyenne and Arapahoe Transportation Company" was formed: forty wagons were sent out, with harness, by the Government; the Indians furnished the horses; and on the 19th of July the Indians set out in their new *rôle* of "freighters" of their own supplies. They went to Wichita, Kansas—one hundred and sixty-five miles—in six days, with their ponies; loaded sixty-five thousand pounds of supplies into the wagons, and made the return trip in two weeks, all things being delivered in good condition.

This experiment was thoroughly tested; and its results are notable among the many unheeded refutations of the constantly repeated assertion that Indians will not work. The agent of the Cheyennes and the Arapahoes, testifying before a Senate Committee in 1879, says: "We have run a wagon train, driven by Indians, to Wichita, for three years and over, and have never had a drunken Indian yet."

"Do they waste their money, or bring it home?"

"They almost invariably spend it for saddles or clothing, or something of use to them that is not furnished by the Government. * * * They have never stolen an ounce of sugar, coffee, or anything else: they have been careful not to injure or waste anything, and have delivered everything in good faith."

The agent reports not a single case of drunkenness during the year. The manual labor and boarding-school has one hundred and thirteen scholars in it, "all it can accommodate." The children earned four hundred dollars in the year by work of one sort and another, and have "expended the money as judiciously as would white children of their ages." They bought calico, cotton cloth, shoes, hats, several head of cattle, and one horse. They also "bought many delicacies for their friends in camp who were sick and in need."

"One Cheyenne woman tanned robes, traded them for twenty-five two-year-old heifers, and gave them to her daughter in the school. * * * The boys have one hundred and twenty acres of corn under cultivation, ten acres of potatoes, broom-corn, sugar-cane, peanuts, melons, and a good variety of vegetables. They are entitled to one-half the crop for cultivating it."

This is a marvellous report of the change wrought in a people in only two years' time. It proves that the misdemeanors, the hostilities of 1874 and 1875, had been largely forced on them by circumstances.

The winter of 1877 and summer of 1878 were terrible seasons for the Cheyennes. Their fall hunt had proved unsuccessful. Indians from other reservations had hunted the ground over before them, and driven the buffalo off; and the Cheyennes made their way home again in straggling parties, destitute and hungry. Their agent reports that the result of this hunt has clearly proved that "in the future the Indian must rely on tilling the ground as the principal means of support; and if this conviction can be firmly established, the greatest obstacle to advancement in agriculture will be overcome. With the buffalo gone, and their pony herds being constantly decimated by the inroads of horse-thieves, they must soon adopt, in all its varieties, the way of the white man. * * * The usual amount of horse-stealing has prevailed, and the few cases of successful pursuit have only increased the boldness of the thieves and the number of the thefts. Until some other system of law is introduced we cannot hope for a cessation of this grievance."

The ration allowed to these Indians is reported as being "reduced and insufficient," and the small sums they have been able to earn by selling buffalo-hides are said to have been " of material assistance" to them in "supplementing" this ration. But in this year there have been sold only $657 worth of skins by the Cheyennes and Arapahoes together. In 1876 they sold $17,600 worth. Here is a falling off enough to cause very great suffering in a little community of five thousand people. But this was only the beginning of their troubles. The summer proved one of unusual heat. Extreme heat, chills and fever, and "a reduced and insufficient ration," all combined, resulted in an amount of sickness heart-rending to read of. "It is no exaggerated estimate," says the agent, "to place the number of sick people on the reservation at two thousand. Many deaths occurred which might have been obviated had there been a proper supply of anti-malarial remedies at hand. * * * Hundreds applying for treatment have been refused medicine."

The Northern Cheyennes grew more and more restless and unhappy. "In council and elsewhere they profess an intense desire to be sent North, where they say they will settle down as the others have done," says the report; adding, with an obtuseness which is inexplicable, that "no difference has been made in the treatment of the Indians," but that the "compliance" of these Northern Cheyennes has been "of an entirely different nature from that of the other Indians," and that it may be "necessary in the future to compel what so far we have been unable to effect by kindness and appeal to their better natures."

If it is "an appeal to men's better natures" to remove them by force from a healthful Northern climate, which they love and thrive in, to a malarial Southern one, where they are struck down by chills and fever — refuse them medicine which can combat chills and fever, and finally starve them—then, indeed, might be said to have been most forcible appeals made to the "better natures" of these Northern Cheyennes. What might have been predicted followed.

Early in the autumn, after this terrible summer, a band of some three hundred of these Northern Cheyennes took the desperate step of running off and attempting to make their way back to Dakota. They were pursued, fought desperately, but were finally overpowered, and surrendered. They surrendered, however, only on the condition that they should be taken to Dakota. They were unanimous in declaring that they would rather die than go back to the Indian Territory. This was nothing more, in fact, than saying that they would rather die by bullets than of chills and fever and starvation.

These Indians were taken to Fort Robinson, Nebraska. Here they were confined as prisoners of war, and held subject to the orders of the Department of the Interior. The department was informed of the Indians' determination never to be taken back alive to Indian Territory. The army officers in charge reiterated these statements, and implored the department to permit them to remain at the North; but it was of no avail. Orders came—explicit, repeated, finally stern—insisting on the return of these Indians to their agency. The commanding officer at Fort Robinson has been censured severely for the course he pursued in his effort to carry out those orders. It is difficult to see what else he could have done, except to have resigned his post. He could not take three hundred Indians by sheer brute force and carry them hundreds of miles, especially when they were so desperate that they had broken up the iron stoves in their quarters, and wrought and twisted them into weapons with which to resist. He thought perhaps he could starve them into submission. He stopped the issue of food; he also stopped the issue of fuel to them. It was midwinter; the mercury froze in that month at Fort Robinson. At the end of two days he asked the Indians to let their women and children come out that he might feed them. Not a woman would come out. On the night of the fourth day— or, according to some accounts, the sixth—these starving, freezing Indians broke prison, overpowered the guards, and fled, carrying their women and children with them. They held the pursuing troops at bay for several days; finally made a last stand in a deep ravine, and were shot down—men, women, and children together. Out of the whole band there were left alive some fifty women and children and seven men, who, having been confined in another part of the fort, had not had the good fortune to share in this outbreak and meet their death in the ravine. These, with their wives and children, were sent to Fort Leavenworth, to be put in prison; the men to be tried for murders committed in their skirmishes in Kansas on their way to the north. Red Cloud, a Sioux chief, came to Fort Robinson immediately after this massacre, and entreated to be allowed to take the Cheyenne widows and orphans into his tribe to be cared for. The Government, therefore, kindly permitted twenty-two Cheyenne widows and thirty-two Cheyenne children— many of them orphans—to be received into the band of the Ogallalla Sioux.

An attempt was made by the Commissioner of Indian Affairs, in his Report for 1879, to show by tables and figures that these Indians were not starving at the time of their flight from Indian Territory. The attempt only redounded to his own disgrace; it being proved, by the testimony given by a former clerk of the Indian Bureau before the Senate committee appointed to investigate the case of the Northern Cheyennes, that the commissioner had been guilty of absolute dishonesty in his estimates, and that the quantity of beef actually issued to the Cheyenne Agency was hundreds of pounds less than he had reported it, and that the Indians were actually, as they had claimed, " starving."

The testimony given before this committee by some of the Cheyenne prisoners themselves is heart-rending. One must have a callous heart who can read it unmoved.

When asked by Senator Morgan, " Did you ever really suffer from hunger ?" one of the chiefs replied, " We were *always* hungry; we *never* had enough. When they that were sick once in awhile felt as though they could eat something, we had nothing to give them."

" Did you not go out on the plains sometimes and hunt buffalo, with the consent of the agent ?"

" We went out on a buffalo-hunt, and nearly starved while out; we could not find any buffalo hardly; we could hardly get back with our ponies; we had to kill a good many of our ponies to eat, to save ourselves from starving."

" How many children got sick and died ?"

" Between the fall of 1877 and 1878 we lost fifty children. A great many of our finest young men died, as well as many women."

" Old Crow," a chief who served faithfully as Indian scout and ally under General Crook for years, said : " I did not feel like doing anything for awhile, because I had no heart. I did not want to be in this country. I was all the time wanting to get back to the better country where I was born, and where my children are buried, and where my mother and sister yet live. So I have laid in my lodge most of the time with nothing to think about but that, and the affair up north at Fort Robinson, and my relatives and friends who were killed there. But now I feel as though, if I had a wagon and a horse or two, and some land, I would try to work. If I had something, so that I could do something, I might not think so much about these other things. As it is now, I feel as though I would just as soon be asleep with the rest."

The wife of one of the chiefs confined at Fort Leavenworth testified before the committee as follows : " The main thing I complained of was that we didn't get enough to eat ; my children nearly starved to death ; then sickness came, and there was nothing good for them to eat ; for a long time the most they had to eat was corn-meal and salt. Three or four children died every day for awhile, and that frightened us."

(This testimony was taken at Fort Reno, in Indian Territory.)

When asked if there were anything she would like to say to the committee, the poor woman replied : " I wish you would do what you can to get my husband released. I am very poor here, and do not know what is to become of me. If he were released he would come down here, and we would live together quietly, and do no harm to anybody, and make no trouble. But I should never get over my desire to get back north ; I should always want to get back where my children were born, and died, and were buried. That country is better than this in every respect. * * * There is plenty of good, cool water there—pure water—while here the water is not good. 'It is not hot there, nor so sickly. Are you going where my husband is? Can you tell when he is likely to be released?"

The Senators were obliged to reply to her that they were not going where her husband was, and they could not tell when he would be released.

In view of the accounts of the sickness and suffering of these Indians in 1877 and 1878, the reports made in 1879 of the industry and progress at the Cheyenne and Arapahoe Agency are almost incredible. The school children have, by their earnings, bought one hundred head of cattle; 451,000 pounds of freight have been transported by the Indians during the year; they have also worked at making brick, chopping wood, making hay, hauling wood, and splitting and hauling rails; and have earned thereby $7121 25. Two of the girls of the school have been promoted to the position of assistant teachers; and the United States mail contractor between this agency and Fort Elliott, in Texas—a distance of one hundred and sixty-five miles—has operated almost exclusively with full-blooded Indians: "there has been no report of breach of trust on the part of any Indians connected with this trust, and the contractor expresses his entire approval of their conduct."

It is stated also that there was not sufficient clothing to furnish each Indian with a warm suit of clothing, "as promised by the treaty," and that, "by reference to official correspondence, the fact is established that the Cheyennes and Arapahoes are judged as having no legal rights to any lands, having forfeited their treaty reservation by a failure to settle thereon," and their "present reservation not having been, as yet, confirmed by Congress. Inasmuch as the Indians fully understood, and were assured that this reservation was given to them in lieu of their treaty reservation, and have commenced farming in the belief that there was no uncertainty about the matter, it is but common justice that definite action be had at an early day, securing to them what is their right."

It would seem that there could be found nowhere in the melancholy record of the experiences of our Indians a more glaring instance of confused multiplication of injustices than this. The Cheyennes were pursued and slain for venturing to leave this very reservation, which, it appears, is not their reservation at all, and they have no legal right to it. Are there any words to fitly characterize such treatment as this from a great, powerful, rich nation, to a handful of helpless people?

CHAPTER IV.

THE NEZ PERCÉS.

BOUNDED on the north, south, and east by snow-topped mountains, and on the west by shining waters; holding in its rocky passes the sources of six great rivers; bearing on its slopes and plains measureless forests of pine and cedar and spruce; its meadows gardens of summer bloom and fruit, and treasure-houses of fertility,—lies Oregon: wide, healthful, beautiful, abundant, and inviting, no wonder it was coveted and fought for.

When Lewis and Clarke visited it, eighty years ago, they found living there many tribes of Indians, numbering in all, at the lowest estimates, between twenty and thirty thousand; of all these tribes the Nez Percés were the richest, noblest, and most gentle.

To the Cayuses, one of the most warlike of these tribes, Messrs. Lewis and Clarke presented an American flag, telling them it was an emblem of peace. The gay coloring and beauty of the flag, allied to this significance, made a deep impression on the poetic minds of these savages. They set the flag up in a beautiful valley called the Grande Ronde — a fertile basin some twenty-five miles in diameter, surrounded by high walls of basaltic rock, and watered by a branch of the Snake River: around this flag they met their old enemies the Shoshones, and swore to keep perpetual peace with them; and the spot became consecrated to an annual meeting of the tribes—a sort of fair, where the Cayuse, Nez Percé, and Walla Walla Indians came every summer and traded their roots, skins, elk and buffalo

meats, for salmon and horses, with the Shoshones. It was a
beautiful spot, nearly circular, luxuriantly covered with grass,
the hill wall around it thick grown with evergreen trees, chiefly
larch.   The Indians called it Karpkarp, which being translated
is "Balm of Gilead."

The life of these Indians was a peculiar one. Most of them
had several homes, and as they lived only a part of the year in
each, were frequently spoken of by travellers as nomadic tribes,
while in fact they were as wedded to their homes as any civilized inhabitants of the world; and their wanderings were as
systematic as the removals of wealthy city people from town
homes to country places. If a man were rich enough, and fond
enough of change, to have a winter house in New York, a house
for the summer in Newport, and one for autumn in the White
Mountains, nobody would think of calling him a nomad; still
less if he made these successive changes annually, with perfect
regularity, owing to opportunities which were offered him at
regularly recurring intervals in these different places to earn
his living; which was the case with the Oregon Indians.

As soon as the snow disappears in the spring there is in
certain localities, ready for gathering, the "pohpoh"—a small
bulb, like an onion. This is succeeded by the "spatlam," and
the "spatlam" by the "cammass" or "ithwa," a root like a
parsnip, which they make into fine meal. In midsummer come
the salmon in countless shoals up the rivers. August is the
month for berries, of which they dry great quantities for winter use. In September salmon again—coming down stream
now, exhausted and ready to die, but in sufficiently good condition to be dried for the winter. In October comes the "me-
sani," another root of importance in the Indian larder. After
this they must depend on deer, bears, small game, and wild-
fowl. When all these resources fail, there is a kind of lichen
growing on the trees, of which they can eat enough to keep
themselves from starving, though its nutritive qualities are very

small. Thus each season had its duty and its appointed place of abode, and year after year the same month found them in the same spot.

In 1833 a delegation from these Oregon Indians went to St. Louis, and through Mr. Catlin, the artist, made known their object, which was "to inquire for the truth of a representation which they said some white men had made among them, that our religion was better than theirs, and that they would all be lost if they did not embrace it." Two members of this delegation were Nez Percés—"Hee-oh'ks-te-kin" and "H'co-a-h'co-a-h'cotes-min," or "Rabbit-skin Leggings," and "No Horns on his Head." Their portraits are to be found in "Catlin's American Indians." One of these died on his way home; but the other journeyed his thousands of miles safely back, and bore to his tribe the news "that the report which they had heard was well founded, and that good and religious men would soon come among them to teach this religion, so that they could all understand and have the benefits of it."

Two years later the Methodist Episcopal Society and the American Board both sent missionaries to Oregon. Before this the religion of the fur-traders was the only white man's religion that the Indians had had the opportunity of observing. Eleven different companies and expeditions, besides the Hudson's Bay and the North-west Companies, had been established in their country, and the Indians had become only too familiar with their standards and methods. It was not many years after the arrival of the missionaries in Oregon that a traveller there gave the following account of his experience with a Nez Percé guide:

"Creekie (so he was named) was a very kind man; he turned my worn-out animals loose, and loaded my packs on his own; gave me a splendid horse to ride, and intimated by significant gestures that we would go a short distance that afternoon. I gave my assent, and we were soon on our way; hav-

ing ridden about ten miles, we camped for the night. I noticed, during the ride, a degree of forbearance toward each other which I had never before observed in that race. When we
halted for the night the two boys were behind; they had been
frolicking with their horses, and, as the darkness came on, lost
the trail. It was a half-hour before they made their appearance, and during this time the parents manifested the most
anxious solicitude for them. One of them was but three years
old, and was lashed to the horse he rode; the other only seven
years of age—young pilots in the wilderness at night. But
the elder, true to the sagacity of his race, had taken his course,
and struck the brook on which we were encamped within three
hundred yards of us. The pride of the parents at this feat,
and their ardent attachment to the children, were perceptible
in the pleasure with which they received them at their even-
ning fire, and heard the relation of their childish adventures.
The weather was so pleasant that no tent was spread. The
willows were bent, and the buffalo-robes spread over them.
Underneath were laid other robes, on which my Indian host
seated himself, with his wife and children on one side and
myself on the other. A fire burnt brightly in front. Water
was brought, and the evening ablutions having been performed,
the wife presented a dish of meat to her husband and one to
myself. There was a pause. The woman seated herself between her children. The Indian then bowed his head and
prayed to God. A wandering savage in Oregon, calling on
Jehovah in the name of Jesus Christ! After the prayer he
gave meat to his children and passed the dish to his wife.
While eating, the frequent repetition of the words Jehovah and
Jesus Christ, in the most reverential manner, led me to suppose that they were conversing on religious topics, and thus
they passed an hour. Meanwhile the exceeding weariness of a
long day's travel admonished me to seek rest. I had slumber-
ed I know not how long, when a strain of music awoke me.

The Indian family was engaged in its evening devotions. They were singing a hymn in the Nez Percés language. Having finished, they all knelt and bowed their faces on the buffalo-robe, and Creekie prayed long and fervently. Afterward they sung another hymn, and retired. To hospitality, family affection, and devotion, Creekie added honesty and cleanliness to a great degree, manifesting by these fruits, so contrary to the nature and habits of his race, the beautiful influence of the work of grace on the heart."

The earliest mention of the Nez Percés in the official records of the Indian Bureau is in the year 1843. In that year an agent was sent out to investigate the condition of the Oregon tribes, and he reports as follows: "The only tribes from which much is to be hoped, or anything to be feared in this part of Oregon, are the Walla Wallas, Cayuses, and Nez Percés, inhabiting a district on the Columbia and its tributaries, commencing two hundred and forty miles from its mouth, and stretching four hundred and eighty miles in the interior."

The Nez Percés, living farther inland, "inhabit a beautiful grazing district, not surpassed by any I have seen for verdure, water privileges, climate, or health. This tribe forms an honorable exception to the general Indian character—being more noble, industrious, sensible, and better disposed toward the whites and their improvements in the arts and sciences; and though brave as Cæsar, the whites have nothing to dread at their hands in case of their dealing out to them what they conceive to be right and equitable."

When this agent arrived at the missionary station among the Nez Percés, he was met there by a large body of the Indians with twenty-two of their chiefs. The missionaries received him "with joyful countenances and glad hearts;" the Indians, "with civility, gravity, and dignified reserve."

He addressed them at length, explaining to them the kind intentions of the Government toward them. They listened with "gravity, fixed attention, and decorum." Finally an aged chief, ninety years of age, arose and said: "I speak to-day; perhaps to-morrow I die. I am the oldest chief of the tribe. I was the high chief when your great brothers, Lewis and Clarke, visited this country. They visited me, and honored me with their friendship and counsel. I showed them my numerous wounds, received in bloody battle with the Snakes. They told me it was not good; it was better to be at peace; gave me a flag of truce; I held it up high. We met, and talked, but never fought again. Clarke pointed to this day—to you and this occasion. We have long waited in expectation; sent three of our sons to Red River school to prepare for it; two of them sleep with their fathers; the other is here, and can be ears, mouth, and pen for us. I can say no more; I am quickly tired; my voice and limbs tremble. I am glad I live to see you and this day; but I shall soon be still and quiet in death."

At this council the Nez Percés elected a head chief named Ellis, and adopted the following Code of Laws:

Art. 1. Whoever wilfully takes life shall be hung.

Art. 2. Whoever burns a dwelling-house shall be hung.

Art. 3. Whoever burns an out-building shall be imprisoned six months, receive fifty lashes, and pay all damages.

Art. 4. Whoever carelessly burns a house or any property shall pay damages.

Art. 5. If any one enter a dwelling without permission of the occupant, the chiefs shall punish him as they think proper. Public rooms are excepted.

Art. 6. If any one steal, he shall pay back twofold; and if it be the value of a beaver-skin or less, he shall receive twenty-five lashes; and if the value is over a beaver-skin, he shall pay back twofold, and receive fifty lashes.

Art. 7. If any one take a horse and ride it, without permission, or take any article and use it, without liberty, he shall pay for the use of it, and receive from twenty to fifty lashes, as the chief shall direct.

Art. 8. If any one enter a field and injure the crops, or throw down the fence, so that cattle or horses go in and do damage, he shall pay all damages, and receive twenty-five lashes for every offence.

Art. 9. Those only may keep dogs who travel or live among the game. If a dog kill a lamb, calf, or any domestic animal, the owner shall pay the damage, and kill the dog.

Art. 10. If an Indian raise a gun or other weapon against a white man, it shall be reported to the chiefs, and they shall punish him. If a white man do the same to an Indian, it shall be reported to Dr. White, and he shall punish or redress it.

Art. 11. If an Indian break these laws, he shall be punished by his chiefs; if a white man break them, he shall be reported to the agent, and punished at his instance.

These laws, the agent says, he "proposed one by one, leaving them as free to reject as to accept. They were greatly pleased with all proposed, but wished a heavier penalty to some, and suggested the dog-law, which was annexed."

In a history of Oregon written by one W. H. Gray, of Astoria, we find this Indian agent spoken of as a "notorious blockhead." Mr. Gray's methods of mention of all persons toward whom he has antagonism or dislike are violent and undignified, and do not redound either to his credit as a writer or his credibility as a witness. But it is impossible to avoid the impression that in this instance he was not far from the truth. Surely one cannot read, without mingled horror and incredulity, this programme of the whipping-post, offered as one of the first instalments of the United States Government's "kind intentions" toward these Indians; one of the first practical illustrations given them of the kind of civilization the United States Government would recommend and introduce.

We are not surprised to read in another narrative of affairs in Oregon, a little later, that "the Indians want pay for being whipped, the same as they did for praying—to please the missionaries—during the great revival of 1839. * * * Some of the influential men in the tribe desired to know of what benefit this whipping-system was going to be to them. They said they were willing it should continue, provided they were to receive shirts and pants and blankets as a reward for being whipped. They had been whipped a good many times, and had got nothing for it, and it had done them no good. If this state of things was to continue, it was all good for nothing, and they would throw it away."

The Secretary of War does not appear to have seen this aspect of his agent's original efforts in the line of jurisprudence. He says of the report which includes this astounding 'code, merely that "it furnishes some deeply interesting and curious details respecting certain of the Indian tribes in that remote part of our territories," and that the conduct of the Nez Percés on the occasion of this important meeting "impresses one most agreeably."

A report submitted at the same time by the Rev. Mr. Spaulding, who had lived six years as missionary among the Nez Percés, is much pleasanter reading. He says that "nearly all the principal men and chiefs are members of the school; that they are as industrious in their schools as on their farms. They cultivate their lands with much skill and to good advantage, and many more would do so if they had the means. About one hundred are printing their own books with the pen. This keeps up a deep interest, as they daily have new lessons to print; and what they print must be committed to memory as soon as possible. A good number are now so far advanced in reading and printing as to render much assistance in teaching. Their books are taken home at night, and every lodge becomes a school-room. Their lessons are Scripture lessons; no others (except the laws) seem to interest them."

Even this missionary seems to have fallen under some strange glamour on the subject of the whipping-code; for he adds: "The laws which you so happily prepared, and which were unanimously adopted by the people, I have printed in the form of a small school-book. A great number of the school now read them fluently."

In the next year's report of the Secretary of War we read that "the Nez Percé tribe have adopted a few simple and plain laws as their code, which will teach them self-restraint, and is the beginning of government on their part." The Secretary also thinks it "very remarkable that there should so soon be several well supported, well attended, and well conducted schools in Oregon." (Not at all remarkable, considering that the Congregationalists, the Methodist Episcopalians, and the Roman Catholics have all had missionaries at work there for eight years.)

In 1846, the Nez Percés, with the rest of the Oregon tribes, disappear from the official records of the Indian Bureau. " It will be necessary to make some provision for conducting our relations with the Indian tribes west of the Rocky Mountains," it is said ; but, "the whole subject having been laid before Congress, it was not deemed advisable to continue a service that was circumscribed in its objects, and originally designed to be temporary." The founder of the whipping-post in Oregon was therefore relieved from his duties, and it is to be hoped his laws speedily fell into disuse. The next year all the Protestant missions in Oregon were abandoned, in consequence of the frightful massacre by the Cayuses of the missionary families living among them.* But the Nez Percés, though deprived of their teaching, did not give up the faith and the practice they had taught them. Six years later General Benjamin Alvord bore the following testimony to their religious character:

"In the spring of 1853 a white man, who had passed the previous winter in the country of the Nez Percés, came to the military post at the Dalles, and on being questioned as to the manners and customs of the tribe, he said that he wintered

---

* See Appendix, Art. XIII.

with a band of several hundred in number, and that the whole party assembled every evening and morning for prayer, the exercises being conducted by one of themselves in their own language. He stated that on Sunday they assembled for exhortation and worship."

In 1851 a superintendent and three agents were appointed for Indian service in Oregon. Treaties were negotiated with some of the tribes, but they were not ratified, and in 1853 there was, in consequence, a wide-spread dissatisfaction among all the Indians in the region. "They have become distrustful of all promises made them by the United States," says the Oregon superintendent, "and believe the design of the Government is to defer doing anything for them till they have wasted away. The settlement of the whites on the tracts which they regarded as secured to them by solemn treaty stipulations, results in frequent misunderstandings between them and the settlers, and occasions and augments bitter animosities and resentments. I am in almost daily receipt of complaints and petitions for a redress of wrongs from both parties."

Governor Stevens, of Washington Territory, in charge of the Northern Pacific Railroad Explorations and Survey, wrote, this year, "These hitherto neglected tribes, whose progress from the wild wanderers of the plains to kind and hospitable neighbors is personally known to you, are entitled, by every consideration of justice and humanity, to the fatherly care of the Government."

In Governor Stevens's report is to be found a comprehensive and intelligible account of all the Indian tribes in Oregon and Washington Territory. The greater part of the Nez Percés' country was now within the limits of Washington Territory, only a few bands remaining in Oregon. They were estimated to number at least eighteen hundred, and were said to be a "rich and powerful tribe, owning many horses." Every year they crossed the mountains to hunt buffalo on the plains of the Missouri.

In 1855 there was a general outbreak of hostilities on the part of the Oregon Indians. Tribe after tribe, even among those who had been considered friendly, fell into the ranks of the hostiles, and some base acts of treachery were committed. The Oregon settlers, menaced with danger on all sides, became naturally so excited and terrified that their actions were hasty and ill-advised. "They are without discipline, without order, and similar to madmen," says one official report. "Every day they run off the horses and the cattle of the friendly Indians. I will soon no longer be able to restrain the friendly Indians. They are indignant at conduct so unworthy of the whites, who have made so many promises to respect and protect them if they remain faithful friends. I am very sure, if the volunteers are not arrested in their brigand actions, our Indians will save themselves by flying to the homes of their relations, the Nez Percés, who have promised them help; and then all these Indians of Oregon would join in the common defence until they be entirely exterminated."

It is difficult to do full justice to the moral courage which is shown by Indians who remain friendly to whites under such circumstances as these. The traditions of their race, the powerful influence of public sentiment among their relatives and friends, and, in addition, terror for their own lives—all combine in times of such outbreaks to draw even the friendliest tribes into sympathy and co-operation with those who are making war on whites.

At this time the hostile Indians in Oregon sent word to the Nez Percés, "Join us in the war against the whites, or we will wipe you out." They said, "We have made the whites run out of the country, and we will now make the friendly Indians do the same."

"What can the friendly Indians do?" wrote the colonel of a company of Washington Territory Volunteers; "they have no ammunition, and the whites will give them none; and the hostiles say to them, 'We have plenty; come and join us, and save your lives.' The Nez Percés are very much alarmed; they say, 'We have no ammunition to defend ourselves with if we are attacked.'"

The Oregon superintendent writes to General Wool (in command at this time of the Department of the Pacific), imploring him to send troops to Oregon to protect both friendly Indians and white settlers, and to enable this department to maintain guarantees secured to these Indians by treaty stipulations. He says that the friendly Indians are "willing to submit to almost any sacrifice to obtain peace, but there may be a point beyond which they could not be induced to go without a struggle."

This outbreak terminated after some sharp fighting, and about equal losses on both sides, in what the Oregon superintendent calls "a sort of armistice," which left the Indians "much emboldened," with the impression on their minds that they have the "ability to contend successfully against the entire white race."

Moreover, "the non-ratification of the treaties heretofore made to extinguish their title to the lands necessary for the occupancy and use of our citizens, seems to have produced no little disappointment; and the continued extension of our settlements into their territory, without any compensation being made to them, is a constant source of dissatisfaction and hostile feeling.

"It cannot be expected that Indians situated like those in Oregon and Washington Territory, occupying extensive sections of country where, from the game and otherwise, they derive a comfortable support, will quietly and peaceably submit, without any equivalent, to be deprived of their homes and possessions, and to be driven off to some other locality where they cannot find their usual means of subsistence. Such a proceeding is not only contrary to our policy hitherto, but is repugnant alike to the dictates of humanity and the principles of natural justice.

"The principle of recognizing and respecting the usufruct right of the Indians to the lands occupied by them has not been so strictly adhered to in the case of the tribes in the Territories of Oregon and Washington. When a territorial government was first provided for Oregon—which then embraced the present Territory of Washington—strong inducements were held out to our people to emigrate and settle there without the usual arrangements being made in advance for the extinguishment of the title of the Indians who occupied and claimed the lands. Intruded upon, ousted of their homes and possessions without any compensation, and deprived in most cases of their accustomed means of support, without any arrangement having been made to enable them to establish and maintain themselves in other locations, it is not a matter of surprise that they have committed many depredations upon our citizens, and been exasperated to frequent acts of hostility."

As was to be expected, the armistice proved of no avail; and in 1858 the unfortunate Territories had another Indian war on their hands. In this war we find the Nez Percés fighting on the side of the United States against the hostile Indians. One of the detachments of United States troops was saved from destruction only by taking refuge with them. Nearly destitute of ammunition, and surrounded by hundreds of hostile Indians, the little company escaped by night; and "after a ride of ninety miles mostly at a gallop, and without a rest, reached Snake River," where they were met by this friendly tribe, who "received them with open arms, succored the wounded men, and crossed in safety the whole command over the difficult and dangerous river."

The officer in command of the Nez Percé band writes as follows, in his report to the Indian Commissioner:

"Allow me, my dear sir, while this general war is going on, to point you to at least a few green spots where the ravages of war do not as yet extend, and which thus far are untainted

and unaffected, with a view of so retaining them that we may
hereafter point to them as oases in this desert of war.   These
green spots are the Nez Percés, the Flat-heads, and Pend
d'Oreilles.   In this connection I refer with grateful pride to
an act of Colonel Wright, which embodies views and motives
which, endorsed and carried out by the Government, must redound to his credit and praise, and be the means of building
up, at no distant day, a bold, brave, warlike, and numerous
people.

" Before leaving Walla-Walla, Colonel Wright assembled the
Nez Percé people, told them his object was to war with and
punish our enemies; but as this great people were and ever
had been our friends, he wanted their friendship to be as en-
during as the mountains around which they lived; and in order
that no difference of views or difficulty might arise, that their
mutual promises should be recorded."

With this view he there made a treaty of friendship with
them, and thirty of the bravest warriors and chiefs at once mar-
shalled themselves to accompany him against the enemy.

When Colonel Wright asked these Indians what they wanted, " their reply was worthy of a noble race—' Peace, ploughs,
and schools.' "   At this time they had no agent appointed to
attend to their welfare; they were raising wheat, corn, and
vegetables with the rude means at their command, and still
preserved the faith and many of the practices taught them by
the missionaries thirteen years before.

In 1859 peace was again established in Oregon, and the Indians " considered as conquered."   The treaties of 1855 were
ratified by the Senate, and this fact went far to restore tranquillity in the territories.   Congress was implored by the superintendents to realize " the importance of making the appropriations for fulfilling those treaty stipulations at the earliest practicable moment;" that it may " prevent the recurrence of another savage war, necessarily bloody and devastating to our

settlements, extended under the authority and sanction of our Government." With marvellous self-restraint, the superintendents do not enforce their appeals by a reference to the fact that, if the treaties had been fulfilled in the outset, all the hostilities of the last four years might probably have been avoided.

The reservation secured to the Nez Percés was a fine tract of country, one hundred miles long and sixty in width—well watered, timbered, and of great natural resources. Already the Indians had begun to practice irrigation in their fields; had large herds of horses, and were beginning to give attention to improving the breed. Some of them could read and write their own language, and many of them professed Christianity, and were exemplary in their conduct—a most remarkable fact, proving the depth of the impression the missionary teachings must have made. The majority of them wore the American costume, and showed "their progress in civilization by attaching little value to the gewgaws and trinkets which so generally captivate the savage."

In less than two years the peace of this noble tribe was again invaded; this time by a deadly foe—the greed of gold. In 1861 there were said to be no less than ten thousand miners in the Nez Percé country prospecting for gold. Now arose the question, What will the Government do? Will it protect the rights of the Indians or not?

"To attempt to restrain miners would be like attempting to restrain the whirlwind," writes the superintendent of Washington Territory; and he confesses that, "seeing the utter impossibility of preventing miners from going to the mines," he has refrained from taking any steps which, by a certain want of success, would tend to weaken the force of the law.

For the next few years the Nez Percés saw with dismay the steady stream of settlers pouring into their country. That they did not resist it by force is marvellous, and can only be explained by the power of a truly Christian spirit.

"Their reservation was overrun by the enterprising miners; treaty stipulations were disregarded and trampled under foot; towns were established thereon, and all the means that cupidity could invent or disloyalty achieve were resorted to to shake their confidence in the Government. They were disturbed in the peaceable possession of what they regarded as their vested rights, sacredly secured by treaty. They were informed that the Government was destroyed, and that whatever treaties were made would never be carried out. All resistance on their part proved unavailing, and inquietude and discontent predominated among them," says the Governor of Idaho, in 1865. Shortly after, by the organization of that new Territory, the Nez Percés' reservation had been removed from the jurisdiction of Washington Territory to that of Idaho.

A powerful party was organized in the tribe, advocating the forming of a league with the Crows and Blackfeet against the whites. The non-arrival of promised supplies; the non-payment of promised moneys; the unchecked influx of miners throughout the reservation, put strong weapons into the hands of these disaffected ones. But the chiefs "remained firm and unwavering in their devotion to the Government and the laws. They are intelligent—their head chief, Sawyer, particularly so —and tell their people to still wait patiently." And yet, at this very time, there was due from the United States Government to this chief Sawyer six hundred and twenty-five dollars! He had for six months been suffering for the commonest necessaries of life, and had been driven to disposing of his vouchers at fifty cents on the dollar to purchase necessaries. The warriors also, who fought for us so well in 1856, were still unpaid; although in the seventh article of the treaty of 1863 it had been agreed that "the claims of certain members of the Nez Percé tribe against the Government, for services rendered and horses furnished by them to the Oregon Mounted Volunteers, as appears by certificates issued by W. H. Fauntleroy, Acting Regimental Quartermaster, and commanding Oregon Volunteers, on the 6th of March, 1856, at Camp Cornelius, and amounting to $4665, shall be paid to them in full in gold coin."

How many communities of white men would remain peaceable, loyal, and friendly under such a strain as this?

In 1866 the Indian Bureau report of the state of our diplomatic relations with the Nez Percés is that the treaty concluded with them in 1863 was ratified by the Senate, " with an amendment which awaited the action of the Indians. The ratification of this treaty has been delayed for several years for various reasons, partly arising from successive changes in the Superintendent of Indian Affairs in Idaho, whose varying opinions on the subject of the treaty have caused doubts in the minds of senators. A later treaty had been made, but, on careful consideration of the subject, it was deemed advisable to carry into effect that of 1863. The Nez Percés claimed title to a very large district of country comprised in what are now organized as Oregon, Washington, and Idaho, but principally within the latter Territory ; and already a large white population is pressing upon them in the search for gold. They are peaceable, industrious, and friendly, and altogether one of the most promising of the tribes west of the Rocky Mountains, having profited largely by the labors of missionaries among them."

By the treaty ratified in this year they give up " all their lands except a reservation defined by certain natural boundaries, and agree to remove to this reservation within one year. Where they have improvements on lands outside of it, such improvements are to be appraised and paid for. The tillable lands are to be surveyed into tracts of twenty acres each, and allotted to such Indians as desire to hold lands in severalty. The Government is to continue the annuities due under former treaties, and, in addition, pay the tribe, or expend for them for certain specific purposes having their improvement in view, the sum of $262,500, and a moderate sum is devoted to homes and salaries for chiefs. The right of way is secured through the reservation, and the Government undertakes to reserve all important springs and watering-places for public use."

In this same year the Governor of Idaho writes, in his annual report to the Department of the Interior: "Prominent among the tribes of Northern Idaho stand the Nez Percés, a majority of whom boast that they have ever been the faithful friends of the white man. But a few over half of the entire tribe of the Nez Percés are under treaty. The fidelity of those under treaty, even under the most discouraging circumstances, must commend itself to the favorable consideration of the Department. The non-payment of their annuities has had its natural effect on the minds of some of those under treaty; but their confiding head chief, Sawyer, remains unmoved, and on all occasions is found the faithful apologist for any failure of the Government. Could this tribe have been kept aloof from the contaminating vices of white men, and had it been in the power of the Government promptly to comply with the stipulations of the treaty of 1855, there can be no doubt but that their condition at this time would have been a most prosperous one, and that the whole of the Nez Percé nation would by this time have been willing to come under treaty, and settle on the reservation with those already there."

In 1867 the patience of the Nez Percés is beginning to show signs of wearing out. The Governor of Idaho writes: "This disaffection is great, and serious trouble is imminent. It could all be settled by prompt payment by the Government of their just dues; but if delayed too long I greatly fear open hostilities. They have been patient, but promises and explanations are losing force with them now. * * * Their grievances are urged with such earnestness that even Sawyer, who has always been our apologist, has in a measure abandoned his pacific policy, and asks boldly that we do them justice. * * * Even now it may not be too late; but, if neglected, war may be reasonably expected. Should the Nez Percés strike a blow, all over our Territory and around our boundaries will blaze the signal-fires and gleam the tomahawks of the savages—Kootenays, Pen d'Oreilles, Cœur d'Alenes, Blackfeet, Flat-heads, Spokanes, Pelouses, Bannocks, and Shoshones will be involved."

This disaffection, says the agent, "began to show itself soon after the visit of George C. Haigh, Esq., special agent, last December, to obtain their assent to the amendments to the treaty of June 9th, 1863—the non-ratification of that treaty had gone on so long, and promises made them by Governor Lyon that it would not be ratified, and that he was authorized to make a new treaty with them by which they would retain all of their country, as given them under the treaty of 1851, except the site of the town of Lewiston. They had also been informed in March, 1866, that Governor Lyon would be here in the June following, to pay them back-annuities due under the treaty of 1855. The failure to carry out these promises, and the idea they have that the stipulations of the treaty of 1863 will be carried out in the same manner, is one of the causes of their bad feeling. It showed itself plainly at the council lately held, and is on the increase. If there is the same delay in carrying out the stipulations of the treaty of 1863 that there has been in that of 1855, some of the chiefs with their bands will join the hostile Indians. There are many things it is impossible to explain to them. They cannot understand why the $1185 that was promised by Governor Lyon to the Indian laborers on the church is not paid. He told them when the walls were up they should receive their pay. These laborers were poor men, and such inducements were held out to them that they commenced the work in good faith, with the full expectation of receiving their pay when their labors ceased."

The head chief Sawyer's pay is still in arrears. For the last quarter of 1863, and the first and second of 1864, he has received no pay. No wonder he has ceased to be the "apologist" of the Government, which four years ago promised him an annuity of $500 a year.

Spite of this increasing disaffection the Nez Percés are industrious and prosperous. They raised in this year 15,000 bushels of wheat. "Many of them carried their wheat to be ground to the mills, while many sold the grain to packers for feed, while much of it is boiled whole for food. Some few of the better class have had their wheat ground, and sold the flour in the mining-camps at lower prices than packers could lay it down in the camps. Some have small pack-trains running through the summer; one in particular, Cru-cru-lu-ye, runs some fifteen animals; he sometimes packs for whites, and again runs on his own account. A Clearwater Station merchant a short time ago informed me of his buying some oats of Cru-cru-lu-ye last fall. After the grain had been weighed, and emptied out of the sacks, the Indian brought the empty sacks to the scales to have them weighed, and the tare deducted, saying he only wanted pay for the oats. Their sales of melons, tomatoes, corn, potatoes, squashes, green pease, etc., during the summer, in the different towns and mining-camps, bring in some $2000 to $3000. Their stock of horses and cattle is increasing fast, and with the benefits to be derived from good American stallions, and good bulls and cows, to be distributed to them under the stipulations of the treaty of 1863, they will rapidly increase in wealth."

In 1869 their reservation is still unsurveyed, and when the Indians claim that white settlers are establishing themselves inside the lines there is no way of proving it, and the agent says all he can do is to promise that "the white man's heart shall be better;" and thus the matter will rest until another disturbance arises, when the same complaints are made, and the same answers given as before—that "the white man's heart shall be better, and the boundary-line shall be surveyed."

Other treaty stipulations are still unfulfilled; and the non-treaty party, while entirely peaceable, is very strong, and immovably opposed to treaties.

In 1870, seven years after it was promised, the long deferred survey of the reservation was made. The superintendent and the agent both remonstrated, but in vain, against the manner in which it was done; and three years later a Board of Special Commissioners, appointed to inquire into the condition of the Indians in Idaho, examined the fence put up at that time, and reported that it was "a most scandalous fraud. It is a post-and-board fence. The posts are not well set. Much of the lumber is deficient in width and length. The posts are not dressed. The lumber laps at any joint where it may chance to meet, whether on the posts or between them, and the boards are not jointed on the posts where they meet; they are lapped and fastened generally with one nail, so that they are falling down rapidly. The lumber was cut on the reservation. The contract price of the fence was very high; the fencing done in places of no value to any one, for the reason that water cannot be had for irrigation. The Government cannot be a party to such frauds on the people who intrust it with their property."

In this year a commission was sent to Oregon to hold council with the band of Nez Percés occupying Wallowa Valley, in Oregon, "with a view to their removal, if practicable, to the Nez Percé Reservation in Idaho. They reported this removal to be impracticable, and the Wallowa Valley has been withdrawn from sale, and set apart for their use and occupation by Executive order."*

This commission report that one of the most troublesome questions in the way of the Government's control of Indian af-

---

* Report of the Secretary of the Interior for 1873.

fairs in Idaho is the contest between the Catholic and Protestant churches. This strife is a great detriment to the Indians.
To illustrate this, they quote Chief Joseph's reason for not
wishing schools on his reservation. He was the chief of the
non-treaty band of Nez Percés occupying the Wallowa Valley,
in Oregon:

"Do you want schools and school-houses on the Wallowa
Reservation?" asked the commissioners.

Joseph. "No, we do not want schools or school-houses on
the Wallowa Reservation."

Com. "Why do you not want schools?"

Joseph. "They will teach us to have churches."

Com. "Do you not want churches?"

Joseph. "No, we do not want churches."

Com. "Why do you not want churches?"

Joseph. "They will teach us to quarrel about God, as the
Catholics and Protestants do on the Nez Percé Reservation,
and at other places. We do not want to learn that. We may
quarrel with men sometimes about things on this earth, but we
never quarrel about God. We do not want to learn that."

Great excitement prevailed among the settlers in Oregon at
the cession of the Wallowa Valley to the Indians. The presence of United States soldiers prevented any outbreak; but the
resentment of the whites was very strong, and threats were
openly made that the Indians should not be permitted to occupy it; and in 1875 the Commissioner of Indian Affairs
writes:

"The settlements made in the Wallowa Valley, which has
for years been the pasture-ground of the large herds of horses
owned by Joseph's band, will occasion more or less trouble
between this band and the whites, until Joseph is induced or
compelled to settle on his reservation."

It is only two years since this valley was set apart by Executive order for the use and occupation of these Indians; already

the Department is contemplating "compelling" them to leave it and go to the reservation in Idaho. There were stormy scenes there also during this year. Suits were brought against all the employés of the Lapwai Agency, and a claim set up for all the lands of the agency, and for many of the Indian farms, by one Langford, representing the old claim of the missionaries, to whom a large tract of ground had been ceded some thirty years before. He attempted to take forcible possession of the place, and was ejected finally by military force, after the decision of the Attorney-general had been given that his claim was invalid.

The Indian Bureau recommended a revocation of the executive order giving the Wallowa Valley to Joseph and his band. In June of this year President Grant revoked the order, and in the autumn a commission was sent out "to visit these Indians, with a view to secure their permanent settlement on the reservation, their early entrance on a civilized life, and to adjust the difficulties then existing between them and the settlers."

It is worth while to study with some care the reasons which this commission gave to Chief Joseph why the Wallowa Valley, which had been given to him by Executive order in 1873, must be taken away from him by Executive order in 1875:

"Owing to the coldness of the climate, it is not a suitable location for an Indian reservation. * * * It is now in part settled by white squatters for grazing purposes. * * * The President claimed that he extinguished the Indian title to it by the treaty of 1863. * * * It is embraced within the limits of the State of Oregon. * * * The State of Oregon could not probably be induced to cede the jurisdiction of the valley to the United States for an Indian reservation. * * * In the conflicts which might arise in the future, as in the past, between him and the whites, the President might not be able to justify or defend him. * * * A part of the valley had already been surveyed and opened to settlement: * * * if, by some arrangement, the white settlers in the valley could be induced to leave it, others would come."

To all these statements Joseph replied that he "asked nothing of the President. He was able to take care of himself. He did not desire Wallowa Valley as a reservation, for that would subject him and his band to the will of, and dependence on, another, and to laws not of their own making. He was disposed to live peaceably. He and his band had suffered wrong rather than do wrong. One of their number was wickedly slain by a white man during the last summer, but he would not avenge his death."

"The serious and feeling manner in which he uttered these sentiments was impressive," the commissioners say, and they proceeded to reply to him "that the President was not disposed to deprive him of any just right, or govern him by his individual will, but merely subject him to the same just and equal laws by which he himself as well as all his people were ruled."

What does it mean when commissioners sent by the President to induce a band of Indians to go on a reservation to live, tell them that they shall be subjected on that reservation "merely to the same just and equal laws" by which the President and "all his people are ruled?" And still more, what is the explanation of their being so apparently unaware of the enormity of the lie that they leave it on official record, signed by their names in full? It is only explained, as thousands of other things in the history of our dealings with the Indians are only to be explained, by the habitual indifference, carelessness, and inattention with which questions relative to Indian affairs and legislation thereon are handled and disposed of, in whatever way seems easiest and shortest for the time being. The members of this commission knew perfectly well that the instant Joseph and his band moved on to the reservation they became subject to laws totally different from those by which the President and "all his people were ruled," and neither "just" nor "equal:" laws forbidding them to go beyond certain bounds without a pass from the agent; laws making them really just as much prisoners as convicts in a prison—the only difference being that the reservation is an unwalled out-of-door prison; laws giving that agent power to summon military power at any moment, to enforce any command he might choose to lay on them, and to shoot them if they refused to obey.* "The same just and equal laws by which the President himself and all his people are ruled!" Truly it is a psychological phenomenon that four men should be found willing to leave it on record under their own signatures that they said this thing.

Farther on in the same report there is an enumeration of some of the experiences which the Nez Percés who are on the Idaho Reservation have had of the advantages of living there, and of the manner in which the Government has fulfilled its promises by which it induced them to go there; undoubtedly these were all as well known to Chief Joseph as to the commissioners. For twenty-two years he had had an opportunity to study the workings of the reservation policy. They say:

"During an interview held with the agent and the treaty Indians, for the purpose of ascertaining whether there were sufficient unoccupied tillable lands for Joseph's band on the reservation, and for the further purpose of securing their co-operation to aid us in inducing Joseph to come upon the reservation, facts were brought to our attention of a failure on the part of the Government to fulfil its treaty stipulations with these Indians. The commission therefore deem it their duty to call the attention of the Government to this subject.

"1st. Article second of the treaty of June 9th, 1863, provides that no white man—excepting such as may be employed by the

---

* Witness the murder of Big Snake on the Ponca Reservation, Indian Territory, in the summer of 1879.

Indian Department—shall be permitted to reside upon the reservation without permission of the tribe, and the superintendent and the agent.   Nevertheless, four white men are occupying or claiming large tracts on the reservation.

"It is clearly the duty of the Government to adjust and quiet these claims, and remove the parties from the reservation.   Each day's delay to fulfil this treaty stipulation adds to the distrust of the Indians in the good faith of the Government.

" 2d. Article third of the same treaty of 1863 provides for the survey of the land suitable for cultivation into lots of twenty acres each ; while a survey is reported to have been early made, no measures were then, or have been since, taken to adjust farm limits to the lines of the surveyed lots.

" 3d. Rules and regulations for continuing the possession of these lots and the improvements thereon in the families of deceased Indians, have not been prescribed, as required by the treaty.

"4th. It is also provided that certificates or deeds for such tracts shall be issued to individual Indians.

"The failure of the Government to comply with this important provision of the treaty causes much uneasiness among the Indians, who are little inclined to spend their labor and means in improving ground held by the uncertain tenure of the pleasure of an agent.

" 5th. Article seventh of the treaty provides for a payment of four thousand six hundred and sixty-five dollars in gold coin to them for services and horses furnished the Oregon Mounted Volunteers in 1856.   It is asserted by the Indians that this provision of the treaty has hitherto been disregarded by the Government."

The commissioners say that "every consideration of justice and equity, as well as expediency, demands from the Government a faithful and literal compliance with all its treaty obligations toward the Indians. A failure to do this is looked upon as bad faith, and can be productive of only bad results."

At last Chief Joseph consented to remove from the Wallowa Valley with his band, and go to the Lapwai Reservation. The incidents of the council in which this consent was finally wrung from him, are left on record in Chief Joseph's own words, in an article written by him (through an interpreter) and published in the *North American Review* in 1874. It is a remarkable contribution to Indian history.

It drew out a reply from General O. O. Howard, who called his paper "The true History of the Wallowa Campaign;" published in the *North American Review* two months after Chief Joseph's paper.

Between the accounts given by General Howard and by Chief Joseph of the events preceding the Nez Percé war, there are noticeable discrepancies.

General Howard says that he listened to the "oft-repeated dreamer nonsense of the chief, 'Too-hool-hool-suit,' with no impatience, but finally said to him: 'Twenty times over I hear that the earth is your mother, and about the chieftainship of the earth. I want to hear it no more.'"

Chief Joseph says: "General Howard lost his temper, and said 'Shut up! I don't want to hear any more of such talk.'

"Too-hool-hool-suit answered, 'Who are you, that you ask us to talk, and then tell me I sha'n't talk? Are you the Great Spirit? Did you make the world?'"

General Howard, quoting from his record at the time, says: "The rough old fellow, in his most provoking tone, says something in a short sentence, looking fiercely at me. The interpreter quickly says: 'He demands what person pretends to divide this land, and put me on it?' In the most decided voice I said, 'I am the man. I stand here for the President, and there is no spirit, bad or good, that will hinder me.   My orders are plain, and will be executed.'"

Chief Joseph says: "General Howard replied, 'You are an impudent fellow, and I will put you in the guard-house,' and then ordered a soldier to arrest him."

General Howard says: "After telling the Indians that this bad advice would be their ruin, I asked the chiefs to go with me to look at their land. 'The old man (Too-hool-hool-suit) shall not go. I will leave him with Colonel Perry.' He says, 'Do you want to scare me with reference to my body?' I said, 'I will leave your body with Colonel Perry.' I then arose and led him out of the council, and gave him into the charge of Colonel Perry."

Chief Joseph says: "Too-hool-hool-suit made no resistance. He asked General Howard, 'Is that your order? I don't care. I have expressed my heart to you. I have nothing to take back. I have spoken for my country. You can arrest me, but you cannot change me, or make me take back what I have said.' The soldiers came forward and seized my friend, and took him to the guard - house. My men whispered among themselves whether they should let this thing be done. I counselled them to submit. * * * Too-hool-hool-suit was prisoner for five days before he was released."

General Howard, it will be observed, does not use the word "arrested," but as he says, later, "Too-hool-hool-suit was released on the pledge of Looking-glass and White Bird, and on his own earnest promise to behave better," it is plain that Chief Joseph did not misstate the facts. This Indian chief, therefore, was put under military arrest, and confined for five days, for uttering what General Howard calls a " tirade " in a council to which the Indians had been asked to come for the purpose of consultation and expression of sentiment.

Does not Chief Joseph speak common-sense, as well as natural feeling, in saying, "I turned to my people and said, 'The arrest of Too-hool-hool-suit was wrong, but we will not resent the insult. We were invited to this council to express our hearts, and we have done so.' "

If such and so swift penalty as this, for "tirades" in council, were the law of our land, especially in the District of Columbia, it would be "no just cause of complaint" when Indians suffer it. But considering the frequency, length, and safety of "tirades" in all parts of America, it seems unjust not to permit Indians to deliver them. However, they do come under the head of "spontaneous productions of the soil;" and an Indian on a reservation is "invested with no such proprietorship" in anything which comes under that head.*

Chief Joseph and his band consented to move. Chief Joseph says: "I said in my heart that, rather than have war, I would give up my country. I would give up my father's grave. I would give up everything rather than have the blood of white men upon the hands of my people."

It was not easy for Joseph to bring his people to consent to move. The young men wished to fight. It has been told that, at this time, Chief Joseph rode one day through his village, with a revolver in each hand, saying he would shoot the first one of his warriors that resisted the Government. Finally, they gathered all the stock they could find, and began the move. A storm came, and raised the river so high that some of the cattle could not be taken across. Indian guards were put in charge of the cattle left behind. White men attacked these guards and took the cattle. After this Joseph could no longer restrain his men, and the warfare began, which lasted over two months. It was a masterly campaign on the part of the Indians. They were followed by General Howard; they had General Crook on their right, and General Miles in front, but they were not once hemmed in; and, at last, when they surrendered at Bear

---

* Annual Report of the Indian Commissioner for 1878, p. 69.

Paw Mountain, in the Montana Hills, it was not because they
were beaten, but because, as Joseph says, "I could not bear to
see my wounded men and women suffer any longer; we had
lost enough already. * * * We could have escaped from Bear
Paw Mountain if we had left our wounded, old women and
children, behind. We were unwilling to do this. We had
never heard of a wounded Indian recovering while in the hands
of white men. * * * I believed General Miles, or I never would
have surrendered. I have heard that he has been censured for
making the promise to return us to Lapwai. He could not
have made any other terms with me at that time. I could
have held him in check until my friends came to my assistance,
and then neither of the generals nor their soldiers would ever
have left Bear Paw Mountain alive. On the fifth day I went
to General Miles and gave up my gun, and said, 'From where
the sun now stands, I will fight no more.' My people needed
rest; we wanted peace."

The terms of this surrender were shamefully violated. Joseph
and his band were taken first to Fort Leavenworth and then to
the Indian Territory. At Leavenworth they were placed in the
river bottom, with no water but the river water to drink.

"Many of my people sickened and died, and we buried them
in this strange land," says Joseph. "I cannot tell how much
my heart suffered for my people while at Leavenworth. The
Great Spirit Chief who rules above seemed to be looking some
other way, and did not see what was being done to my people."

Yet with a marvellous magnanimity, and a clear-headed sense
of justice of which few men would be capable under the circumstances, Joseph says: "I believe General Miles would have
kept his word if he could have done so. I do not blame him
for what we have suffered since the surrender. I do not know
who is to blame. We gave up all our horses, over eleven hundred, and all our saddles, over one hundred, and we have not
heard from them since. Somebody has got our horses."

This narrative of Chief Joseph's is profoundly touching; a very Iliad of tragedy, of dignified and hopeless sorrow; and it stands supported by the official records of the Indian Bureau.

"After the arrival of Joseph and his band in Indian Territory, the bad effect of their location at Fort Leavenworth manifested itself in the prostration by sickness at one time of two hundred and sixty out of the four hundred and ten; and 'within a few months' in the death of 'more than one-quarter of the entire number.'"*

"It will be borne in mind that Joseph has never made a treaty with the United States, and that he has never surrendered to the Government the lands he claimed to own in Idaho. * * * Joseph and his followers have shown themselves to be brave men and skilful soldiers, who, with one exception, have observed the rules of civilized warfare. * * * These Indians were encroached upon by white settlers, on soil they believed to be their own, and when these encroachments became intolerable, they were compelled in their own estimation to take up arms."†

Chief Joseph and a remnant of his band are still in Indian Territory, waiting anxiously the result of the movement now being made by the Ponca chief, Standing Bear, and his friends and legal advisers, to obtain from the Supreme Court a decision which will extend the protection of the civil law to every Indian in the country.

Of the remainder of the Nez Percés (those who are on the Lapwai Reservation), the report of the Indian Bureau for 1879 is that they "support themselves entirely without subsistence from the Government; procure of their own accord, and at their own expense, wagons, harness, and other farming implements beyond the amount furnished by the Government under

---

* Annual Report of the Indian Commissioner for 1878, p. 33.
† Same Report, p. 34.

their treaty," and that "as many again as were taught were turned away from school for lack of room."

The Presbyterian Board of Foreign Missions has contributed during this year $1750 for missionary work among them, and the Indians themselves have raised $125.

Their reservation is thus described: "The majority of land comprising the reservation is a vast rolling prairie, affording luxuriant pasturage for thousands of their cattle and horses. The Clearwater River, flowing as it does directly through the reserve, branching out in the North, Middle, and South Forks, greatly benefits their locations that they have taken in the valleys lying between such river and the bluffs of the higher land, forming in one instance—at Kaimaih—one of the most picturesque locations to be found in the whole North-west. Situated in a valley on either side of the South Fork, in length about six miles, varying in width from one-half to two miles; in form like a vast amphitheatre, surrounded on all sides by nearly perpendicular bluffs rising two thousand feet in height, it forms one of the prettiest valleys one can imagine. A view from the bluff reveals a living panorama, as one sees the vast fields of waving grain surrounding well-built and tasty cottages adorned with porches, and many of the conveniences found among industrious whites. The sight would lead a stranger, not knowing of its inhabitance by Indians, to inquire what prosperous white settlement was located here. It is by far the most advanced in the ways of civilization and progress of any in the Territory, if not on the coast."

How long will the white men of Idaho permit Indians to occupy so fair a domain as this? The small cloud, no larger than a man's hand, already looms on their horizon. The closing paragraph of this (the last) report from the Nez Percés is:

"Some uneasiness is manifest about stories set afloat by renegade whites, in relation to their treatment at the expiration of their treaty next July, but I have talked the matter over, and they will wait patiently to see the action on the part of the Government. They are well civilized; but one mistake on the part of the Government at this time would destroy the effects of the past thirty years' teachings. Give them time and attention; they will astonish their most zealous friends in their progress toward civilization."

CHAPTER V.

THE SIOUX.

THE word Sioux is a contraction from the old French word
"Nadouessioux," or "Enemies," the name given by the French
traders to this most powerful and warlike of all the North-western tribes. They called themselves "Dakota," or "many in
one," because so many bands under different names were joined
together. At the time of Captain Carver's travels among the
North American Indians there were twelve known bands of
these "Nadouwessies." They entertained the captain most
hospitably for seven months during the winter of 1766–'7;
adopted him as one of their chiefs; and when the time came
for him to depart, three hundred of them accompanied him
for a distance on his journey, and took leave with expressions of friendship for him, and good-will toward the Great
Father, the English king, of whom he had told them. The
chiefs wished him to say to the king "how much we desire
that traders may be sent to abide among us with such things
as we need, that the hearts of our young men, our wives, and
children may be made glad. And may peace subsist between
us so long as the sun, the moon, the earth, and the waters shall
endure;" and "acquaint the Great King how much the Nadouwessies wish to be counted among his good children."

Nothing in all the history of the earliest intercourse between
the friendly tribes of North American Indians and the Europeans coming among them is more pathetic than the accounts
of their simple hospitality, their unstinted invitations, and their

guileless expressions of desire for a greater knowledge of the white men's ways.

When that saintly old bigot, Father Hennepin, sailed up the Illinois River, in 1680, carrying his "portable chapel," chalice, and chasuble, and a few holy wafers "in a steel box, shut very close," going to teach the savages "the knowledge of the Captain of Heaven and Earth, and to use fire-arms, and several other things relating to their advantage," the Illinois were so terrified that, although they were several thousand strong, they took to flight "with horrid cries and howlings." On being reassured by signs and words of friendliness, they slowly returned—some, however, not until three or four days had passed. Then they listened to the good man's discourses with "great attention; afterward gave a great shout for joy," and "expressed a great gratitude;" and, the missionaries being footsore from long travel, the kindly creatures fell to rubbing their legs and feet "with oil of bears, and grease of wild oxen, which after much travel is an incomparable refreshment; and presented us some flesh to eat, putting the three first morsels into our mouths with great ceremonies."

It was a pity that Father Hennepin had no more tangible benefit than the doctrine of the "efficacy of the Sacraments" to communicate to the hospitable Illinois in return for their healing ointments. Naturally they did not appreciate this, and he proceeded on his way disheartened by their "brutish stupidity," but consoling himself, however, with the thought of the infants he had baptized. Hearing of the death of one of them, he says he is "glad it had pleased God to take this little Christian out of the world," and he attributed his own "preservation amidst the greatest dangers" afterward to "the care he took for its baptism." Those dangers were, indeed, by no means inconsiderable, as he and his party were taken prisoners by a roaming party of these Indians, called in the Father's quaint old book "Nadouwessians." He was forced to accompany them on their expeditions, and was in daily danger of being murdered by the more riotous and hostile members of the band. He found these savages on the whole "good-natured men, affable, civil, and obliging," and he was indebted for his life to the good-will of one of the chiefs, who protected him again and again at no inconsiderable danger to himself. The only evidence of religion among the Nadouwessies which he mentions is that they never began to smoke without first holding the pipe up to the sun, saying, "Smoke, sun!" They also offered to the sun the best part of every beast they killed, carrying it afterward to the cabin of their chief; from which Father Hennepin concluded that they had "a religious veneration for the sun."

The diplomatic relations between the United States Government and the Sioux began in the year 1815. In that year and the year following we made sixteen "treaties" of peace and friendship with different tribes of Indians—treaties demanding no cessions of land beyond the original grants which had been made by these tribes to the English, French, or Spanish governments, but confirming those to the United States; promising "perpetual peace," and declaring that "every injury or act of hostility committed by one or other of the contracting parties shall be mutually forgiven and forgot." Three of these treaties were made with bands of the Sioux—one of them with "the Sioux of the Leaf, the Sioux of the Broad Leaf, and the Sioux who shoot in the Pine-tops."

In 1825 four more treaties were made with separate Sioux bands. By one of those treaties—that of Prairie du Chien—boundaries were defined between the Chippewas and the Sioux, and it was hoped that their incessant feuds might be brought to an end. This hostility had continued unabated from the time of the earliest travellers in the country, and the Sioux had been slowly but steadily driven south and west by the victorious Chippewas. A treaty could not avail very much toward keeping peace between such ancient enemies as these. Fighting went on as before; and white traders, being exposed to the attacks of all war-parties, suffered almost more than the Indians themselves. The Government consoled itself for this spectacle of bloody war, which it was powerless to prevent, by the thought that the Indians would "probably fight on until some one or other of the tribes shall become too reduced and feeble to carry on the war, when it will be lost as a separate power" —an equivocal bit of philosophizing which was unequivocally stated in these precise words in one of the annual reports of the War Department.

In the third Article of the next treaty, also at Prairie du Chien, in 1830, began the trouble which has been from that day to this a source of never ending misunderstanding and of many fierce outbreaks on the part of the Sioux. Four of the bands by this article ceded and relinquished to the United States "forever" a certain tract of country between the Mississippi and the Des Moines River. In this, and in a still further cession, two other bands of Sioux, who were not fully represented at the council, must join; also, some four or five other tribes. Landed and "undivided" estate, owned in common by dozens of families, would be a very difficult thing to parcel out and transfer among white men to-day, with the best that fair intentions and legal skill combined could do; how much more so in those days of unsurveyed forests, unexplored rivers, owned and occupied in common by dozens of bands of wild and ignorant Indians, to be communicated with only by interpreters. Misconstructions and disputes about boundaries would have been inevitable, even if there had been all possible fairmindedness and good-will on both sides; but in this case there was only unfairmindedness on one side, and unwillingness on the other. All the early makers of treaties with the Indians congratulated themselves and the United States on the getting of acres of valuable land by the million for next to nothing, and, as years went on, openly lamented that "the Indians were beginning to find out what lands were worth;" while the Indians, anxious, alarmed, hostile at heart, seeing themselves harder and harder pressed on all sides, driven "to provide other sources for supplying their wants besides those of hunting, which must soon entirely fail them,"* yielded mile after mile with increasing sense of loss, which they were powerless to prevent, and of resentment which it would have been worse than impolitic for them to show.

The first annuities promised to the Sioux were promised by this treaty—$3000 annually for ten years to the Yankton and Santee bands; to the other four, $2000. The Yankton and Santee bands were to pay out of their annuity $100 yearly to the Otoes, because part of some land which was reserved for the half-breeds of the tribe had originally belonged to the Otoes. "A blacksmith, at the expense of the United States; also, instruments for agricultural purposes; and iron and steel to the amount of $700 annually for ten years to some of the bands, and to the amount of $400 to the others; also, $3000 a year 'for educational purposes,' and $3000 in presents distributed at the time," were promised them.

It was soon after these treaties that the artist Catlin made his famous journeys among the North American Indians, and gave to the world an invaluable contribution to their history, perpetuating in his pictures the distinctive traits of their faces and their dress, and leaving on record many pages of unassailable testimony as to their characteristics in their native state. He spent several weeks among the Sioux, and says of them: "There is no tribe on the continent of finer looking men, and few tribes who are better and more comfortably clad and supplied with the necessaries of life. * * * I have travelled several years already among these people, and I have not had my scalp

---

* Treaty of Prairie du Chien.

taken, nor a blow struck me, nor had occasion to raise my hand against an Indian; nor has my property been stolen as yet to my knowledge to the value of a shilling, and that in a country where no man is punishable by law for the crime of stealing. * * * That the Indians in their native state are drunken, is false, for they are the only temperance people, literally speaking, that ever I saw in my travels, or expect to see. If the civilized world are startled at this, it is the fact that they must battle with, not with me. These people manufacture no spirituous liquor themselves, and know nothing of it until it is brought into their country, and tendered to them by Christians.

"That these people are naked, is equally untrue, and as easily disproved with the paintings I have made, and with their beautiful costumes which I shall bring home. I shall be able to establish the fact that many of these people dress not only with clothes comfortable for any latitude, but that they dress also with some considerable taste and elegance. * * * Nor am I quite sure that they are entitled to the name of 'poor' who live in a country of boundless green fields, with good horses to ride; where they are all joint tenants of the soil together; where the Great Spirit has supplied them with an abundance of food to eat."

Catlin found six hundred families of the Sioux camped at one time around Fort Pierre, at the mouth of the Teton River, on the west bank of the Missouri. There were some twenty bands, each with their chief, over whom was one superior chief, called Ha-won-je-tah (the One Horn), whose portrait is one of the finest in Catlin's book. This chief took his name, "One Horn," from a little shell which he wore always on his neck. This shell had descended to him from his father, and he said "he valued it more than anything which he possessed: affording a striking instance of the living affection which these people often cherish for the dead, inasmuch as he chose to carry this name through life in preference to many others and more honorable ones he had a right to have taken from different battles and exploits of his extraordinary life." He was the fleetest man in the tribe; "could run down a buffalo, which he had often done on his own legs, and drive his arrow to the heart."

This chief came to his death, several years later, in a tragic way. He had been in some way the accidental cause of the death of his only son—a very fine youth—and so great was the anguish of his mind at times that he became insane. In one of these moods he mounted his favorite war-horse, with his bow and arrows in his hand, and dashed off at full speed upon the prairies, repeating the most solemn oath that he would slay the first living thing that fell in his way, be it man or beast, friend or foe. No one dared follow him, and after he had been absent an hour or two his horse came back to the village with two arrows in its body covered with blood. Fears of the most serious kind were now entertained for the fate of the chief, and a party of warriors immediately mounted their horses and retraced the animal's tracks to the place of the tragedy, where they found the body of their chief horribly mangled and gored by a buffalo-bull, whose carcass was stretched by the side of him.

A close examination of the ground was then made by the Indians, who ascertained by the tracks that their unfortunate chief, under his unlucky resolve, had met a buffalo-bull in the season when they are very stubborn, and unwilling to run from any one, and had incensed the animal by shooting a number of arrows into him, which had brought him into furious combat. The chief had then dismounted and turned his horse loose, having given it a couple of arrows from his bow, which sent it home at full speed, and then had thrown away his bow and quiver, encountering the infuriated animal with his knife alone, and the desperate battle had resulted in the death of both.

Many of the bones of the chief were broken, and his huge antagonist lay dead by his side, weltering in blood from a hundred wounds made by the chief's long and two-edged knife.

Had the provisions of these first treaties been fairly and promptly carried out, there would have been living to-day among the citizens of Minnesota thousands of Sioux families, good and prosperous farmers and mechanics, whose civilization would have dated back to the treaty of Prairie du Chien.

In looking through the records of the expenditures of the Indian Bureau for the six years following this treaty, we find no mention of any specific provisions for the Sioux in the matter of education. The $3000 annually which the treaty promised should be spent "on account of the children of the said tribes and bands," is set down as expended on the "Choctaw Academy," which was in Kentucky. A very well endowed institution that must have been, if we may trust to the fiscal reports of the Indian Bureau. In the year 1836 there were set down as expended on this academy: On account of the Miamis, $2000; the Pottawattomies, $5000; the Sacs, Foxes, and others, $3000; the Choctaws, $10,000; the Creeks, east, $3000; the Cherokees, west, $2000; the Florida Indians, $1000; the Quapaws, $1000; the Chickasaws, $3000; the Creeks, $1000: being a total of $31,000.

There were in this year one hundred and fifty-six pupils at the Choctaw Academy, sixteen of them being from the Sacs, Foxes, Sioux, and others represented in the Treaty of Prairie du Chien of 1830. For the education of these sixteen children, therefore, these tribes paid $3000 a year. The Miamis paid more in proportion, having but four youths at school, and $2000 a year charged to them. The Pottawattomies, on a treaty provision of $5000, educated twenty.

In 1836 Congress appropriated $2000 "for the purpose of extinguishing the Indian title between the State of Missouri and the Missouri River. The land owned here by the Indians was a long, narrow belt of country, separated from the rest of the Indian country by the Missouri River. The importance of it to the State of Missouri was evident—an " obvious convenience and necessity." The citizens of Missouri made representations to this effect ; and though the President is said to have been " unwilling to assent, as it would be in disregard of the guarantee given to the Indians in the Treaty of Prairie du Chien, and might be considered by them as the first step in a series of efforts to obtain possession of their new country," he nevertheless consented that the question of such a cession should be submitted to them. Accordingly, negotiations were opened, and nearly all the Indians who had rights in these lands, " seeing that from their local position they could never be made available for Indian purposes," relinquished them.*

In 1837 the Government invited deputations of chiefs from many of the principal tribes to come to Washington. It was " believed to be important to exhibit" to them "the strength of the nation they would have to contend with" if they ventured to attack our borders, " and at the same time to impress upon them the advantages which flow from civilization." Among these chiefs came thirty chiefs and headmen of the Sioux ; and, being duly " impressed," as was most natural, concluded treaties by which they ceded to the United States " all their land east of the Mississippi River, and all their islands in the same." These chiefs all belonged to the Medawakanton band, " community of the Mysterious Lakes."

The price of this cession was $300,000, to be invested for them, and the interest upon this sum, at five per cent., to be paid to them " annually forever ;" $110,000 to be distributed among the persons of mixed blood in the tribe ; $90,000 to be

---

* For this relinquishment the Government gave to the Lower Sioux presents to the amount of $400, and to the upper bands $530 in goods.

devoted to paying the just debts of the tribe; $8230 to be expended annually for twenty years in stock, implements, on physicians, farmers, blacksmiths, etc.; $10,000 worth of tools, cattle, etc., to be given to them immediately, "to enable them to break up and improve their lands;" $5300 to be expended annually for twenty years in food for them, "to be delivered at the expense of the United States;" $6000 worth of goods to be given to them on their arrival at St. Louis.

In 1838 the Indian Bureau reports that all the stipulations of this treaty have been complied with, "except those which appropriate $8230 to be expended annually in the purchase of medicines, agricultural implements, and stock; and for the support of a physician, farmers, and blacksmiths," and "bind the United States to supply these Sioux as soon as practicable with agricultural implements, tools, cattle, and such other articles as may be useful to them, to an amount not exceeding $10,000, to enable them to break up and improve their lands." The fulfilment or non-fulfilment of these stipulations has been left to the discretion of the agent; and the agent writes that it "must be obvious to any one that a general personal intercourse" on his part "is impracticable," and that "his interviews with many of the tribes must result from casualty and accident." This was undoubtedly true; but it did not, in all probability, occur to the Indians that it was a good and sufficient reason for their not receiving the $18,000 worth of goods promised.

Five thousand seven hundred and eighty-nine dollars were expended the next year under this provision of the treaty, and a few Indians, who "all labored with the hoe," raised their own crops without assistance. Six thousand bushels of corn in all were housed for the winter; but the experiment of turning hunters into farmers in one year was thought not to be, on the whole, an encouraging one. The "peculiar habits of indolence, and total disregard and want of knowledge of the value and uses of time and property," the agent says, "almost forbid hope." A more reasonable view of the situation would have seen in it very great hope. That out of five hundred warriors a few score should have been already found willing to work was most reassuring, and promised well for the future of the tribe.

For the next ten years affairs went on badly with the Sioux; they were continually attacked by the Chippewas, Ottawas, and others, and continually retaliated. The authorities took a sensible view of this state of things, as being the easiest way of securing the safety of the whites. "So long as they (the Indians) are at war with each other they will not feel a disposition to disturb the peace and safety of our exposed frontier settlements," wrote Governor Dodge, in 1840.

Whiskey traders flocked faster and faster into the neighborhood; fur traders, also, found it much more for their interest to trade with drunken Indians than with sober ones, and the Sioux grew rapidly demoralized. Their annuities were in arrears; yet this almost seemed less a misfortune than a blessing, since both money, goods, and provisions were so soon squandered for whiskey.

In 1842 several of the bands were reduced to a state of semi-starvation by the failure of corn crops, and also by the failure of the Senate to ratify a treaty they had made with Governor Doty in 1841.* Depending on the annuities promised in this treaty, they had neglected to make their usual provisions for the winter. Frosts, which came in June, and drought, which followed in July, combined to ruin their crops. For several years the water had been rapidly decreasing in all the lakes and streams north-west of Traverse de Sioux: the musk-rat ponds, from which the Indians used to derive considerable revenue, had dried up, and the musk-rats had gone, nobody knew where; the beaver, otter, and other furry creatures had

---

* Never ratified.

been hunted down till they were hard to find; the buffalo had long since been driven to new fields, far distant. Many of the Indians were too poor to own horses on which to hunt. They were two hundred miles from the nearest place where corn could be obtained, even if they had money to pay for it. Except for some assistance from the Government, they would have died by hundreds in the winter of this year.

In 1849 the "needs" of the white settlers on the east side of the Mississippi made it imperative that the Sioux should be again removed from their lands. "The desirable portions of Minnesota east of the Mississippi were already so occupied by a white population as to seem to render it absolutely necessary to obtain without delay a cession from the Indians on the west side of the river, for the accommodation of our citizens emigrating to that quarter, a large portion of whom would probably be compelled to precipitate themselves on that side of the Mississippi."

Commissioners were accordingly sent to treat with the Indians owning these desired lands. In the instructions given to these commissioners there are some notable sentences: "Though the proposed purchase is estimated to contain some twenty millions of acres, and some of it no doubt of excellent quality," there are "sound reasons why it is comparatively valueless to the Indians, and a large price should not be paid for it." Alive to the apparent absurdity of the statement that lands which are "absolutely necessary" for white farmers are "comparatively valueless" to Indians whom the Government is theoretically making every effort to train into farmers, and who have for the last ten years made appreciable progress in that direction, the commissioner adds, "With respect to its being valuable to the United States, it is more so for the purpose of making room for our emigrating citizens than for any other; and only a small part of it is now actually necessary for that object. * * * The extent of the proposed cession should be no criterion of the amount that should be paid for it. On a full consideration of the whole matter, it is the opinion of this office that from two to two and a half cents an acre would be an ample equivalent for it." Some discretion is left to the commissioners as to giving more than this if the Indians are "not satisfied;" but any such increase of price must be "based on such evidence and information as shall fully satisfy the President and Senate."*

Reading farther on in these instructions, we come at last to the real secret of this apparent niggardliness on the part of the Government. It is not selfishness at all; it is the purest of philanthropy. The Government has all along been suffering in mind from two conflicting desires—" the desire to give these Indians an equivalent for their possessions," and, on the other hand, " the well-ascertained fact that no greater curse can be inflicted on a tribe so little civilized as the Sioux than to have large sums of money coming to them as annuities." * * * On the whole, the commissioner says that we are called on, " as a matter of humanity and duty toward this helpless race, to make every exertion in our power not to place much money at their discretion." The Government is beginning very well in this direction, it must be admitted, when it proposes to pay for Mississippi Valley lands in Minnesota only two and a half cents per acre. " Humanity and duty " allied could hardly do more at one stroke than that.

We cannot ascribe to the same philanthropy, however, the withholding from 1837 to 1850 the $3000 a year which the treaty of 1837 provided should be expended " annually " as the President might direct, and which was not expended at all, because President after President directed that it should be ap-

---

* " Chrysostom was of opinion, and not without reason, that, in contracts, as often as we strive earnestly to buy anything for less than it is worth, or to have more than our just measure or weight, there was in that fact a kind of theft."—GROTIUS on Contracts.

plied to educational purposes; and there being no evident and easy way of expending it in that manner, it was allowed to accumulate, until in 1850 it amounted, according to the report of Governor Ramsey, of Minnesota, to $50,000. The governor also thinks better than the United States Government does of the country to be relinquished this year by the Sioux. He says that it will be "settled with great rapidity, possessing as it does from its situation considerable prospective commercial as well as agricultural advantages." It was evidently very cheap at two and a half cents an acre.

In this same code of instructions by the Indian Bureau there is a record of another instance of the Government's disregard of treaty stipulations. At the time of the treaty of Prairie du Chien, in 1850, the Sioux chiefs had requested that a certain tract be set apart and bestowed upon the half-breeds of their nation. This was provided for in the ninth Article of that treaty; but the Government refused to give to the half-breeds any title to this land, except "in the same manner as other Indian titles are held." It was agreed, however, that the President might "assign to any of said half-breeds, to be held by him or them in fee-simple, any portion of said tract not exceeding a section of six hundred and forty acres to an individual." This tract of land was known as the "Half-breed Reservation on Lake Tepin."

The half-breeds had made almost unintermitting efforts to have these assignments made, but the Government had as constantly refused to do it. The Indian Bureau now assigns two reasons why this treaty stipulation was never fulfilled: 1st, that "the half-breeds, or most of them, would be speculated upon by designing persons, and cheated out of their reservations;" 2d, that, "on account of the quality of the lands, some would necessarily have much better reservations than others, which would engender dissatisfaction and heart-burning among themselves as well as against the United States." The Bureau felicitates itself that "the only title they now have to this land, therefore, is that by which other Indians hold their lands, viz., the occupant or usufruct right, and this they enjoy by the permission of the United States." Such being the case, and as the Government would probably never find it expedient and advisable to make the assignment referred to, this tract, whatever may be the character of the land, must be and would continue comparatively worthless to them.

Nevertheless, it appears that in 1841 one of the three treaties made with the Sioux, but not ratified, was with these very half-breeds for this same "valueless" tract of 384,000 acres of land; that they were to be paid $200,000 for it, and also to be paid for all the improvements they had made on it; and that the treaty commissioners are still instructed "to allow them for it now whatever sum the commissioners deem it to be" fairly worth; "under no circumstances," however, "to exceed the sum stipulated in 1841." Putting this all into plain English, it simply means that in 1830 the Government promised to let a band of men take out tracts of land in fee-simple, and settle down like other men on their homesteads; that for ten years the men begged to do so, and were refused; that at the end of ten years, thinking there was no hope of anything better, they agreed to sell the whole tract back to the Government for $200,000; that this bargain, also, the Government did not fulfil (the treaties never being ratified), and nine years later was found congratulating itself on the fact that, by reason of all these unfulfilled agreements, the land was still "held only in the same manner as other Indian titles are held"—i. e., not "held" at all—only used on sufferance of the Government, and could be taken possession of at any time at the Government's pleasure. (This matter was supposed to be finally settled in 1854 by a law of Congress; but in 1856 the thing appears to have been still unsettled. A commission had been sent out to investigate it, and the report was that "the subject has been one of some difficulty and intricacy; but the final report of the commissioners has just been received, and steps will be taken at once to cause the scrip to issue to the parties entitled thereto.")

A little farther on in this same notable document is a mention of another tract, of which it is now "desirable to extinguish the title." This was set apart by the tenth Article of that same old treaty for the half-breeds of the Omahas, Otoes, Iowas, and Yankton and Santee Sioux. This contains about 143,000 acres, but is "supposed to be of much less value than that on Lake Tepin:" much less value than "valueless;" but the "amount to be paid for it is left to the discretion" of the commissioners.

At this time the bands of the Medewakanton Sioux were occupying a tract of over two hundred miles along the west shore of the Mississippi, reaching also some twenty-five miles up the St. Peter's. The Yanktons, Santees, and other bands lived high up the St. Peter's, reaching over into the lands west of the Missouri, out of reach of ordinary facilities of intercourse. These bands were often in great distress for food, owing to the failure of the buffalo. They never lost an occasion to send imploring messages to the Great Father, urging him to help them. They particularly ask for hoes, that they may plant corn. In his report for 1850 the superintendent of the territory embracing these Indians says: "The views of most of those who have lived the longest among the Indians agree in one respect—that is, that no great or beneficial change can take place in their condition until the General Government has made them amenable to local laws—laws which will punish the evil-disposed, and secure the industrious in their property and individual rights."

Superintendents, agents, commissioners, secretaries, all reiteratedly recommending this one simple and necessary step toward civilization—the Indians themselves by hundreds imploring for titles to their farms, or at least "hoes"—why did the United States Government keep on and on in its obstinate way, feeding the Indian in gross and reckless improvidence with one hand, plundering him with the other, and holding him steadily down at the level of his own barbarism? Nay, forcing him below it by the newly added vices of gambling and drunkenness, and yet all the while boasting of its desire to enlighten, instruct, and civilize him.   It is as inexplicable as it is infamous: a phenomenal thing in the history of the world.

In the summer of 1851 the desired treaties were made, the upper and lower bands of Sioux being treated with separately at Traverse de Sioux and at Mendota.   The upper bands were soon disposed of, though "some few of them, having been taught to read," had become impressed with the idea that their country was of immense value, and at first demanded six million dollars for the lands to be ceded.   The treaty with the lower bands—the Medawakantons and Wahpacootas—was "exceedingly difficult of attainment" on account of, firstly, "their proximity to the flourishing settlements on the east side of the Mississippi producing necessarily frequent contact with the whites, whose ideas of the great value of the country had been imparted to these Indians; secondly, their great experience in Indian diplomacy, being in the enjoyment already of liberal annuities under former stipulations"—all these things rendered them as "indifferent to the making of another treaty at present as the whites on their borders were anxious that their lands should he acquired."   In consequence of this indomitable common-sense on the part of the Indians the sessions of the commissioners were tedious and long; not until a month had passed did they prevail on these Indians to sign away the coveted lands, "the garden-spot of the Mississippi Valley," and they were obliged to more than treble the number of cents per acre which they had been instructed to pay.   For thirty-five millions of acres of land they agreed to pay nominally $3,075,000, which would be between eight and nine cents an acre.   But as

$2,500,000 was to be held in trust, and only the interest at five per cent. to be paid to the Indians, and this only for the term of fifty years, at which time the principal was to revert to the Government, it will be easily reckoned that the Indians would receive, all told, only about six and one-quarter cents an acre. And taking into account the great value of the relinquished lands, and the price the Government would undoubtedly obtain for them, it will be readily conceded that Governor Ramsey was not too sanguine when he stated, in his report to the Interior Department, that the "actual cost to the Government of this magnificent purchase is only the sum paid in hand" ($575,000).

The governor says that it was "by no means the purpose" of the commission "to act other than justly and generously toward the Indians;" that "a continuation of the payment of large sums of interest annually would do them no further good" after fifty years had expired, and would be "inconsistent with sound governmental policy." He says that the Dakota nation, although warlike, is "friendly to the whites," and that it may be reasonably expected that, "by a judicious expenditure of the civilization and improvement funds provided for in these treaties," they will soon take the lead "in agriculture and other industrial pursuits."

One of the provisions of this treaty forbade the introduction of ardent spirits into the new reservation. This was put in in accordance with the "earnest desire" of the chiefs, who requested that "some stringent measures should be taken by the Government to exclude all kinds of liquors from their new home."

By this treaty the four great bands of Minnesota Sioux were all to be "consolidated together on one reservation in the upper part of the Mississippi Valley." This region was thought to be "sufficiently remote to guarantee" them against any pressure from the white population for many years to come. Farms were to be opened for them, mills and schools to be established,

and dwelling-houses erected.   They were to have now a chance
to own "that domestic country called home, with all the living
sympathies and all the future hopes and projects which people
it."   From this time "a new era was to be dated in the history of the Dakotas: an era full of brilliant promise."   The
tract of territory relinquished by them was "larger than the
State of New York, fertile and beautiful beyond description,"
far the best part of Minnesota.   It is "so far diversified in natural advantages that its productive powers may be considered
almost inexhaustible. * * * Probably no tract on the surface of
the globe is equally well watered. * * * A large part is rich
arable land ; portions are of unsurpassed fertility, and eminent-
ly adapted to the production in incalculable quantities of the
cereal grains.   The boundless plains present inexhaustible fields
of pasturage, and the river bottoms are richer than the banks
of the Nile.   In the bowels of the earth there is every indication of extensive mineral fields."

It would seem that the assertion made only a few lines before this glowing paragraph—"to the Indians themselves the
broad regions which have been ceded are of inconsiderable
value"—could not be true.   It would seem that for eight thousand people, who, according to this same writer, "have outlived
in a great degree the means of subsistence of the hunter
state," and must very soon "resort to the pursuits of agriculture," nothing could have been more fortunate than to have
owned and occupied thirty-five millions of acres of just such
land as this.

They appear to be giving already some evidence of a disposition to turn this land to account.   The reports from the different farms and schools show progress in farming industry
and also in study.   The farming is carried on with difficulty,
because there are only a few carts and ploughs, which must be
used in turn by the different farmers, and therefore must come
to some quite too late to be of use, and there is much quarrel-

ling among them owing to this trouble. Nevertheless, these bands have raised over four thousand bushels of corn in the year. There is also a great opposition to the schools, because the Indians have been told that the accumulated fifty thousand dollars which is due to them would be paid to them in cash if it were not for the schools. Nevertheless, education is slowly progressing; in this year fifty copies of a little missionary paper called *The Dakota Friend* were subscribed for in the one mission station of Lac qui Parle, and sixty scholars were enrolled at the school. The blacksmith at St. Peter's reports that he has made during the year 2506 pieces of one sort and another for the Indians, and repaired 1430 more. Evidently a community keeping blacksmiths so busy as this are by no means wholly idle themselves.

It is worth while to dwell upon these seemingly trivial details at this point in the history of the Minnesota Sioux, because they are all significant to mark the point in civilization they had already reached, and the disposition they had already shown toward industry before they were obliged to submit to their first great removal. Their condition at the end of two years from the ratification of these treaties is curtly told in the official reports of the Indian Bureau:

" The present situation of that portion of the Sioux Indians parties to the treaties of July 23d and August 5th, 1851, is peculiar, unfortunate, and to them must prove extremely injurious. By these treaties they reluctantly parted with a very large extent of valuable country, which it was of the greatest importance to the Government to acquire. An insignificant portion of it near its western boundary, not deemed necessary or desirable for a white population for many years, if at all, was agreed to be reserved and assigned to them for their future residence. The Senate amended the treaties, striking out this provision, allowing ten cents an acre in lieu of the reservations, and requiring the President, with the assent of the Indians, if they agreed to the amendments, to assign them such tracts of country, beyond the limits of that ceded, as might be satisfactory for their future home.   To the amendments was appended a proviso 'that the President may, by the consent of the Indians, vary the conditions aforesaid, if deemed expedient.' The Indians were induced to agree to the amendments ; ' confiding in the justice, liberality, and humanity of the President and the Congress of the United States, that such tracts of country will be set apart for their future occupancy and home as will be to them acceptable and satisfactory.'   Thus, not only was the assent of the Indians made necessary to a country being assigned to them without the limits of that ceded, but, by the authority given to the President to vary the conditions of the amendments to the treaties, he was empowered, with the consent of the Indians, to place them upon the designated reservations, or upon any other portion of the ceded territory, ' if deemed expedient.'

" To avoid collisions and difficulties between the Indians and the white population which rapidly commenced pouring into the ceded country, it became necessary that the former should vacate at least a large portion of it without delay, while there was neither the time nor the means to make the requisite explorations to find a suitable location for them beyond the limits of the cession.

" Under these pressing and embarrassing circumstances the late President determined to permit them to remain five years on the designated reservations, if they were willing to accept this alternative.   They assented, and many of them have been already removed.   However unavoidable this arrangement, it is a most unfortunate one.   The Indians are fully aware of its temporary character, and of the uncertainty as to their future position, and will consequently be disinclined and deterred from any efforts to make themselves comfortable and improve their condition.   The inevitable result must be that, at the end of the time limited, they will be in a far worse condition than now, and the efforts and expenditures of years to infuse into them a spirit of improvement will all have been in vain.

"The large investments in mills, farms, mechanic shops, and other improvements required by the treaties to be made for their benefit, will be entirely wasted if the Indians are to remain on their reservations only during the prescribed five years. At the very period when they would begin to reap the full advantage of these beneficial provisions they would have to remove. Another unfortunate feature of this arrangement, if temporary, is that the Indians will have expended the considerable sums set apart in the treaties for the expenses of their removal to a permanent home, and for subsistence until they could otherwise provide it, leaving nothing for these important and necessary purposes in the event of another emigration. In view of these facts and considerations, no time should be lost in determining upon some final and permanent arrangement in regard to them."

The Governor of Minnesota also writes at this time: "The doubtful tenure by which this tribe hold their supposed reservation is well understood by their chiefs and headmen, and is beginning to give deep dissatisfaction, and throwing daily more and more obstacles in the way of their removal. This reservation will not be wanted for white men for many years.

"There is not wood, or timber, or coal sufficient for the purposes of civilization, except immediately on the St. Peter's and its tributaries. From near the vicinity of the new agency there commences a vast prairie of more than one hundred miles in extent, entirely destitute of timber, and I feel confident that we never shall be able to keep any very large number of them at their new agency, or near there.

"Already the fund set apart for the removal and subsistence the first year of the Sissetons and Wah-pa-tons has been expended, and all their provisions eaten up. Seventeen thousand dollars and upward have been expended by Governor Ramsey, and one year in advance of the time fixed by the treaty for their removal. This expenditure was made while he was getting them to sign the Senate amendments to the treaty of 1851, which they were very reluctant to do, and which not more than half the chiefs have signed. These Indians want the Government to confirm this reservation to them. I would recommend that this be done as the only means to satisfy them, and humanity demands it."

Here is a picture of a helpless people! Forced to give up the "garden-spot of the State," and accept in its stead an "insignificant tract, on the greater part of which there is not wood, or timber, or coal sufficient for civilization;" and then, before the ink of this treaty is dry, told that even from this insignificant tract they must promise to move at the end of five years. What words could characterize such a transaction between man and man? There is not a country, a people, a community in which it would be even attempted! Was it less base, or more, being between a strong government and a feeble race?

From the infamy of accomplishing this purpose the United States was saved. Remonstrances, and still more the resistance of the Indians, prevailed, and in 1854 we find the poor creatures expressing "much satisfaction" that the President has decreed that they are to remain permanently on their "insignificant tract."

The Upper Missouri Sioux are still suffering and destitute; a few of them cultivating little patches of ground, depending chiefly on the chase, and on roots and wild berries; when these resources fail there is nothing left for them but to starve, or to commit depredations on white settlers. Some of the bands, nevertheless, have scrupulously observed the stipulations of the Fort Laramie treaty in 1851, show a "strong desire for improvement," and are on the most friendly terms with the whites. These peaceable and friendly bands are much distressed, as well they may be, at the reckless course pursued by others of their tribe. They welcome the presence of the soldiers sent to chastise the offenders, and gladly render all the service to them they can, even against their relatives and friends.

In 1855 it is stated that "various causes have combined to prevent the Minnesota Sioux from deriving, heretofore, much substantial benefit from the very liberal provisions of the treaties of 1851. Until after the reservations were permanently assured to the Indians (1854) it would have been highly improper to have made the expenditures for permanent improvements, and since then the affairs of the agency have not been free from confusion."

"Large sums of money have been expended for these Sioux, but they have been indolent, extravagant, intemperate, and have wasted their means without improving, or seeming to desire to improve their condition."

Both these statements are made in grave good faith; certainly without any consciousness of their bearing on each other. It is not stated, however, what specific means the Sioux could have employed "to improve their condition," had they "desired" to do so.

The summer of 1857 was one which will long be remembered by the citizens of Minnesota. It was opened by terrible massacres, which were all the work of a strolling outcast band of Sioux, not more than fifteen in number. They had been driven out of their tribe some sixteen years previous, and had been ever since then leading a wandering and marauding life. The beginning of the trouble was a trivial difficulty between one of the white settlers on Rock River and an Indian. The settler's dog bit the Indian, and the Indian shot the dog. For this the white settlers beat the Indian severely, and then went to the camp and by force took away all the guns of the band. This was at a season of the year when to be without guns meant simply to be without food, and the Indians were reduced at once to a condition of great suffering. By some means they either repossessed themselves of their guns or procured others, and, attacking the settlement, killed all the inhabitants except four women, whom they carried away with them, and treated with the utmost barbarity. The inevitable results of such horrors followed. The thousands of peaceable Indians in Minnesota, who did not even know of this outrage, were all held in one common terror and hatred by the general public; only the very great firmness and discretion of the military officers sent to deal with the outbreak saved Minnesota from a general uprising and attack from all the Sioux bands, who were already in a state of smouldering discontent by reason of the non-payment of their annuities. However, they obeyed the demands of the Government that they themselves should pursue this offending band, and either capture or exterminate it. They killed four, and took three prisoners, and then returned "much jaded and worn," and said they could do no more without the help of United States soldiers; and that they thought they had now done enough to show their loyalty, and to deserve the payment of their annuities. One of the chiefs said: "The man who killed white people did not belong to us, and we did not expect to be called to account for the people of another band. We have always tried to do as our Great Father tells us." Another said: "I am going to speak of the treaty. For fifty years we were to be paid $50,000 per annum. We were also promised $300,000 that we have not seen. I wish to say to my Great Father we were promised these things, but have not seen them yet. Why does not the Great Father do as he promised?"

These hostilities were speedily brought to an end, yet the situation was by no means reassuring for the Indians. But one sentiment seemed to inspire the whole white population, and this was the desire to exterminate the entire Indian race.

"For the present," writes the superintendent, "it is equally important to protect the Indians from the whites as the whites from the Indians;" and this in spite of the fact that all the leading bands of the treaty Sioux had contributed warriors to go in pursuit of the murderers, had killed or captured all they could find, and stood ready to go again after the remaining eight, if the United States troops would go also and assist them. Spite of the exertions of one of the chiefs of the Lower Sioux, "Little Crow," who, the superintendent says, labored with him "night and day in organizing the party, riding continually between the lower and upper agencies," so that they "scarcely slept" till the war-party had set out on the track of the murderers; spite of the fact that the whole body of the Sioux, without exception, "received the intelligence with as much indignation and disapprobation as the whites themselves, and did their best to stand clear of any suspicion of or connection with the affair—spite of all this, they were in continual danger of being shot at sight by the terrified and unreasoning settlers. One band, under the chief Sleepy Eyes, were returning to their homes from a hunt; and while they were "wondering what the panic among the whites meant" (they having heard nothing of the massacre), were fired into by some of the militia volunteers.

The next day a white settler was found killed near that spot —presumably by some member of Sleepy Eyes' band. This excitement slowly abated, and for the next four years a steady improvement was visible in the Minnesota Sioux. Hundreds of them threw aside the blanket—the distinctive badge of their wild state; schools were well attended, and farms were well tilled. That there was great hostility to this civilization, on the part of the majority of the tribe, cannot be denied; but that was only natural—the inevitable protest of a high-spirited and proud race against abandoning all its race distinctions. When we see the men of Lorraine, or of Montenegro, ready to

die for the sake merely of being called by the name of one
power rather than by that of another, we find it heroic, and
give them our sympathies; but when the North American Indian is ready to die rather than wear the clothes and follow
the ways of the white man, we feel for him only unqualified
contempt, and see in his instinct nothing more than a barbarian's incapacity to appreciate civilization. Is this just?

In 1861 the Commissioner of Indian Affairs, visiting these
Sioux, reports: "I was much surprised to find so many of the
Sioux Indians wearing the garb of civilization, many of them
living in frame or brick houses, some of them with stables or
out-houses, and their fields indicating considerable knowledge
of agriculture." Their condition, he says, affords "abundant
evidence of what may be accomplished among the Sioux Indians by steadily adhering to a uniform, undeviating policy.

"The number that live by agricultural pursuits is yet small
compared with the whole; but their condition is so much better
than that of the wild Indian, that they, too, are becoming convinced that it is the better way to live; and many are coming
in, asking to have their hair cut, and for a suit of clothes, and
to be located on a piece of land where they can build a house
and fence in their fields."

Many more of them would have entered on the agricultural
life had the Government provided ways and means for them to
do so.   In this same report is a mention of one settlement of
two thousand Indians at Big Stone Lake, who "have been
hitherto almost entirely neglected.   These people complain
that they have lived upon promises for the last ten years, and
are really of opinion that white men never perform what they
promise.   Many of them would go to work if they had any
reasonable encouragement."

The annuities are still in arrears.   Every branch of the industries and improvements attempted suffers for want of the promised funds, and from delays in payments expected.   The worst

result, however, of these delays in the fulfilment of treaty stipulations was the effect on the Indians. A sense of wrong in
the past and distrust for the future was ever deepening in their
minds, and preparing them to be suddenly thrown by any small
provocation into an antagonism and hostility grossly disproportionate to the apparent cause. This was the condition of the
Minnesota Sioux in the summer of 1862.*

The record of the massacres of that summer is scarcely equal-
led in the history of Indian wars. Early in August some bands
of the Upper Sioux, who had been waiting at their agency nearly two months for their annuity payments, and had been suffering greatly for food during that time—so much so that "they
dug up roots to appease their hunger, and when corn was turned
out to them they devoured it uncooked, like wild animals"—became desperate, broke into the Government warehouse, and took
some of the provisions stored there. This was the real beginning of the outbreak, although the first massacre was not till
the 18th. When that began, the friendly Indians were powerless to resist—in fact, they were threatened with their lives if
they did not join. Nevertheless, some of them rescued whole
families, and carried them to places of safety; others sheltered
and fed women and children in their own lodges; many fled,
leaving all their possessions behind—as much victims of the outbreak as the Minnesota people themselves. For three days the
hostile bands, continually re-enforced, went from settlement to
settlement, killing and plundering. A belt of country nearly
two hundred miles in length and about fifty in width was entirely abandoned by the population, who flocked in panic to
the towns and forts. Nearly a thousand were killed — men,
women, and children—and nameless outrages were committed
on many. Millions of dollars' worth of property were destroyed. The outbreak was quickly quelled by military force,

* See Appendix, Art. VI.

and a large number of Indians captured. Many voluntarily surrendered, bringing with them over two hundred whites that they had taken prisoners. A military commission tried these Indians, and sentenced over three hundred to be hung. All but thirty-nine were reprieved and put into prison. The remainder were moved to Dakota, to a barren desert, where for three years they endured sufferings far worse than death. The remainder escaped to the Upper Missouri region or to Canada.*

Minnesota, at a terrible cost to herself and to the United States Government, was at last free from the presence of Indians within her borders — Indians who were her enemies only because they had been treated with injustice and bad faith.

During this time the bands of Sioux in the Upper Missouri region had been more or less hostile, and military force in continual requisition to subdue them. Re-enforced by the Minnesota refugees, they became more hostile still, and in the summer of 1863 were in almost incessant conflict. In 1864 the Governor of Dakota Territory writes to the Department that the war is spreading into Nebraska and Kansas, and that if provision is not made for the loyal treaty Indians in that region before long, they also will join the hostiles. One band of the Sioux—the Yanktons—has been persistently loyal, and rendered great service through all the troubles. Fifty of these Yankton Sioux had been organized by General Sibley into a company of scouts, and had proved " more effective than twice the number of white soldiers." The only cost to the Government " of this service on the part of the Yanktons had been fifty suits of condemned artillery uniforms, arms, and rations in part to the scouts themselves."

In 1865 the Government, having spent about $40,000,000 on these campaigns, began to cast about for cheaper, if not

---

* All the Winnebagoes were removed from Minnesota at the same time.

more humane methods, and, partly at the instance of the Governor of Dakota, who knew very well that the Indians desired peace, sent out a commission to treat with them. There were now, all told, some 14,000 Sioux in this region, nearly 2000 being the refugees from Minnesota.

The report of this commission is full of significant statements. There seems to be no doubt that the great majority of the Indians are anxious for peace; but they are afraid to meet the agents of the Government, lest they be in some way betrayed. Such bands as are represented, however, gladly assent to a treaty of peace and good-will. The commissioners speak with great feeling of the condition of the loyal Yanktons. "No improvements have been made on their lands, and the commissioners were obliged to issue provisions to them to keep them from starving. * * * No crops met the eye, nor is there the semblance of a school-house."

Yet by Article four of the treaty with the Yankton Sioux the United States Government had agreed to expend $10,000 in erecting a suitable building or buildings, and to establish and maintain one or more normal labor schools; and it is to be read in the United States Statutes at Large that in each of the years 1860, 1861, 1862, and 1863, Congress appropriated $65,000, as per treaty, for the benefit of the Yankton Sioux.

"With the exception of a few miserable huts, a saw-mill, and a small amount of land enclosed, there are few vestiges of improvement. * * * They are reduced to the necessity of hunting for a living, and, unless soon reassured and encouraged, they will be driven to despair, and the great discontent existing among them will culminate in another formidable Indian war."

Nine treaties were concluded by this commission with as many different bands of Sioux, the Indians pledging themselves to abstain from all hostilities with each other and with the whites, and the Government agreeing to pay to the Indians fifteen dollars a head per annum, and to all who will settle down to farming twenty-five dollars a head.

In the winter following these treaties all these Indians faithfully kept their promises, in spite of terrible sufferings from cold and from lack of food. Some of them were at the old Crow Creek Reservation in Dakota, where they were "kept from absolute starvation only by the issue to them of such scanty supplies as could be spared from the stores at Fort Sully, and from the agency." It is much to the credit of these Indians that, in spite of their manifold sufferings, scarcely a case of stealing occurred among them, they being determined to keep their faith to the Government.

"They will run like chickens to gather the offal from the slop buckets that are carried from the garrison kitchens; while they pass a pile of corn and hundreds of loose cattle without touching a thing, except when told they may gather up the grains of corn from the ground where the rats in their depredations have let it fall from the sacks," says the report of one of the commissioners.

In the summer of 1865 still further treaties were concluded with the Indians of the plains, and all the Sioux, with the exception of those in the British possessions, were now pledged to peace. This summer also saw the first recognition on the part of the Government of its flagrant injustice toward the friendly Minnesota Sioux who were moved to Crow Creek, Dakota, at the time of the massacre. There were nearly one thousand of these—mostly old men, women, and children—many of them the widows and children of those who had been hung or were in prison at Davenport. For three years they had been "quiet and patient in their sufferings."

The two hundred prisoners in Davenport had also shown "an excellent disposition and entire submission," although many of them were known and proved to have been "absolutely guiltless of any acts of hostility; and not only this, but deserving of reward for the rescue of white captives." Certificates, petitions, and letters showing these facts were forwarded from Iowa to the Department, but the commissioner says, in his report for 1866, that "they have been mislaid in their passage through the various departments, and cannot be found !"

There was still another class of these Indians deserving of help from the Government — some two hundred and fifty friendly farmer Indians, who were living in 1862 quietly on their farms, "who have acted as scouts for the Government; who never committed any acts of hostility, nor fled with those who did commit them," and have still remained friendly through these four years, "while compelled to a vagabond life by the indiscriminate confiscation of all their land and property."

"The crops belonging to these farmer Indians were valued at $125,000, and they had large herds of stock of all kinds, fine farms, and improvements. The United States troops engaged in suppressing the massacre, also the prisoners taken by them—in all, some 3500 men—lived for fifty days on this property."

Strong efforts were made by Bishop Whipple and others to obtain from the Government some aid for these friendly Indians, and the sum of $7500 was appropriated by Congress for that purpose. The letter of Bishop Whipple, who was requested to report on the division of this sum, is so eloquent a summing up of the case of these Indians, that it ought to be placed on permanent record in the history of our country. He writes:

"There is positive injustice in the appropriation of so miserable a pittance. * * * A much larger sum would not pay the amount which we honestly owe these men. The Government was the trustee of the Upper and Lower Sioux. It held several millions of dollars for their benefit—the joint property of the tribes. These friendly Sioux had abandoned their wild life, and adopted the dress, habits, and customs of civilization; and in doing this, which placed them in open opposition to the traditions of their tribes, they were pledged the protection of the Government. By a mistaken policy, by positive neglect to provide a government, by the perversion of funds due them for the sale of one-half their reservations, by withholding their annuities until two months after they were due (which was caused by the use of a part of these funds for claims), by permitting other causes of dissatisfaction to go on unheeded, we provoked the hostility of the wild Indians, and it went on until it ripened in massacre. These farmer Indians had been pledged a patent for their farms : unless we violated our solemn pledge, these lands were theirs by a title as valid as any title could be. They had large crops, sufficient to support General Sibley's army for a number of weeks. They lost all they had —crops, stock, clothing, furniture. In addition to this, they were deprived of their share in these annuities, and for four years have lived in very great suffering. You can judge whether $5000 shall be deemed a just reward* for the bravery and fidelity of men who, at the risk of their own lives, were instrumental in saving white captives, and maintained their friendship to the whites.

"I submit to you, sir, and through you hope to reach all who fear God and love justice, whether the very least we can do for all the friendly Sioux is not to fulfil the pledges we made years ago, and give to each of them a patent of eighty acres of land, build them a house, and provide them cattle, seeds, and implements of husbandry ?"

In 1866 all these Sioux were removed, and, in spite of the

---

* Two thousand five hundred of the seven thousand five hundred dollars had been especially set aside by the Government (unjust in its rewards as in its punishments) for Chief Other Day, who was really less deserving than many others.

protestations of the Nebraska citizens, settled on reservations on the Niobrara River, in Northern Nebraska. It soon became evident that this place was undesirable for a reservation, both on account of its previous occupancy by the whites and scarcity of timber.

In the fall they removed again to the mouth of Bazile Creek. Temporary buildings were again erected, and here they spent the winters of 1866 and 1867. In February they were cheered by the invitation sent their chiefs and headmen to visit Washington. They went, feeling sure that they should get a home for themselves and people. "All they got was a promise that a commission should be sent out to visit them the next year." They were told, however, to move to Breckenridge, on the west bank of the Missouri, plant crops there, and were promised that, if they liked the place, they should have it "secured to them as a permanent home." Accordingly, the "agency buildings" were once more removed, and two hundred acres of land were planted. Before the crops were harvested the commission arrived, and urged the Indians to move farther up the Missouri. The Indians being averse to this, however, they were allowed to remain, and told that if they would cultivate the soil like white men—take lands in severalty—the Government would assist them. The Indians gladly consented to this, and signed a treaty to that effect. But in 1868 their agent writes: "That treaty is not yet ratified, and, instead of assistance to open farms, their appropriation has been cut down one half. After paying for supplies purchased on credit last year, it is entirely insufficient for clothing and subsistence, and leaves nothing for opening farms, procuring cattle," etc. These Indians, only five years previous, had been living on good farms, and had $125,000 worth of stock, implements, etc. No wonder their agent writes: "Leave them without a home a few years longer. and you offer strong inducements for them to become idle and worthless."

It is an intricate and perplexing task to attempt now to follow the history of the different bands of the Sioux tribe through all their changes of location and affiliation—some in Dakota, some in Nebraska, and some on the Upper Arkansas with the hostile Cheyennes and Arapahoes—signing treaties one summer, and on the war-path the next—promised a home in spring, and ordered off it before harvest—all the time more and more hemmed in by white settlers, and more and more driven out of their buffalo ranges by emigrations—liable at any time to have bodies of United States soldiers swoop down on them and punish whole bands for depredations committed by a handful of men, perhaps of a totally distinct band—the wonder is not that some of them were hostile and vindictive, but that any of them remained peaceable and friendly. Bandied about from civil authorities to military—the War Department recommending " that all Indians not on fixed reservations be considered at war," and proceeded against accordingly, and the Interior Department neglecting to provide them with "fixed reservations," or to define or enforce the boundaries of even their temporary reservations—tricked, cheated on all sides—starving half the time—there is not a tribe of all the perse-cuted tribes of Indians that has a more piteous record than the Sioux. Nevertheless, we find many of the bands, in 1870, ad-vancing in civilization. In the Yankton band nearly one hun-dred children are in school, and eight hundred acres of land are under cultivation. The Lower Yanktons are peaceful and quiet, although they are near the Brulés, who are always rov-ing and hostile. The Sissetons and Wahpetons, who were by a treaty of 1867 placed on reservations in Dakota, are "indus-trious, and fast advancing in agricultural pursuits." Four schools are in operation among them. The Yanktons are " anxious to farm, and state that the Government has promised to assist and teach them to farm; that they are and have been ready for some time, but as yet the agent has not received any instructions or funds to permit of their accomplishing their desire."

Two events, important in the history of the Sioux tribe, happened in 1869 and 1870. One was the visit of a delegation of chiefs and headmen from several of the bands, under the leadership of the chief Red Cloud, to Washington, Philadelphia, and New York. They had thus an opportunity of relating all their grievances, and of receiving the Government's declarations of good intentions toward them. Red Cloud, after his return home, became an ardent and determined advocate of peace and loyalty. The other was the withdrawal of a portion of the Santee Sioux from their band, for the purpose of taking up farms under the Homestead Act, and becoming independent citizens. The story of this experiment, and the manner in which it was met by the United States Government, is best told in the words of Dr. Williamson, a missionary, who had lived thirty-five years among them, and who pleaded thus warmly for them in a letter addressed to the Department in the summer of 1870: "Several considerations have influenced the Dakotas in going to the Big Sioux River: 1st. The soil and climate are more similar to that to which they have been accustomed in Minnesota, their former home, than is that of their reservation on the Missouri; 2d. Feeling that they were men capable of sustaining themselves if a fair opportunity is afforded them, they felt that it was degrading to live as sinecures and pensioners dependent on Government for food and clothing; 3d. And chiefly a desire to make homes for their families where they could be subjected to, and protected by, the laws of the United States, the same as all other men are. This they thought could not be the case on their reservation.

"These Sioux were parties to the treaties made in 1851, by which they and other bands ceded to the United States all the best settled parts of Minnesota west of the Mississippi for less than one-hundredth part of its present value, and much less

than the lands were worth to them as hunting-grounds.   And
while as hunters they needed no protection of the law, they
knew that as agriculturists they could not live without it; and
they positively refused to sell their hunting-grounds till the
Commissioner of the United States promised that they should
be protected in their persons and property the same as white
men.   Government never accorded to them this protection,
which, in the view of the Indians, was a very important consideration in selling the lands.   This neglect on the part of the
Government led to yearly complaints, and the massacres of
1862. * * * These Sioux were most of them previous to the
war living in comfortable homes, with well-cultivated farms
and teams," and were receiving by annuity provisions, either in
money or the equivalent, about $50 a head annually, from in-
terest on their money invested in the bonds of the Government.   These Indians, in taking up their new homesteads, were
required by the Department to renounce, on oath, all claims on
the United States for annuities.   Without doubt, citizenship
of the United States, the protection of our laws, is worth a
great sum; but is it wise or right in our Government to require these natives of the country to purchase, at a price of several thousands of dollars, that which is given without money or
price to every immigrant from Asia, Europe, or Africa that
asks for it?

"Besides their annuities, there is due them from the Government the proceeds of the sale of their old reservation on the
Minnesota River, which is more than forty miles long and ten
wide; which, after paying expenses of survey and sale, are, according to a law of the United States, to be expended in as-
sisting them to make homes elsewhere; and as these lands were
valued at $1 25 an acre and upward, and are rapidly selling,
the portion which will be due each of the Indians cannot be
less than $200 or $300—or $1000 for each family.   The oath
required of them is supposed to bar them from any claim to

this also. Now, I cannot see how this decision of the Indian Department is consistent either with justice or good policy, and it is certainly inconsistent with both the spirit and letter of Articles six and ten of a treaty between the United States of America and different bands of Sioux Indians, concluded in 1868, and ratified and proclaimed February, 1869. * * * What I ask for them is that our Government restore to them a part of what we took from them, and give them the same chance to live and thrive which we give to all the other inhabitants of our country, whether white or black. * * * That some aid is very necessary must be obvious to you, who know how difficult it is for even white men, trained to work, and with several hundred dollars in property, to open a new farm in this Western wilderness. Their number is probably greater than you are aware of. When I administered the Lord's Supper there on the first Sabbath of this month, there were present seventy-seven communicants of our church, besides quite a number of other persons. * * * It is owing to the Santee Sioux—partly to those on the Big Sioux River, chiefly to those near Fort Wadsworth—that in the last five years not a single white inhabitant of Minnesota or Iowa has been murdered by the wild Indians, while many have been cut off in every frontier State and Territory south-west of the Missouri. So long as the Christian Sioux can be kept on the frontier, the white settlements are safe. * * * In conclusion, I wish again to call your attention to the fact that these Indians on the Big Sioux purchase citizenship at a very great sum, and to entreat you to do all in your power to secure for them that protection of person or property for which they bargain, and without which nothing our Government can do will make them prosperous or happy."

No attention was paid to this appeal; and the next year the indefatigable missionary sent a still stronger one, setting forth that this colony now numbered fifty families; had been under the instruction of the American Board of Commissioners

for Foreign Missions for many years; had a church of one
hundred members; a native preacher, partly supported by
them; had built log-cabins on their claims, and planted farms,
"many of them digging up the ground with hoes and spades."

Dr. Williamson reiterates the treaty provisions under which he
claims that these Indians are entitled to aid. The sixth Article
of the treaty of 1868 closes as follows: "Any Indian or Indians receiving a patent for land under the foregoing provisions, shall thereby and henceforth become and be a citizen of the
United States, and be entitled to all the privileges and immunities of such citizenship, and shall at the same time retain all
his rights and benefits accruing to Indians under this treaty."

This treaty goes on to provide most liberally for all Indians
adopting the civilized mode of life. Article eighth specially
provides for supplying them with seed and agricultural implements, and this is what they most of all need.

The encouragement held forth in this treaty was one great
motive in leading these people to break tribal influences, so
deleterious to improvement, and adopt our democratic civilization. Is it not base tyranny to disappoint them? They are
the first Sioux, if not the first Indians in the United States to
adopt the spirit and life of our American civilization. They
have of their own accord done just what the Government has
been for generations trying to get the Indians to do. And
now will the Government refuse this helping hand? To our
shame, it has for two years refused. And why? Because the
Indians said, "If we become civilized, it is necessary for us to
break up tribal relations, and settle down like white men."

In 1873 the Government at last yielded to this request,
and sent out oxen, wagons, ploughs, etc., enough to stock thirty farms. In 1874, Dr. Williamson, having been appointed a
special agent for them, reports their progress: "They all live
in log-houses and wear citizens' dress. * * * One hundred and
nineteen can read their own language fluently. They all go to

church regularly. They have broken one hundred and seventy-seven acres of new prairie. Twenty new houses have been built. * * * They have cut and hauled two hundred cords of wood, hauling some of it forty miles to market. * * * They have done considerable freighting with their teams, going sometimes a hundred miles away. They have earned thirty-five hundred dollars, catching small furs. * * * One Indian has the contract for carrying the mail through Flandreau, for which he receives one thousand dollars a year. * * * It is but a few miles from Flandreau to the far-famed pipe-stone quarry, and these Indians make many little sums by selling pipes, rings, ink-glasses, etc., made of this beautiful red stone. * * * They are anxious to be taught how to make baskets, mats, cloth; and the young men ask to be taught the blacksmith and carpenter trades."

This is a community that only five years before had pushed out into an unbroken wilderness without a dollar of money, without a plough, to open farms. "Without ploughs, they had to dig the sod with their hoes, and at the same time make their living by hunting. They suffered severe hardships, and a number of their best men perished in snow-storms. Believing they were carrying out the wishes of the Great Father, as expressed in the treaty of 1868, to which they were parties, they were disappointed when for three years no notice was taken of them." There is something pathetic in the gratitude they are said now to feel for the niggardly gift of a few oxen, wagons, and ploughs. They have apparently given over all hope of ever obtaining any of the money due them on account of their lands sold in Minnesota. No further allusion is made to it by Dr. Williamson.

From the Yankton Sioux this year comes a remarkable report: "We have no jail, no law except the treaty and the agent's word, yet we have no quarrels, no fighting, and, with one or two exceptions, not a single case of drunkenness during the year. This I consider remarkable, when we take into consideration the fact that the reservation is surrounded by ranches where liquors of all kinds can be obtained." Is there another village of two thousand inhabitants in the United States of which this can be said?

In this year a commission was sent to treat with some of the wilder bands of Sioux for the relinquishment of their right to hunt and roam over a large part of their unneeded territory in Kansas and Nebraska. Some of the chiefs consented. Red Cloud's band refused at first; "but on being told that the right would soon be taken from them," after a delay of two days they "agreed to accept," merely stipulating that their share of the twenty-five thousand dollars promised should be paid in horses and guns. They insisted, however, on this proviso: "That we do not surrender any right of occupation of the country situated in Nebraska north of the divide, which is south of and near to the Niobrara River and west of the one hundredth meridian."

It was a significant fact that, when these Sioux gave up this hunting privilege, "they requested that nearly all the $25,000 they received in compensation for this relinquishment should be expended in cows, horses, harness, and wagons," says the Commissioner of Indian Affairs in 1875.

There are still some thousand or more of hostile Sioux roaming about under the famous chief Sitting Bull—living by the chase when they can, and by depredations when they must; occasionally, also, appearing at agencies, and drawing rations among the other Indians unsuspected. The remainder of the bands are steadily working their way on toward civilization. The Santees are a Christian community; they have their industrial-schools, Sabbath-schools, and night-schools; they publish a monthly paper in the Dakota tongue, which prints twelve hundred copies. The Yanktons have learned to weave, and have made cloth enough to give every Indian woman in the tribe one good dress. The Flandreau citizen Sioux have a

Presbyterian church of one hundred and thirty-five members, and pay half the salary of the native preacher. On the occasion of an anniversary meeting of the Dakota missionaries there, these people raised one hundred dollars to pay for their entertainment. These three bands are far the most advanced, but all the others are making steady progress.

In 1876 the news from the Sioux on the agencies is that, owing to the failure of appropriations, the Indian Bureau had been unable to send the regular supplies, and the Indians, being in "almost a starving condition," had been induced, by the "apparent purpose of the Government to abandon them to starvation," to go north in large numbers, and join the hostile camps of Sitting Bull. This was in the spring; again in midsummer the same thing happened, and many of the Indians, growing still more anxious and suspicious, left their agencies to join in the war.

Congress would probably have paid little attention at this time to the reading of this extract from "Kent's Commentaries:" "Treaties of peace, when made by the competent power, are obligatory on the whole nation. If the treaty requires the payment of money to carry it into effect, and the money cannot be raised but by an act of the legislature, the treaty is morally obligatory upon the legislature to pass the law; and to repeal it would be a breach of the public faith."

A disturbed and unsettled condition of things prevailed at all the Sioux agencies, consequent on this state of things. Companies of troops were stationed at all of them to guard against outbreaks. Owing to lack of funds, the Yanktons were obliged to give up their weaving and basket-making. At the Standing Rock Agency, after the Indians had planted eight hundred and seventy-two dollars' worth of seeds—of corn, potatoes, and other vegetables—the grasshoppers came and devoured them. "Many of these Indians, with their whole families, stood all day in their fields fighting these enemies, and in

several places succeeded so far as to save a considerable part of
their crops." The Santees were made very anxious and unhappy by fresh rumors of their probable removal. Public sentiment at the East, knowing no difference between different tribes
of Sioux, regarded it as maudlin sentimentalism to claim for the
Santees any more rights than for the hostiles that had murdered
General Custer. One of the agents in Dakota writes :

"The recent troubles in the Indian country, and the existing
uncertainty as to the future intentions of the Government
toward the Indians, occasion considerable uneasiness among
them. * * * Reports are circulated that no further assistance
will be rendered by the Government, as the Great Council in
Washington refuses to furnish money unless the Indians are
turned over to the War Department. Every inducement is
held out to encourage secession from the agencies, and strength-
en the forces of the hostile camp. It is not surprising that, in
view of the non-arrival of supplies, and the recent order of the
War Department to arrest parties leaving and arriving, that
people less credulous than Indians would feel undecided and
uneasy. * * * It must be remembered that the whole Sioux
nation is related, and that there is hardly a man, woman, or
child in the hostile camp who has not blood relations at one or
the other of the agencies."

Contrast the condition into which all these friendly Indians
are suddenly plunged now, with their condition only two years
previous : martial law now in force on all their reservations ;
themselves in danger of starvation, and constantly exposed to the
influence of emissaries from their friends and relations, urging
them to join in fighting this treacherous government that had
kept faith with nobody—neither with friend nor with foe ;
that made no discriminations in its warfare between friends and
foes ; burning villages occupied only by women and children ;
butchering bands of Indians living peacefully under protection
of its flag, as at Sand Creek, in Colorado—no wonder that

one of the military commander's official reports says, "The hostile body was largely re-enforced by accessions from the various agencies, where the malcontents were, doubtless, in many cases, driven to desperation by starvation and the heartless frauds perpetrated on them;" and that the Interior Department is obliged to confess that, "Such desertions were largely due to the uneasiness which the Indians had long felt on account of the infraction of treaty stipulations by the white invasion of the Black Hills, seriously aggravated at the most critical period by irregular and insufficient issues of rations, necessitated by inadequate and delayed appropriations."

It was at this time that Sitting Bull made his famous reply: "Tell them at Washington if they have one man who speaks the truth to send him to me, and I will listen to what he has to say."

The story of the military campaign against these hostile Sioux in 1876 and 1877 is to be read in the official records of the War Department, so far as statistics can tell it. Another history, which can never be read, is written in the hearts of widowed women in the Sioux nation and in the nation of the United States.

Before midsummer the Sioux war was over. The indomitable Sitting Bull had escaped to Canada—that sanctuary of refuge for the Indian as well as for the slave. Here he was visited in the autumn by a commission from the United States, empowered by the President to invite him with his people to return, and be "assigned to agencies," and treated "in as friendly a spirit as other Indians had been who had surrendered." It was explained to him that every one of the Indians who had surrendered had "been treated in the same manner as those of your nation who, during all the past troubles, remained peaceably at their agencies." As a great part of those who had fled from these same agencies to join Sitting Bull had done so because they were starving, and the

Government knew this (had printed the record of the fact in the reports of two of its Departments), this was certainly a strange phraseology of invitation for it to address to Sitting Bull. His replies and those of his chiefs were full of scathing sarcasm. Secure on British soil, they had for once safe freedom of speech as well as of action, and they gave the United States Commissioners very conclusive reasons why they chose to remain in Canada, where they could "trade with the traders and make a living," and where their women had "time to raise their children." *

The commissioners returned from their bootless errand, and the Interior Department simply entered on its records the statement that "Sitting Bull and his adherents are no longer considered wards of the Government." It also enters on the same record the statement that "in the months of September and October, 1876, the various Sioux agencies were visited by a commission appointed under the Act of Congress, August 15th of that year, to negotiate with the Sioux for an agreement to surrender that portion of the Sioux Reservation which included the Black Hills, and certain hunting privileges outside that reserve, guaranteed by the treaty of 1868; to grant a right of way across their reserve ; and to provide for the removal of the Red Cloud and Spotted Tail bands to new agencies on the Missouri River. The commission were also authorized to take steps to gain the consent of the Sioux to their removal to the Indian Territory. * * * The commission were successful in all the negotiations with which they were charged, and the Indians made every concession that was desired by the Government, although we were engaged at that very time in fighting their relatives and friends." The only comment needed on this last paragraph is to suggest that a proper list of errata for that page should contain: "For 'although' read 'because!'" "On behalf of the United States the agreement thus entered into pro-

---

* See Appendix, Art. V.

vided for subsisting the Sioux on a stated ration until they should become self-supporting; for furnishing schools, and all necessary aid and instruction in agriculture and the mechanical arts, and for the allotment of lands in severalty."

In accordance with this act, a commission was sent to select a location on the Missouri River for the two new Sioux agencies (the Red Cloud and Spotted Tail).

"For the former the site chosen is the junction of Yellow Medicine and Missouri rivers, and at that point agency buildings have just been erected," says the Report of the Indian Bureau for 1877. "For the latter the old Ponca Reserve was decided on, where the agency buildings, storehouses, one hundred and fifty Indian houses, and five hundred acres of cultivated fields, left vacant by the Poncas, offer special advantages for present quarters."

The commissioner says : "The removal of fourteen thousand Sioux Indians at this season of the year, a distance of three hundred miles from their old agencies in Nebraska to their new quarters near the Missouri River, is not a pleasant matter to contemplate. Neither the present Secretary of the Interior nor the present Commissioner of Indian Affairs is responsible for the movement, but they have carried out the law faithfully though reluctantly. The removal is being made in accordance with the Act of August 15th, 1876. It is proper to say here that I cannot but look on the necessity thus imposed by law on the executive branch of the Government as an unfortunate one, and the consequences ought to be remedied as speedily as possible.

"Let us for a moment consider that the Spotted Tail Agency was in 1871 on the west bank of the Missouri River, where the whites became exceedingly troublesome, and the river afforded abundant facilities for the introduction of intoxicating liquors. In 1874 the Red Cloud and Spotted Tail agencies were removed to what a subsequent survey proved to be the State of Nebraska—the former agency one hundred and sixty-five miles from Cheyenne, and the latter one hundred and eight miles from Sidney, the nearest points on the Union Pacific Railroad. Here the usual ill-fortune attending the removal of these Indians was again exemplified in placing the agencies on absolutely barren land, where there was no possibility of cultivating the soil, no hope of their being enabled to become self-supporting, and where they have of necessity been kept in the hopeless condition of paupers."

In the hope of placing these Indians upon arable land, where they might become civilized and self-supporting, the determination was hastily taken to remove them back to the Missouri River. This step was taken without a proper examination of other points on their reservation, where it is stated that "a sufficient quantity of excellent wheat lands can be found on either bank of the White River, and where there is also timber sufficient in quantity and quality for all practical purposes. * * * The Indian chiefs, in their interview with the President in September last, begged that they might not be sent to the Missouri River, as whiskey-drinking and other demoralization would be the consequence. This was the judgment of the best men of the tribe; but the necessity was one that the President could not control. The provisions and supplies for the ensuing winter had been placed, according to law, on the Missouri, and, owing to the lateness of the season, it was impossible to remove them to the old agencies. Accordingly, the necessities of the case compelled the removal of these Indians in the midst of the snows and storms of early winter, which have already set in."

If there were absolutely no other record written of the management of Indian affairs by the Interior Department than this one page of the history of these two bands of the Sioux tribe, this alone would be enough to show the urgent need of an entirely new system. So many and such hasty, ill-considered, uninformed, capricious, and crue⌊ decisions of arbitrary power could hardly be found in a seven years' record of any known tyrant; and there is no tyrant whose throne would not have been rocked, if not upset, by the revolutions which would have followed on such oppressions.

There is a sequel to this story of the removal of the Red Cloud and Spotted Tail bands—a sequel not recorded in the official reports of the Department, but familiar to many men in the Western country. Accounts of it—some humorous, some severe—were for some time floating about in Western newspapers.

The Red Cloud and Spotted Tail bands of Sioux consented to go to the old Ponca Reserve only after being told that all their supplies had been sent to a certain point on the Missouri River with a view to this move; and it being too late to take all this freight northward again, they would starve if they stayed where they were. Being assured that they would be allowed to go back in the spring, and having a written pledge from General Crook (in whose word they had implicit faith) that the Government would fulfil this promise, they at last very reluctantly consented to go to the Ponca Reserve for the winter. In the spring no orders came for the removal. March passed, April passed—no orders. The chiefs sent word to their friend, General Crook, who replied to them with messages sent by a swift runner, begging them not to break away, but to wait a little longer. Finally, in May, the Commissioner of Indian Affairs went himself to hold a council with them. When he rose to speak, the chief Spotted Tail sprung up, walked toward him, waving in his hand the paper containing the promise of the Government to return them to White Clay Creek, and exclaimed, " All the men who come from Washington are liars, and the bald-headed ones are the worst of all! I don't want to hear one word from you—you are a bald-headed old liar! You have but one thing to do here, and that is to give an order for us to return to White Clay Creek. Here are your written words; and if you don't give this order, and everything here is not on wheels inside of ten days, I'll order my young men to tear down and burn everything in this part of the country! I don't want to hear anything more from you, and I've got nothing more to say to you:" and he turned his back on the commissioner and walked away. Such language as this would not have been borne from unarmed and helpless Indians; but when it came from a chief with four thousand armed warriors at his back, it was another affair altogether. The order was written. In less than ten days everything was "on wheels," and the whole body of these Sioux on the move to the country they had indicated; and the Secretary of the Interior says, naïvely, in his Report for 1868, "The Indians were found to be quite determined to move westward, and the promise of the Government in that respect was faithfully kept."

The reports from all the bands of Sioux for the past two years have been full of indications of their rapid and encouraging improvement. "The most decided advance in civilization has been made by the Ogallalla and Brulé Sioux," says the Report of the Indian Bureau for 1879. "Their progress during the last year and a half has been simply marvellous."

And yet this one band of Ogallalla Sioux has been moved, since 1863, eight times. Is it not a wonder that they have any heart to work, any hope of anything in the future?

"It is no longer a question," says this same report, "whether Indians will work. They are steadily asking for opportunities to do so, and the Indians who to-day are willing and anxious to engage in civilized labor are largely in the majority; * * * there is an almost universal call for lands in severalty; * * * there is a growing desire to live in houses; the demand for agricultural implements and appliances, and for wagons and harness for farming and freighting purposes, is constantly increasing."

That all this should be true of these wild, warlike Sioux, after so many years of hardships and forced wanderings and removals, is incontrovertible proof that there is in them a native strength of character, power of endurance, and indomitable courage, which will make of them ultimately a noble and superior race of people, if civilization will only give them time to become civilized, and Christians will leave them time and peace to learn Christianity.

CHAPTER VI.

THE PONCAS.

IN 1803 Captain Lewis and Lieutenant Clarke, of the First United States Infantry, were commissioned by Congress to explore the river Missouri from its mouth to its source, to " seek the best water communication from thence to the Pacific Ocean," and to enter into conference with all the Indian tribes on their route, with a view to the establishment of commerce with them. They report the " Poncars " as " the remnant of a nation once respectable in point of numbers; they formerly resided on a branch of the Red River of Lake Winnipeg; being oppressed by Sioux, they removed to the west side of the Missouri, on Poncar River, where they built and fortified a village, and remained some years ; but, being pursued by their ancient enemies, the Sioux, and reduced by continual wars, they have joined and now live with the Mahas (Omahas), whose language they speak." Their numbers are estimated by Lewis and Clarke as being only about two hundréd, all told ; but this small estimate is probably to be explained by the fact that at this time the tribe was away on its annual buffalo-hunt, and their village had been so long empty and quiet that a buffalo was found grazing there. A few years later the tribe is reckoned at four hundred : in a census of the Indian tribes, taken by General Porter in 1829, they are set down at six hundred. The artist Catlin, who visited them a few years later, rated them a little less. He gives an interesting account of the chief of the tribe, named Shoo-de-ga-cha (Smoke), and his young and pretty wife, Hee-la'h-dee (the Pure Fountain), whose portraits he painted.

He says : " The chief, who was wrapped in a buffalo-robe, is a
noble specimen of native dignity and philosophy. I conversed
much with him, and from his dignified manners, as well as from
the soundness of his reasoning, I became fully convinced that
he deserved to be the sachem of a more numerous and prosperous tribe. He related to me with great coolness and frankness
the poverty and distress of his nation—and with the method of
a philosopher predicted the certain and rapid extinction of his
tribe, which he had not the power to avert. Poor, noble chief,
who was equal to and worthy of a greater empire ! He sat on
the deck of the steamer, overlooking the little cluster of his
wigwams mingled among the trees, and, like Caius Marius
weeping over the ruins of Carthage, shed tears as he was des-
canting on the poverty of his ill-fated little community, which
he told me had ' once been powerful and happy ; that the buffaloes which the Great Spirit had given them for food, and
which formerly spread all over their green prairies, had all been
killed or driven out by the approach of white men, who wanted
their skins ; that their country was now entirely destitute of
game, and even of roots for food, as it was one continuous prairie ; and that his young men, penetrating the countries of their
enemies for buffaloes, which they were obliged to do, were cut
to pieces and destroyed in great numbers. That his people had
foolishly become fond of fire-water, and had given away everything in their country for it ; that it had destroyed many of
his warriors, and would soon destroy the rest ; that his tribe
was too small and his warriors too few to go to war with the
tribes around them ; that they were met and killed by the Sioux
on the north, by the Pawnees on the west, by the Osages and
Konzas on the south, and still more alarmed from the constant
advance of the pale faces—their enemies from the east—with
whiskey and small-pox, which already had destroyed four-fifths
of his tribe, and would soon impoverish and at last destroy the
remainder of them.' In this way did this shrewd philosopher

lament over the unlucky destiny of his tribe, and I pitied him with all my heart."

The day before Catlin arrived at this village this old chief's son—the young Hongs-kay-de—had created a great sensation in the community by accomplishing a most startling amount of bigamy in a single day. Being the chief's son, and having just been presented by his father with a handsome wigwam and nine horses, he had no difficulty whatever in ingratiating himself with the fathers of marriageable daughters, and had, with ingenious slyness, offered himself to and been accepted by four successive fathers-in-law, promising to each of them two horses—enjoining on them profound secrecy until a certain hour, when he would announce to the whole tribe that he was to be married. At the time appointed he appeared, followed by some of his young friends leading eight horses. Addressing the prospective father-in-law who stood nearest him, with his daughter by his side, he said, "You promised me your daughter: here are the two horses." A great hubbub immediately arose; the three others all springing forward, angry and perplexed, claiming his promises made to them. The triumphant young Turk exclaimed, "You have all now acknowledged your engagements to me, and must fulfil them. Here are your horses." There was nothing more to be said. The horses were delivered, and Hongs-kay-de, leading two brides in each hand, walked off with great dignity to his wigwam.

This was an affair totally unprecedented in the annals of the tribe, and produced an impression as profound as it could have done in a civilized community, though of a different character —redounding to the young prince's credit rather than to his shame—marking him out as one daring and original enough to be a "Big Medicine." Mr. Catlin says that he visited the bridal wigwam soon afterward, and saw the "four modest little wives seated around the fire, seeming to harmonize very well." Of the prettiest one—"Mong-shong-shaw" (the Bending Willow)—he took a portrait, and a very sweet-faced young woman she is too, wrapped in a beautifully ornamented fur robe, much handsomer and more graceful than the fur-lined circulars worn by civilized women.

The United States' first treaty with this handful of gentle and peaceable Indians was made in 1817. It was simply a treaty of peace and friendship.

In 1825 another was made, in which the Poncas admit that "they reside within the territorial limits of the United States, acknowledge their supremacy, and claim their protection." They also admit "the right of the United States to regulate all trade and intercourse with them." The United States, on their part, "agree to receive the Poncar tribe of Indians into their friendship and under their protection, and to extend to them from time to time such benefits and acts of kindness as may be convenient, and seem just and proper to the President of the United States."

After this there is little mention, in the official records of the Government, of the Poncas for some thirty years. Other tribes in the Upper Missouri region were so troublesome and aggressive that the peaceable Poncas were left to shift for themselves as they best could amidst all the warring and warring interests by which they were surrounded. In 1856 the agent of the Upper Platte mentions incidentally that their lands were being fast intruded upon by squatters; and in 1857 another agent reports having met on the banks of the Missouri a large band of Poncas, who made complaint that all the Indians on the river were receiving presents and they were overlooked; that the men from the steamboats cut their trees down, and that white settlers were taking away all their land. In 1858 the Commissioner for Indian Affairs writes: "Treaties were entered into in March and April last with the Poncas and Yankton Sioux, who reside west of Iowa, for the purpose of extinguishing their title to all the lands occupied and claimed by them, except small portions on which to colonize and domesticate them. This proceeding was deemed necessary in order to obtain such control over these Indians as to prevent their interference with our settlements, which are rapidly extending in that direction. These treaties were duly laid before the Senate at its last regular session, but were not, it is understood, finally acted on by that body.

" Relying on the ratification of their treaty, and the adoption of timely measures to carry out its provisions in their favor, the Poncas proceeded in good faith to comply with its stipulations by abandoning their settlements and hunting-grounds, and withdrawing to the small tract reserved for their future home. Being without a crop to rely upon, and having been unsuccessful in their usual summer hunt, they were reduced to a state of desperation and destitution. As nothing had been done for them under the treaty, they concluded it was void, and threatened to fall back upon their former settlements, some of the most important of which had, in the mean time, been taken possession of by numerous white persons."

The Poncas never heard of Grotius or Vattel; but, in assuming that the treaty was void because it was not fulfilled, they only acted on the natural principles of the law of nations and of treaties, as laid down by all authorities. Thucydides said: " They are not the first breakers of a league who, being deserted, seek for aid to others, but they that perform not by their deeds what they have promised to do upon their oaths."

In consequence of this delay to fulfil the treaty provisions, the Government was forced to step in at the last moment and " incur a heavy expense " in furnishing the Poncas with food enough to keep them from starving; and in 1859, under this pressure, the Senate ratified the treaty. By it the Poncas ceded and relinquished to the United States all the lands they had ever owned or claimed, " wherever situate," except a small tract between the Ponca and Niobrara rivers. In consideration of this cession, the United States Government agreed "to protect the Poncas in the possession of this tract of land, and their persons and property thereon, during good behavior on their part; to pay them annuities annually for thirty years—$12,000 for the first five years, then $10,000 for ten years, then $8000 for fifteen years; to expend $20,000 for their subsistence during the first year, for building· houses, etc.; to establish schools, and to build mills, mechanics' shops, etc.; to give $20,000 for the payment of the existing obligations of the tribe."

Two years later the agent newly appointed to take charge of the Poncas reports to the Department the amount of improvements made on the reservation : " One saw and grist-mill ; two agency houses—story and a half houses—without inside lining or plastering, 16 by 26 and 18 by 32 feet in size ; six small round log-houses (three with a small shed for a stable), a light log-corral for cattle, and a canvas shed for storing under ; and about sixty acres of ground, broken, comprised all the improvements."

Evidently a very small part of the $20,000 had been spent as yet. He did not find an Indian on the reservation. From fear of the Sioux (who in 1860 had stolen from them more than half the horses they owned) they had moved down the Niobrara River, some twenty miles nearer the Missouri. It was with the greatest difficulty that the agent induced them to return ; and after they did so, they huddled their tents close about the agency buildings, and could not be induced to go half a mile away unless accompanied by some of the white employés.

As the agent had no food to feed them with, and no money to buy any (spite of the appropriation of $20,000 for subsistence and house-building), he induced them to go off on a hunt; but in less than a month they came straggling back, " begging for provisions for their women and children, whom they had left on the plains half-starved, having been unable to find any game, or any food except wild-turnips. Some of them went to visit the Omahas, others the Pawnees, where they remained until the little corn they had planted produced roasting-ears. In the mean time those who were here subsisted mainly on wild-cherries and plums and the wild-turnip, and traded away most of their blankets and annuity goods for provisions."

In 1863 the reports are still more pitiful. "They started on their summer hunt toward the last of May, immediately after the first hoeing of their corn. At first they were successful and found buffaloes; but afterward, the ground being occupied by the Yanktons, who were sent south of the Niobrara by the general commanding the district, and who were about double the number, and with four times as many horses, they soon consumed what meat they had cured, and were compelled to abandon the chase. They commenced to return in the latter part of July. They went away with very high hopes, and reasonably so, of a large crop, but returned to see it all withered and dried up. In the mean time the plains had been burnt over, so that they could not discover the roots they are in the habit of digging. Even the wild-plums, which grow on bushes down in ravines and gullies, are withered and dried on the limbs. The building I occupy was constantly surrounded by a hungry crowd begging for food. * * * I am warned by military authority to keep the Poncas within the limits of the reservation; but this is an impossibility. There is nothing within its limits, nor can anything be obtained in sufficient quantity, or brought here soon enough to keep them from starving. * * * The Poncas have behaved well—quite as well, if not better than, under like circumstances, the same number of whites would have done. I have known whole families to live for days together on nothing but half-dried corn-stalks, and this when there were cattle and sheep in their sight."

At this time martial law was in force on many of the Indian

reservations, owing to the presence of roving bands of hostile Sioux, driven from Minnesota after their outbreak there.

The Poncas through all these troubles remained loyal and peaceable, and were "unwavering in their fidelity to their treaty," says the Indian Commissioner.

In December of this year what the governmental reports call " a very unfortunate occurrence " took place in Nebraska. A party of Poncas, consisting of four men, six women, three boys, and two girls, returning from a visit to the Omahas, had camped for the night about twelve miles from their own reservation. In the night a party of soldiers from a military post on the Niobrara River came to their camp, and began to insult the squaws, "offering money with one hand, and presenting a revolver with the other." The Indians, alarmed, pulled up their lodge, and escaped to a copse of willows near by. The soldiers fired at them as they ran away, and then proceeded to destroy all their effects. They cut the lodge covers to pieces, burnt the saddles and blankets, cut open sacks of beans, corn, and dried pumpkin, and strewed their contents on the ground, and went away, taking with them a skin lodge-covering, beaver-skins, buffalo-robes, blankets, guns, and all the small articles. The Indians' ponies were hid in the willows. Early in the morning they returned with these, picked up all the corn which had not been destroyed, and such other articles as they could find, packed their ponies as best they might, and set off barefooted for home. After they had gone a few miles they stopped and built a fire to parch some corn to eat. Some of the women and children went to look for wild-beans, leaving three women and a child at the camp. Here the soldiers came on them again. As soon as the Indians saw them coming they fled. The soldiers fired on them, wounding one woman by a ball through her thigh ; another, with a child on her back, by two balls through the child's thighs, one of which passed through the mother's side. These women were fired on as they were crossing the river on the ice. The soldiers then took possession of the six ponies and all the articles at the camp, and left. The squaws and children who were looking for beans were half a mile below; a little dog belonging to them barked and revealed their hiding-place in the willows. The soldiers immediately turned on them, dismounted, and, making up to them, deliberately shot them dead as they huddled helplessly together—three women and a little girl!

One of the boys, a youth, ran for the river, pursued by the soldiers. On reaching the river he dived into the water through a hole in the ice; as often as he lifted his head they fired at him. After they went away he crawled out and escaped to the agency. One of the murdered women, the mother of this boy, had three balls in her head and cheek, her throat cut, and her head half-severed by a sabre-thrust; another, the youngest woman, had her cloth skirt taken off and carried away, and all her other clothes torn from her body, leaving it naked!

The men who did this deed belonged to Company B of the Seventh Iowa Cavalry.

The outrage was promptly reported to the Department, and the general commanding the Nebraska District detailed an officer to examine into it. There was some correspondence between the military authorities relative to it, but with no result; and in the report of the next year the Indian Commissioner says: "Attention was called last year to the fact that the murderers of several of this loyal and friendly tribe had not been discovered and punished. I trust that, as there seems to be no probability that this will be done, a special appropriation may be made for presents to the relatives of the deceased."

In 1865 a supplementary treaty was made with the Poncas, extending their reservation down the Niobrara to the Missouri River; and the Government agreed to pay them $15,000, for the purpose of indemnifying them for the loss they had sustained in this outrage and in others. For the ratification of this treaty also they waited two years; and in 1867 the Superintendent of the Dakota Territory says: "Schools would have been in operation at the Ponca Agency before this time but for the long delay in ratifying the supplementary treaty of 1865; and now that this measure has fortunately been accomplished, there can be no further necessity for delay, and it is confidently believed another year will witness the foundation and rapid progress of an English school at this agency."

This superintendent, having been in office only one year, was probably not familiar with the provisions of the treaty of 1859 with the Poncas, in which, by Article three, the United States Government had promised "to establish and maintain for ten years, at an annual expense not to exceed $5,000, one or more manual labor schools for the education and training of the Ponca youth in letters, agriculture, mechanics, and housewifery."

This educational annuity has but one more year to run; whatever may have been done with it up to this time, it really is now being spent on schools, and it seems a great pity that it should soon cease. The Governor of Dakota, in 1868, evidently thinks so too, for he writes to the Department, in the autumn of 1868: "A school has been in successful operation at this agency (the Ponca) for the past nine months, with an average attendance of about fifty scholars, and with every evidence of advancement in the primary department of an English education. But just at this interesting period of its existence we are notified by the agent that with this fiscal year all funds for school as well as for agricultural purposes cease, agreeably to the terms and conditions of their original treaty. This will be a serious and irreparable calamity if not remedied by the most generous action of the Government. If funds for this purpose cannot be otherwise procured, the Poncas are willing and anxious to transfer their old reservation to the Government for a moderate extension of these important and indispensable benefits."

The governor also says that in the past year the Poncas have paid out of their annuity money for all the improvements which had been made on lands occupied by certain white settlers, who were ejected from their new reservation by the terms of the last treaty.

In the report for 1869 we read that the Ponca school has been "discontinued for want of funds." The Department earnestly recommends an appropriation of $25,000 to put it in operation again. The new Governor of Dakota seconds the recommendation, and regrets to say that, "for the enlightenment of the 35,000 Indians embraced in the Dakota Superintendency, there is not one school in operation."

In 1870 an appropriation of $5,000 was made by the Department from a general educational fund, for the purpose of resuming this school. The condition of the Poncas now is, on the whole, encouraging; they are "not only willing, but extremely anxious to learn the arts by which they may become self-supporting, and conform to the usages of white men. With the comparatively small advantages that have been afforded them, their advancement has been very great."

In the summer of 1869 they built for themselves sixteen very comfortable log-houses; in the summer of 1870 they built forty-four more; with their annuity money they bought cookstoves, cows, and useful implements of labor. They worked most assiduously in putting in their crops, but lost them all by drought, and are in real danger of starvation if the Government does not assist them. All this while they see herds of cattle driven across their reservation to feed the lately hostile Sioux—flour, coffee, sugar, tobacco, by the wagon-load, distributed to them—while their own always peaceable, always loyal, long-suffering tribe is digging wild roots to eat, and in actual danger of starvation. Nevertheless they are not discouraged, knowing that but for the drought they would have had ample food from their farms, and they make no attempts to retaliate

on the Sioux for raiding off their horses and stock, because
they hope "that the Government will keep its faith with
them," and that suitable remuneration for these losses will be
made them, according to the treaty stipulations.

For the next two years they worked industriously and well;
three schools were established; a chapel was built by the Episcopal mission; the village began to assume the appearance of
permanence and thrift; but misfortune had not yet parted
company with the Poncas. In the summer of 1873 the Missouri River suddenly overflowed, washed away its banks hundreds of yards back, and entirely ruined the Ponca village.
By working night and day for two weeks the Indians saved
most of the buildings, carrying them half a mile inland to be
sure of safety. The site of their village became the bed of the
main channel of the river; their cornfields were ruined, and
the lands for miles in every direction washed and torn up by
the floods.

" For nearly two weeks," the agent writes, " the work of sal-
vage from the ever-threatening destruction occupied our whole
available force night and day. We succeeded in carrying from
the river bank to near half a mile inland the whole of the
agency buildings, mechanics' houses, stabling, and sheds—
more than twenty houses—nearly every panel of fencing.
The Poncas worked well and long, often through the night;
and the fact that the disaster did not cost us ten dollars of actual loss is to be attributed to their labor, continuous and persevering—working sometimes over the swiftly-flowing waters,
terrible and turbid, on the edge of the newly-formed current
but a few inches below them, and into which a fall would have
been certain death, even for an Indian."

In one year after this disaster they had recovered themselves
marvellously; built twenty new houses; owned over a hundred
head of cattle and fifty wagons, and put three hundred acres of
land under cultivation (about three acres to each male in the

tribe). But this year was not to close without a disaster. First came a drought; then three visitations of locusts, one after the other, which so completely stripped the fields that "nothing was left but a few prematurely dry stalks and straw." One hundred young trees which had been set out—box-elder, soft maple, and others—withered and died.

In 1875 the locusts came again, destroyed the corn and oats, but left the wheat. Much of this crop, however, was lost, as there was only one reaping-machine on the agency, and it could not do all of the work. Many of the Indians saved a part of their crop by cutting it with large butcher-knives; but this was slow, and much of the wheat dried up and perished before it could be harvested by this tedious process.

This year was also marked by a flagrant instance of the helplessness of Indians in the courts. Two Poncas were way-laid by a party of Santees, one of the Poncas murdered, and the other seriously wounded. This occurred at the Yankton Agency, where both parties were visiting. When the case was brought up before the courts, a motion was made to quash the indictment for want of jurisdiction, and the judge was obliged to sustain the motion, there being under the present laws no jurisdiction whatever "over crimes committed by one Indian on the person or property of another Indian in the Indian country."

In 1876 the project of consolidating all the Indians in the United States upon a few reservations began to be discussed and urged. If this plan were carried out, it would be the ·destiny of the Poncas to go to the Indian Territory. It was very gratuitously assumed that, as they had been anxious to be allowed to remove to Nebraska and join the Omahas, they would be equally ready to remove to Indian Territory—a process of reasoning whose absurdity would be very plainly seen if it were attempted to apply it in the case of white men.

After a series of negotiations, protestations, delays, and bewilderments, the tribe at last gave what the United States Government chose to call a " consent " to the removal. The story of the influences, deceits, coercions brought to bear on these unfortunate creatures before this was brought about, is one of the most harrowing among the harrowing records of our dealings with the Indians. A party of chiefs were induced, in the first place, to go, in company with a United States inspector— Kemble by name—to the Indian Territory, to see whether the country would suit them. It was distinctly promised to them that, if it did not suit them, they should then be permitted to go to Washington and consult with the President as to some further plan for their establishment.

The story of this journey and of its results is best told in the words of one of the Ponca chiefs, Standing Bear. No official document, no other man's narrative—no, not if a second Homer should arise to sing it—could tell the story so well as he tells it :

" We lived on our land as long as we can remember. No one knows how long ago we came there. The land was owned by our tribe as far back as memory of men goes.

" We were living quietly on our farms. All of a sudden one white man came. We had no idea what for. This was the inspector. He came to our tribe with Rev. Mr. Hinman. These two, with the agent, James Lawrence, they made our trouble.

" They said the President told us to pack up—that we must move to the Indian Territory.

" The inspector said to us : ' The President says you must sell this land. He will buy it and pay you the money, and give you new land in the Indian Territory.'

" We said to him : ' We do not know your authority. You have no right to move us till we have had council with the President.'

" We said to him : ' When two persons wish to make a bargain, they can talk together and find out what each wants, and then make their agreement.'

" We said to him : ' We do not wish to go. When a man owns anything, he does not let it go till he has received payment for it.'

" We said to him : ' We will see the President first.'

" He said to us : ' I will take you to see the new land. If you like it, then you can see the President, and tell him so. If not, then you can see him and tell him so.' And he took all ten of our chiefs down. I went, and Bright Eyes' uncle went. He took us to look at three different pieces of land. He said we must take one of the three pieces, so the President said. After he took us down there he said : ' No pay for the land you left.'

" We said to him : ' You have forgotten what you said before we started. You said we should have pay for our land. Now you say not. You told us then you were speaking truth.' All these three men took us down there. The man got very angry. He tried to compel us to take one of the three pieces of land. He told us to be brave. He said to us : ' If you do not accept these, I will leave you here alone. You are one thousand miles from home. You have no money. You have no interpreter, and you cannot speak the language.' And he went out and slammed the door. The man talked to us from long before sundown till it was nine o'clock at night.

" We said to him : ' We do not like this land. We could not support ourselves. The water is bad. Now send us to Washington, to tell the President, as you promised.'

" He said to us : ' The President did not tell me to take you to Washington ; neither did he tell me to take you home.'

" We said to him : ' You have the Indian money you took to bring us down here. That money belongs to us. We would like to have some of it. People do not give away food for nothing. We must have money to buy food on the road.'

"He said to us : 'I will not give you a cent.'

"We said to him : 'We are in a strange country. We cannot find our way home. Give us a pass, that people may show us our way.'

"He said : 'I will not give you any.'

"We said to him : 'This interpreter is ours. We pay him. Let him go with us.'

"He said : 'You shall not have the interpreter. He is mine, and not yours.'

"We said to him : 'Take us at least to the railroad; show us the way to that.'

"And he would not. He left us right there. It was winter. We started for home on foot. At night we slept in hay-stacks. We barely lived till morning, it was so cold. We had nothing but our blankets. We took the ears of corn that had dried in the fields; we ate it raw. The soles of our moccasins wore out. We were barefoot in the snow. We were nearly dead when we reached the Otoe Reserve. It had been fifty days. We stayed there ten days to strengthen up, and the Otoes gave each of us a pony. The agent of the Otoes told us he had received a telegram from the inspector, saying that the Indian chiefs had run away; not to give us food or shelter, or help in any way. The agent said : 'I would like to understand. Tell me all that has happened. Tell me the truth.' "

(This Otoe agent afterward said that when the chiefs entered his room they left the prints of their feet in blood on the floor as they came in.)

"Then we told our story to the agent and to the Otoe chiefs —how we had been left down there to find our way.

"The agent said : 'I can hardly believe it possible that any one could have treated you so. That inspector was a poor man to have done this. If I had taken chiefs in this way, I would have brought them home; I could not have left them there.'

"In seven days we reached the Omaha Reservation. Then

we sent a telegram to the President : asked him if he had authorized this thing. We waited three days for the answer. No answer came.

"In four days we reached our own home. We found the inspector there. While we were gone, he had come to our people and told them to move.

"Our people said : 'Where are our chiefs? What have you done with them? Why have you not brought them back? We will not move till our chiefs come back.'

"Then the inspector told them : 'To-morrow you must be ready to move. If you are not ready you will be shot.' Then the soldiers came to the doors with their bayonets, and ten families were frightened. The soldiers brought wagons ; they put their things in and were carried away. The rest of the tribe would not move.

"When we got there, we asked the inspector why he had done this thing, and he got very angry.

"Then we said to him : 'We did not think we would see your face again, after what has passed. We thought never to see your face any more. But here you are.'

"We said to him : 'This land is ours. It belongs to us. You have no right to take it from us. The land is crowded with people, and only this is left to us.'

"We said to him : 'Let us alone. Go away from us. If you want money, take all the money which the President is to pay us for twelve years to come. You may have it all, if you will go and leave us our lands.'

"Then, when he found that we would not go, he wrote for more soldiers to come.

"Then the soldiers came, and we locked our doors, and the women and children hid in the woods. Then the soldiers drove all the people the other side of the river, all but my brother Big Snake and I. We did not go ; and the soldiers took us and carried us away to a fort and put us in jail.

There were eight officers who held council with us after we got there. The commanding officer said: 'I have received four messages telling me to send my soldiers after you. Now, what have you done?'

"Then we told him the whole story. Then the officer said: 'You have done no wrong. The land is yours; they had no right to take it from you. Your title is good. I am here to protect the weak, and I have no right to take you; but I am a soldier, and I have to obey orders.'

"He said: 'I will telegraph to the President, and ask him what I shall do. We do not think these three men had any authority to treat you as they have done. When we own a piece of land, it belongs to us till we sell it and pocket the money.'

"Then he brought a telegram, and said he had received answer from the President. The President said he knew nothing about it.

"They kept us in jail ten days. Then they carried us back to our home. The soldiers collected all the women and children together; then they called all the chiefs together in council; and then they took wagons and went round and broke open the houses. When we came back from the council we found the women and children surrounded by a guard of soldiers.

"They took our reapers, mowers, hay-rakes, spades, ploughs, bedsteads, stoves, cupboards, everything we had on our farms, and put them in one large building. Then they put into the wagons such things as they could carry. We told them that we would rather die than leave our lands; but we could not help ourselves. They took us down. Many died on the road. Two of my children died. After we reached the new land, all my horses died. The water was very bad. All our cattle died; not one was left. I stayed till one hundred and fifty-eight of my people had died. Then I ran away with thirty of my people, men and women and children. Some of the children were orphans. We were three months on the road. We were weak and sick and starved. When we reached the Omaha Reserve the Omahas gave us a piece of land, and we were in a hurry to plough it and put in wheat. While we were working the soldiers came and arrested us. Half of us were sick. We would rather have died than have been carried back; but we could not help ourselves."

Nevertheless they were helped. The news of their arrest, and the intention of the Government to take them back by force to Indian Territory, roused excitement in Omaha. An Omaha editor and two Omaha lawyers determined to test the question whether the Government had a legal right to do it. It seemed a bold thing, almost a hopeless thing, to undertake. It has passed into a proverb that Providence is on the side of the heaviest battalions: the oppressed and enslaved in all ages have felt this. But there are times when a simple writ of habeas corpus is stronger than cannon or blood-hounds; and this was one of these times. Brought into the District Court of the United States for the District of Nebraska, these Poncas were set free by the judge of that court. Will not the name of Judge Dundy stand side by side with that of Abraham Lincoln in the matter of Emancipation Acts?

The Government attorney, the Hon. G. M. Lambertson, made an argument five hours long, said to have been both "ingenious and eloquent," to prove that an Indian was not entitled to the protection of the writ of habeas corpus, "*not* being a person or citizen under the law."

Judge Dundy took several days to consider the case, and gave a decision which strikes straight to the root of the whole matter—a decision which, when it is enforced throughout our land, will take the ground out from under the feet of the horde of unscrupulous thieves who have been robbing, oppressing, and maddening the Indians for so long, that to try to unmask and expose their processes, or to make clean their methods, is a task before which hundreds of good men—nay, whole denominations of good men—disheartened, baffled, and worn-out, have given up.

When Standing Bear found that by the decision of Judge Dundy he was really a free man, and could go where he pleased, he made a speech which should never be forgotten or left out in the history of the dealings of the United States Government with the Indians.

After a touching expression of gratitude to the lawyers who had pleaded his cause, he said : " Hitherto, when we have been wronged, we went to war to assert our rights and avenge our wrongs. We took the tomahawk. We had no law to punish those who did wrong, so we took our tomahawks and went to kill. If they had guns and could kill us first, it was the fate of war. But you have found a better way. You have gone into the court for us, and I find that our wrongs can be righted there. Now I have no more use for the tomahawk. I want to lay it down forever."

Uttering these words with eloquent impressiveness, the old chief, stooping down, placed the tomahawk on the floor at his feet ; then, standing erect, he folded his arms with native dignity, and continued : " I lay it down. I have no more use for it. I have found a better way."

Stooping again and taking up the weapon, he placed it in Mr. Webster's hands, and said : " I present it to you as a token of my gratitude. I want you to keep it in remembrance of this great victory which you have gained. I have no further use for it. I can now seek the ways of peace."

The first use that Standing Bear made of his freedom was to endeavor to procure the freedom of his tribe, and establish their legal right to their old home in Dakota. Accompanied by a young and well-educated Omaha girl and her brother as interpreters, and by Mr. Tibbles, the champion and friend to whom he owed his freedom, he went to the Eastern States, and told the story of the sufferings and wrongs of his tribe to large audiences in many of the larger cities and towns. Money was generously subscribed everywhere for the purpose of bringing suits to test the question of the Poncas' legal right to the lands which the United States Government had by treaty ceded to them in specified "townships," thus giving to them the same sort of title which would be given to any corporation or individual.

Very soon this movement of Standing Bear and his companions began to produce on the community a strong effect, shown by the interest in their public meetings, and by expressions of strong feeling in the newspapers. This attracted the attention of the authorities at Washington. Letters were published contradicting many of Standing Bear's assertions; statements were circulated injurious to the reputation of all members of the party. A careful observer of the whole course of the Department of the Interior in this matter could not fail to come to the conclusion that for some mysterious, unexplained, and unexplainable reason the Department did not wish—in fact, was unwilling—that the Ponca tribe should be reinstated on its lands. Discussions on the matter grew warm. The inspector who had been concerned in their removal published long letters reflecting equally on the veracity of Standing Bear and of the Secretary of the Interior. Standing Bear replied in a few pithy words, which were conclusive in their proving of the falsity of some of the inspector's statements. The Secretary, also, did not think it beneath his dignity to reply in successive newspaper articles to the inspector's reflections upon him; but the only thing that was made clear by this means was that either the Secretary or the inspector, or both, said what was not true.

In Boston the interest in the Ponca case reached such a height that a committee was appointed to represent the case in

Washington, and to secure legislation upon it. Standing Bear and his party went to Washington, and, in spite of the secret hostility of the Interior Department, produced a powerful impression upon Congress. Senator Dawes, of Massachusetts, and Senator Morgan, of Alabama, both became warm advocates of their cause. The subject once started, case after case came up for investigation; and the Congressional committees called for evidence in regard to several of the more striking instances of injustice to Indians.

White Eagle, one of the Ponca chiefs, who had lost his wife and four children, and who was himself fast sinking under disease developed by the malarial Indian Territory, came to Washington and gave eloquent testimony in behalf of his tribe. The physicians there predicted that he had not three months to live. A bill was introduced into Congress for restoring to the Poncas their old reservation in Dakota, and putting their houses, farms, etc., in the same good condition they were at the time of their removal.

The story of that removal was written out in full at the time by the agent who superintended it. That he should forward this report to the Department of the Interior was natural; but that the Department of the Interior should have been willing to publish it to the country, to have it on the official record of its management of Indian affairs for the year 1877, is strange. It will make a fitting conclusion to this sketch of the history of the Ponca tribe. The name of this agent was E. A. Howard. He calls the report "Journal of the March."

" *May* 21*st*. Broke camp at seven o'clock and marched to Crayton, a distance of thirteen miles. Roads very heavy. The child that died yesterday was here buried by the Indians, they preferring to bury it than to have it buried by the white people.

" *May* 22*d*. Broke camp at seven o'clock and marched to

Neligh, a distance of about twenty-five miles. The day was cool, and, the road being high and comparatively good, the travel was made without much inconvenience.

"*May* 23*d*. The morning opened with light rain; but at eight o'clock a terrific thunder-storm occurred of two hours' duration, which was followed by steady rain throughout the day, in consequence of which we remained in camp. During the day a child died, and several women and children were reported sick, and medical attendance and medicine were procured for them.

"*May* 24*th*. Buried the child that died yesterday in the cemetery at Neligh, giving it a Christian burial. Broke camp at ten o'clock and marched about eight miles, crossing the Elk-horn River about two miles below Oakdale Village. Were unable to cross at Neligh, the road being about two feet under water and the bridges being washed away. The road was fearfully bad, and much time and labor were expended in making the road and bridges at all passable over the Elk-horn flats, where the crossing was effected.

"*May* 25*th*. Broke camp at six o'clock and marched twenty miles, to a point on Shell Creek. No wood at this place, and none to be had except what little had been picked up and brought in by the trains. Weather cold, damp, and dreary. The Indians during the day behaved well, and marched splendidly.

"*May* 26*th*. The morning opened with a heavy continuous rain, which prevailed until ten o'clock. Broke camp at eleven o'clock and marched eight miles farther down Shell Creek, when it again commenced raining, and we went into camp. The evening set in cold and rainy, and no wood to be had except what was purchased of a settler.

"*May* 27*th*. The morning opened cold, with a misty rain. Rain ceased at half-past seven o'clock, and we broke camp at eight and marched eight miles farther down Shell Creek, when, a heavy thunder-storm coming on, we again went into camp. Several of the Indians were here found to be quite sick, and having no physician, and none being attainable, they gave us much anxiety and no little trouble. The daughter of Standing Bear, one of the.chiefs, was very low of consumption, and moving her with any degree of comfort was almost impossible, and the same trouble existed in transporting all the sick.

" *May* 28*th.* Last evening I gave orders to break camp at five o'clock this morning, intending, if practicable, to reach Columbus before night ; but a heavy thunder-storm prevailed at that time. Broke camp at seven o'clock. Marched seven miles, when we came to a slough confluent to Shell Creek, which was only made passable after two hours of active work in cutting willow-brush and bringing a large quantity of wheat straw from a distance of thirty rods, with which we covered the road thickly. After crossing the slough we marched to a point on Shell Creek and camped, having made about fourteen miles during the day.

" *May* 29*th.* Broke camp at seven o'clock and crossed Shell Creek. For about five miles the road led over a divide, and was quite good ; but in coming down on the flats, which extended for five miles between the Bluffs and Columbus, we found the roads for the entire distance almost impassable, owing to the many deep, miry sloughs which cross the road, and the generally flooded and yielding condition of the soil aside from the sloughs. Teams had to be frequently doubled, in order to get the wagons through. The difficulties were finally overcome, and the train marched into Columbus at two o'clock, and went into camp at Soap Fork, having made a march of about ten miles, the march of five miles across the flats occupying about seven hours. Major Walker, who had accompanied us from the Niobrara River to this place with twenty-five soldiers, under orders from the War Department, took leave of us, and returned to Dakota."

It was asserted again and again by the Secretary of the Interior, and by the inspector, E. C. Kemble, that these Indians were not removed by force—that they consented to go.

In another part of this same report this agent says :

"On the 15th" (six days before the "march" began) "I held another council, which was largely attended by the chiefs, headmen, and soldiers of the tribe, and which was of more than four hours' duration. At this council the Indians maintained that the Government had no right to move them from the reservation, and demanded, as an inducement or equivalent for them to give up the reservation and move to the Indian Territory—first, the payment to them by the Government of the sum of $3,000,000 ; and, second, that, before starting, I should show to them the sum of $40,000 which they had been told had been appropriated by the Government for their removal. To all of which I replied positively in the negative, telling them that I would not accede to nor consider any demands that they might make ; but that I would take under my consideration reasonable requests that they might submit touching their removal, and, as their agent, do what I could for them in promoting their welfare ; that I demanded that they should at all times listen to my words ; that they should go with me to their new home ; and that *they should without delay give me their final answer whether they would go peaceably or by force.* The Indians refused to give answer at this time ; the council closed without definite results ; and the Indians dispersed with a sullen look and determined expression."

This evidently was not the "consent" of which we have heard. We come to it presently.

"On the following morning, however, May 16th, they sent word to me, at an early hour, that they had considered my words, and had concluded to go with me, and that they wanted assistance in getting the old and infirm, together with their property, over the Niobrara River, which was much swollen by the rains and at a low temperature."

What a night must these helpless creatures have passed before this "consent" was given! Seven hundred people, *more than half of them women and children;* a farming people, not armed with rifles, as the Ogallalla Sioux were, when, one year later, on this same ground, the Chief Spotted Tail told Commissioner Hayt that, if he did not give an order to have his tribe on the way back to White Clay Creek in ten days, his young men would go on the war-path at once; and the much-terrified commissioner wrote the order then and there, and the Sioux were allowed to go where they had chosen to go. Behold the difference between the way our Government treats the powerful and treats the weak! What could these Ponca farmers do? They must, "without delay," give their "final answer whether they would go peaceably or *by force.*" What did *"by force"* mean? It was *"by force"* that the Government undertook to compel the Cheyennes to go to Indian Territory; and in that Cheyenne massacre the Cheyenne men, women, children, and babies were all shot down together!

What could these Ponca farmers do? What would any father, brother, husband have done under the circumstances? He would have "consented" to go.

The agent, as was wise, took them at their word, quickly, and that very day, "at five o'clock P.M., had the entire tribe, with their effects, across the river, off the reservation, and in camp in Nebraska."

The agent should have said, "with part of their effects," for it was only a part, and a very small part, that this helpless *consenting* party were allowed to take with them. All their agricultural implements and most of their furniture were left behind.

"It was a hard day's work," the getting the tribe and their "effects" across the river, the agent says; "the river being about forty rods wide, and the current so swift that it was found impossible to move the goods across in any other way

than by packing them on the shoulders of the men, the quick-
sand bottom rendering it unsafe to trust them on the backs
of animals; even the wagons having to be drawn across by
hand."

Let us dwell for a moment on this picture. Seven hundred
helpless, heart-broken people beginning their sad journey by
having to ford this icy stream with quicksands at bottom.
The infirm, the sick, the old, the infants, all carried "by packing them on the shoulders of the men!" What a scene! The
Honorable Secretary of the Interior said, in one of the letters
in his newspaper controversy with the inspector in regard to
the accounts of this removal, that " the highly-colored stories
which are told about the brutal military force employed in
compelling their [the Poncas'] removal from Dakota to the
Indian Territory are sensational fabrications; at least, the official record, which is very full, and goes into minute details,
does not in the least bear them out."

There was never any accusation brought against the "military force" of "brutality" in this removal. The brutality
was on the part of the Government. The simple presence
of the "military force" was brutal. It meant but one thing.
The Indians understood it, and the Government intended that
they should understand it; and when the agent of the Government said to these Indians that they must give him their "final
answer whether they would go peaceably or by force," he intended that they should understand it. Has anybody any
doubt what were the orders under which that "military force"
was there? any doubt what it would have been the military
duty of Major Walker to have done in case the Poncas had
refused to "consent" to go?

And now let us return to the "Official Record," which is,
indeed, as the Honorable Secretary of the Interior says, "very
full," and "goes into minute details," and let us see in how
much it will "bear us out;" and when we have done with this

"Official Record," let us ask ourselves if any imagination could have invented so " highly-colored " a " story " as it tells.

"*June 2d.* Broke camp at seven o'clock and marched seventeen miles, going into camp near Ulysses. Roads in bad condition.

"*June 3d.* Had some trouble in getting started. Broke camp at eleven o'clock and marched eight miles. Went into camp on Blue River. Many people sick, one of whom was reported in a dying condition. Had bad roads. Rained during afternoon.

"*June 4th.* Broke camp at six o'clock. Marched fifteen miles, and went into camp on Lincoln Creek, near Seward.

"*June 5th.* Broke camp at seven o'clock. Marched fourteen miles, and went into camp near Milford. Daughter of Standing Bear, Ponca chief, died at two o'clock, of consumption.

"*June 6th.* Remained in camp all day, for the purpose of obtaining supplies. Prairie Flower, wife of Shines White and daughter of Standing Bear, who died yesterday, was here given Christian burial, her remains being deposited in the cemetery at Milford, Nebraska, a small village on Blue River.

"In this connection I wish to take official knowledge and recognition of the noble action performed by the ladies of Milford, in preparing and decorating the body of the deceased Indian woman for burial in a style becoming the highest civilization. In this act of Christian kindness they did more to ameliorate the grief of the husband and father than they could have done by adopting the usual course of this untutored people and presenting to each a dozen ponies. It was here that, looking on the form of his dead daughter thus arrayed for the tomb, Standing Bear was led to forget the burial-service of his tribe, and say to those around him that he was desirous of leaving off the ways of the Indian and adopting those of the white men.

"*June 7th.* Quite a heavy rain during the afternoon. The storm, most disastrous of any that occurred during the removal of the Poncas under my charge, came suddenly upon us while in camp on the evening of this day. It was a storm such as I never before experienced, and of which I am unable to give an adequate description. The wind blew a fearful tornado, demolishing every tent in camp, and rending many of them into shreds, overturning wagons, and hurling wagon-boxès, camp-equipages, etc., through the air in every direction like straws. Some of the people were taken up by the wind and carried as much as three hundred yards. Several of the Indiaris were quite seriously hurt, and one child died the next day from injuries received, and was given Christian burial. The storm caused a delay until the 8th for repairs, and for medical attendance upon the injured.

"*June 8th.* Broke camp at Milford and marched seven miles. Roads very bad. Child died during the day.

"*June 9th.* Put the child that died yesterday in the coffin and sent it back to Milford, to be buried in the same grave with its aunt, Prairie Flower. Broke camp at seven o'clock and marched to within three miles of Crete.

"*June 10th.* Broke camp at seven o'clock and marched one mile beyond De Witt, where I employed a physician to visit camp and prescribe for the sick. A woman had a thumb accidentally cut off, which caused further commotion in the camp.

"*June 12th.* Broke camp at seven o'clock and marched to within two miles of Otoe Agency. Crossed Wolf Creek with a part of the train, the crossing being very difficult; but the Indians worked splendidly."

"The Indians worked splendidly!" Is not this a well-nigh incredible record of patience and long-suffering? These poor creatures, marching from ten to twenty-five miles a day, for twenty-two days, through muddy sloughs, swollen rivers, in tempests and floods and dreary cold, leaving their wives and their children dead by the way—dead of the sufferings of the march—are yet docile, obedient, and "work splendidly !"

"*June* 13*th*. After considerable time we succeeded in building a bridge over Wolf Creek out of drift-timber, and succeeded in crossing the balance of the train. Broke camp and marched three miles, and went into camp again near Otoe Agency.

"*June* 14*th*. Water-bound, and had to remain in camp all day waiting for creek to run down. The Otoe Indians came out to see the Poncas, and gave them ten ponies.

"*June* 15*th*. Still water-bound. Remained in camp all day.

"*June* 16*th*. Broke camp at seven o'clock and reached Marysville, Kansas, where we went into camp. During the march a wagon tipped over, injuring a woman quite severely. Indians out of rations, and feeling hostile."

What wonder that the Indians felt hostile ? Hunger added to all the rest of their direful misery !

"*June* 18*th*. Broke camp at seven o'clock. Marched nine miles and went into camp at Elm Creek. Little Cottonwood died. Four families determined to return to Dakota. I was obliged to ride nine miles on horseback to overtake them, to restore harmony, and settle difficulty in camp. Had coffin made for dead Indian, which was brought to camp at twelve o'clock at night from Blue Rapids. A fearful thunder-storm during the night, flooding the camp-equipage."

This is a "highly-colored" story, indeed ! The darkness ; the camp flooded by the driving rain ; thunder and lightning ; a messenger arriving at midnight with a coffin ; the four families of desperate fugitives setting out to flee back to their homes ! What "sensational fabrication" could compete with this ?

"*June* 19*th*. The storm of last night left the roads in an impassable condition, and, in consequence, was obliged to remain in camp all day. Buried Little Cottonwood in a cemetery about five miles from camp. * * *

"*June 25th.* Broke camp at six o'clock. Marched to a point about fifteen miles farther up Deep Creek. Two old women died during the day. * * *

"*June 30th.* Broke camp at six o'clock. Passed through Hartford, and camped about six miles above Burlington. A child of Buffalo Chief died during the day. * * *

"*July 2d.* Broke camp at six o'clock. Made a long march of fifteen miles for Noon Camp, for reason that no water could be got nearer. An Indian became hostile, and made a desperate attempt to kill White Eagle, head chief of the tribe. For a time every male in camp was on the war-path, and for about two hours the most intense excitement prevailed, heightened by continued loud crying by all the women and children."

This Indian, who is reported here as having "become hostile," no doubt, tried to kill White Eagle for having allowed the tribe to be brought into all this trouble. It is the general feeling among the less intelligent members of a tribe that their chiefs are bound, under all circumstances, to see that they come to no harm.

"*July 9th.* Broke camp at six o'clock, passing through Baxter Springs at about one o'clock. Just after passing Baxter Springs a terrible thunder-storm struck us. The wind blew a heavy gale and the rain fell in torrents, so that it was impossible to see more than four or five rods distant, thoroughly drenching every person and every article in the train, making a fitting end to a journey commenced by wading a river and thereafter encountering innumerable storms.

"During the last few days of the journey the weather was exceedingly hot, and the teams terribly annoyed and bitten by green-head flies, which attacked them in great numbers. Many of the teams were nearly exhausted, and, had the distance been but little farther, they must have given out. The people were all nearly worn out from the fatigue of the march, and were heartily glad that the long, tedious journey was at an end, that

they might take that rest so much required for the recuperation of their physical natures." Now let us see what provision
the Government had made for that "rest" and "recuperation,"
surely " much required " and fairly earned. Not one dollar had
been appropriated for establishing them in their new home; not
one building had been put up. This people was set down in a
wilderness without one provision of any kind for their shelter.

"It is a matter of astonishment to me," says Agent Howard
(p. 100 of this " Report "), " that the Government should have
ordered the removal of the Ponca Indians from Dakota to the
Indian Territory without having first made some provision for
their settlement and comfort. Before their removal was carried
into effect an appropriation should have been made by Congress sufficient to have located them in their new home, by
building a comfortable home for the occupancy of every family
of the tribe. As the case now is, no appropriation has been
made by Congress except of a sum little more than sufficient
to remove them; and the result is that these people have been
placed on an uncultivated reservation, to live in their tents as
best they may, and await further legislative action."

This journal of Mr. Howard's is the best record that can ever
be written of the sufferings of the Poncas in their removal
from their homes. It is "highly colored;" but no one, however much it may be for his interest to do so, can call it "a
sensational fabrication," or can discredit it in the smallest particular, for it is an "official record," authorized and endorsed
by being published in the "Annual Report" of the Secretary
of the Interior.

The remainder of the Ponca tribe is still in Indian Territory,
awaiting anxiously the result of the efforts to restore to them
their old homes, and to establish the fact of their indisputable
legal right to them.*

---

* See Appendix, Art. II., for later facts in the history of the Poncas.

CHAPTER VII.

THE WINNEBAGOES.

THE Winnebagoes belonged to the Dakota family, but, so far as can be known, were naturally a peace-loving people, and had no sympathy with the more warlike tribes of their race. The Algonquins gave them the name of Winnebagoes, or " people of the salt-water ; " and as the Algonquin word for salt-water and stinking-water was the same, the French called them " Les Puants," or " Stinkards." The Sioux gave them a more melodious and pleasing name, " O-ton-kah," which signified " The large, strong people."

Bancroft, in his account of the North American tribes, says : " One little community of the Dakota (Sioux) family had penetrated the territories of the Algonquins : the Winnebagoes dwelling between Green Bay and the lake that bears their name preferred to be environed by Algonquins than to stay in the dangerous vicinity of their own kindred."

One of the earliest mentions that is found of this tribe, in the diplomatic history of our country, is in the reports given of a council held in July, 1815, at " Portage des Sioux," in Missouri, after the treaty of Ghent. To this council the Winnebagoes refused to send delegates ; and their refusal was evidently considered a matter of some moment. The commissioners "appointed to treat with the North-western Indians " at this time reported that they found " the Indians much divided among themselves in regard to peace with the United States." Some of them " spoke without disguise of their opposition to military establishments on the Mississippi," and many of them, "among whom were the Winnebagoes, utterly refused to send deputies to the council." This disaffection was thought by the commissioners to be largely due to the influence of British traders, who plied the Indians with gifts, and assured them that war would soon break out again between the United States and Great Britain. It is probable, however, that the Winnebagoes held themselves aloof from these negotiations more from a general distrust of white men than from any partisan or selfish leaning to the side of Great Britain; for when Dr. Jedediah Morse visited them, only seven years later, he wrote : " There is no other tribe which seems to possess so much jealousy of the whites, and such reluctance to have intercourse with them, as this."

Spite of this reluctance they made, in 1816, a treaty " of peace and friendship with the United States," agreeing " to remain distinct and separate from the rest of their nation or tribe, giving them no assistance whatever until peace shall be concluded between the United States and their tribe or nation." They agreed also to confirm and observe all the lines of British, French, or Spanish cessions of land to the United States.

In 1825 the United States Government, unable to endure the spectacle of Indians warring among themselves, and massacring each other, appears in the North-western country as an unselfish pacificator, and compels the Sacs, Foxes, Chippewas, and Sioux, including the Winnebagoes, to make a treaty of peace and friendship with each other and with the United States. The negotiations for this treaty occupied one month ; which does not seem a long time when one considers that the boundaries of all the lands to be occupied by these respective tribes were to be defined, and that in those days and regions definitions of distance were stated in such phrases as "a half day's march," " a long day's march," " about a day's paddle in a canoe," "to a point where the woods come out into the meadows," "to a point on Buffalo River, half way between its

source and its mouth." These were surely precarious terms
for peace to rest upon, especially as it was understood by all
parties that "no tribe shall hunt within the actual limits of
any other without their consent."

At the close of this treaty there occurred a curious incident,
which Schoolcraft calls "an experiment on the moral sense of
the Indians with regard to intoxicating liquors." "It had been
said by the tribes that the true reason for the Commissioners of
the United States speaking against the use of ardent spirits by
the Indians, and refusing to give it to them, was the fear of expense, and not a sense of its bad effects. To show them that
the Government was above such a petty motive, the commissioners had a long row of tin camp-kettles, holding several gal-
lons each, placed on the grass; and then, after some suitable
remarks, each kettle was spilled out in their presence. The
thing was ill-relished by the Indians, who loved the whiskey
better than the joke."

At this time the lands of the Winnebagoes lay between the
Rock and the Wisconsin rivers, along the shore of Winnebago
Lake, and the Indians claimed that the whole lake belonged
to them. It was here that President Morse had found them
living in 1822. He gives the following graphic picture of their
pleasant home: "They have five villages on the Lake, and
fourteen on Rock River. The country has abundance of
springs, small lakes, ponds, and rivers; a rich soil, producing
corn and all sorts of grain. The lakes abound with fine-fla-
vored, firm fish." Of the Indians themselves, he says: "They
are industrious, frugal, and temperate. They cultivate corn,
potatoes, pumpkins, squashes, and beans, and are remarkably
provident. They numbered five hundred and eighty souls."

In 1827 a third treaty was signed by the Winnebagoes,
Chippewas, and Menomonies with the United States and with
each other. This treaty completed the system of boundaries
of their lands, which had been only partially defined by the two

previous treaties. Of these three treaties Schoolcraft says: "These three conferences embody a new course and policy for keeping the tribes in peace, and are founded on the most enlarged consideration of the aboriginal right of fee-simple to the soil. They have been held exclusively at the charge and expense of the United States, and contain no cession of territory."

They were the last treaties of their kind. In 1828 the people of Northern Illinois were beginning to covet and trespass on some of the Indian lands, and commissioners were sent to treat with the Indians for the surrender of such lands. The Indians demurred, and the treaty was deferred; the United States in the mean time agreeing to pay to the four tribes $20,000, "in full compensation for all the injuries and damages sustained by them in consequence of the occupation of any part of the mining country."

In 1829 a benevolent scheme for the rescue of these hard-pressed tribes of the North-western territory was proposed by Mr. J. D. Stevens, a missionary at Mackinaw. He suggested the formation of a colony of them in the Lake Superior region. He says — and his words are as true to-day, in 1879, as they were fifty years ago : " The Indian is in every view entitled to sympathy. The misfortune of the race is that, seated on the skirts of the domain of a popular government, they have no vote to give. They are politically a nonentity. * * * The whole Indian race is not worth one white man's vote. If the Indian were raised to the right of giving his suffrage, a plenty of politicians on the frontiers would enter into plans to better him ; whereas now the subject drags along like an incubus in Congress."

It did, indeed. Appropriations were sadly behindhand. The promises made to the Indians could not be fulfilled, simply because there was no money to fulfil them with. In 1829 a Washington correspondent writes to Mr. Schoolcraft : " There is a screw loose in the public machinery somewhere. In 1827 we were promised $48,000 for the Indian service, and got $30,000 ; in 1828 $40,000, and got $25,000." A little later the Secretary of War himself writes : " Our annual appropriation has not yet passed; and when it will, I am sure I cannot tell."

In 1830 the all-engrossing topic of Congress is said to be " the removal of the Indians. It occupies the public mind throughout the Union, and petitions and remonstrances are pouring in without number."

Meantime the Indians were warring among themselves, and also retaliating on the white settlers who encroached upon their lands. The inevitable conflict had begun in earnest, and in September of 1832 the Winnebagoes were compelled to make their first great cession of territory to the United States. In exchange for it they accepted a tract west of the Mississippi, and before the 1st of June, 1833, most of those who were living on the ceded lands had crossed the river to their new homes. Their title to this new country was not so good as they probably supposed, for the treaty expressly stated that it was granted to them " to be held as other Indian lands are held."

Article three of this treaty said, " As the country hereby ceded by the Winnebagoes is more extensive and valuable than that given by the United States in exchange," the United States would pay to the Winnebagoes $10,000 annually in specie for twenty-seven years. The Government also promised to put up buildings for them, send teachers, make various allowances for stock, implements, tobacco, etc., and to furnish them with a doctor.

The Winnebagoes agreed to deliver up some of their number who had murdered white settlers. Lands were granted by patent to four Winnebagoes by name—two men and two women; for what reason, does not appear in the treaty.

Five years later the Winnebagoes ceded to the United States all their lands east of the Mississippi, and also relinquished the right to occupy, "except for hunting," a portion of that which they owned on the west side. For this cession and relinquishment they were to receive $200,000 ; part of this sum to be expended in paying their debts, the expense of their removal and establishment in their new homes, and the rest to be invested by the United States Government for their benefit.

In 1846 the Winnébagoes were forced to make another treaty, by which they finally ceded and sold to the United States "all right, title, interest, claim, and privilege to all lands heretofore occupied by them ; " and accepted as their home, " to be held as other Indian lands are held," a tract of 800,000 acres north of St. Peter's, and west of the Mississippi. For this third removal they were to be paid $190,000—$150,000 for the lands they gave up, and $40,000 for relinquishing the hunting privilege on lands adjacent to their own. Part of this was to be expended in removing them, and the balance was to be "left in trust" with the Government at five per cent. interest.

This reservation proved unsuited to them. The tribe were restless and discontented; large numbers of them were continually roaming back to their old homes in Iowa and Wisconsin, and in 1855 they gladly made another treaty with the Government, by which they ceded back to the United States all the land which the treaty of 1846 had given them, and took in exchange for it a tract eighteen miles square on the Blue Earth River. The improved lands on which they had been living, their mills and other buildings, were to be appraised and sold to the highest bidder, and the amount expended in removing them, subsisting them, and making them comfortable in their new home. This reservation, the treaty said, should be their "permanent home ; " and as this phrase had never before been used in any of their treaties, it is to be presumed that the

Winnebagoes took heart at hearing it. They are said to have "settled down quietly and contentedly," and have gone to work immediately, "ploughing, planting, and building."

The citizens of Minnesota did not take kindly to their new neighbors. "An indignation meeting was held; a petition to the President signed; and movements made, the object of all which was to oust these Indians from their dearly-purchased homes," says the Report of the Indian Commissioner for 1855.

Such movements, and such a public sentiment on the part of the population surrounding them, certainly did not tend to encourage the Winnebagoes to industry, or to give them any very sanguine hopes of being long permitted to remain in their "permanent home." Nevertheless they worked on, doing better and better every year, keeping good faith with the whites and with the Government, and trusting in the Government's purpose and power to keep faith with them. The only serious faults with which they could be charged were drunkenness and gambling, and both of these they had learned of the white settlers. In the latter they had proved to be apt scholars, often beating professional gamblers at their own game.

They showed the bad effects of their repeated removals, also, in being disposed to wander back to their old homes. Sometimes several hundred of them would be roaming about in Wisconsin. But the tribe, as a whole, were industrious, quiet, always peaceable and loyal, and steadily improving. They took hold in earnest of the hard work of farming; some of them who could not get either horses or ploughs actually breaking up new land with hoes, and getting fair crops out of it. Very soon they began to entreat to have their farms settled on them individually, and guaranteed to them for their own; and the Government, taking advantage of this desire on their part, made a treaty with them in 1859, by which part of their lands were to be "allotted" to individuals in "severalty," as they had requested, and the rest were to be sold, the proceeds to be partly expended in improvements on their farms, and partly to be "left in trust" with the Government. This measure threw open hundreds of thousands of acres of land to white settlers, and drew the belt of greedy civilization much tighter around the Indians. Similar treaties to this had been already made with some of the Sioux tribes and with others. It was evident that "the surplus land occupied by the Indians was required for the use of the increasing white population," and that it was "necessary to reduce the reservations."

There is in this treaty of 1859 one extraordinary provision: "In order to render unnecessary any further treaty engagements or arrangements with the United States, it is hereby agreed and stipulated that the President, with the assent of Congress, shall have full power to modify or change any of the provisions of former treaties with the Winnebagoes, in such manner and to whatever extent he may judge to be necessary and expedient for their welfare and best interest."

It is impossible to avoid having a doubt whether the chiefs and headmen of the Winnebago tribe who signed this treaty ever heard that proviso. It is incredible that they could have been so simple and trustful as to have assented to it.

Prospects now brightened for the Winnebagoes. With their farms given to them for their own, and a sufficient sum of money realized by the sale of surplus lands to enable them to thoroughly improve the remainder, their way seemed open to prosperity and comfort. They "entered upon farming with a zeal and energy which gave promise of a prosperous and creditable future."

"Every family in the tribe has more or less ground under cultivation," says their agent. He reports, also, the minutes of a council held by the chiefs, which tell their own story:

"When we were at Washington last winter, we asked our Great Father to take $300,000 out of the $1,100,000, so that we could commence our next spring's work. We do not want all of the $1,100,000, only sufficient to carry on our improve-ments. This money we ask for we request only as a loan; and when our treaty is ratified, we want it replaced. We want to buy cattle, horses, ploughs, and wagons; and this money can be replaced when our lands are sold. We hope you will get this money: we want good farms and good houses. Many have already put on white man's clothes, and more of us will when our treaty is ratified.

"Father, we do not want to make you tired of talk, but hope you will make a strong paper, and urgent request of our Great Father in respect to our wishes."

In 1860 the Commissioner of Indian Affairs writes: "The Winnebagoes continue steadily on the march of improvement. * * * The progress of the Winnebagoes in agricultural growths is particularly marked with success. There have been raised by individuals as high as sixty acres of wheat on a single farm. * * * The agent's efforts have been directed to giving to each Indian his own allotment of land. * * * Wigwams are be-coming as scarce as houses were two years ago. * * * All In-dians who had horses ploughed and farmed their own lands. * * * The Indians were promised that new and comfortable houses should be built for them. The treaty not yet being ratified, I have no funds in my hands that could be made ap-plicable to this purpose. * * * The greater part of the Indians have entreated me to carry out the meaning of the commission-er on his visit here, and the reasons for my not doing so do not seem comprehensible to them. * * * The school is in a flourishing condition."

In 1861 the commissioner writes that the allotment of lands in severalty to the Winnebagoes has been "substantially accomplished;" but that the sales of the remaining lands have not yet been made, owing to the unsettled condition of the country, and therefore the funds on which the Indians were depending for the improvements of their farms have not been

paid to them. They complain bitterly that the provisions of
the treaty of 1859 have not been fulfilled. "It has been two
years and a half since this treaty was concluded," says the
agent, "and the Indians have been told from one season to
another that something would be done under it for their benefit, and as often disappointed, till the best of them begin to
doubt whether anything will be done. * * * The Indians who
have had their allotments made are ' clamoring for their certificates.' "

Drunkenness is becoming one of the serious vices of the
tribe. They are surrounded on all sides by white men who
traffic in whiskey, and who are, moreover, anxious to reduce
the Indians to as degraded a state as possible. "There are
some circumstances connected with the location of this tribe
which make it more difficult to protect them from the ravages
of liquor-selling than any other tribe. They are closely surrounded by a numerous white population, and these people
feel very indignant because the Indians are settled in their
midst, and are disposed to make it as uncomfortable for them
to remain here as they can, hoping at some future time they
may be able to cause their removal."

The time was not far distant. In 1862 we find the Winnebagoes in trouble indeed. A ferocious massacre of white settlers by the Sioux had so exasperated the citizens of Minnesota, that they demanded the removal of all Indians from the
State. The people were so excited that not an Indian could
step outside the limits of the reservation without the risk of
being shot at sight. The Winnebagoes had utterly refused to
join the Sioux in their attack on the whites, and had been
threatened by them with extermination in consequence of this
loyalty. Thus they were equally in danger from both whites
and Indians: their position was truly pitiable.

In the Annual Report of the Interior Department for 1862
the condition of things is thus described: "While it may be

true that a few of the Winnebagoes were engaged in the atrocities of the Sioux, the tribe, as such, is no more justly responsible for their acts than our Government would be for a pirate who happened to have been born on our territory. Notwithstanding this, the exasperation of the people of Minnesota appears to be nearly as great toward the Winnebagoes as toward the Sioux. They demand that the Winnebagoes as well as the Sioux shall be removed from the limits of the State. The Winnebagoes are unwilling to move. Yet the Minnesota people are so excited that not a Winnebago can leave his reservation without risk of being shot; and as they have never received their promised implements of agriculture, and the game on their reservation is exhausted, and their arms have been taken from them, they are starving."

Their agent writes: "These Indians have been remaining here in a continuous state of suspense, waiting for the Government to cause the stipulations of the treaty of 1859 to be carried into operation: such has been their condition for three years and a half, and they do not understand why it is so. * * * The fact that a very few of the Winnebagoes were present and witnessed, if they did not take part in, the massacre at the Lower Sioux Agency, has caused the Winnebagoes themselves to be universally suspected of disloyalty. * * * The hostile feelings of the white people are so intense, that I am necessitated to use extra efforts to keep the Indians upon their own lands. I have been notified by the whites that the Indians will be massacred if they go out of their own country; and it is but a few days since an Indian was killed while crossing the Mississippi River, for no other reason than that he was an Indian, and such is the state of public opinion that the murderer goes unpunished."

As to the loyalty of the tribe, the agent says: "There is no tribe of Indians more so." There is "no doubt of their loyalty as a tribe. * * * In consequence of a threat made by the

Sioux, immediately upon their outbreak, that they (the Sioux) would exterminate the Winnebagoes unless they joined them in a raid against the white people, the Winnebagoes have lived in fear of an attack from the Sioux, and have almost daily implored me for protection. * * * To further assure them, I requested of the Governor of the State that two companies of United States infantry be stationed here in their midst, which has allayed their fears. * * * Notwithstanding the nearness of the belligerent Sioux, and the unfriendly feelings of the white people, and other unfortunate circumstances, I am confident that my Indians will remain loyal to the last. * * * They have been informed that, notwithstanding their fidelity to the Government and the people, the people of this State are memorializing Congress to remove them out of the State—which they consider very unjust under the circumstances, for they have become attached to this location and would not leave it willingly, and think their fidelity ought to entitle them to respect and kind treatment."

The "popular demand" of the people of Minnesota triumphed. In February, 1863, Congress passed an act authorizing the "peaceful and quiet removal of the Winnebago Indians from the State of Minnesota, and the settling of them on a new reserve." It was determined to locate them "on the Missouri River somewhere within a hundred miles of Fort Randall, where it is not doubted they will be secure from any danger of intrusion from whites." All their guns, rifles, and pistols were to be taken from them, "securely boxed up," labelled "with the names of their respective owners." The Department impressed it on the agent in charge of the removal that it was "absolutely necessary that no time should be lost in the emigrating of these Indians." The hostile Sioux were to be removed at the same time, and to a reservation adjoining the reservation of the Winnebagoes. The reports of the Indian Bureau for 1863 tell the story of this removal.*

---

* See Appendix, Art. VI.

The commissioner says: " The case of the Winnebagoes is one of peculiar hardship. I am still of the opinion that this tribe was in no manner implicated in or responsible for the cruel and wanton outbreak on the part of the Sioux; but its consequences to the tribe have been as disastrous as unmerited. In obedience to the Act of Congress, and the popular demand of the people of Minnesota, they have been removed to a new location upon the Missouri River, adjoining that selected for the Sioux. Contrasting the happy homes, and the abundant supply for all their wants which they have left behind them, with the extreme desolation which prevails throughout the country, including their present location, and their almost defenceless state, as against the hostile savages in their vicinity, their present condition is truly pitiable; and it is not surprising that they have become to some extent discouraged, and are dissatisfied with their new homes. It cannot be disguised that their removal, although nominally peaceable and with their consent, was the result of the overwhelming pressure of the public sentiment of the community in which they resided; and it is to be feared that it will be many years before their confidence in the good faith of our Government, in its professed desire to ameliorate and improve their condition, will be restored. Their misfortunes and good conduct deserve our sympathy."

The Act of Congress above mentioned provides for the peaceable removal of the Indians. In its execution some of the members of the tribe were found unwilling to leave their homes; and as there was neither the disposition nor the power to compel them to accompany their brethren, they remained upon their old reservation. The most of them are represented as having entirely abandoned the Indian habits and customs, and as being fully qualified by good conduct and otherwise for civilized life. Many of them are enlisted in the military service, and all are desirous of retaining possession

of the homes allotted to them under the provisions of their
treaty.

"The trust lands belonging to the tribe have been placed in
the market, and from the amount already sold has been realized
$82,537 62. An appraisement has also been had of the lands
of the diminished reserve, and the same will soon be placed in
the market."

In the Report of the Superintendent of the North-west Territory for the same year is the following summing up of their
case: "The case of these Winnebago Indians is one of peculiar
hardship. Hurried from their comfortable homes in Minnesota,
in 1863, almost without previous notice, huddled together on
steamboats with poor accommodations, and transported to
the Crow Creek Agency in Dakota Territory at an expense to
themselves of more than $50,000, they were left, after a very
imperfect and hasty preparation of their new agency for their
reception, upon a sandy beach on the west bank of the Missouri River, in a country remarkable only for the rigors of its
winter climate and the sterility of its soil, to subsist themselves where the most industrious and frugal white man would
fail, five years out of six, to raise enough grain upon which to
subsist a family. The stern alternative was presented to this
unfortunate people, thus deprived of comfortable homes (on
account of no crime or misdemeanor of their own), of abandoning this agency, or encountering death from cold or starvation.
They wisely chose the former; and after encountering hardships and sufferings too terrible to relate, and the loss of several hundred of their tribe by starvation and freezing, they
arrived at their present place of residence [the Omaha Agen-
cy] in a condition which excited the active sympathy of all
who became acquainted with the story of their wrongs. There
they have remained, trusting that the Government would redeem its solemn promise to place them in a position west of
the Missouri which should be as comfortable as the one which
they occupied in Minnesota.

"This tribe is characterized by frugality, thrift, and industry to an extent unequalled by any other tribe of Indians in the North-west. Loyal to the Government, and peaceable toward their neighbors, they are entitled to the fostering care of the General Government. The improvement of the homes which they have voluntarily selected for their future residence will place them in a short time beyond the reach of want, and take from the Government the burden of supplying their wants at an actual expense of $100,000."

It was in May, 1863, that the Winnebagoes gathered at Fort Snelling, ready for their journey. The chiefs are said to have "acquiesced in the move as a matter of necessity, for the protection of their people," but some of them "actually shed tears on taking leave." Colonel Mix, who was in charge of this removal, wrote to Washington, urgently entreating that tents at least might be provided for them on their arrival at their new homes in the wilderness. He also suggests that it is a question whether they ought to be settled so near the hostile Sioux, especially as just before leaving Minnesota some of the tribe had "scalped three Sioux Indians, thinking it would propitiate them in the kind regards of their Great Father at Washington, and, as a consequence, they would perhaps be permitted to remain in Minnesota."

The removal was accomplished in May and June. There were, all told, 1945 of the Winnebagoes. They arrived to find themselves in an almost barren wilderness—a dry, hard soil, "too strong for ploughs;" so much so, that it was "difficult to get a plough to run a whole day without breaking." A drought had parched the grass, so that in many places where the previous year several tons of good hay to an acre had been raised there was not now "pasturage for a horse." The cottonwood timber, all which could be procured, was "crooked, difficult to handle, full of wind-shakes, rots, etc." The channel of the Missouri River here was so "changeable," and the banks so low, that it was "dangerous to get too near." They were obliged therefore to settle half a mile away from the river. No wonder that on July 1st the Winnebagoes are reported as "not pleased with their location, and anxious to return to Minnesota, or to some other place among the whites." They gathered together in council, and requested Superintendent Thompson to write to their Great Father for permission "to move among the whites again. * * * They have lived so long among the whites that they are more afraid of wild Indians than the whites are." The superintendent hopes, however, they will be more contented as soon as he can get them comfortable buildings. But on July 16th we find Brigadier-general Sulley, commander of the North-western expedition against Indians, writing to the Department in behalf of these unfortunate creatures. General Sulley having been detained in camp near Crow Creek on account of the low water, the chiefs had gone to him with their tale of misery. "They stated that nothing would grow here. They dare not go out to hunt for fear of other tribes, and they would all starve to death. This I believe to be true, without the Government intends to ration them all the time. The land is sandy, dry, and parched up. * * * The land is poor; a low, sandy soil. I don't think you can depend on a crop of corn even once in five years, as it seldom rains here in the summer. * * * I find them hard at work making canoes, with the intention of quitting the agency and going to join the Omahas or some other tribe down the river. They said they had been promised to be settled on the Big Sioux River. * * * I told them they must stay here till they get permission from Washington to move; that, if they attempted it, they would be fired on by my troops stationed down the river."

This is a graphic picture of the condition of a band of two thousand human beings, for whose "benefit" $82,537 62 had just been realized from sale of their lands by the Government, to say nothing of the property they owned in lands yet unsold, and in annuity provisions of previous treaties to the amount of over $1,000,000 capital! Is not their long suffering, their patience, well-nigh incredible?

Spite of the dread of being fired on by the United States troops, they continued to make canoes and escape in them from this "new home" in the desert, and in October the Department of the Interior began to receive letters containing paragraphs like this: "I have also to report that small detachments of Winnebagoes are constantly arriving in canoes, locating on our reserve, and begging for food to keep them from starving."—*Agent for Omaha Agency.*

These are the men who only one year before had been living in comfortable homes, with several hundred acres of good ground under cultivation, and "clamoring for certificates" of their "allotted" farms—now shelterless, worse than homeless, escaping by canoe-loads, under fire of United States soldiers, from a barren desert, and "clamoring" for food at Indian agencies!

The Department of the Interior promptly reports to the Superintendent of Indian Affairs in Minnesota this "information," and calls it "astounding." The Department had "presumed that Agent Balcombe would adopt such measures as would induce the Winnebagoes to remain upon their reservation," and had "understood that ample arrangements had been made for their subsistence." It, however, ordered the Omaha agent to feed the starving refugees till spring, and it sent word to those still remaining on the reservation that they must not "undertake to remove without the consent of their Great Father, as it is his determination that a home that shall be healthy, pleasant, and fertile, shall be furnished to them at the earliest practicable moment."

This was in the autumn of 1863. In one year no less than 1222 of the destitute Winnebagoes had escaped and made their way to the Omaha Reservation in Nebraska. Here the

Superintendent of the Northern Superintendency held a council with them.

"They expressed," he says, "a strong desire to have some arrangement made by which they would be allowed to occupy a portion of that reservation. It was represented that the Omahas wished it also. * * * I found that I could not gain their consent to go back to their reservation, and I had no means within my reach of forcing them back, even if I had deemed it proper to do so." The superintendent recommended, therefore, that they be subsisted where they were "until some arrangement be made for their satisfaction, or some concert of action agreed upon between the War Department and the Interior Department by which they can be kept on their reservation after they shall have been moved there."

In September of this same year the agent for the Winnebago Reserve wrote that the absence of a protecting force had been one of the reasons of the Indians leaving in such numbers. "Both the Winnebagoes and Sioux who have stayed here have lived in fear and trembling close to the stockade, and have refused to separate and live upon separate tracts of land."

He gives some further details as to the soil and climate. "The region has been subject, as a general rule, to droughts, and the destructive visits of grasshoppers and other insects. The soil has a great quantity of alkali in it; it is an excessively dry climate; it very seldom rains, and dews are almost unknown here: almost destitute of timber. * * * It is generally supposed that game is plenty about here. This is an erroneous impression. There are but a very few small streams, an entire absence of lakes, and an almost entire destitution of timber—the whole country being one wilderness of dry prairie for hundreds of miles around; hence there is but a very little small game, fish, or wild fruit to be found. In former times the buffalo roamed over this country, but they have receded, and very seldom come here in any numbers. * * * The Indians

must have horses to hunt them: horses they have not. The
Winnebagoes had some when they first arrived, but they were
soon stolen by the hostile Sioux."

Agent Balcombe must have led a hard life on this reservation. Exposed to all the inconveniences of a remote frontier,
three hundred miles from any food-raising country; receiving
letters from the Interior Department expressing itself "astound-
ed" that he does not "induce the Indians in his charge to remain on their reservation;" and letters from citizens, and petitions from towns in Wisconsin, Minnesota, Iowa, and Nebraska, imploring him to "gather up" all the wandering Winnebagoes who have been left behind; unprovided with any proper
military protection, and surrounded by hostile Indians — no
wonder that he recommends to the Government "to remove
and consolidate" the different tribes of Indians into "one territory" as soon as possible.

The effects of this sojourn in the wilderness upon the Winnebagoes were terrible. Not only were they rendered spiritless
and desperate by sufferings, they were demoralized by being
brought again into conflict with the wild Sioux. They had
more than one skirmish with them, and, it is said, relapsed so
far into the old methods of their barbaric life that at one of
their dances they actually roasted and ate the heart of a Sioux
prisoner! Yet in less than a year after they were gathered together once more on the Omaha Reservation, and began again
to have hopes of a "permanent home," we find their chiefs and
headmen sending the following petition to Washington :

"OUR GREAT FATHER AT WASHINGTON, ALL GREETING, —
From the chiefs, braves, and headmen of your dutiful children
the Winnebagoes.

"Father, we cannot see you. You are far away from us.
We cannot speak to you. We will write to you; and, Father,
we hope you will read our letter and answer us.

"Father: Some years ago, when we had our homes on Turkey River, we had a school for our children, where many of them learned to read and write and work like white people, and we were happy.

"Father: Many years have passed away since our school was broken up; we have no such schools among us, and our children are growing up in ignorance of those things that should render them industrious, prosperous, and happy, and we are sorry. Father: It is our earnest wish to be so situated no longer. It is our sincere desire to have again established among us such a school as we see in operation among your Omaha children. Father: As soon as you find a permanent home for us, will you not do this for us? And, Father, as we would like our children taught the Christian religion, as before, we would like our school placed under the care of the Presbyterian Board of Foreign Missions. And last, Father, to show you our sincerity, we desire to have set apart for its establishment, erection, and support, all of our school-funds and whatever more is necessary.

"Father: This is our prayer. Will not you open your ears and heart to us, and write to us?"

This letter was signed by thirty-eight of the chiefs and headmen of the Winnebagoes.

In March, 1865, a new treaty was made between the United States and this long-suffering tribe of Indians, by which, in consideration of their "ceding, selling, and conveying" to the United States all their right in the Dakota Reserve, the United States agreed "to set apart for the occupation and future home of the Winnebago Indians forever" a certain tract of 128,000 acres in Nebraska—a part of the Omaha Reservation which the Omahas were willing to sell. The United States also agreed to erect mills, break land, furnish certain amounts of seeds, tools, guns, and horses, oxen and wagons, and to subsist the tribe for one year, as some small reparation for the terrible losses and sufferings they had experienced. From this word "forever" the Winnebagoes perhaps took courage.

At the time of their removal from Minnesota, among the fugitives who fled back to Wisconsin was the chief De Carry. He died there, two years later, in great poverty. He was very old, but remarkably intelligent; he was the grandson of Ho-po-ko-e-kaw, or "Glory of the Morning," who was the queen of the Winnebagoes in 1776, when Captain Carver visited the tribe. There is nothing in Carver's quaint and fascinating old story more interesting than his account of the Winnebago country. He stayed with them four days, and was entertained by them "in a very distinguished manner." Indeed, if we may depend upon Captain Carver's story, all the North-western tribes were, in their own country, a gracious and hospitable people. He says: "I received from every tribe of them the most hospitable and courteous treatment, and am convinced that, till they are contaminated by the example and spirituous liquors of their more refined neighbors, they will retain this friendly and inoffensive conduct toward strangers."

He speaks with great gusto of the bread that the Winnebago women made from the wild maize. The soft young kernels, while full of milk, are kneaded into a paste, the cakes wrapped in bass-wood leaves, and baked in the ashes. "Better flavored bread I never ate in any country," says the honest captain.

He found the Winnebagoes' home truly delightful. The shores of the lake were wooded with hickory, oak, and hazel. Grapes, plums, and other fruits grew in abundance. The lake abounded in fish; and in the fall of the year with geese, ducks, and teal, the latter much better flavored than those found nearer the sea, as they "acquire their excessive fatness by feeding on the wild rice which grows so plentifully in these parts."

How can we bear to contrast the picture of this peace,

plenty, and gracious hospitality among the ancient Winnebagoes with the picture of their descendants—only two generations later—hunted, driven, starved? And how can we bear
to contrast the picture of the drunken, gambling Winnebago
of Minnesota with this picture which Captain Carver gives of
a young Winnebago chief with whom he journeyed for a few
days?

Captain Carver, after a four days' visit with the Winnebagoes, and "having made some presents to the good old queen,
and received her blessing," went on his way. Two months
later, as he was travelling to the Falls of St. Anthony, he encountered a young Winnebago chief going on an embassy to
some of the bands of the "Nadouwessies" (Sioux). This young
chief, finding that Captain Carver was about to visit the Falls,
agreed to accompany him, "his curiosity having been often excited by the accounts he had received from some of his chiefs.
He accordingly left his family (for the Indians never travel without their households) at this place under charge of my Mohawk
servant, and we proceeded together by land, attended only by
my Frenchman, to this celebrated place. We could distinctly
hear the noise of the water full fifty miles before we reached
the Falls; and I was greatly pleased and surprised when I approached this astonishing work of nature; but I was not long
at liberty to indulge these emotions, my attention being called
off by the behavior of my companion. The prince had no
sooner gained the point that overlooks this wonderful cascade
than he began with an audible voice to address the Great Spirit, one of whose places of residence he imagined this to be.
He told him that he had come a long way to pay his adorations to him, and now would make him the best offerings in
his power. He accordingly threw his pipe into the stream;
then the roll that contained his tobacco; after these the brace-
lets he wore on his arms and wrists; next an ornament that en-
circled his neck, composed of beads and wires; and at last the

ear-rings from his ears; in short, he presented to his god every
part of his dress that was valuable.   During this he frequently
smote his breast with great violence, threw his arms about, and
appeared to be much agitated.   All this while he continued
his adorations, and at length concluded them with fervent petitions that the Great Spirit would constantly afford us his protection on our travels, giving us a bright sun, a blue sky, and
clear, untroubled waters; nor would he leave the place till we
had smoked together with my pipe in honor of the Great
Spirit.

"I was greatly surprised at beholding an instance of such
elevated devotion in so young an Indian. * * * Indeed, the whole
conduct of this young prince at once charmed and amazed me.
During the few days we were together his attention seemed to
be totally employed in yielding me every assistance in his
power, and even in so short a time he gave me innumerable
proofs of the most generous and disinterested friendship, so
that on our return I parted from him with the greatest reluctance."

In 1866 the report from the Winnebagoes is that they are
"improving;" manifest "a good degree of industry;" that the
health of the tribe is generally poor, but "as good as can be
expected when we remember their exposures and sufferings
during the last three years."   The tribe has "diminished some
four or five hundred since they left Minnesota."   One hundred soldiers have returned, "who have served with credit to
themselves and to their tribe in the defence of their country."
No school has yet been established on the agency, and this is
said to be "their greatest want."

The superintendent writes: "The appropriations under the
late treaty have all been made, and the work of fitting up the
reservation is progressing.   It affords me the highest personal
satisfaction to assure the Department that this deeply-wronged
and much-abused tribe will soon be in all respects comfortable

and self-sustaining. They entered upon their new reservation late last May, and during the present year they have raised at least twenty thousand bushels of corn."

In 1867 the Commissioner of Indian Affairs says: "The Winnebagoes have a just claim against the Government on account of their removal from Minnesota, the expenses of which *were borne out of their own tribal funds.* The Government is clearly bound in all honor to refund to them moneys thus expended."

It would seem that there could have been no question in the beginning as to who should pay the costs of such a removal as that. It should not even have been a tax on the general Government, but on the State of Minnesota, which demanded it— especially as there was no shadow of doubt that the demand was made—not because the citizens of Minnesota had any real fear of the peaceable and kindly Winnebagoes (who were as much in terror of the Sioux as they were themselves), but because they "coveted the splendid country the Winnebagoes were occupying, and the Sioux difficulties furnished the pretext to get rid of them with the aid of Congressional legislation."

Some members of the tribe who remained in Minnesota still claimed their "allotted" lands; "their share of all moneys payable to the Winnebagoes under treaty stipulations, and that their share of the funds of the tribe be capitalized and paid to them in bulk; their peculiar relations as Indians be dissolved, and they left to merge themselves in the community where they have cast their lot." The commissioner urges upon the Government compliance with these requests.

In 1868 a school was opened on the Winnebago Agency, and had a daily attendance of one hundred and fifty scholars. The tribe adopted a code of laws for their government, and the year was one of peace and quietness, with the exception of some dissatisfaction on the part of the Indians in regard to three hundred cows, which, having been sent to the agency in

fulfilment of one of the provisions of the treaty, were nevertheless ordered by the Indian Bureau to be " kept as Department
stock." The Indians very naturally held that they had a right
to these cows; nevertheless, they continued peaceable and contented, in the feeling that they had " at last found a home,"
where they might " hope to remain and cultivate the soil with
the feeling that it is theirs, and that their children will not in
a few days be driven from their well-tilled and productive
lands." They are, however, " growing exceedingly anxious for
the allotment of their lands in severalty."

In 1869 " preparations " were " being made for allotting the
lands to heads of families."

In 1870 " the allotment of land in severalty to the Indians has
been nearly completed, each head of a family receiving eighty
acres. * * * The Indians anxiously look for the patents to these,
as many have already commenced making improvements. * * *
At least thirty have broken four acres of prairie apiece, and
several have built houses. * * * Three schools are in operation,
and four hundred acres of ground under cultivation."

In this year comes also an interesting report from the stray
Winnebagoes left behind in Wisconsin. They and the stray
Pottawottomies who are in the same neighborhood are " remarkably quiet and inoffensive, giving no cause of complaint;
on the contrary, the towns and villages where they trade their
berries, maple-sugar, etc., are deriving considerable benefit from
them : a number have been employed in lumbering, harvesting,
and hop-picking. A number of mill-owners and lumbermen
have informed me that the Indians they have employed in their
business have been steady, good hands. * * * There are nearly one thousand of these Winnebagoes. Some of them have
bought land; others are renting it; and all express an anxiety
that the 'Great Father' should give them a reservation in this
region, and allow them to remain."

In 1871 the Nebraska Winnebagoes deposed their old chiefs,

and elected twelve new ones, to serve one year; these were mainly from the younger members of the tribe who were in favor of civilization and progress. This was an important step toward breaking up the old style of tribal relations.

In 1872 we hear again from the "strays" in Wisconsin. The whites having complained of them, Congress has appropriated funds to move them to their respective tribes " west of the Mississippi;" but the removal has not been undertaken " for various reasons," and the commissioner doubts " whether it can be accomplished without additional and severe legislation on the part of Congress, as the Indians are attached to the country, and express great repugnance to their contemplated removal from it."

The poor creatures are not wanted anywhere. Spite of their being " steady, good hands " for hired labor, and useful to towns and villages in furnishing fruits and fish, the Wisconsin people do not want them in their State. And the agent of the Winnebago Reservation writes, earnestly protesting against their being brought there. He thinks they are in moral tone far below the Indians under his charge. Moreover, he says " the prejudice in the surrounding country is such " that he believes it would be bad policy to remove any " more Indians " there. Nebraska does not like Indians any better than Wisconsin does, or Minnesota did. He adds also that his Indians " would be greatly stimulated to improve their claims if they could secure the titles for them. They have waited three years since the first allotments were made. It is difficult to make them believe that it requires so long a time to prepare the patents, and they are beginning to fear that they are not coming."

In 1873 the Winnebagoes are cited as a " striking example of what can be accomplished in a comparatively short time in the way of civilizing and Christianizing Indians. * * * Their beautiful tract of country is dotted over with substantially-built cottages; the farmers own their wagons, horses, harness, furniture of their houses — dress in civilized costume, raise crops—and several hundred Winnebago men assisted the farmers in adjoining counties during the late harvest in gathering their grain crop, and proved themselves efficient and satisfactory workmen."

In the winter of 1874 the Wisconsin "strays" were moved down to the Nebraska Reservation. They were discontented, fomented dissatisfaction in the tribe, and in less than a year more than half of them had wandered back to Wisconsin again; a striking instance of the differences in the Government's methods of handling different bands of Indians. The thirty Poncas who ran away from Indian Territory were pursued and arrested, as if they had been thieves escaping with stolen property; but more than five hundred Winnebagoes, in less than one year, stroll away from their reserve, make their way back to Wisconsin, and nothing is done about it.

In 1875 there are only two hundred and four of the Wisconsin "strays" left on the Nebraska Reservation. All the others are "back in their old haunts, where a few seem to be making a sincere effort to take care of themselves by taking land under the Homestead Act."

The Nebraska Winnebagoes are reported as being "nearly civilized;" all are engaged in civilized pursuits, "the men working with their own hands, and digging out of the ground three-fourths of their subsistence." They have raised in this year 20,000 bushels of corn, 5800 bushels of wheat, and 6000 bushels of oats and vegetables. They have broken 800 acres of new land, and have built 3000 rods of fencing. Nearly one-sixth of the entire tribe is in attendance at schools. The system of electing chiefs annually works well; the chiefs, in their turn, select twelve Indians to serve for the year as policemen, and they prove efficient in maintaining order.

What an advance in six years! Six years ago there were but twenty-three homes and only 300 acres of land under cultivation on the whole reservation; the people were huddled together in ravines and bottom-lands, and were dying of disease and exposure.

In 1876 the Winnebagoes are reported again as "fast emerging from a condition of dependence upon their annual appropriations. * * * Each head of a family has a patent for eighty acres of land. Many have fine farms, and are wholly supporting themselves and families by their own industry. * * * The issue of rations has been discontinued, except to the Wisconsin branch of the tribe and to the sick-list."

In what does this report differ from the report which would be rendered from any small farming village in the United States? The large majority "wholly supporting themselves and their families by their own industry;" a small minority of worthless or disabled people being fed by charity—i. e., being fed on food bought, at least in part, by interest money due on capital made by sales of land in which they had a certain reckonable share of ownership. Every one of the United States has in nearly every county an almshouse, in which just such a class of worthless and disabled persons will be found; and so crowded are these almshouses, and so appreciable a burden is their support on the tax-payers of State and county, that there are perpetual disputes going on between the authorities of neighboring districts as to the ownership and responsibility of individual paupers: for the paupers in civilized almshouses are never persons who have had proceeds of land sales "invested" for their benefit, the interest to be paid to them "annually forever." It is for nobody's interest to keep them paupers, or to take care of them as such.

We now find the Winnebagoes once more quietly established in comfortable homes—as they were, in their own primitive fashion, in 1822, when Dr. Morse visited them on the shores of their beautiful lake; as they were, after our civilized fashion, in 1862, on the healthful and fertile up-lands of Minnesota. In their present home they seem to have reason, at last, to feel secure, to anticipate permanence, safety, and success. Their lands have been allotted to them in severalty: each head of a family has his patent for eighty acres. They are, in the main, self-supporting.

How does the United States Government welcome this success, this heroic triumph of a patient people over disheartening obstacles and sufferings?

In the Annual Report of the Secretary of the Interior for 1876 the Secretary says: "As a matter of economy, the greatest saving could be made by uniting all the Indians upon a few reservations; the fewer, the better." He says that there is land enough in the Indian Territory to give every Indian—man, woman, and child—in the country seventy-five acres apiece. He says, "The arguments are all in favor of the consolidation." He then goes on to enumerate those arguments: "Expensive agencies would be abolished; the Indians themselves can be more easily watched over and controlled; evil-designing men be the better kept away from them, and illicit trade and barter in arms and ammunition and whiskey prevented. Goods could be supplied at a greater saving; the military service relieved; the Indians better taught, and friendly rivalry established among them—those most civilized hastening the progress of those below them; and *most of the land now occupied as reserves reverting to the General Government, would be open to entry and sale.*"

Here are nine reasons given for removing all Indians to Indian Territory. Five of these reasons ostensibly point to benefits likely to accrue from this removal to the Indians. The other four point to benefits likely to accrue to the Government; the first three of these last are, simply, "saving;" the fourth is the significant one, "gain"—"most of the land reverting to the General Government would be open to entry and sale."

It was before this necessity of opening Indian lands "to entry and sale" that the Winnebagoes had been fleeing, from
1815 to 1863. It seems they are no safer now. There is evidently as much reason for moving them out of Nebraska as
there was for moving them out of Wisconsin and Minnesota.

The Secretary goes on to say: "As soon as the Indian is
taught to toil for his daily bread, and realize the sense of proprietorship in the results of his labor, it cannot but be further
to his advantage to be able to appreciate that his labor is expended upon his individual possessions and for his personal
benefit. * * * The Indian must be made to see the practical advantage to himself of his work, and feel that he reaps the full
benefit of it. Everything should teach him that he has a home;
* * * a hearth-stone of his own, around which he can gather his
family, and in its possession be entirely secure and independent."

The logical relation of these paragraphs to the preceding one
is striking, and the bearing of the two together on the case of
the Winnebagoes is still more striking.

In the same report the Commissioner for Indian Affairs
says: "If legislation were secured giving the President authority to remove any tribe or band, or any portion of a tribe or
band, whenever in his judgment it was practicable, to any one
of the reservations named, and if Congress would appropriate
from year to year a sum sufficient to enable him to take advantage of every favorable opportunity to make such removals, I
am confident that a few years' trial would conclusively demon-
strate the entire feasibility of the plan. I believe that all the
Indians in Kansas, Nebraska, and Dakota, and a part at least
of those in Wyoming and Montana, could be induced to remove to the Indian Territory."

He adds "that the Indian sentiment is opposed to such removal is true," but he thinks that, "with a fair degree of per-
sistence," the removal "can be secured." No doubt it can.

Later in the same report, under the head of "Allotments in

Severalty," he says : " It is doubtful whether any high degree of civilization is possible without individual ownership of land. The records of the past, and the experience of the present, testify that the soil should be made secure to the individual by all the guarantees which law can devise, and that nothing less will induce men to put forth their best exertions. It is essential that each individual should feel that his home is his own; * * * that he has a direct personal interest in the soil on which he lives, and that that interest will be faithfully protected for him and for his children by the Government."

The commissioner and the secretary who wrote these clear statements of evident truths, and these eloquent pleas for the Indians' rights, both knew perfectly well that hundreds of Indians had had lands " allotted to them " in precisely this way, and had gone to work on the lands so allotted, trusting " that that interest would be faithfully protected by the Government ;" and that these " allotments," and the " certificates " of them, had proved to be good for nothing as soon as the citizens of a State united in a " demand " that the Indians should be moved. The commissioner and the secretary knew perfectly well, at the time they wrote these paragraphs, that in this one Winnebago tribe in Nebraska, for instance, " every head of a family owned eighty acres of land," and was hard at work on it—industrious, self-supporting, trying to establish that "hearthstone " around which, as the secretary says, he must "gather his family, and in its possession be entirely secure and independent." And yet the secretary and the commissioner advise the moving of this Winnebago tribe to Indian Territory with the rest: " all the Indians in Kansas, Nebraska, and Dakota " could probably be "induced to move," they say.

These quotations from this report of the Interior Department are but a fair specimen of the velvet glove of high-sounding phrase of philanthropic and humane care for the Indian, by which has been most effectually hid from the sight of the

American people the iron hand of injustice and cruelty which has held him for a hundred years helpless in its grasp.

In this same year an agent on one of the Nebraska agencies writes feelingly and sensibly :

" Nothing has tended to retard the progress of this tribe in the line of opening farms for themselves so much as the unsettlement occasioned by a continued agitation of the subject of selling their reservation and the removal of the tribe. * * * The improvement that has been made at this agency during the past three years in the direction of developing among the Indians the means of self-support, seems to have caused an uneasiness that has been prolific of a great deal of annoyance, inasmuch as it has alarmed this speculative element around us with the fear that the same (continued) will eventually plant the Indians on their present fertile land so firmly that they cannot be removed, and thus they be deprived of the benefits of manipulating the sale of their reservation."

Nevertheless, the Winnebagoes keep on in their work—building houses, school-buildings, many of them of brick made on the ground.

In this year (1876) they experienced a great injustice in the passing of an Act of Congress fixing the total amount to be expended for pay of employés at any one agency at not more than $10,000. This necessitated the closing of the fine building they had built at a cost of $20,000 for the purpose of an industrial boarding-school.

In this year's report their agent gives a resumé of the financial condition of the tribe: " By treaty proclaimed June 16th, 1838, the Winnebagoes ceded to the United States all their land east of the Mississippi, in consideration of which they were to receive $1,100,000. The balance of this, after making certain payments, was to be invested for their benefit, on which the United States guaranteed to pay them an annual interest of not less than five per cent.

"The Winnebagoes receive no support from the Government, other than from the interest appropriated annually on what remains of these funds. This in 1870 amounted to over $50,000. Since then the half-breeds, numbering one hundred and sixty persons, members of the tribe remaining in Minnesota at the time of the removal of the Indians from that State in 1863, have, in accordance with the provisions of the act making appropriations for the Indian service, approved March 3d, 1871, been paid their proportion of the principal of all Winnebago funds, as shown on the books of the Treasury at that time, including the proportion of $85,000, on which but five more instalments of interest were to be paid, per fourth Article treaty October 13th, 1846. In computing this proportion, the whole number of the tribe considered as being entitled to participate in the benefits of the tribal funds was 1531; which number included only those located on the Winnebago reservation in Nebraska at that time, in addition to the one hundred and sixty already spoken of. By this Act of Congress the Nebraska Winnebagoes, who comprise only that portion of the tribe which has complied with treaty stipulations, and quietly acquiesced in the demands of the Government, were deprived of nearly one-eighth part of their accustomed support.

"Other reductions were afterward made for the purchase of a reservation adjoining the old one in this State, and for removing to it the wandering bands of Winnebagoes in Wisconsin. These were supposed to have numbered in all nearly one thousand persons. They had not been in the habit of receiving any attention or acknowledgment from the Government since they, as a tribal organization, had declined to treat with it. Nearly all of them objected to removing from Wisconsin to their new reservation in Nebraska, and, as a natural consequence, soon returned after being compelled to do so. At the present time there are probably less than one hundred of the number remaining here. For the past three years the sum to which the

Wisconsin Winnebagoes would have been entitled had they remained on their reservation, amounting in all to $48,521 07, has been set apart, awaiting such act of Congress as will give relief in the premises; thus reducing the total amount received per annum by that portion of the tribe living on the reservation to but little more than one-half of what it was seven years ago. It seems needless to say that they are very much dissatisfied at this, and that when they refer to the subject I have some difficulty in satisfying them as to the justice of the governmental policy in setting apart funds (to be expended at some future time) for the benefit of certain individuals who persist in absenting themselves from their reservation, while others, who are absent but a few months, are deprived of all advantages from issues of supplies or payments that may have been made during their absence."

This case is a good illustration of the working of the trustee relation between the United States Government and its wards.

In 1877 we find the Secretary of the Interior still recommending that the Indians be "gradually gathered together on smaller reservations," to the end that "greater facilities be afforded for civilization." He reiterates that "the enjoyment and pride of individual ownership of property is one of the most effective civilizing agencies," and recommends that "allotments of small tracts of land should be made to the heads of families on all reservations, to be held in severalty under proper restrictions, so that they may have fixed homes."

The commissioner also recommends "a steady concentration of the smaller bands of Indians on the larger reservations." He calls attention again to the fact that there are 58,000 square miles in the Indian Territory "set apart for the use of Indians, and that there they can be fed and clothed at a greatly diminished expense; and, better than all, can be kept in obedience, and taught to become civilized and self-supporting."

In 1878 the Commissioner of Indian Affairs reports that a

bill has been drawn "providing for the removal and consolidation of certain Indians in the States of Oregon, Colorado, Iowa,
Kansas, Nebraska, Wisconsin, and Minnesota, and the Territories of Washington and Dakota. * * * A reduction of twenty-
five reservations and eleven agencies will thus be effected. * * *
There will be restored to the public domain 17,642,455 acres
of land." He says that "further consolidations of like character are not only possible, but expedient and advisable. * * *
There is a vast area of land in the Indian Territory not yet occupied."

With the same ludicrous, complacent logic as before, he proceeds to give as the reason for uprooting all these Indians from
the homes where they are beginning to thrive and take root,
and moving them again—for the third, fourth, fifth, sixth, or
seventh time, as it may be—the fact that, "among the most
radical defects of the policy formerly pursued with the Indians,
has been the frequent changes in their location which have
been made. * * * Permanent homes, sufficient aid to enable
them to build houses, cultivate the soil, and to subsist them
until they have harvested their first crops, will wean them entirely from their old methods of life, and in the course of a
few years enable them to become entirely self-supporting. * * *
Among the more forcible arguments which can be presented
in connection with this subject is the fact that the expenses
attending the removal and consolidation of the Indians, as herein proposed, *will be more than met from the sale of lands va-
cated.* * * * Much of the land now owned by these Indians is
valuable only for its timber, and may be sold at an appraised
value for an amount far in excess of the price fixed by law,
and yet leave a large margin of profit to the purchaser into
whose hands the lands will fall. * * * I can see no reason why
the Government should not avail itself of these facts, and in
effecting the consolidation of the Indians, and the opening of
the lands for settlement, sell the same for an amount sufficient

to support the Indians in their new locations, without any actual drain on the Treasury in the future. * * * The lands belong
to the Indians, and they are clearly entitled to receive the full
value of the same when sold."

In this sentence we reach the high-water mark of the sophistry and dishonesty of the Department's position. "The
lands belong to the Indians," but we will compel them to "restore to the public domain" (*i. e.*, to give up to white settlers)
17,642,455 acres of them. The Indians "are clearly entitled
to receive the full value of the same when sold," but we will
compel them to expend that "full value" in removing to a
place where they do not want to go, opening new lands, building new houses, buying new utensils, implements, furniture and
stock, and generally establishing themselves, "without any actual drain on the Treasury" of the United States: and the
Department of the Interior "can see no reason why the Government should not avail itself of these facts."

All this is proposed with a view to the benefit of the Indians.
The report goes on to reiterate the same old story that the Indians must have "a perfect title to their lands;" that they have
come to feel that they are at any time liable to be moved,
"whenever the pressure of white settlers upon them may create
a demand for their lands," and that they "decline to make any
improvements on their lands, even after an allotment in severalty has been made, until they have received their patents for
the same," and that even "after the issue of patents the difficulties surrounding them do not cease." Evidently not, since,
as we have seen, it is now several years since every head of a
family among these Winnebagoes, whose "removal" the commissioner now recommends, secured his "patent" for eighty
acres of land.

Finally, the commissioner says: "Every means that human
ingenuity can devise, legal or illegal, has been resorted to for
the purpose of obtaining possession of Indian lands." Of this

there would seem to be left no doubt in the mind of any intelligent person, after reading the above quotations.

It is not to be wondered that when the news of such schemes as these reaches the Indians on their reservations great alarm and discontent are the result. We find in the reports from the Nebraska agencies for this year unmistakable indications of disheartenment and anxiety. The Winnebagoes are reported to be very anxious to be made citizens. A majority are in favor of it, "provided the Government will adopt certain measures which they consider necessary for the care and protection of their property."

They have had a striking illustration of the disadvantage of not being citizens, in an instance of the unpunished murder of one of their number by a white man. The story is related by the agent tersely and well, and is one of the notable incidents in the history of the relation between the United States Government and its wards.

"Henry Harris, a Winnebago in good standing, an industrious man and a successful farmer, was employed by Joseph Smith, a white man, to cut wood on his land in Dakota County, a short distance north of the reservation. While alone and thus engaged, on the 29th of last January, Harris was shot through the heart with a rifle-ball. I had his dead body taken before the coroner of the county, and at the inquest held before that officer it was shown, to the satisfaction of the jury that rendered a verdict in accordance therewith, that the Indian came to his death at the hands of one D. Balinska, who had been for many years leading a hermit's life on a tract of land that he owned adjoining the reservation, and who had threatened Harris's life a few months before, when they quarrelled about damages for corn destroyed by Balinska's horse. There being snow on the ground at the time of the murder, Balinska was tracked from his home to the place where, under cover, he did the shooting; and his shot-pouch, containing a moulded ball of the same weight as the one cut from the body of the Indian, was found near by and identified. Notwithstanding this direct evidence, which was laid before the Grand-jury of Dakota County, that honorable body was unwilling to find a ' true bill;' for the reason, as I understand, that it was only an Indian that was killed, and it would not be popular to incur the expense of bringing the case to trial. This is but another illustration of the difficulty of punishing a white man for a wrong committed against an Indian. I need hardly say that the Indians, when comparing this murder with that of a white man, committed eight years ago by five of their young men— who, upon less direct evidence, were sentenced to imprisonment in the State Penitentiary for life—are struck with the wonderful difference in the application of the same law to whites and Indians."

The report from the Winnebago Agency for 1879 tells the story of the sequel to this unpunished murder of Henry Harris. The agent says: " In my last report I referred to the murder of one of our best Indian farmers by a white man, who was afterward arrested and discharged without trial, though there was no question as to his guilt. As a sequel to this, one white man is known to have been killed last May by Holly Scott, a nephew of the murdered Indian; and another white man is supposed to have been killed by Eddy Priest and Thomas Walker, two young Indians who have left for Wisconsin. The murdered white men had temporarily stopped with the Indians. Their antecedents are unknown, and they are supposed to have belonged to the fraternity of tramps. Holly Scott was arrested by the Indian police, and turned over to the authorities of Dakota County for trial, the State Legislature having at its last session extended the jurisdiction of that county over this reservation, by what authority I am unable to say.

" The effect of these murders was to unsettle the Indians, nearly all industry being suspended for several weeks. They feared that the white people would do as they did in Minnesota in 1862, after the Sioux massacre, when the Winnebagoes were driven from their homes in Minnesota. * * * A number of our most quiet and industrious men became alarmed, and moved their families to Wisconsin, encouraged in so doing by the hope of receiving from the Government a share of the funds which have been set apart from the annual appropriations during the past four years for the benefit of the Wisconsin Winnebagoes, and which they suppose aggregate a large amount which will soon be paid in cash."

This brings the story of the Winnebagoes down to the present time. What its next chapter may be is saddening to think. It is said by those familiar with the Nebraska Indians that, civilized though they be, they will all make war to the knife if the attempt is made by the Government to rob them of their present lands on the plea again of offering them a "permanent home." That specious pretence has done its last duty in the United States service. No Indian is left now so imbecile as to believe it once more.

Whether the Winnebagoes' "patents" in Nebraska would, in such a case, prove any stronger than did their "certificates" in Minnesota, and whether the Winnebagoes themselves, peaceable and civilized though they be, would side with the United States Government, or with their wronged and desperate brethren, in such an uprising, it would be hard to predict.

CHAPTER VIII.

THE CHEROKEES.

THE Cherokees were the Eastern Mountaineers of America. Their country lay along the Tennessee River, and in the highlands of Georgia, Carolina, and Alabama—the loveliest region east of the Mississippi River. Beautiful and grand, with lofty mountains and rich valleys fragrant with flowers, and forests of magnolia and pine filled with the singing of birds and the melody of streams, rich in fruits and nuts and wild grains, it was a country worth loving, worth fighting, worth dying for, as thousands of its lovers have fought and have died, white men as well as red, within the last hundred years.

When Oglethorpe came with his cargo of Madeira wine and respectable paupers from England in 1733, and lived in tents in midwinter on the shores of the Savannah River, one of the first conditions of safety for his colossal almshouse, in shape of a new colony, was that all the Indians in the region should become its friends and allies.

The reputation of his goodness and benevolence soon penetrated to the fastnesses of their homes, and tribe after tribe sent chiefs and headmen to greet him with gifts and welcome. When the Cherokee chief appeared, Oglethorpe said to him, "Fear nothing. Speak freely." "I always speak freely," answered the mountaineer. "Why should I fear? I am now among friends: I never feared, even among my enemies."

The principal intention of the English trustees who incorporated the Georgia colony was to provide a home for worthy persons in England who were " in decayed circumstances."

Among other great ends which they also avowed was "the civilization of the savages." In one of Oglethorpe's first reports to the trustees he says: "A little Indian nation—the only one within fifty miles—is not only in amity, but desirous to be subjects to his Majesty King George; to have lands given to them among us, and to breed their children at our schools. Their chief and his beloved man, who is the second man in the nation, desire to be instructed in the Christian religion."

The next year he returned to England, carrying with him eight Indian chiefs, to show them " so much of Great Britain and her institutions as might enable them to judge of her power and dignity. * * * Nothing was neglected," we are told, "that was likely to awaken their curiosity or impress them with a sense of the power and grandeur of the nation." They were received by the Archbishop of Canterbury, and by the Fellows of Eton, and for a space of four months were hospitably entertained, and shown all the great sights of London and its vicinity.

The tribes at home were much gratified by these attentions paid to their representatives, and sent out to the trustees a very curious missive, expressing their thanks and their attachment to General Oglethorpe. This letter was the production of a young Cherokee chief. It was written in black and red hieroglyphs on a dressed buffalo-skin. Before it was sent to England it was exhibited in Savannah, and the meaning of the hieroglyphs translated by an interpreter in a grand gathering of fifty Indian chiefs and all the principal people of Savannah. Afterward the curious document was framed and hung up in the Georgia Office in Westminster.

When the Wesleyan missionaries arrived in Georgia, two years later, some of the chiefs who had made this visit to England went to meet them, carrying large jars of honey and of milk as gifts, to " represent their inclinations;" and one of the chiefs said to Mr. Wesley, "I am glad you are come. When I was in England I desired that some one would speak the Great Word to me. I will go up and speak to the wise men of our nation, and I hope they will hear. But we would not be made Christians as the Spaniards make Christians; we would be taught before we are baptized."

In those early days Wesley was an intolerant and injudicious enthusiast. His missionary work in the Georgia Colony was anything but successful in the outset, either among the whites or the Indians, and there was ample justification for the reply which this same Indian chief made later when urged to embrace the doctrines of Christianity.

"Why, these are Christians at Savannah. Those are Christians at Frederica. Christians get drunk! Christians beat men! Christians tell lies! Me no Christian!" On another occasion Wesley asked him what he thought he was made for. "He that is above," answered the chief, "knows what he made us for. We know nothing; we are in the dark; but white men know much. And yet white men build great houses, as if they were to live forever. But white men cannot live forever. In a little time white men will be dust as well as I."

For twenty years Oglethorpe's colony struggled on under great difficulties and discouragements. Wars with France and with Spain; tiresome squabbles with and among Methodist missionaries, all combined to make Oglethorpe's position hard. Again and again England would have lost her colony except for the unswerving fidelity of the Indian allies; they gathered by hundreds to fight for Oglethorpe. In one expedition against the frontier, four hundred Creeks and six hundred Cherokees set out in one day, under an urgent call for help sent by Indian runners to their towns. His Indian friends were the only friends Oglethorpe had who stood by him past everything: nothing could shake their fidelity.

"He is poor; he can give you nothing," said the St. Augustine Spaniards to a Creek chief at this time; "it is foolish

for you to go to him:" and they showed to the Indian a fine
suit of scarlet clothes, and a sword, which they were about to
give to a chief of the Tennessees who had become their ally.

But the Creek answered, "We love him. It is true, he does
not give us silver; but he gives us everything we want that he
has. He has given me the coat off his back, and the blanket
from under him."

At last the trustees of the Georgia Colony lost patience:
very bitterly they had learned that paupers, however worthy,
are not good stuff to build new enterprises of. In eighteen
years the colony had not once furnished a sufficient supply of
subsistence for its own consumption: farms which had been
cultivated were going to ruin; and the country was rapidly de-
generating in every respect. Dishonest traders had tampered
with and exasperated the Indians, so that their friendliness
could no longer be implicitly trusted. For everything that
went wrong the English Company was held responsible, and
probably there were no happier men in all England on the 20th
of June, 1752, than were the Georgia trustees, who on that
day formally resigned their charter, and washed their hands of
the colony forever.

The province was now formed into a royal government, and
very soon became the seat of frightful Indian wars. The new
authorities neither understood nor kept faith with the Indians:
their old friend Oglethorpe had left them forever, and the same
scenes of treachery and massacre which were being enacted at
the North began to be repeated with heart-sickening similarity
at the South. Indians fighting Indians—fighting as allies to-
day with the French, to-morrow with the English; treaties
made, and broken as soon as made; there was neither peace
nor safety anywhere.

At last, in 1763, a treaty was concluded with the chiefs and
headmen of five tribes, which seemed to promise better things.
The Cherokees and Creeks granted to the King of England a

large tract of land, cleared off their debts with the sum paid for it, and observed its stipulations faithfully for several years, until peace was again destroyed, this time by no fault of the Indians, in consequence of the revolt of the American Colonies against Great Britain. The English loyalists in Georgia now availed themselves of the Indians' old habit of allegiance to the Crown. One of their leading agents took a Cherokee woman as his mistress, placed her at the head of his table, gave her the richest dress and equipage that the country could afford, and distributed through her lavish gifts to all the Indians he could reach. When war actually broke out he retreated with her into the fastnesses of the Cherokee nation, where he swayed them at his will. Attempts to capture him were repelled by the Cherokees with ferocity. Prisoners taken by them at this time were tortured with great cruelty; one instance is recorded (in a journal kept by another prisoner, who escaped alive) of a boy about twelve years of age who was suspended by the arms between two posts, and raised about three feet from the ground. "The mode of inflicting the torture was by light-wood splints of about eighteen inches long, made sharp at one end and fractured at the other, so that the torch might not be extinguished by throwing it. After these weapons of death were prepared, and a fire made for the purpose of lighting them, the scene of horror commenced. It was deemed a mark of dexterity, and accompanied by shouts of applause, when an Indian threw one of these torches so as to make the sharp end stick into the body of the suffering youth without extinguishing the torch. This description of torture was continued for two hours before the innocent victim was relieved by death."

These are sickening details, and no doubt will be instinctively set down by most readers as proof of innate cruelty peculiar to the Indian race. Let us, therefore, set side by side with them the record that in this same war white men (British officers) confined white men ("rebels") in prison-ships, starved, and otherwise maltreated them till they died, five or six a day, then threw their dead bodies into the nearest marsh, and had them "*trodden down in the mud*—from whence they were soon exposed by the washing of the tides, and at low-water the prisoners beheld the carrion-crows picking the bones of their departed companions!" Also, that white men (British officers) were known at that time to have made thumb-screws out of musket-locks, to torture Georgia women, wives of "rebels," to force them to reveal the places where their husbands were in hiding. Innate cruelty is not exclusively an Indian trait.

The Cherokees had the worst of the fighting on the British side during the Revolution. Again and again their towns were burnt, their winter stores destroyed, and whole bands reduced to the verge of starvation. At one time, when hard pressed by the American forces, they sent to the Creeks for help; but the shrewd Creeks replied, "You have taken the thorns out of our feet; you are welcome to them." The Creeks, having given only limited aid to the British, had suffered much less severely. That any of the Indians should have joined the "rebel" cause seems wonderful, as they had evidently nothing to gain by the transfer of their allegiance to what must have appeared to them for a long time to be the losing side in the contest. For three years and a half Savannah was in the possession of the British, and again and again they had control of the entire State. And to show that they had no compunction about inciting the Indians to massacres they left many a written record —such, for instance, as this, which is in a letter written by General Gage from Boston, June, 1775: "We need not be tender of calling on the savages to attack the Americans."*

The first diplomatic relations of the United States Government with the Cherokees were in the making of the treaty of Hopewell, in 1785. At the Hopewell council the United States

---

* See Appendix, Art. X.

commissioners said: "Congress is now the sovereign of all our country which we now point out to you on the map. They want none of your lands, nor anything else which belongs to you; and as an earnest of their regard for you, we propose to enter into articles of a treaty perfectly equal and conformable to what we now tell you. * * * This humane and generous act of the United States will no doubt be received by you with gladness, and held in grateful remembrance; and the more so, as many of your young men, and the greater number of your warriors, during the late war, were our enemies, and assisted the King of Great Britain in his endeavors to conquer our country."

The chiefs complained bitterly of the encroachments of white settlers upon lands which had been by old treaties distinctly reserved to the Cherokees. They demanded that some of these settlers should be removed; and when the commissioners said that the settlers were too numerous for the Government to remove, one of the chiefs asked, satirically, "Are Congress, who conquered the King of Great Britain, unable to remove those people?"

Finally, the chiefs agreed to accept payment for the lands which had been taken. New boundaries were established, and a general feeling of good-will and confidence was created. One notable feature in this council was the speech of an Indian woman, called the "war-woman of Chota." (Chota was the Cherokees' city of refuge. All murderers were safe so long as they lived in Chota. Even Englishmen had not disdained to take advantage of its shelter; one English trader who had killed an Indian, having fled, lived there for many months, his own house being but a short distance away. After a time he resolved to return home, but the headmen of the tribe assured him that, though he was entirely safe there, he would surely be killed if he left the town.) The chief who brought this "war-woman" to the council introduced her as "one of our beloved women who has borne and raised up warriors." She proceeded to say, " I am fond of hearing that there is a peace, and I hope you have now taken us by the hand in real friendship. I have a pipe and a little tobacco to give the commissioners to smoke in friendship. I look on you and the red people as my children. Your having determined on peace is most pleasing to me, for I have seen much trouble during the late war. I am old, but I hope yet to bear children who will grow up and people our nation, as we are now to be under the protection of Congress, and shall have no disturbance."

A brief summary of the events which followed on the negotiation of this treaty may be best given in the words of a report made by the Secretary of War to the President four years later. In July, 1789, General Knox writes as follows of the Cherokees : " This nation of Indians, consisting of separate towns or villages, are seated principally on the head-waters of the Tennessee, which runs into the Ohio. Their hunting-grounds extend from the Cumberland River along the frontiers of Virginia, North and South Carolina, and part of Georgia.

" The frequent wars they have had with the frontier people of the said States have greatly diminished their number. The commissioners estimated them in November, 1785, at 2000 warriors, but they were estimated in 1787 at 2650 ; yet it is probable they may be lessened since by the depredations committed on them.

" The United States concluded a treaty with the Cherokees at Hopewell, on the Keowee, the 28th of November, 1785, which is entered on the printed journals of Congress April 17th, 1786. The negotiations of the commissioners on the part of the United States are hereunto annexed, marked A. It will appear by the papers marked B. that the State of North Carolina, by their agent, protested against the said treaty as infringing and violating the legislative rights of that State.

" By a variety of evidence which has been submitted to the

last Congress, it has been proved that the said treaty has been entirely disregarded by the white people inhabiting the frontiers, styling themselves the State of Franklin. The proceedings of Congress on the 1st of September, 1788, and the proclamation they then issued on this subject, will show their sense of the many unprovoked outrages committed against the Cherokees.

" The information contained in the papers marked C., from Colonel Joseph Martin, the late agent to the Cherokees, and Richard Winn, Esq., will further evince the deplorable situation of the Cherokees, and the indispensable obligation of the United States to vindicate their faith, justice, and national dignity.

" The letter of Mr. Winn, the late superintendent, of the 1st of March, informs that a treaty will be held with the Cherokees on the third Monday of May, at the Upper War-ford on French Broad River. But it is to be observed that the time for which both he and Colonel Joseph Martin, the agent to the Cherokees and Chickasaws, were elected has expired, and therefore they are not authorized to act on the part of the Union. If the commissioners appointed by North Carolina, South Carolina, and Georgia, by virtue of the resolve of Congress of the 26th of October, 1787, should attend the said treaty, their proceedings thereon may soon be expected. But, as part of the Cherokees have taken refuge within the limits of the Creeks, it is highly probable they will be under the same direction; and, therefore, as the fact of the violation of the treaty cannot be disputed, and as the commissioners have not power to replace the Cherokees within the limits established in 1785, it is not probable, even if a treaty should be held, as stated by Mr. Winn, that the result would be satisfactory."

This is the summing up of the situation. The details of it are to be read in copious volumes of the early history of Tennessee, North and South Carolina, and Georgia—all under the head of " Indian Atrocities." To very few who read those records does it occur that the Indians who committed these "atrocities" were simply ejecting by force, and, in the contests arising from this forcible ejectment, killing men who had usurped and stolen their lands—lands ceded to them by the United States Government in a solemn treaty, of which the fifth Article was as follows:

"If any citizen of the United States or other person, not being an Indian, shall attempt to settle on any of the lands westward or southward of the said boundaries which are hereby allotted to the Indians for their hunting-grounds, or having already settled and will not remove from the same within six months after the ratification of this treaty, such person shall forfeit the protection of the United States, and the Indians *may punish him or not as they please.*"

It is evident that it is necessary to go back to the days of the first treaties with our Indians to possess ourselves of the first requisites for fair judgment of their conduct toward white men. What would a community of white men, situated precisely as these Cherokees were, have done? What did these very Southern colonists themselves do to Spaniards who encroached on their lands? Fought them; killed them; burnt their houses over their heads, and drove them into the sea!

In a later communication in the same year to the President, the Secretary says: "The disgraceful violation of the treaty of Hopewell with the Cherokees requires the serious consideration of Congress. If so direct and manifest contempt of the authority of the United States be suffered with impunity, it will be in vain to attempt to extend the arm of the Government to the frontiers. The Indian tribes can have no faith in such imbecile promises, and the lawless whites will ridicule a government which shall on paper only make Indian treaties and regulate Indian boundaries."

The President, thus entreated, addressed himself to the Senate, and asked their advice. He recapitulated the facts as set forth by General Knox, "that upward of five hundred families are settled on the Cherokee lands," and asks,

"1st. Is it the judgment of the Senate that overtures shall be made to the Cherokees to arrange a new boundary, so as to embrace the settlements made by the white people since the treaty of Hopewell in November, 1785?

"2d. If so, shall compensation to the amount of $—— annually, or of $—— in gross, be made to the Cherokees for the land they shall relinquish, holding the occupiers of the land accountable to the United States for its value?

"3d. Shall the United States stipulate solemnly to guarantee the new boundary which may be arranged?"

The Senate thereupon resolved that the President should, at his discretion, cause the Hopewell treaty to be carried out, or make a new one; but, in case a new one was made, the "Senate do advise and consent solemnly to guarantee the same."

Accordingly, in July, 1791, a new treaty—the treaty of Holston—was made with the Cherokees, new boundaries established, and $1000 a year promised to the tribe for the lands relinquished.

By the seventh Article of this treaty the United States "solemnly guarantee to the Cherokee nation all their lands not hereby ceded: the eighth Article reiterates the old permission that if any citizen of the United States or other person (not an Indian) shall settle on the Cherokees' lands, the Cherokees may punish him as they please. Article ninth says that no citizen or inhabitant of the United States shall hunt or destroy game on the Cherokee lands, or go into the Cherokee country without a passport from the governor or some other authorized person.

The next year the Cherokees sent an embassy to Philadelphia to ask for an increase of $500 in their annuity. One of the chiefs said that he had told Governor Blunt the year before that he would not consent to selling the lands for $1000 a year. "It would not buy a breech-clout for each of my nation;" which was literally true.

To this additional annuity the Senate consented, and with this the chiefs said they were "perfectly satisfied." But they begged for the ploughs, hoes, cattle, etc., which had been promised in the treaty. They said, "Game is going fast away from among us. We must plant corn and raise cattle, and we want you to assist us."

In 1794 it was necessary to make another treaty, chiefly to declare that the Holston treaty was in "full force and binding." It had not been "fully carried into execution by reason of misunderstandings," it was said. This was very true; white settlers had gone where they pleased, as if it did not exist; Cherokees had murdered them, as they were, by their treaty, explicitly permitted to do. The whites had retaliated by unprovoked attacks on friendly Indians, and the Indians had retaliated again. The exasperated Indians implored Congress to protect them: the still more exasperated whites demanded of Congress to protect them. The Secretary of War writes despairingly, that "The desire of too many frontier white people to seize by force or fraud on the neighboring Indian lands continues to be an unceasing cause of jealousy and hatred on the part of the Indians; and it would appear, upon a calm investigation, that until the Indians can be quieted on this point, and rely with confidence on the protection of their lands by the United States, no well-grounded hope of tranquillity can be entertained."

In this miserable manner, unjust equally to the white men and to the Indians, affairs went on for several years, until in 1801 it became absolutely necessary that in some way a definite understanding of boundaries, and an authoritative enforcement of rights on both sides, should be brought about; accordingly, commissioners were sent by the President "to obtain the consent of the Cherokees" to new grants of land and establishment of boundaries. The instructions given to these commissioners are remarkable for their reiterated assertion of the Indians' unquestioned right to do as they please about ceding these lands. Such phrases as these: "Should the Indians refuse to cede to the United States any of the above-designated lands," and "you will endeavor to prevail upon them to cede," and "you will endeavor to procure the consent of the Indians," are proof of the fulness of the recognition the United States Government at that time gave of the Indians' "right-of occupancy;" also of the realization on the part of the Government that these Indian nations were powers whose good-will it was of importance to conciliate. "It is of importance," the instructions say, "that the Indian nations generally should be convinced of the certainty in which they may at all times rely upon the friendship of the United States, and that the President will never abandon them or their children;" and, "It will be incumbent on you to introduce the desires of the Government in such a manner as will permit you to drop them, as you may find them illy received, without giving the Indians an opportunity to reply with a decided negative, or raising in them unfriendly and inimical dispositions. You will state none of them in the tone of demands, but in the first instance merely mention them as propositions which you are authorized to make, and their assent to which the Government would consider as new testimonials of their friendship."

Nevertheless, the Cherokees did reply with "a decided negative." They utterly refused to cede any more lands, or to give their consent to the opening of any more roads through their territory. But it only took four years to bring them to the point where they were ready to acquiesce in the wishes of the Government, and to make once more the effort to secure to themselves an unmolested region, by giving up several large tracts of land and a right of way on several roads. In 1805 they concluded another treaty, ceding territory for which the United States thought it worth while to pay $15,000 immediately, and an annuity of $3000.

Ten years later (in 1816) they gave up all their lands in South Carolina, and the United States became surety that South Carolina should pay to them $5000 for the same. In the autumn of the same year they made still another cession of lands to the United States Government, for which they were to have an annuity of $6000 a year for ten years, and $5000 as compensation for the improvements they surrendered.

In 1817 an important treaty was concluded, making still further cessions of lands, and defining the position of a part of the Cherokee nation which had moved away, with the President's permission, to the Arkansas River in 1809. The eighth Article of this treaty promises that the United States will give to every head of an Indian family residing on the east side of the Mississippi, who may wish to become a citizen, "a reservation of six hundred and forty acres of land, in which they will have a life estate, with a reversion in fee-simple to their children."

What imagination could have foreseen that in less than twenty years the chiefs of this Cherokee nation would be found piteously pleading to be allowed to remain undisturbed on these very lands? In the whole history of our Government's dealings with the Indian tribes, there is no record so black as the record of its perfidy to this nation. There will come a time in the remote future when, to the student of American history, it will seem well-nigh incredible. From the beginning of the century they had been steadily advancing in civilization. As far back as 1800 they had begun the manufacture of cotton cloth, and in 1820 there was scarcely a family in that part of the nation living east of the Mississippi but what understood the use of the card and spinning-wheel. Every family had its farm under cultivation. The territory was laid off into districts, with a council-house, a judge, and a marshal in each district. A national committee and council were the supreme authority in the nation. Schools were flourishing in all the villages. Printing-presses were at work.

Their territory was larger than the three States of Massachusetts, Rhode Island, and Connecticut combined. It embraced the North-western part of Georgia, the North-east of Alabama, a corner of Tennessee and of North Carolina. They were enthusiastic in their efforts to establish and perfect their own system of jurisprudence. Missions of several sects were established in their country, and a large number of them had professed Christianity, and were living exemplary lives.

There is no instance in all history of a race of people passing in so short a space of time from the barbarous stage to the agricultural and civilized. And it was such a community as this that the State of Georgia, by one high-handed outrage, made outlaws!—passing on the 19th of December, 1829, a law "to annul all laws and ordinances made by the Cherokee nation of Indians;" declaring " all laws, ordinances, orders, and regulations of any kind whatever, made, passed, or enacted by the Cherokee Indians, either in general council or in any other way whatever, or by any authority whatever, null and void, and of no effect, as if the same had never existed ; also, that no Indian, or descendant of any Indian residing within the Creek or Cherokee nations of Indians, shall be deemed a competent witness in any court of this State to which a white man may be a party."

What had so changed the attitude of Georgia to the Indians within her borders? Simply the fact that the Indians, finding themselves hemmed in on all sides by fast thickening white settlements, had taken a firm stand that they would give up no more land. So long as they would cede and cede, and grant and grant tract after tract, and had millions of acres still left to cede and grant, the selfishness of white men took no alarm ;

but once consolidated into an empire, with fixed and inalienable boundaries, powerful, recognized, and determined, the Cherokee nation would be a thorn in the flesh to her white neighbors.   The doom of the Cherokees was sealed on the day when
they declared, once for all, officially as a nation, that they would
not sell another foot of land.   This they did in an interesting
and pathetic message to the United States Senate in 1822.

Georgia, through her governor and her delegates to Congress,
had been persistently demanding to have the Cherokees compelled to give up their lands.   She insisted that the United
States Government should fulfil a provision, made in an old
compact of 1802, to extinguish the Indian titles within her
limits as soon as it could be peaceably done.   This she demanded should be done now, either peaceably or otherwise.

"We cannot but view the design of those letters," says this
message, "as an attempt bordering on a hostile disposition toward the Cherokee nation to wrest from them by arbitrary
means their just rights and liberties, the security of which is
solemnly guaranteed to them by these United States. * * * We
assert under the fullest authority that all the sentiments expressed in relation to the disposition and determination of the
nation never to cede another foot of land, are positively the
production and voice of the nation. * * * There is not a spot
out of the limits of any of the States or Territories thereof,
and within the limits of the United States, that they would
ever consent to inhabit; because they have unequivocally determined never again to pursue the chase as heretofore, or to
engage in wars, unless by the common call of the Government
to defend the common rights of the United States. * * * The
Cherokees have turned their attention to the pursuits of the
civilized man: agriculture, manufactures, and the mechanic arts
and education are all in successful operation in the nation at
this time; and while the Cherokees are peacefully endeavoring
to enjoy the blessings of civilization and Christianity on the

soil of their rightful inheritance, and while the exertions and labors of various religious societies of these United States are successfully engaged in promulgating to them the words of truth and life from the sacred volume of Holy Writ, and under the patronage of the General Government, they are threatened with removal or extinction. * * * We appeal to the magnanimity of the American Congress for justice, and the protection of the rights and liberties and lives of the Cherokee people. We claim it from the United States by the strongest obligation which imposes it on them—by treaties: and we expect it from them under that memorable declaration, 'that all men are created equal; that they are endowed by their Creator with certain inalienable rights; that among these are life, liberty, and the pursuit of happiness.'"

The dignified and pathetic remonstrances of the Cherokee chiefs, their firm reiterations of their resolve not to part with their lands, were called by the angry Georgian governor "tricks of vulgar cunning," and "insults from the polluted lips of outcasts and vagabonds;" and he is not afraid, in an official letter to the Secretary of War, to openly threaten the President that, if he upholds the Indians in their rejection of the overtures for removal, the "consequences are inevitable," and that, in resisting the occupation of the Cherokee lands by the Georgians, he will be obliged to "make war upon, and shed the blood of brothers and friends."

To these Cherokees Mr. Jefferson had written, at one time during his administration, "I sincerely wish you may succeed in your laudable endeavors to save the remnant of your nation by adopting industrious occupations, and a government of regular law. In this you may always rely on the counsel and assistance of the United States."

In 1791 he had written to General Knox, defining the United States' position in the matter of Indian lands: "Government should firmly maintain this ground, that the Indians have a right to the occupation of their lands independent of the States within whose chartered lines they happen to be; that until they cede them by treaty, or other transaction equivalent to treaty, no act of a State can give a right to such lands. * * * The Government is determined to exert all its energy for the patronage and protection of the rights of the Indians."

And the year before General Washington had said to the Six Nations: "In future you cannot be defrauded of your lands. No State or person can purchase your lands unless at some public treaty held under the authority of the United States. The General Government will never consent to your being defrauded; but it will protect you in all your just rights. * * * You possess the right to sell, and the right of refusing to sell your lands. * * * The United States will be true and faithful to their engagements."

What could Cherokee men and women have thought when, only thirty years later, they found this United States Government upholding the State of Georgia in her monstrous pretensions of right to the whole of their country, and in her infamous cruelties of oppression toward them? when they found this United States Government sending its agents to seduce and bribe their chiefs to bargain away their country; even stooping to leave on the public records of official instructions to a commissioner such phrases as these: "Appeal to the chiefs and influential men—not together, but apart, at their own houses;" "make offers to them of extensive reservations in fee-simple, and other rewards, to obtain their acquiescence;" "the more careful you are to secure from even the chiefs the official character you bear, the better;" "enlarge on the advantage of their condition in the West: there the Government would protect them." This the Secretary of War called "moving on them in the line of their prejudices."

In a report submitted to the War Department in 1825 by Thomas L. McKenney is a glowing description of the Cherokee country and nation at that time: "The country is well watered; abundant springs of pure water are found in every part; a range of majestic and lofty mountains stretch themselves across it. The northern part is hilly and mountainous; in the southern and western parts there are extensive and fertile plains, covered partly with tall trees, through which beautiful streams of water glide. These plains furnish immense pasturage, and numberless herds of cattle are dispersed over them; horses are plenty; numerous flocks of sheep, goats, and swine cover the valleys and the hills. On Tennessee, Ustanula, and Canasagi rivers Cherokee commerce floats. The climate is delicious and healthy; the winters are mild; the spring clothes the ground with the richest scenery; flowers of exquisite beauty and variegated hues meet and fascinate the eye in every direction. In the plains and valleys the soil is generally rich, producing Indian-corn, cotton, tobacco, wheat, oats, indigo, and sweet and Irish potatoes. The natives carry on considerable trade with the adjoining States; some of them export cotton in boats down the Tennessee to the Mississippi, and down that river to New Orleans. Apple and peach orchards are quite common, and gardens are cultivated, and much attention paid to them. Butter and cheese are seen on Cherokee tables. There are many public roads in the nation, and houses of entertainment kept by natives. Numerous and flourishing villages are seen in every section of the country. Cotton and woollen cloths are manufactured: blankets of various dimensions, manufactured by Cherokee hands, are very common. Almost every family in the nation grows cotton for its own consumption. Industry and commercial enterprise are extending themselves in every part. Nearly all the merchants in the nation are native Cherokees. Agricultural pursuits engage the chief attention of the people. Different branches in mechanics are pursued. The population is rapidly increasing. * * * White men in the nation enjoy all the immunities and privileges of the Cherokee people, except that they are not eligible to public offices. * * *. The Christian religion is the religion of the nation.   Presbyterians, Methodists, Baptists, and Moravians are the most numerous sects.   Some of the most influential characters are members of the Church, and live consistently with their professions.   The whole nation is penetrated with gratitude for the aid it has received from the United States Government, and from different religious societies.   Schools are increasing every year; learning is encouraged and rewarded; the young class acquire the English, and those of mature age the Cherokee system of learning. * * * Our relations with all nations are of the most friendly character.   We are out of debt, and our public revenue is in a flourishing condition.   Besides the amount arising from imports, perpetual annuity is due from the United States in consideration of lands ceded in former periods.   Our system of government, founded on republican principles by which justice is equally distributed, secures the respect of the people.   New Town, pleasantly situated in the centre of the nation, and at the junction of the Canasagi and Gusuwati, two beautiful streams, is the seat of government.   The legislative power is vested in what is denominated in native dialect Tsalagi Tinilawige, consisting of a national committee and council.   Members of both branches are chosen by and from the people for a limited period.   In New Town a printing-press is soon to be established; also a national library and museum.   An immense concourse of people frequent the seat of government when the Tsalagi Tinilawige is in session, which takes place once a year.

"The success which has attended the philological researches of one in the nation whose system of education has met with universal approbation among the Cherokees certainly entitles him to great consideration, and to rank with the benefactors of man.   His name is Guess, and he is a native and unlettered Cherokee; but, like Cadmus, he has given to his people the alphabet of their language. It is composed of eighty-six characters, by which in a few days the older Indians, who had despaired of deriving an education by means of the schools, and who are not included in the existing school system, may read and correspond."*

Never did mountaineers cling more desperately to their homes than did the Cherokees. The State of Georgia put the whole nation in duress, but still they chose to stay. Year by year high-handed oppressions increased and multiplied; military law reigned everywhere; Cherokee lands were surveyed, and put up to be drawn by lottery; missionaries were arrested and sent to prison for preaching to Cherokees; Cherokees were sentenced to death by Georgia juries, and hung by Georgia executioners. Appeal after appeal to the President and to Congress for protection produced only reiterated confessions of the Government's inability to protect them—reiterated proposals to them to accept a price for their country and move away. Nevertheless they clung to it. A few hundreds went, but the body of the nation still protested and entreated. There is nothing in history more touching than the cries of this people to the Government of the United States to fulfil its promises to them. And their cause was not without eloquent advocates. When the bill for their removal was before Congress, Frelinghuysen, Sprague, Robbins, Storrs, Ellsworth, Evans, Huntington, Johns, Bates, Crockett, Everett, Test—all spoke warmly against it; and, to the credit of Congress be it said, the bill passed the Senate by only one majority.

The Rev. Jeremiah Evarts published a series of papers in the *National Intelligencer* under the signature of William Penn, in which he gave a masterly analysis and summing up of the case, recapitulated the sixteen treaties which the Government had made with the Cherokees, all guaranteeing to them their

* See Appendix, Art. IX.

lands, and declared that the Government had "arrived at the bank of the Rubicon," where it must decide if it would or would not save the country from the charge of bad faith. Many of his eloquent sentences read in the light of the present time like prophecies. He says, "in a quarter of a century the pressure upon the Indians will be much greater from the boundless prairies, which must ultimately be subdued and inhabited, than it would ever have been from the borders of the present Cherokee country;" and asks, pertinently, "to what confidence would such an engagement be entitled, done at the very moment that treaties with Indians are declared not to be binding, and for the very reason that existing treaties are not strong enough to bind the United States." Remonstrances poured in upon Congress, petitions and memorials from religious societies, from little country villages, all imploring the Government to keep its faith to these people.

The Cherokees' own newspaper, *The Phœnix*, was filled at this time with the records of the nation's suffering and despair.

"The State of Georgia has taken a strong stand against us, and the United States must either defend us and our rights or leave us to our foe. In the latter case she will violate her promise of protection, and we cannot in future depend upon any guarantee to us, either here or beyond the Mississippi.

"If the United States shall withdraw their solemn pledges of protection, utterly disregard their plighted faith, deprive us of the right of self-government, and wrest from us our land, then, in the deep anguish of our misfortunes, we may justly say there is no place of security for us, no confidence left that the United States will be more just and faithful toward us in the barren prairies of the West than when we occupied the soil inherited from the Great Author of our existence."

As a last resort the Cherokees carried their case before the Supreme Court, and implored that body to restrain the State of Georgia from her unjust interference with their rights.

The reports of the case of the Cherokee Nation *vs.* the State of Georgia fill a volume by themselves, and are of vital importance to the history of Indian affairs. The majority of the judges decided that an Indian tribe could not be considered as a foreign nation, and therefore could not bring the suit. Judge Thompson and Judge Story dissented from this opinion, and held that the Cherokee tribe did constitute a foreign nation, and that the State of Georgia ought to be enjoined from execution of its unjust laws. The opinion of Chancellor Kent coincided with that of Judges Thompson and Story. Chancellor Kent gave it as his opinion that the cases in which the Supreme Court had jurisdiction would "reach and embrace every controversy that can arise between the Cherokees and the State of Georgia or its officers under the execution of the act of Georgia."

But all this did not help the Cherokees; neither did the fact of the manifest sympathy of the whole court with their wrongs. The technical legal decision had been rendered against them, and this delivered them over to the tender mercies of Georgia: no power in the land could help them. Fierce factions now began to be formed in the nation, one for and one against the surrender of their lands. Many were ready still to remain and suffer till death rather than give them up; but wiser counsels prevailed, and in the last days of the year 1835 a treaty was concluded with the United States by twenty of the Cherokee chiefs and headmen, who thereby, in behalf of their nation, relinquished all the lands claimed or possessed by them east of the Mississippi River.

The preamble of this treaty is full of pathos: "*Whereas*, The Cherokees are anxious to make some arrangement with the Government of the United States whereby the difficulties they have experienced by a residence within the settled parts of the United States under the jurisdiction and laws of the State governments may be terminated and adjusted; and with a view to reuniting their people in one body, and securing a permanent home for themselves and their posterity in the country selected by their forefathers without the territorial limits of the State sovereignties, and where they can establish and enjoy a government of their choice, and perpetuate such a state of society as may be most consonant with their views, habits, and condition, and as may tend to their individual comfort and their advancement in civilization."

By this treaty the Cherokees gave up a country " larger than the three States of Massachusetts, Rhode Island, and Connecticut combined, and received therefor five millions of dollars and seven millions of acres of land west of the Mississippi." This the United States " guaranteed, and secured to be conveyed in patent," and defined it by exact boundaries; and, " in addition to the seven millions of acres of land thus provided for and bounded," the United States did " further guarantee to the Cherokee nation a perpetual outlet west, and a free and unmolested use of all the country west of the western boundary of said seven millions of acres, as far west as the sovereignty of the United States and their rights of soil extend."

The fifth Article of this treaty is, " The United States hereby covenant and agree that the lands ceded to the Cherokee nation in the foregoing article shall in no future time, without their consent, be included within the territorial limits or jurisdiction of any State or Territory."

In the sixth Article is this promise: " The United States agree to protect the Cherokee nation from domestic strife and foreign enemies, and against intestine wars between the several tribes."

Even after this treaty was made a great part of the nation refused to sanction it, saying that it did not represent their wish; they would never carry it out; hundreds refused to receive any longer either money or supplies from the United States agents, lest they should be considered to have thereby committed themselves to the treaty.

In 1837 General Wool wrote from the Cherokee country that the people "uniformly declare that they never made the treaty in question. * * * So determined are they in their opposition that not one of all those who were present, and voted in the council held but a day or two since at this place, however poor or destitute, would receive either rations or clothing from the United States, lest they might compromise themselves in regard to the treaty. These same people, as well as those in the mountains of North Carolina, during the summer past preferred living on the roots and sap of trees rather than receive provisions from the United States. Thousands, I have been informed, had no other food for weeks."

For two years—to the very last moment allowed them by the treaty—they clung to their lands, and at last were removed only by military force. In May, 1838, General Scott was ordered to go with a sufficient military force to compel the removal. His proclamation "to the Cherokee people remaining in North Carolina, Georgia, Tennessee, and Alabama" opens thus:

"CHEROKEES,—The President of the United States has sent me with a powerful army to cause you, in obedience to the treaty of 1835, to join that part of your people who are already established on the other side of the Mississippi. Unhappily the two years which were allowed for the purpose you have suffered to pass away without following, and without making any preparation to follow; and now, or by the time that this solemn address shall reach your distant settlements, the emigration must be commenced in haste, but I hope without disorder. I have no power, by granting a further delay, to correct the error that you have committed. The full-moon of May is already on the wane, and before another shall have passed away every Cherokee man, woman, and child in those States must be in motion to join their brethren in the West."

The tone of this proclamation, at once firm and kindly, could not fail to profoundly impress the unfortunate people to whom

it was addressed. " My troops," said the humane and sympa-
thizing general, " already occupy many positions in the country
that you are to abandon, and thousands and thousands are approaching from every quarter, to render resistance and escape
alike hopeless. All those troops, regular and militia, are your
friends. Receive them and confide in them as such; obey
them when they tell you that you can remain no longer in this
country. Soldiers are as kind-hearted as brave, and the desire
of every one of us is to execute our painful duty in mercy. * * *

" Chiefs, headmen, and warriors, will you then, by resistance,
compel us to resort to arms? God forbid. Or will you by
flight seek to hide yourselves in mountains and forests, and
thus oblige us to hunt you down? Remember that in pursuit it may be impossible to avoid conflicts. The blood of the
white man or the blood of the red man may be spilt; and if
spilt, however accidentally, it may be impossible for the dis-
creet and humane among you or among us to prevent a general
war and carnage. Think of this, my Cherokee brethren! I
am an old warrior, and have been present at many a scene of
slaughter; but spare me, I beseech you, the horror of witness-
ing the destruction of the Cherokees. Do not even wait for
the close approach of the troops, but make such preparations
for emigration as you can, and hasten to this place, to Ross's
Landing, or to Guinter's Landing, where you will be received
in kindness by officers selected for the purpose. * * * This is
the address of a warrior to warriors. May its entreaties be
kindly received, and may the God of both prosper the Americans and Cherokees, and preserve them long in peace and
friendship with each other."

The reply of the council of the Cherokee nation to this proclamation is worthy to be put on record. They make no further protest against going; they simply ask the privilege of
undertaking the whole charge of the removal themselves. They
say: " The present condition of the Cherokee people is such

that all dispute as to the time of emigration is set at rest. Being already severed from their homes and their property, their persons being under the absolute control of the commanding general, and being altogether dependent on the benevolence and humanity of that high officer for the suspension of their transportation to the West at a season and under circumstances in which sickness and death were to be apprehended to an alarming extent, all inducements to prolong their stay in this country are taken away. And however strong their attachment to the homes of their fathers may be, their interests and their wishes are now to depart as early as may be consistent with their safety."

The council therefore submitted to General Scott several propositions: 1st. "That the Cherokee nation will undertake the whole business of removing their people to the west of the river Mississippi." Their estimates of cost, and arrangement as to time, intervals, etc., were wise and reasonable. To their estimate of $65,880 as the cost for every thousand persons transported General Scott objected, thinking it high. He said that he was "confident" that it would be found that out of every thousand there would be "at least five hundred strong men, women, boys, and girls not only capable of marching twelve or fifteen miles a day, but to whom the exercise would be beneficial; and another hundred able to go on foot half that distance daily." He also objected to the estimate of the ration at sixteen cents as too high.

The council replied that they believed the estimate reasonable, "having the comfortable removal of our people solely in view, and endeavoring to be governed, as far as that object will allow, by the rates of expenditure fixed by the officers of the Government. After the necessary bedding, cooking-utensils, and other indispensable articles of twenty persons—say, four or five families—are placed in a wagon, with subsistence for at least two days, the weight already will be enough to exclude, in our opinion, more than a very few persons being hauled. The great distance to be travelled, liability to sickness on the way of grown persons, and the desire of performing the trip in as short a time as possible, induce us still to think our estimate of that item not extravagant. * * * Whatever may be necessary in the emigration of our people to their comfort on the way, and as conducive to their health, we desire to be afforded them; at the same time it is our anxious wish, in the management of this business, to be free at all times from the imputation of extravagance." They added that the item of soap had been forgotten in their first estimate, and must now be included, at the rate of three pounds to every hundred pounds of rations.

General Scott replied, " as the Cherokee people are exclusively interested in the cost as well as the comfort of the removal," he did not feel himself at liberty to withhold his sanction from these estimates. In the report of the Indian Commissioner, also, it is stated that "the cost of removal, according to the Indian estimate, is high;" but the commissioner adds, "as their own fund pays it, and it was insisted on by their own confidential agents, it was thought it could not be rejected."

Noble liberality! This nation of eighteen thousand industrious, self-supporting people, compelled at the point of the bayonet to leave their country and seek new homes in a wilderness, are to be permitted, as a favor, to spend on their journey to this wilderness as much of their own money as they think necessary, and have all the soap they want.

The record which the United States Government has left in official papers of its self-congratulations in the matter of this Cherokee removal has an element in it of the ludicrous, spite of the tragedy and shame.

Says the Secretary of War: " The generous and enlightened policy evinced in the measures adopted by Congress toward that people during the last session was ably and judiciously carried into effect by the general appointed to conduct their removal. The reluctance of the Indians to relinquish the land of their birth in the East, and remove to their new homes in the West, was entirely overcome by the judicious conduct of that officer, and they departed with alacrity under the guidance of their own chiefs. The arrangements for this purpose made by General Scott, in compliance with his previous instructions, although somewhat costly to the Indians themselves, met the entire approbation of the Department, as it was deemed of the last importance that the Cherokees should remove to the West voluntarily, and that upon their arrival at the place of their ultimate destination they should recur to the manner in which they had been treated with kind and grateful feelings. Humanity no less than good policy dictated this course toward these children of the forest; and in carrying out in this instance with an unwavering hand the measures resolved upon by the Government, in the hope of preserving the Indians and of maintaining the peace and tranquillity of the whites, it will always be gratifying to reflect that this has been effected not only without violence, but with every proper regard for the feelings and interests of that people."

The Commissioner of Indian Affairs says, in his report: "The case of the Cherokees is a striking example of the liberality of the Government in all its branches. * * * A retrospect of the last eight months in reference to this numerous and more than ordinarily enlightened tribe cannot fail to be refreshing to well-constituted minds."

A further appropriation had been asked by the Cherokee chiefs to meet the expense of their removal (they not thinking $5,000,000 a very munificent payment for a country as large as all Massachusetts, Rhode Island, and Connecticut together), and Congress had passed a law giving them $1147 67 more, and the commissioner says of this: "When it is considered that by the treaty of December, 1835, the sum of $5,000,000 was stipulated to be paid them as the full value of their lands, after that amount was declared by the Senate of the United States to be an ample consideration for them, the spirit of this whole proceeding cannot be too much admired. By some the measure may be regarded as just; by others generous: it perhaps partook of both attributes. If it went farther than naked justice could have demanded, it did not stop short of what liberality approved. * * * If our acts have been generous, they have not been less wise and politic. A large mass of men have been conciliated; the hazard of an effusion of human blood has been put by; good feeling has been preserved, and we have quietly and gently transported eighteen thousand friends to the west bank of the Mississippi."

To dwell on the picture of this removal is needless. The fact by itself is more eloquent than pages of detail and description could make it. No imagination so dull, no heart so hard as not to see and to feel, at the bare mention of such an emigration, what horrors and what anguish it must have involved. "Eighteen thousand friends!" Only a great magnanimity of nature, strengthened by true Christian principle, could have prevented them from being changed into eighteen thousand bitter enemies.

For some years after this removal fierce dissensions rent the Cherokee nation. The party who held that the treaty of 1835 had been unfair, and that the nation still had an unextinguished right to its old country at the East, felt, as was natural, a bitter hatred toward the party which, they claimed, had wrongfully signed away the nation's lands. Several of the signers of the treaty, influential men of the nation, were murdered. Party-spirit ran to such a height that the United States Government was compelled to interfere; and in 1846, after long negotiations and dissensions, a new treaty was made, by the terms and concessions of which the anti-treaty party were appeased, a general amnesty provided for, and comparative harmony restored to the nation.

The progress of this people in the ten years following this removal is almost past belief. In 1851 they had twenty-two primary schools, and had just built two large houses for a male and female seminary, in which the higher branches of education were to be taught. They had a temperance society with three thousand members, and an auxiliary society in each of the eight districts into which the country was divided. They had a Bible Society and twelve churches; a weekly newspaper, partly in English, partly in Cherokee; eight district courts, two circuit courts, and a supreme court. Legislative business was transacted as before by the national council and committee, elected for four years. Nearly one thousand boys and girls were in the public schools.

In 1860 the agitation on the subject of slavery began to be felt, a strong antislavery party being organized in the nation. There were stormy scenes also in that part of the country nearest the Kansas line. For several years white settlers had persisted in taking up farms there, and the Cherokees had in vain implored the Government to drive them away. The officer at last sent to enforce the Cherokees' rights and dislodge the squatters was obliged to burn their cabins over their heads before they would stir, so persuaded were they of the superior right of the white man over the Indian. "The only reason the settlers gave for not heeding the notices was that they had been often notified before to quit the reservation; and, no steps having been taken to enforce obedience, they supposed they would be allowed to remain with like security in this instance."

"It is surprising," says the Commissioner of Indian Affairs, "to see the growing disposition on the part of our citizens to wholly disregard our treaty obligations with Indian tribes within our borders; and it is to be hoped that in future their rights will be held more sacred, or that the Government will in every instance promptly see that they are observed and respected."

In the first year of the Civil War a large number of the

Cherokees took up arms on the rebel side.   That this was not from any love or liking for the Southern cause, it would seem, must be evident to any one who believed that they were possessed of memories. The opportunity of fighting against Georgians could not but have been welcome to the soul of a Cherokee, even if he bought it at the price of fighting.on the side of the government which had been so perfidious to his nation. Their defection was no doubt largely due to terror. The forts in their vicinity were surrendered to the rebels; all United States troops were withdrawn from that part of the country. They had no prospect of protection from the Government, and, as if to leave them without one incentive to loyalty, the Government suspended the payment of their annuities.

The Confederate Government stepped in, artfully promising to pay what the Northern Government refused. It would have taken a rare loyalty, indeed, to have stood unmoved in such circumstances as these; yet thousands of the Indians in Indian Territory did remain loyal, and fled for their lives to avoid being pressed into the rebel service; almost half of the Creek nation, many Seminoles, Chickasaws, Quapaws, Cherokees, and half a dozen others—over six thousand in all—fled to Kansas, where their sufferings in the winter of 1862 were heart-rending.

That the Cherokees did not lightly abandon their allegiance is on record in the official history of the Department of the Interior. The Report of the Indian Bureau for 1863 says: "The Cherokees, prior to the Rebellion, were the most numerous, intelligent, wealthy, and influential tribe of this superintendency (the southern). For many months they steadily resisted the efforts made by the rebels to induce them to abandon their allegiance to the Federal Government; but being wholly unprotected, and without the means of resistance, they were finally compelled to enter into treaty stipulations with the rebel authorities. This connection was, however, of short duration, for upon the first appearance of United States forces in their country an entire regiment of Indian troops, raised ostensibly for service in the rebel army, deserted and came over to us, and have ever since been under our command, and upon all occasions have proved themselves faithful and efficient soldiers." In the course of the next year, however, many more joined the rebels: it was estimated that between six and seven thousand of the wealthier portion of the nation co-operated in one way or another with the rebels. The result was that at the end of the war the Cherokee country was ruined.

"In the Cherokee country," says the Report of the Indian Bureau for 1865, "where the contending armies have moved to and fro; where their foraging parties have gone at will, sparing neither friend nor foe; where the disloyal Cherokees in the service of the rebel government were determined that no trace of the homesteads of their loyal brethren should remain for their return; and where the swindling cattle-thieves have made their ill-gotten gains for two years past, the scene is one of utter desolation."

The party feeling between the loyal and disloyal Cherokees ran as high as it did between the loyal and disloyal whites, and it looked for a time as if it would be as impossible to make the two opposing parties in the Cherokee nation agree to live peaceably side by side with each other, as it would to make discharged soldiers from Georgia and from Maine settle down in one village together. But after long and troublesome negotiations a treaty was concluded in 1866, by which all the necessary points seemed to be established of a general amnesty and peace.

That the Indians were at a great disadvantage in the making of these new treaties it is unnecessary to state. The peculiarity of the Government's view of their situation and rights is most näively stated in one of the reports for 1862. Alluding to the necessity of making at no very distant time new treaties with all these Southern tribes, one of the Indian superintendents says: " While the rebelling of a large portion of most of these tribes abrogates treaty obligations, and places them at our mercy, the very important fact should not be forgotten that the Government first wholly failed to keep its treaty stipulations with those people, and in protecting them, by withdrawing all the troops from the forts in Indian Territory, and leaving them at the mercy of the rebels. It is a well-known fact that self-preservation in many instances compelled them to make the best terms they could with the rebels."

Nevertheless they are " at our mercy," because their making the " best terms they could with the rebels abrogates treaty obligations."   The trite old proverb about the poorness of rules that do not work both ways seems to be applicable here.

With a recuperative power far in advance of that shown by any of the small white communities at the South, the Cherokees at once addressed themselves to rebuilding their homes and reconstructing their national life.   In one year they established fifteen new schools, set all their old industries going, and in 1869 held a large agricultural fair, which gave a creditable exhibition of stock and farm produce.   Thus a second time they recovered themselves, after what would seem to be well-nigh their destruction as a people.   But the Indian's fate of perpetual insecurity, alarm, and unrest does not abandon them. In 1870 they are said to be "extremely uneasy about the security of their possession of the lands they occupy."   When asked why their high-schools are not re-established, reforms introduced into the administration of justice, desirable improvements undertaken, the reply inevitably comes, " We expect to have our lands taken away: what is the use of all that when our doom as a nation is sealed ?"

"Distrust is firmly seated in their minds.   National apathy depresses them, and until they realize a feeling of assurance that their title to their lands will be respected, and that treaties are an inviolable law for all parties, the Cherokees will not make the efforts for national progress of which they are capable."

When their delegates went to Washington, in 1866, to make the new treaty, they were alarmed by the position taken by the Government that the nation, as a nation, had forfeited its rights. They were given to understand that "public opinion held them responsible for complicity in the Rebellion; and, although they could point to the fact that the only countenance the rebels received came from less than one-third of the population, and cite the services of two Cherokee regiments in the Union cause, it was urged home to them that, before being rehabilitated in their former rights by a new treaty, they were not in a position to refuse any conditions imposed. Such language from persons they believed to possess the power of injuring their people intimidated the Cherokee delegates. They sold a large tract in South-eastern Kansas at a dollar an acre to an association of speculators, and it went into the possession of a railroad company. They also acceded, against the wishes of the Cherokee people, to a provision in the treaty granting right of way through the country for two railroads. This excited great uneasiness among the Indians."

And well it might. The events of the next few years amply justified this uneasiness. The rapacity of railroad corporations is as insatiable as their methods are unscrupulous. The phrase "extinguishing Indian titles" has become, as it were, a mere technical term in the transfer of lands. The expression is so common that it has probably been one of the agencies in fixing in the minds of the people the prevalent impression that extinction is the ultimate and inevitable fate of the Indian; and this being the case, methods and times are not, after all, of so much consequence; they are merely foreordained conditions of the great foreordained progression of events. This is the only explanation of the unconscious inhumanity of many good men's modes of thinking and speaking in regard to the Indians being driven from home after home, and robbed of tract after tract of their lands.

In the Report of the Indian Bureau for 1875 is an account of a remnant of the Cherokee tribe in North Carolina: "They number not far from seventeen hundred, and there are probably in other parts of North Carolina, and scattered through Georgia and Tennessee, between three and four hundred more. These Cherokees have had an eventful history. When the main portion of the tribe was compelled to remove west of the Mississippi they fled to the mountains, and have steadily refused to leave their homes. The proceeds of their lands, which were sold in accordance with a treaty with the main body of the Cherokees, have been mainly expended in the purchase of lands, and providing funds for the Western Cherokees. At various times previous to the year 1861 the agent for the Eastern Cherokees, at their request, purchased lands with their funds, upon which they might make their homes. These purchases, though probably made with good intent, carelessly left the title in their agent personally, and not in trust. By this neglect, when subsequently the agent became insolvent, all their lands were seized and sold for his debts. By special legislation of Congress their case has been brought before the courts of North Carolina, and their rights to a certain extent asserted, and they are enabled to maintain possession of their lands; and, by the use of their own funds in extinguishing liens, are now in possession of above seventy thousand acres of fair arable, timber, and grazing lands. They have shown themselves capable of self-support, and, I believe, have demonstrated the unwisdom of removing Indians from a country which offers to them a home, and where a white man could make a living. This is shown by the fact that they are now, though receiving scarcely any Government aid, in a more hopeful condition, both as to morals, and industry, and personal property, than the Cherokees who removed West."

The Report of the Indian Bureau for 1876 fully bears out
this statement. The North Carolina Cherokees have, indeed,
reason to be in a more hopeful condition, for they have their
lands secured to them by patent, confirmed by a decision of
State courts; but this is what the Department of the Interior
has brought itself to say as to the Western Cherokees' lands,
and those of all other civilized tribes in the Indian Territory:
"By treaty the Government has ceded to the so-called civilized
tribes—the Cherokees, Creeks, Choctaws, Chickasaws, and Seminoles — a section of country altogether disproportionate in
amount to their needs. * * * The amount susceptible of cultivation must be many-fold greater than can ever be cultivated by
the labor of the Indians. But the Indians claim, it is understood, that they hold their lands by sanctions so solemn that it
would be a gross breach of faith on the part of the Government to take away any portion thereof without their consent;
and that consent they apparently propose to withhold."

Let us set side by side with this last paragraph a quotation
from the treaty by virtue of which "the Indians claim, it is
understood, that they hold" these lands, which they now "apparently propose to withhold." We will not copy it from the
original treaty; we will copy it, and a few other sentences with
it, from an earlier report of this same Department of the Interior. Only so far back as 1870 we find the Department in a
juster frame of mind toward the Cherokees. "A large part of
the Indian tribes hold lands to which they are only fixed by
laws that define the reservations to which they shall be confined. It cannot be denied that these are in a great measure
dependent on the humanity of the American people. * * * But
the Cherokees, and the other civilized Indian nations no less,
hold lands in perpetuity by titles defined by the supreme law
of the land. The United States agreed 'to possess the Cherokees, and to guarantee it to them forever,' and that guarantee
'was solemnly pledged of seven million acres of land.' The

consideration for this territory was the same number of acres elsewhere located. The inducement to the bargain set forth in the treaty was 'the anxious desire of the Government of the United States to secure to the Cherokee nation of Indians a permanent home, and which shall, under the most solemn guarantee of the United States, be and remain theirs forever—a home that shall never in all future time be embarrassed by having extended around it the lines or placed over it the jurisdiction of a Territory or State, or be pressed upon by the extension in any way of the limits of any existing State.' To assure them of their title, a patent for the Territory was issued."

This was the view of the Department of the Interior in 1870. In 1876 the Department says that affairs in the Indian Territory are "complicated and embarrassing, and the question is directly raised whether an extensive section of country is to be allowed to remain for an indefinite period practically an uncultivated waste, or whether the Government shall determine to reduce the size of the reservation."

The phrase "whether the Government shall determine to reduce the size of the reservation" sounds much better than "whether the Government shall rob the Indians of a few millions of acres of land;" but the latter phrase is truth, and the other is the spirit of lying.

The commissioner says that the question is a difficult one, and should be "considered with calmness, and a full purpose to do no injustice to the Indians." He gives his own personal opinion on it "with hesitancy," but gives it nevertheless, that "public policy will soon require the disposal of a large portion of these lands to the Government for the occupancy either of other tribes of Indians or of white people. There is a very general and growing opinion that observance of the strict letter of treaties with Indians is in many cases at variance with their own best interests and with sound public policy." He adds, however, that it must not be understood from this recommendation that it is "the policy or purpose of this office to in any way encourage the spirit of rapacity which demands the throwing open of the Indian Territory to white settlement." He says, "the true way to secure its perpetual occupancy by Indians is to fill it up with other Indians, to give them lands in severalty, and to provide a government strong and intelligent enough to protect them effectually from any and all encroachments on the part of the whites."

Comment on these preposterously contradictory sentences would be idle. The best comment on them, and the most fitting close to this sketch of the Cherokee nation, is in a few more quotations from the official reports of the Indian Bureau.

Of this people, from whom the Department of the Interior proposes, for "public policy," to take away "a large portion" of their country, it has published within the last three years these records:

"It has been but a few years since the Cherokees assembled in council under trees or in a rude log-house, with hewed logs for seats. Now the legislature assembles in a spacious brick council-house, provided with suitable committee-rooms, senate chamber, representative hall, library, and executive offices, which cost $22,000.

"Their citizens occupy neat hewed double log-cabins, frame, brick, or stone houses, according to the means or taste of the individual, with ground adorned by ornamental trees, shrubbery, flowers, and nearly every improvement, including orchards of the choicest fruits. Some of these orchards have existed for nearly twenty years, and are now in a good, fruitful condition. Their women are usually good house-keepers, and give great attention to spinning and weaving yarns, jeans, and linsey, and make most of the pants and hunter-jackets of the men and boys. The farmers raise most of their own wool and cotton, and it is not an uncommon sight, in a well-to-do Cherokee farmer's house, to see a sewing-machine and a piano.

"They have ample provision for the education of all their children to a degree of advancement equal to that furnished by an ordinary college in the States. They have seventy-five common day-schools, kept open ten months in the year, in the different settlements. For the higher education of their young men and women they have two commodious and well-furnished seminaries, one for each sex; and, in addition to those already mentioned, they have a manual labor school and an orphan asylum. The cost of maintaining these schools the past year (1877) was, as reported by the superintendent of public instruction, $73,441 65, of which $41,475 was paid as salary to teachers.

"They have twenty-four stores, twenty-two mills, and sixty-five smith-shops, owned and conducted by their own citizens.

"Their constitution and laws are published in book form; and from their printing-house goes forth among the people in their own language, and also in English, the *Cherokee Advocate*, a weekly paper, which is edited with taste and ability.

"They have (and this is true also of the Choctaws, Creeks, Chickasaws, and Seminoles) a constitutional government, with legislative, judicial, and executive departments, and conducted upon the same plan as our State governments, the entire expenses of which are paid out of their own funds, which are derived from interest on various stocks and bonds—the invested proceeds of the sale of their lands, and held in trust by the Government of the United States—which interest is paid the treasurers of the different nations semi-annually, and by them disbursed on national warrants issued by the principal chief and secretary, and registered by the auditors.

"They are an intelligent, temperate, and industrious people, who live by the honest fruits of their labor, and seem ambitious to advance both as to the development of their lands and the conveniences of their homes. In their council may be found men of learning and ability; and it is doubtful if their rapid progress from a state of wild barbarism to that of civilization and enlightenment has any parallel in the history of the world.   What required five hundred years for the Britons to accomplish in this direction they have accomplished in one hundred years."

Will the United States Government determine to " reduce the size of the reservation ?"

CHAPTER IX.

MASSACRES OF INDIANS BY WHITES.

I.—*The Conestoga Massacre.*

WHEN the English first entered Pennsylvania messengers from the Conestoga Indians met them, bidding them welcome, and bringing gifts of corn and venison and skins. The whole tribe entered into a treaty of friendship with William Penn, which was to last " as long as the sun should shine or the waters run into the rivers."

The records of Pennsylvania history in the beginning of the eighteenth century contain frequent mention of the tribe. In 1705 the governor sent the secretary of his council, with a delegation of ten men, to hold an interview with them at Conestoga, for purposes of mutual understanding and confidence. And in that same year Thomas Chalkley, a famous Quaker preacher, while sojourning among the Maryland Quakers, was suddenly seized with so great a "concern" to visit these Indians that he laid the matter before the elders at the Nottingham meeting; and, the idea being "promoted" by the elders, he set off with an interpreter and a party of fourteen to make the journey. He says: "We travelled through the woods about fifty miles, carrying our provisions with us; and on the journey sat down by a river and spread our food on the grass, and refreshed ourselves and horses, and then went on cheerfully and with good-will and much love to the poor Indians. And when we came they received us kindly, treating us civilly in their way. We treated about having a meeting with them in a religious way; upon which they called a council, in which they were very grave, and spoke, one after another, without any heat or jarring. Some of the most esteemed of their women speak in their councils."

When asked why they suffered the women to speak, they replied that "some women were wiser than some men." It was said that they had not for many years done anything without the advice of a certain aged and grave woman, who was always present at their councils. The interpreter said that she was an empress, and that they gave much heed to what she said. This wise queen of Conestoga looked with great favor on the Quakers, the interpreter said, because they "did not come to buy or sell, or get gain;" but came "in love and respect" to them, "and desired their well-doing, both here and hereafter." Two nations at this time were represented in this Conestoga band—the Senecas and the Shawanese.

The next year the governor himself, anxious to preserve their inalienable good-will, and to prevent their being seduced by emissaries from the French, went himself to visit them. On this occasion one of the chiefs made a speech, still preserved in the old records, which contains this passage: "Father, we love quiet; we suffer the mouse to play; when the woods are rustled by the wind, we fear not; when the leaves are disturbed in ambush, we are uneasy; when a cloud obscures your brilliant sun, our eyes feel dim; but when the rays appear, they give great heat to the body and joy to the heart. Treachery darkens the chain of friendship; but truth makes it brighter than ever. This is the peace we desire."

A few years later a Swedish missionary visited them, and preached them a sermon on original sin and the necessity of a mediator. When he had finished, an Indian chief rose and replied to him; both discourses being given through an interpreter. The Swede is said to have been so impressed with the Indian's reasoning that, after returning to Sweden, he wrote out his own sermon and the Indian's reply in the best Latin at his command, and dedicated the documents to the University of Upsal, respectfully requesting them to furnish him with some arguments strong enough to confute the strong reasonings of this savage.

"Our forefathers," said the chief, "were under a strong persuasion (as we are) that those who act well in this life will be rewarded in the next according to the degrees of their virtues; and, on the other hand, that those who behave wickedly here will undergo such punishments hereafter as were proportionate to the crimes they were guilty of. This has been constantly and invariably received and acknowledged for a truth through every successive generation of our ancestors. It could not, then, have taken its rise from fable; for human fiction, however artfully and plausibly contrived, can never gain credit long among people where free inquiry is allowed, which was never denied by our ancestors. * * * Now we desire to propose some questions. Does he believe that our forefathers, men eminent for their piety, constant and warm in their pursuit of virtue, hoping thereby to merit eternal happiness, were all damned? Does he think that we who are zealous imitators in good works, and influenced by the same motives as we are, earnestly endeavoring with the greatest circumspection to tread the path of integrity, are in a state of damnation? If that be his sentiment, it is surely as impious as it is bold and daring. * * * Let us suppose that some heinous crimes were committed by some of our ancestors, like to that we are told of another race of people. In such a case God would certainly punish the criminal, but would never involve us that are innocent in the guilt. Those who think otherwise must make the Almighty a very whimsical, evil-natured being. * * * Once more: are the Christians more virtuous, or, rather, are they not more vicious than we are? If so, how came it to pass that they are the objects of God's beneficence, while we are neglected? Does he daily confer his favors without reason and with so much partiality?   In a word, we find the Christians much more depraved in their morals than we are; and we judge from their doctrine by the badness of their lives."

It is plain that this Indian chief's speech was very much Latinized in the good Swede's hands; but if the words even approached being a true presentation of what he said, it is wonderful indeed.

In 1721 His Excellency Sir William Keith, Bart., Governor of the Province of Pennsylvania, went with an escort of eighty horsemen to Conestoga, and spent several days in making a treaty with the representatives of the Five Nations, "the Indians of Conestoga and their friends."   He was entertained at "Captain Civility's cabin."   When he left them, he desired them to give his "very kind love and the love of all our people to your kings and to all their people."   He invited them to visit him in Philadelphia, saying, "We can provide better for you and make you more welcome.   People always receive their friends best at their own homes."   He then took out a coronation medal of the King, and presented it to the Indian in these words: "That our children when we are dead may not forget these things, but keep this treaty between us in perpetual remembrance, I here deliver to you a picture in gold, bearing the image of my great master, the King of all the English.   And when you return home, I charge you to deliver this piece into the hands of the first man or greatest chief of all the Five Nations, whom you call Kannygoodk, to be laid up and kept as a token to our children's children that an entire and lasting friendship is now established forever between the English in this country and the great Five Nations."

At this time the village of Conestoga was described as lying "about seventy miles west of Philadelphia.   The land thereabout being exceeding rich, it is now surrounded with divers fine plantations and farms, where they raise quantities of wheat, barley, flax, and hemp, without the help of any dung."

The next year, also, was marked by a council of great significance at Conestoga.   In the spring of this year an Indian
called Saanteenee had been killed by two white men, brothers,
named Cartledge.   At this time it was not only politic but
necessary for the English to keep on good terms with as many
Indians as possible.   Therefore, the old record says, "Policy
and justice required a rigid inquiry" into this affair, and the
infliction of "exemplary punishment."

Accordingly, the Cartledges were arrested and confined in
Philadelphia, and the high-sheriff of Chester County went, with
two influential men of the province, to Conestoga, to confer
with the Indians as to what should be done with them.   The
Indians were unwilling to decide the matter without advice
from the Five Nations, to whom they owed allegiance.   A
swift runner (Satcheecho) was, therefore, sent northward with
the news of the occurrence; and the governor, with two of his
council, went to Albany to hear what the Five Nations had to
say about it.   What an inconceivable spectacle to us to-day:
the governments of Pennsylvania and New York so fully recognizing an Indian to be a "person," and his murder a thing
to be anxiously and swiftly atoned for if possible!

Only a little more than a hundred and fifty years lie between
this murder of Saanteenee in Conestoga and the murder of Big
Snake on the Ponca Reservation in 1880.   Verily, Policy has
kept a large assortment of spectacles for Justice to look through
in a surprising short space of time.

On the decision of the king and chiefs of the Five Nations
hung the fate of the murderers.   Doubtless the brothers Cartledge made up their minds to die.   The known principles of
the Indians in the matter of avenging injuries certainly left
them little room for hope.   But no!   The Five Nations took
a different view.   They "desired that the Cartledges should
not suffer death, and the affair was at length amicably settled,"
says the old record.   "One life," said the Indian king, "on

this occasion, is enough to be lost. There should not two die."

This was in 1722. In 1763 there were only twenty of these Conestoga Indians left—seven men, five women, and eight children. They were still living in their village on the Shawanee Creek, their lands being assured to them by manorial gift; but they were miserably poor—earned by making brooms, baskets, and wooden bowls a part of their living, and begged the rest. They were wholly peaceable and unoffending, friendly to their white neighbors, and pitifully clinging and affectionate, naming their children after whites who were kind to them, and striving in every way to show their gratitude and good-will.

Upon this little community a band of white men, said by some of the old records to be "Presbyterians," from Paxton, made an attack at daybreak on the 14th of December. They found only six of the Indians at home—three men, two women, and a boy. The rest were away, either at work for the white farmers or selling their little wares. "These poor defenceless creatures were immediately fired upon, stabbed, and hatcheted to death; the good Shebaes, among the rest, cut to pieces in his bed. All of them were scalped and otherwise horribly mangled, then their huts were set on fire, and most of them burnt down."

"Shebaes was a very old man, having assisted at the second treaty held with Mr. Penn, in 1701, and ever since continued a faithful friend to the English. He is said to have been an exceeding good man, considering his education; being naturally of a most kind, benevolent temper."

From a manuscript journal kept at this time, and belonging to the great-granddaughter of Robert Barber, the first settler in Lancaster County, are gathered the few details known of this massacre. "Some of the murderers went directly from the scene of their crime to Mr. Barber's house. They were strangers to him; but, with the hospitality of those days, he made a fire for them and set refreshments before them.

"While they warmed themselves they inquired why the Indians were suffered to live peaceably here.   Mr. Barber said they were entirely inoffensive, living on their own lands and injuring no one.   They asked what would be the consequence if they were all destroyed.   Mr. Barber said he thought they would be as liable to punishment as if they had destroyed so many white men.   They said *they* were of a different opinion, and in a few minutes went out.   In the mean time two sons of Mr. Barber's, about ten or twelve years old, went out to look at the strangers' horses, which were hitched at a little distance from the house.

"After the men went the boys came in, and said that they had tomahawks tied to their saddles which were all bloody, and that they had Christy's gun.   Christy was a little Indian boy about their own age.   They were much attached to him, as he was their playmate, and made bows and arrows for them."

While the family were talking over this, and wondering what it could mean, a messenger came running breathless to inform them of what had happened.   Mr. Barber went at once to the spot, and there he found the murdered Indians lying in the smouldering ruins of their homes, "like half-consumed logs."   He, "with some trouble, procured their bodies, to administer to them the rights of sepulture."

"It was said that at the beginning of the slaughter an Indian mother placed her little child under a barrel, charging it to make no noise, and that a shot was fired through the barrel which broke the child's arm, and still it kept silent."

The magistrates of Lancaster, shocked, as well they might be, at this frightful barbarity, sent messengers out immediately, and took the remaining Indians, wherever they were found, brought them into the town for protection, and lodged them in the newly-erected workhouse or jail, which was the strongest building in the place.   The Governor of Pennsylvania issued a proclamation, ordering all judges, sheriffs, and "all His Majesty's liege subjects in the province," to make every effort to apprehend the authors and perpetrators of this crime, also their abettors and accomplices. But the "Paxton Boys" held magistrates and governor alike in derision. Two weeks later they assembled again, fifty strong, rode to Lancaster, dismounted, broke open the doors of the jail, and killed every Indian there.

"When the poor wretches saw they had no protection nigh, nor could possibly escape, and being without the least weapon of defence, they divided their little families, the children clinging to their parents. They fell on their faces, protested their innocence, declared their love to the English, and that in their whole lives they had never done them injury. And in this posture they all received the hatchet. Men, women, and children were every one inhumanly murdered in cold blood. * * * The barbarous men who committed the atrocious act, in defiance of government, of all laws, human and divine, and to the eternal disgrace of their country and color, then mounted their horses, huzzaed in triumph, as if they had gained a victory, and rode off unmolested. * * * The bodies of the murdered were then brought out and exposed in the street till a hole could be made in the earth to receive and cover them. But the wickedness cannot be covered, and the guilt will lie on the whole land till justice is done on the murderers. The blood of the innocent will cry to Heaven for vengeance."

These last extracts are from a pamphlet printed in Philadelphia at the time of the massacre; printed anonymously, because "so much had fear seized the minds of the people" that neither the writer nor the printer dared to give "name or place of abode."

There are also private letters still preserved which give accounts of the affair. A part of one from William Henry, of Lancaster, to a friend in Philadelphia, is given in "Rupp's His-

tory of Lancaster County." He says, "A regiment of High-
landers were at that time quartered at the barracks in the
town, and yet these murderers were permitted to break open
the doors of the city jail and commit the horrid deed. The
first notice I had of the affair was that, while at my father's
store near the court-house, I saw a number of people running
down-street toward the jail, which enticed me and other lads
to follow them. At about six or eight yards from the jail we
met from twenty-five to thirty men, well mounted on horses,
and with rifles, tomahawks, and scalping-knives, equipped for
murder. I ran into the prison-yard, and there, oh, what a horrid sight presented itself to my view! Near the back door of
the prison lay an old Indian and his squaw, particularly well
known and esteemed by the people of the town on account of
his placid and friendly conduct. His name was Will Soc.
Around him and his squaw lay two children, about the age of
three years, whose heads were split with the tomahawk and
their scalps taken off. Toward the middle of the jail-yard,
along the west side of the wall, lay a stout Indian, whom I particularly noticed to have been shot in his breast. His legs
were chopped with the tomahawk, his hands cut off, and finally
a rifle-ball discharged in his mouth, so that his head was blown
to atoms, and the brains were splashed against and yet hanging
to the wall for three or four feet around. This man's hands
and feet had been chopped off with a tomahawk. In this
manner lay the whole of them—men, women, and children—
spread about the prison-yard, shot, scalped, hacked, and cut to
pieces."

After this the Governor of Pennsylvania issued a second
proclamation, still more stringent than the first, and offering a
reward of $600 for the apprehension of any three of the
ringleaders.

But the "Paxton Boys" were now like wild beasts that had
tasted blood. They threatened to attack the Quakers and all

persons who sympathized with or protected Indians. They openly mocked and derided the governor and his proclamations, and set off at once for Philadelphia, announcing their intention of killing all the Moravian Indians who had been placed under the protection of the military there.

Their march through the country was like that of a band of maniacs. In a private letter written by David Rittenhouse at this time, he says, "About fifty of these scoundrels marched by my workshop. I have seen hundreds of Indians travelling the country, and can with truth affirm that the behavior of these fellows was ten times more savage and brutal than theirs. Frightening women by running the muzzles of guns through windows, hallooing and swearing; attacking men without the least provocation, dragging them by the hair to the ground, and pretending to scalp them; shooting dogs and fowls: these are some of their exploits."

It is almost past belief that at this time many people justified these acts. An Episcopalian clergyman in Lancaster wrote vindicating them, "bringing Scripture to prove that it was right to destroy the heathen;" and the "Presbyterians think they have a better justification—nothing less than the Word of God," says one of the writers on the massacre.

"With the Scriptures in their hands and mouths, they can set at naught that express command, 'Thou shalt do no murder,' and justify their wickedness by the command given to Joshua to destroy the heathen. Horrid perversion of Scripture and religion, to father the worst of crimes on the God of Love and Peace!" It is a trite saying that history repeats itself; but it is impossible to read now these accounts of the massacres of defenceless and peaceable Indians in the middle of the eighteenth century, without the reflection that the record of the nineteenth is blackened by the same stains. What Pennsylvania pioneers did in 1763 to helpless and peaceable Indians of Conestoga, Colorado pioneers did in 1864 to help-

less and peaceable Cheyennes at Sand Creek, and have threatened to do again to helpless and peaceable Utes in 1880. The
word "extermination" is as ready on the frontiersman's tongue
to-day as it was a hundred years ago; and the threat is more
portentous now, seeing that we are, by a whole century of
prosperity, stronger and more numerous, and the Indians are,
by a whole century of suffering and oppression, fewer and
weaker. But our crime is baser and our infamy deeper in the
same proportion.

Close upon this Conestoga massacre followed a "removal"
of friendly Indians—the earliest on record, and one whose
cruelty and cost to the suffering Indians well entitle it to a
place in a narrative of massacres.

Everywhere in the provinces fanatics began to renew the
old cry that the Indians were the Canaanites whom God had
commanded Joshua to destroy; and that these wars were a
token of God's displeasure with the Europeans for permitting
the "heathen" to live. Soon it became dangerous for a Moravian Indian to be seen anywhere. In vain did he carry one
of the Pennsylvania governor's passports in his pocket. He
was liable to be shot at sight, with no time to pull his passport
out. Even in the villages there was no safety. The devoted
congregations watched and listened night and day, not knowing at what hour they might hear the fatal warwhoop of hostile members of their own race, coming to slay them; or the
sudden shots of white settlers, coming to avenge on them outrages committed by savages hundreds of miles away.

With every report that arrived of Indian massacres at the
North, the fury of the white people all over the country rose
to greater height, including even Christian Indians in its unreasoning hatred. But, in the pious language of a narrative
written by one of the Moravian missionaries, "God inclined
the hearts of the chief magistrates to protect them. November 6th an express arrived from Philadelphia, bringing an or-

der that all the baptized Indians from Nain and Wechquetank should be brought to Philadelphia, and be protected in that city, having first delivered up their arms."

Two days later both these congregations set out on their sad journey, weeping as they left their homes. They joined forces at Bethlehem, on the banks of the Lecha, and "entered upon their pilgrimage in the name of the Lord, the congregation of Bethlehem standing spectators, and, as they passed, commending them to the grace and protection of God, with supplication and tears."

Four of the Moravian missionaries were with them, and some of the brethren from Bethlehem accompanied them all the way, "the sheriff, Mr. Jennings, caring for them as a father."

The aged, the sick, and the little children were carried in wagons. All the others, women and men, went on foot. The November rains had made the roads very heavy. As the weary and heart-broken people toiled slowly along through the mud, they were saluted with curses and abuse on all sides. As they passed through the streets of Germantown a mob gathered and followed them, taunting them with violent threats of burning, hanging, and other tortures. It was said that a party had been organized to make a serious attack on them, but was deterred by the darkness and the storm. Four days were consumed in this tedious march, and on the 11th of November they reached Philadelphia. Here, spite of the governor's positive order, the officers in command at the barracks refused to allow them to enter. From ten in the forenoon till three in the afternoon there the helpless creatures stood before the shut gate — messengers going back and forth between the defiant garrison and the bewildered and impotent governor; the mob, thickening and growing more and more riotous hour by hour, pressing the Indians on every side, jeering them, reviling them, charging them with all manner of outrages, and threatening to kill them on the spot. The missionaries, brave-ly standing beside their flock, in vain tried to stem or turn the torrent of insult and abuse. All that they accomplished was to draw down the same insult and abuse on their own heads.

Nothing but the Indians' marvellous patience and silence saved them from being murdered by this exasperated mob. To the worst insults they made no reply, no attempt at retaliation or defence. They afterward said that they had comforted themselves "by considering what insult and mockery our Saviour had suffered on their account."

At last, after five hours of this, the governor, unable to compel the garrison to open the barracks, sent an order that the Indians should be taken to Province Island, an island in the Delaware River joined to the main-land by a dam. Six miles more, every mile in risk of their lives, the poor creatures walked. As they passed again through the city, thousands followed them, the old record says, and "with such tumultuous clamor that they might truly be considered as sheep among wolves."

Long after dark they reached the island, and were lodged in some unused buildings, large and comfortless. There they kept their vesper service, and took heart from the fact that the verse for the day was that verse of the beautiful thirty-second psalm which has comforted so many perplexed souls: "I will teach thee in the way thou shalt go."

Here they settled themselves as best they could. The missionaries had their usual meetings with them, and humane people from Philadelphia, "especially some of the people called Quakers," sent them provisions and fuel, and tried in various ways to "render the inconvenience of their situation less grievous."

Before they had been here a month some of the villages they had left were burnt, and the riotous Paxton mob, which had murdered all the peaceful Conestoga Indians, announced its intention of marching on Province Island and killing every In-

dian there. The Governor of Pennsylvania launched proclamation after proclamation, forbidding any one, under severest
penalties, to molest the Indians under its protection, and offering a reward of two hundred pounds for the apprehension of
the ringleaders of the insurgents. But public sentiment was
inflamed to such a degree that the Government was practically powerless. The known ringleaders and their sympathiz-
ers paraded contemptuously in front of the governor's house,
mocking him derisively, and not even two hundred pounds
would tempt any man to attack them. In many parts of Lancaster County parties were organized with the avowed intention of marching on Philadelphia and slaughtering all the Indians under the protection of the Government. Late on the
29th of December rumors reached Philadelphia that a large
party of these rioters were on the road; and the governor, at
daybreak the next day, sent large boats to Province Island,
with orders to the missionaries to put their people on board as
quickly as possible, row to Leek Island, and await further orders. In confusion and terror the congregations obeyed, and
fled to Leek Island. Later in the day came a second letter
from the governor, telling them that the alarm had proved a
false one. They might return to Province Island, where he
would send them a guard; and that they would better keep
the boats, to be ready in case of a similar emergency.

"They immediately returned with joy to their former habi-
tation," says the old record, "comforted by the text for the
day—'The Lord is my strength and my shield; my heart
trusted in him' (Ps. xxviii., 7)—and closed this remarkable
year with prayer and thanksgiving for all the proofs of the
help of God in so many heavy trials."

Four days later the missionaries received a second order for
instant departure. The reports of the murderous intentions of
the rioters being confirmed, and the governor seeing only too
clearly his own powerlessness to contend with them, he had re-

solved to send the Indians northward, and put them under the
protection of the English army, and especially of Sir William
Johnson, agent for the Crown among the Northern Indians.
No time was to be lost in carrying out this plan, for at any moment the mob might attack Province Island.   Accordingly, at
midnight of January 4th, the fugitives set out once more, passed through Philadelphia, undiscovered, to the meeting-house
of the Moravian Brethren, where a breakfast had been provided for them.   Here they were met by the commissary, Mr.
Fox, who had been detailed by the governor to take charge of
their journey.   Mr. Fox, heart-stricken at their suffering appearance, immediately sent out and bought blankets to be distributed among them, as some protection against the cold.
Wagons were brought for the aged, sick, blind, little children,
and the heavy baggage; and again the pitiful procession took
up its march.   Again an angry mob gathered fast on its steps,
cursing and reviling in a terrible manner, only restrained by
fear from laying violent hands on them.   Except for the protection of a military escort they would scarcely have escaped
murderous assault.

At Amboy two sloops lay ready to transport them to New
York; but just as they reached this place, and were preparing
to go on shore, a messenger arrived from the Governor of
New York with angry orders that not an Indian should set
foot in that territory.   Even the ferry-men were forbidden,
under heavy penalties, to ferry one across the river.

The commissioner in charge of them, in great perplexity,
sent to the Governor of Pennsylvania for further orders, placing the Indians, meantime, in the Amboy barracks.   Here they
held their daily meetings, singing and praying with great unc-
tion, until finally many of their enemies were won to a hearty
respect and sympathy for them; even soldiers being heard to
say, " Would to God all the white people were as good Christians as these Indians."

The Pennsylvania governor had nothing left him to do but to order the Indians back again, and, accordingly, says the record, "The Indian congregation set out with cheerfulness on their return, in full confidence that the Lord in his good providence, for wise purposes best known to himself, had ordained their travelling thus to and fro. This belief supported them under all the difficulties they met with in their journeys made in the severest part of winter."

They made the return journey under a large military escort, one party in advance and one bringing up the rear. This escort was composed of soldiers, who, having just come from Niagara, where they had been engaged in many fights with the North-western savages, were at first disposed to treat these defenceless Indians with brutal cruelty; but they were soon disarmed by the Indians' gentle patience, and became cordial and friendly.

The return journey was a hard one. The aged and infirm people had become much weakened by their repeated hardships, and the little children suffered pitiably. In crossing some of the frozen rivers the feeble ones were obliged to crawl on their hands and feet on the ice.

On the 24th of January they reached Philadelphia, and were at once taken to the barracks, where almost immediately mobs began again to molest and threaten them. The governor, thoroughly in earnest now, and determined to sustain his own honor and that of the province, had eight heavy pieces of cannon mounted and a rampart thrown up in front of the barracks. The citizens were called to arms, and so great was the excitement that it is said even Quakers took guns and hurried to the barracks to defend the Indians; and the governor himself went at midnight to visit them, and reassure them by promises of protection.

On February 4th news was received that the rioters in large force were approaching the city. Hearing of the preparations made to receive them, they did not venture to enter. On the night of the 5th, however, they drew near again. The whole city was roused, church-bells rung, bonfires lighted, cannon fired, the inhabitants waked from their sleep and ordered to the town-house, where arms were given to all. Four more cannon were mounted at the barracks, and all that day was spent in hourly expectation of the rebels. But their brave boasts were not followed up by action. Seeing that the city was in arms against them, they halted. The governor then sent a delegation of citizens to ask them what they wanted.

They asserted, insolently, that there were among the Indians some who had committed murders, and that they must be given up. Some of the ringleaders were then taken into the barracks and asked to point out the murderers. Covered with confusion, they were obliged to admit they could not accuse one Indian there. They then charged the Quakers with having taken away six and concealed them. This also was disproved, and finally the excitement subsided.

All through the spring and summer the Indians remained prisoners in the barracks. Their situation became almost insupportable from confinement, unwholesome diet, and the mental depression inevitable in their state. To add to their misery small-pox broke out among them, and fifty-six died in the course of the summer from this loathsome disease.

"We cannot describe," said the missionaries, "the joy and fervent desire which most of them showed in the prospect of seeing their Saviour face to face. We saw with amazement the power of the blood of Jesus in the hearts of poor sinners." This was, no doubt, true; but there might well have entered into the poor, dying creatures' thoughts an ecstasy at the mere prospect of freedom, after a year of such imprisonment and suffering.

At last, on December 4th, the news of peace reached Philadelphia. On the 6th a proclamation was published in all the newspapers that war was ended and hostilities must cease. The joy with which the prisoned Indians received this news can hardly be conceived. It "exceeded all descriptions," says the record, and " was manifested in thanksgivings and praises to the Lord."

It was still unsafe, however, for them to return to their old homes, which were thickly surrounded by white settlers, who were no less hostile now at heart than they had been before the proclamation of peace. It was decided, therefore, that they should make a new settlement in the Indian country on the Susquehanna River. After a touching farewell to their old friends of the Bethlehem congregation, and a grateful leave-taking of the governor, who had protected and supported them for sixteen months, they set out on the 3d of April for their new home in the wilderness. For the third time their aged, sick, and little children were placed in overloaded wagons, for a long and difficult journey—a far harder one than any they had yet taken. The inhospitalities of the lonely wilderness were worse than the curses and revilings of riotous mobs. They were overtaken by severe snow-storms. They camped in icy swamps, shivering all night around smouldering fires of wet wood. To avoid still hostile whites they had to take great circuits through unbroken forests, where each foot of their path had to be cut tree by tree. The men waded streams and made rafts for the women and children. Sometimes, when the streams were deep, they had to go into camp, and wait till canoes could be built. They carried heavy loads of goods for which there was no room in the wagons. Going over high, steep hills, they often had to divide their loads into small parcels, thus doubling and trebling the road. Their provisions gave out. They ate the bitter wild potatoes. When the children cried with hunger, they peeled chestnut-trees, and gave them the sweet-juiced inner bark to suck. Often they had no water except that from shallow, muddy puddles. Once they

were environed by blazing woods, whose fires burnt fiercely for
hours around their encampment.   Several of the party died,
and were buried by the way.

"But all these trials were forgotten in their daily meetings,
in which the presence of the Lord was most sensibly and comfortably felt.   These were always held in the evening, around
a large fire, in the open air."

They celebrated a "joyful commemoration" of Easter, and
spent the Passion-week "in blessed contemplation" of the
sufferings of Jesus, whose "presence supported them under all
afflictions, insomuch that they never lost their cheerfulness
and resignation" during the five long weeks of this terrible
journey.

On the 9th of May they arrived at Machwihilusing, and
"forgot all their pain and trouble for joy that they had reached the place of their future abode. * * * With offers of praise
and thanksgiving, they devoted themselves anew to Him who
had given them rest for the soles of their feet."

"With renewed courage" they selected their home on the
banks of the Susquehanna, and proceeded to build houses.
They gave to the settlement the name of Friedenshutten—a
name full of significance, as coming from the hearts of these
persecuted wanderers : Friedenshutten—"Tents of Peace."

If all this persecution had fallen upon these Indians because
they were Christians, the record, piteous as it is, would be only
one out of thousands of records of the sufferings of Christian
martyrs, and would stir our sympathies less than many another.
But this was not the case.   It was simply because they were
Indians that the people demanded their lives, and would have
taken them, again and again, except that all the power of the
Government was enlisted for their protection.   The fact of
their being Christians did not enter in, one way or the other,
any more than did the fact that they were peaceable.   They
were Indians, and the frontiersmen of Pennsylvania intended

either to drive all Indians out of their State or kill them, just as the frontiersmen of Nebraska and of Colorado now intend to do if they can. We shall see whether the United States Government is as strong to-day as the Government of the Province of Pennsylvania was in 1763; or whether it will try first (and fail), as John Penn did, to push the helpless, hunted creatures off somewhere into a temporary makeshift of shelter, for a temporary deferring of the trouble of protecting them.

Sixteen years after the Conestoga massacre came that of Gnadenhütten, the blackest crime on the long list; a massacre whose equal for treachery and cruelty cannot be pointed out in the record of massacres of whites by Indians.

II.—*The Gnadenhütten Massacre.*

In the year 1779 the congregations of Moravian Indians living at Gnadenhütten, Salem, and Schonbrun, on the Muskingum River, were compelled by hostile Indians to forsake their villages and go northward to the Sandusky River. This movement was instigated by the English, who had become suspicious that the influence of the Moravian missionaries was thrown on the side of the colonies, and that their villages were safe centres of information and supplies. These Indians having taken no part whatever in the war, there was no pretext for open interference with them; but the English agents found it no difficult matter to stir up the hostile tribes to carry out their designs. And when the harassed congregations finally consented to move, the savages who escorted them were commanded by English officers.

"The savages drove them forward like cattle," says an old narrative; "the white brethren and sisters in the midst, surrounded by the believing Indians." "One morning, when the latter could not set out as expeditiously as the savages thought proper, they attacked the white brethren, and forced them to set out alone, whipping their horses forward till they grew wild, and not even allowing mothers time to suckle their children. The road was exceeding bad, leading through a continuance of swamps. Sister Zeisberger fell twice from her horse, and once, hanging in the stirrup, was dragged for some time; but assistance was soon at hand, and the Lord preserved her from harm. Some of the believing Indians followed them as fast as possible, but with all their exertions did not overtake them till night."

For one month these unfortunate people journeyed through the wilds in this way. When they reached the Sandusky Creek the savages left them to take care of themselves as best they might. They were over a hundred miles from their homes, "in a wilderness where there was neither game nor provisions." Here they built huts of logs and bark. They had neither beds nor blankets. In fact, the only things which the savages had left them were their utensils for making maple sugar. It was the middle of October when they reached Sandusky. Already it was cold, and the winter was drawing near. In November Governor De Peyster, the English commander at Fort Detroit, summoned the missionaries to appear before him and refute the accusations brought against their congregations of having aided and abetted the colonies.

"The missionaries answered that they doubted not in the least but that very evil reports must have reached his ears, as the treatment they had met with had sufficiently proved that they were considered as guilty persons, but that these reports were false. * * * That Congress, indeed, knew that they were employed as missionaries to the Indians, and did not disturb them in their labors; but had never in anything given them directions how to proceed."

The governor, convinced of the innocence and single-heartedness of these noble men, publicly declared that " he felt great satisfaction in their endeavors to civilize and Christianize the Indians, and would permit them to return to their congregations." He then gave them passports for their journey back to Sandusky, and appended a permission that they should perform the functions of their office among the Christian Indians without molestation.

This left them at rest so far as apprehensions of attack from hostile Indians were concerned; but there still remained the terrible apprehension of death by starvation and cold. Deep snows lay on the ground. Their hastily-built huts were so small that it was impossible to make large fires in them. Their floors being only the bare earth, whenever a thaw came the water forced itself up and then froze again. Cattle died for lack of food, and their carcasses were greedily devoured; nursing children died for want of nourishment from their starving mothers' breasts; the daily allowance of corn to each adult was one pint, and even this pittance it was found would not last till spring.

Nevertheless, "they celebrated the Christmas holidays with cheerfulness and blessing, and concluded this remarkable year with thanks and praise to Him who is ever the Saviour of his people. But, having neither bread nor wine, they could not keep the communion."

Meantime the corn still stood ungathered in their old fields on the Muskingum River. Weather-beaten, frozen, as it was, it would be still a priceless store to these starving people. The project of going back there after it began to be discussed. It was one hundred and twenty-five miles' journey; but food in abundance lay at the journey's end. Finally it was decided that the attempt should be made. Their first plan was to hide their families in the woods at some distance from the settlements lest there might be some danger from hostile whites. On their way, however, they were met by some of their brethren from Schonbrun, who advised them to go back openly into their deserted towns, assuring them that the Americans were friendly to them now. They accordingly did

so, and remained for several weeks at Salem and Gnadenhütten, working day and night gathering and husking the weather-beaten corn, and burying it in holes in the ground in the
woods for future supply. On the very day that they were to
have set off with their packs of corn, to return to their starving friends and relatives at Sandusky, a party of between one
and two hundred whites made their appearance at Gnadenhütten. Seeing the Indians scattered all through the cornfields, they rode up to them, expressing pleasure at seeing
them, and saying that they would take them into Pennsylvania, to a place where they would be out of all reach of persecution from the hostile savages or the English. They represented themselves as "friends and brothers, who had purposely come out to relieve them from the distress brought on them
on account of their being friends to the American people.
* * * The Christian Indians, not in the least doubting their
sincerity, walked up to them and thanked them for being so
kind ; while the whites again gave assurances that they would
meet with good treatment from them. They then advised
them to discontinue their work and cross over to the town, in
order to make necessary arrangements for the journey, as they
intended to take them out of the reach of their enemies, and
where they would be supplied abundantly with all they stood
in need of."

They proposed to take them to Pittsburg, where they
would be out of the way of any assault made by the English
or the savages. This the Indians heard, one of their missionaries writes, "with resignation, concluding that God would
perhaps choose this method to put an end to their sufferings.
Prepossessed with this idea, they cheerfully delivered their
guns, hatchets, and other weapons to the murderers, who promised to take good care of them, and in Pittsburg to return
every article to its rightful owner. Our Indians even showed
them all those things which they had secreted in the woods,

assisted in packing them up, and emptied all their beehives for these pretended friends."

In the mean time one of the assistants, John Martin by name, went to Salem, ten miles distant, and carried the good news that a party of whites had come from the settlements to carry them to a place of safety and give them protection. "The Salem Indians," says the same narrative, "did not hesitate to accept of this proposal, believing unanimously that God had sent the Americans to release them from their disagreeable situation at Sandusky, and imagining that when arrived at Pittsburg they might soon find a safe place to build a settlement, and easily procure advice and assistance from Bethlehem."

Some of the whites expressed a desire to see the village of Salem, were conducted thither, and received with much friendship by the Indians. On the way they entered into spiritual conversation with their unsuspecting companions, feigning great piety and discoursing on many religious and scriptural subjects. They offered also to assist the Salem Indians in moving their effects.

In the mean time the defenceless Indians at Gnadenhütten were suddenly attacked, driven together, bound with ropes, and confined. As soon as the Salem Indians arrived, they met with the same fate.

The murderers then held a council to decide what should be done with them. By a majority of votes it was decided to kill them all the next day. To the credit of humanity be it recorded, that there were in this band a few who remonstrated, declared that these Indians were innocent and harmless, and should be set at liberty, or, at least, given up to the Government as prisoners. Their remonstrances were unavailing, and, finding that they could not prevail on these monsters to spare the Indians' lives, "they wrung their hands, calling God to witness that they were innocent of the blood of these Christian Indians. They then withdrew to some distance from the scene of slaughter."

The majority were unmoved, and only disagreed as to the method of putting their victims to death. Some were for burning them alive; others for tomahawking and scalping them. The latter method was determined on, and a message was sent to the Indians that, "as they were Christian Indians, they might prepare themselves in a Christian manner, for they must all die to-morrow."

The rest of the narrative is best told in the words of the Moravian missionaries: "It may be easily conceived how great their terror was at hearing a sentence so unexpected. However, they soon recollected themselves, and patiently suffered the murderers to lead them into two houses, in one of which the brethren were confined and in the other the sisters and children. * * * Finding that all entreaties to save their lives were to no purpose, and that some, more blood-thirsty than others, were anxious to begin upon them, they united in begging a short delay, that they might prepare themselves for death, which request was granted them. Then asking pardon for whatever offence they had given, or grief they had occasioned to each other, they knelt down, offering fervent prayers to God their Saviour and kissing one another. Under a flood of tears, fully resigned to his will, they sung praises unto him, in the joyful hope that they would soon be relieved from all pains and join their Redeemer in everlasting bliss. * * * The murderers, impatient to make a beginning, came again to them while they were singing, and, inquiring whether they were now ready for dying, they were answered in the affirmative, adding that they had commended their immortal souls to God, who had given them the assurance in their hearts that he would receive their souls. One of the party, now taking up a cooper's mallet which lay in the house, saying, 'How exactly this will answer for the purpose,' began with Abraham, and continued knocking down one after another until he counted fourteen that he had killed with his own hands. He now handed the instrument to one of his fellow-murderers, saying : ' My arm fails me. Go on in the same way. I think I have done pretty well.' In another house, where mostly women and children were confined, Judith, a remarkably pious aged widow, was the first victim. After they had finished the horrid deed they retreated to a small distance from the slaughterhouses; but, after a while, returning again to view the dead bodies, and finding one of them (Abel), although scalped and mangled, attempting to raise himself from the floor, they so renewed their blows upon him that he never rose again. * * * Thus ninety-six persons magnified the name of the Lord by patiently meeting a cruel death. Sixty-two were grown persons and thirty-four children. Many of them were born of Christian parents in the society, and were among those who in the year 1763 were taken under the protection of the Pennsylvania Government at the time of the riots of the Paxton Boys. * * * Two boys, about fourteen years of age, almost miraculously escaped from this massacre. One of them was scalped and thrown down for dead. Recovering himself, he looked around ; but, with great presence of mind, lay down again quickly, feigning death. In a few moments he saw the murderers return, and again bury their hatchets in the head of Abel, who was attempting to rise, though scalped and terribly mangled. As soon as it was dark, Thomas crept over the dead bodies and escaped to the woods, where he hid himself till night. The other lad, who was confined in the house with the women, contrived unnoticed to slip through a trap-door into the cellar, where he lay concealed through the day, the blood all the while running down through the floor in streams. At dark he escaped through a small window and crept to the woods, where he encountered Thomas, and the two made their way together, after incredible hardships, to Sandusky. To describe the grief and terror of the Indian congregation on hearing that so large a number of its members was so cruelly massacred is impossible. Parents wept and mourned for the loss of their children, husbands for their wives, and wives for their husbands, children for their parents, sisters for brothers, and brothers for sisters. But they murmured not, nor did they call for vengeance on the murderers, but prayed for them. And their greatest consolation was a full assurance that all their beloved relatives were now at home in the presence of the Lord, and in full possession of everlasting happiness."

An account of this massacre was given in the *Pennsylvania Gazette*, of April 17th, 1782. It runs as follows :

"The people being greatly alarmed, and having received intelligence that the Indian towns on the Muskingum had not moved, as reported, a number of men, properly provided, collected and rendezvoused on the Ohio, opposite the Mingo Bottom, with a desire to surprise the above towns.

"One hundred men swam the river, and proceeded to the towns on the Muskingum, where the Indians had collected a large quantity of provisions to supply their war-parties. They arrived at the town in the night, undiscovered, attacked the Indians in their cabins, and so completely surprised them that they killed and scalped upward of ninety—but a few making their escape—about forty of whom were warriors, the rest old women and children. About eighty horses fell into their hands, which they loaded with the plunder, the greatest part furs and skins, and returned to the Ohio without the loss of a man."

III.—*Massacres of Apaches.*

In less than one hundred years from this Gnadenhütten massacre an officer of the United States Army, stationed at Camp Grant, in Arizona Territory, writes to his commanding officer the following letter :

"Camp Grant, Arizona Territory, May 17th, 1871.

"DEAR COLONEL,—Thanks for your kind letter of last week. If I could see you and have a long talk, and answer all your questions, I could come nearer giving you a clear idea of the history of the Indians at this post than by any written account. Having had them constantly under my observation for nearly three months, and the care of them constantly on my mind, certain things have become so much a matter of certainty to me that I am liable to forget the amount of evidence necessary to convince even the most unprejudiced mind that has not been brought in contact with them. I will, however, try and give you a connected account, and if it proves not sufficiently full in detail, you may be sure all its positive statements will be sustained by the testimony of all competent judges who have been at this post and cognizant of the facts.

"Sometime in February a party of five old women came in under a flag of truce, with a letter from Colonel Greene, saying they were in search of a boy, the son of one of the number taken prisoner near Salt River some months before. This boy had been well cared for, and had become attached to his new mode of life, and did not wish to return. The party were kindly treated, rationed while here, and after two days went away, asking permission to return. They came in about eight days, I think, with a still larger number, with some articles for sale, to purchase manta, as they were nearly naked. Before going away they said a young chief would like to come in with a party and have a talk. This I encouraged, and in a few days he came with about twenty-five of his band. He stated in brief that he was chief of a band of about one hundred and fifty of what were originally the Aravapa Apaches; that he wanted peace; that he and his people had no home, and could make none, as they were at all times apprehensive of the approach of the cavalry. I told him he should go to the White Mountains. He said, 'That is not our country, neither are they our people. We are at peace with them, but never have mixed with them. Our fathers and their fathers before them have lived in these mountains, and have raised corn in this valley. We are taught to make mescal, our principal article of food, and in summer and winter here we have a never-failing supply. At the White Mountains there is none, and without it now we get sick. Some of our people have been in at Goodwin, and for a short time at the White Mountains; but they are not contented, and they all say, " Let us go to the Aravapa and make a final peace, and never break it." '

"I told him I had no authority to make any treaty with him, or to promise him that he would be allowed a permanent home here, but that he could bring in his band, and I would feed them, and report his wishes to the Department commander. In the mean time runners had been in from two other small bands, asking the same privileges and giving the same reasons. I made the same reply to all, and by about the 11th of March I had over three hundred here. I wrote a detailed account of the whole matter, and sent it by express to Department Head-quarters, asking for instructions, having only the general policy of the Government in such cases for my guidance. After waiting more than six weeks my letter was returned to me without comment, except calling my attention to the fact that it, was not briefed properly. At first I put them in camp, about half a mile from the post, and counted them, and issued their rations every second day. The number steadily increased until it reached the number of five hundred and ten.

" Knowing, as I did, that the responsibility of the whole movement rested with me, and that, in case of any loss to the Government coming of it, I should be the sufferer, I kept them continually under my observation till I came not only to know the faces of the men, but of the women and children. They were nearly naked, and needed everything in the way of clothing. I stopped the Indians from bringing hay, that I might buy of these. I arranged a system of tickets with which to pay them and encourage them; and to be sure that they were properly treated, I personally attended to the weighing. I also made inquiries as to the kind of goods sold them, and prices. This proved a perfect success; not only the women and children engaged in the work, but the men. The amount furnished by them in about two months was nearly 300,000 pounds.

"During this time many small parties had been out with passes for a certain number of days to burn mescal. These parties were always mostly women, and I made myself sure by noting the size of the party, and from the amount of mescal brought in, that no treachery was intended. From the first I was determined to know not only all they did, but their hopes and intentions. For this purpose I spent hours each day with them in explaining to them the relations they should sustain to the Government, and their prospects for the future in case of either obedience or disobedience. I got from them in return much of their habits of thought and rules of action. I made it a point to tell them all they wished to know, and in the plainest and most positive manner. They were readily obedient, and remarkably quick of comprehension. They were happy and contented, and took every opportunity to show it. They had sent out runners to two other bands which were connected with them by intermarriages, and had received promises from them that they would come in and join them. I am confident, from all I have been able to learn, that but for this unlooked-for butchery, by this time we would have had one thousand persons, and at least two hundred and fifty able-bodied men. As their number increased and the weather grew warmer, they asked and obtained permission to move farther up the Aravapa to higher ground and plenty of water, and opposite to the ground they were proposing to plant. They were rationed every third day. Captain Stanwood arrived about the first of April, and took command of the post. He had received, while *en route*, verbal instructions from General Stoneman to recognize and feed any Indians he might find at the post as prisoners of war. After he had carefully inspected all things pertaining to their conduct and treatment, he concluded to make no changes, but had become so well satisfied of the integrity of their intentions that he left on the 24th with his whole troop for a long scout in the lower part of the Territory. The ranchmen in this vicinity were friendly and kind to them, and felt perfectly secure, and had agreed with me to employ them at a fair rate of pay to harvest their barley. The Indians seemed to have lost their characteristic anxiety to purchase ammunition, and had, in many instances, sold their best bows and arrows. I made frequent visits to their camp, and if any were absent from count, made it my business to know why.

" Such was the condition of things up to the morning of the 30th of April. They had so won on me that, from my first idea of treating them justly and honestly, as an officer of the army, I had come to feel a strong personal interest in helping to show them the way to a higher civilization. I had come to feel respect for men who, ignorant and naked, were still ashamed to lie or steal ; and for women who would work cheerfully like slaves to clothe themselves and children, but, untaught, held their virtue above price. Aware of the lies industriously circulated by the puerile press of the country, I was content to know I had positive proof they were so.

"I had ceased to have any fears of their leaving here, and only dreaded for them that they might be at any time ordered to do so. They frequently expressed anxiety to hear from the general, that they might have confidence to build for themselves better houses ; but would always say, 'You know what we want, and if you can't see him you can write, and do for us what you can.' It is possible that, during this time, individuals from here had visited other bands ; but that any number had ever been out to assist in any marauding expedition I know is false. Or the morning of April 30th I was at breakfast at 7.30 o'clock, when a despatch was brought to me by a sergeant of Company P, 21st Infantry, from Captain Penn, commanding Camp Lowell, informing me that a large party had left Tucson on the 28th with the avowed purpose of killing all the Indians at this post. I immediately sent the two interpreters, mounted, to the Indian camp, with orders to tell the chiefs the exact state of things, and for them to bring their entire party inside the post. As I had no cavalry, and but about fifty infantry (all recruits), and no other officer, I could not leave the post to go to their defence. My messengers returned in about an hour with intelligence that they could find no living Indians.

"Their camp was burning, and the ground strewed with their dead and mutilated women and children. I immediately mounted a party of about twenty soldiers and citizens, and sent them with the post surgeon with a wagon to bring in the wounded, if any could be found. The party returned late in the afternoon, having found no wounded, and without having been able to communicate with any of the survivors. Early the next morning I took a similar party with spades and shovels, and went out and buried the dead immediately in and about the camp. I had, the day before, offered the interpreters, or any one who would do so, $100 to go to the mountains and communicate with them, and convince them that no officer or soldier of the United States Government had been concerned in the vile transaction; and, failing in this, I thought the act of caring for their dead would be an evidence to them of our sympathy, at least, and the conjecture proved correct; for while we were at the work, many of them came to the spot and indulged in expressions of grief too wild and terrible to be described.

"That evening they began to come in from all directions, singly and in small parties, so changed as hardly to be recognizable in the forty-eight hours during which they had neither eaten

nor slept. Many of the men, whose families had all been killed,
when I spoke to them and expressed sympathy for them, were
obliged to turn away, unable to speak, and too proud to show
their grief. The women whose children had been killed or
stolen were convulsed with grief, and looked to me appealingly,
as if I were their last hope on earth. Children, who two days
before had been full of frolic, kept at a distance, expressing
wondering horror.

"I did what I could : I fed them, talked to them, and listened patiently to their accounts. I sent horses to the mountains to bring in two badly wounded women, one shot through
the left leg, one with an arm shattered. These were attended
to, and are doing well, and will recover.

"Their camp was surrounded and attacked at daybreak.
So sudden and unexpected was it, that I found a number of
women shot while asleep beside their bundles of hay, which
they had collected to bring in on that morning. The wounded
who were unable to get away had their brains beaten out
with clubs or stones, while some were shot full of arrows after
having been mortally wounded by gun-shots. The bodies were
all stripped. Of the number buried, one was an old man, and
one was a well-grown boy ; all the rest women and children.
Of the whole number killed and missing—about one hundred
and twenty-five—only eight were men. It has been said that
the men were not there : they were all there. On the 28th
we counted one hundred and twenty-eight men, a small number being absent for mescal, all of whom have since been in.
I have spent a good deal of time with them since the affair,
and have been astonished at their continued unshaken faith in
me, and their perfectly clear understanding of their misfortune. They say, ' We know there are a great many white men
and Mexicans who do not wish us to live at peace. We know
that the Papagos would never have come out against us at
this time unless they had been persuaded to do so.' What

they do not understand is, while they are at peace and are conscious of no wrong intent, that they should be murdered.

"One of the chiefs said : 'I no longer want to live ; my women and children have been killed before my face, and I have been unable to defend them. Most Indians in my place would take a knife and cut their throats ; but I will live to show these people that all they have done, and all they can do, shall not make me break faith with you so long as you will stand by us and defend us, in a language we know nothing of, to a great governor we never have and never shall see.'

"About their captives they say : 'Get them back for us. Our little boys will grow up slaves, and our girls, as soon as they are large enough, will be diseased prostitutes, to get money for whoever owns them. Our women work hard, and are good women, and they and our children have no diseases. Our dead you cannot bring to life ; but those that are living we gave to you, and we look to you, who can write and talk and have soldiers, to get them back.'

"I assure you it is no easy task to convince them of my zeal when they see so little being done. I have pledged my word to them that I never would rest, day or night, until they should have justice, and just now I would as soon leave the army as to be ordered away from them, or be obliged to order them away from here. But you well know the difficulties in the way. You know that parties who would engage in murder like this could and would make statements and multiply affidavits without end in their justification. I know you will use your influence on the right side. I believe, with them, this may be made either a means of making good citizens of them and their children, or of driving them out to a hopeless war of extermination. They ask to be allowed to live here in their old homes, where nature supplies nearly all their wants. They ask for a fair and impartial trial of their faith, and they ask that all their captive childen may be returned to them. Is their demand unreasonable ? "

This letter was written to Colonel T. G. C. Lee, U.S.A., by Lieut. Royal E. Whitman, 3d U.S. Cavalry. It is published in the Report of the Board of Indian Commissioners for 1871. There is appended to it the following affidavit of the post surgeon at Camp Grant :

" On this 16th day of September, 1871, personally appeared Conant B. Brierley, who, being duly sworn according to law, deposeth and saith : ' I am acting-assistant surgeon, U.S.A., at Camp Grant, Arizona, where I arrived April 25th, 1871, and reported to the commanding officer for duty as medical officer. Some four hundred Apache Indians were at that time held as prisoners of war by the military stationed at Camp Grant, and during the period intervening between April 25th and 30th I saw the Indians every day. They seemed very well contented, and were busily employed in bringing in hay, which they sold for manta and such little articles as they desired outside the Government ration. April 29th Chiquita and some of the other chiefs were at the post, and asked for seeds and for some hoes, stating that they had ground cleared and ready for planting. They were told that the garden-seeds had been sent for, and would be up from Tucson in a few days. They then left, and I saw nothing more of them until after the killing.

" ' Sunday morning I heard a rumor that the Indians had been attacked, and learned from Lieutenant Whitman that he had sent the two interpreters to the Indian camp to warn the Indians, and bring them down where they could be protected, if possible. The interpreters returned and stated that the attack had already been made and the Indians dispersed, and that the attacking party were returning.

" ' Lieutenant Whitman then ordered me to go to the Indian camp to render medical assistance, and bring down any wounded I might find. I took twelve men and a wagon, and proceeded without delay to the scene of the murder. On my arrival I found that I should have but little use for the wagon or medicine. The work had been too thoroughly done. The camp had been fired, and the dead bodies of twenty-one women and children were lying scattered over the ground; those who had been wounded in the first instance had their brains beaten out with stones. Two of the squaws had been first ravished, and then shot dead. One infant of some two months was shot twice, and one leg nearly hacked off. * * * I know from my own personal observations that, during the time the Indians were in, after my arrival, they were rationed every three days, and Indians absent had to be accounted for; their faces soon became familiar to me, and I could at once tell when any strange Indian came in.

"'And I furthermore state that I have been among nearly all the tribes on the Pacific coast, and that I have never seen any Indians who showed the intelligence, honesty, and desire to learn manifested by these Indians. I came among them greatly prejudiced against them; but, after being with them, I was compelled to admit that they were honest in their intentions, and really desired peace.

"'C. B. BRIERLEY,
"'Acting Assistant Surgeon, U.S.A.'"

This is not the only instance of cruel outrage committed by white men on the Apaches. In the Report of the Board of Indian Commissioners for 1871 is the following letter from one of the Arizona pioneers, Mr. J. H. Lyman, of Northampton, Mass. Mr. Lyman spent the years of 1840–'41 among the Apaches, and thus briefly relates an occurrence which took place at a time when they were friendly and cordial to all Americans going among them:

"The Indians were then, as now, hostile to the Mexicans of Sonora, and they were constantly making raids into the State and driving off the cattle. The Mexicans feared them, and were unable to meet them man to man. At that time American trappers found the beaver very abundant about the head-waters of the Gila River, among those rich mountain valleys where the Apaches had, and still have, their secure retreats. At the time I speak of there were two companies of trappers in that region. One of the companies, about seventeen men, was under a captain named Johnson. The other company consisted of thirty men, I think. I was trapping on another head of the Gila, several miles north. The valleys were full of Apaches, but all peaceful toward the white men, both Indians and whites visiting each other's camps constantly and fearlessly, with no thought of treachery or evil. Besides the Mexicans, the only enemies of the Apaches were the Piutes and Navajoes, in the north-west. But here in their fastnesses they felt safe from all foes.

"One day Johnson concluded to go down into Sonora on a spree, as was occasionally the way with mountain-men. He there saw the Governor of Sonora, who, knowing that he had the confidence of the Indians, offered him an ounce of gold for every Apache scalp he would bring him. The bargain was struck. Johnson procured a small mountain howitzer, and then, with supplies for his party, returned to his camp. Previous to entering it he loaded his howitzer with a quantity of bullets. On approaching the valley he was met by the Indians, who joyfully welcomed him back, and proceeded at once to prepare the usual feast. While they were boiling and roasting their venison and bear meat, and were gathered in a small group around the fire, laughing and chatting in anticipation of the pleasure they expected in entertaining their guests, Johnson told those of his party who had remained behind of the offer of the governor, and with such details of temptation as easily overcame any scruples such men might have.

"As they were all armed with rifles, which were always in

hand day and night, together with pistols in belt, they needed no preparation. The howitzer, which the Indians might have supposed to be a small keg of whiskey, was placed on the ground and pointed at the group of warriors, squaws, and little children round the fire, watching the roasting meal.

"While they were thus engaged, with hearts full of kindly feelings toward their white friends, Johnson gave the signal. The howitzer was discharged, sending its load of bullets scattering and tearing through the mass of miserable human beings, and nearly all who were not stricken down were shot by the rifles. A very few succeeded in escaping into the ravine, and fled over the dividing ridge into the northern valleys, where they met others of their tribe, to whom they told the horrible story.

"The Apaches at once showed that they could imitate their more civilized brothers. Immediately a band of them went in search of the other company of trappers, who, of course, were utterly unconscious of Johnson's infernal work. They were attacked, unprepared, and nearly all killed ; and then the story that the Apaches were treacherous and cruel went forth into all the land, but nothing of the wrongs they had received."

Is it to be wondered at that the Apaches became one of the most hostile and dangerous tribes on the Pacific coast?

These are but four massacres out of scores, whose history, if written, would prove as clearly as do these, that, in the long contest between white men and Indians, the Indian has not always been the aggressor, and that treachery and cruelty are by no means exclusively Indian traits.

CHAPTER X.

CONCLUSION.

THERE are within the limits of the United States between two hundred and fifty and three hundred thousand Indians, exclusive of those in Alaska. The names of the different tribes and bands, as entered in the statistical tables of the Indian Office Reports, number nearly three hundred. One of the most careful estimates which have been made of their numbers and localities gives them as follows : " In Minnesota and States east of the Mississippi, about 32,500 ; in Nebraska, Kansas, and the Indian Territory, 70,650 ; in the Territories of Dakota, Montana, Wyoming, and Idaho, 65,000 ; in Nevada and the Territories of Colorado, New Mexico, Utah, and Arizona, 84,000 ; and on the Pacific slope, 48,000."

Of these, 130,000 are self-supporting on their own reservations, "receiving nothing from the Government except interest on their own moneys, or annuities granted them in consideration of the cession of their lands to the United States." *

This fact alone would seem sufficient to dispose forever of the accusation, so persistently brought against the Indian, that he will not work.

Of the remainder, 84,000 are partially supported by the Government—the interest money due them and their annuities, as provided by treaty, being inadequate to their subsistence on the reservations where they are confined. In many cases, however, these Indians furnish a large part of their sup-

---

* Annual Report of Indian Commissioner for 1872.

port—the White River Utes, for instance, who are reported by the Indian Bureau as getting sixty-six per cent. of their living by "root-digging, hunting, and fishing;" the Squaxin band, in Washington Territory, as earning seventy-five per cent., and the Chippewas of Lake Superior as earning fifty per cent. in the same way.   These facts also would seem to dispose of the accusation that the Indian will not work.

There are about 55,000 who never visit an agency, over whom the Government does not pretend to have either control or care.   These 55,000 "subsist by hunting, fishing, on roots, nuts, berries, etc., and by begging and stealing ;" and this also seems to dispose of the accusation that the Indian will not "work for a living."   There remains a small portion, about 31,000, that are entirely subsisted by the Government.

There is not among these three hundred bands of Indians one which has not suffered cruelly at the hands either of the Government or of white settlers.   The poorer, the more insignificant, the more helpless the band, the more certain the cruelty and outrage to which they have been subjected.   This is especially true of the bands on the Pacific slope.   These Indians found themselves of a sudden surrounded by and caught up in the great influx of gold-seeking settlers, as helpless creatures on a shore are caught up in a tidal wave.   There was not time for the Government to make treaties ; not even time for communities to make laws.   The tale of the wrongs, the oppressions, the murders of the Pacific-slope Indians in the last thirty years would be a volume by itself, and is too monstrous to be believed.

It makes little difference, however, where one opens the record of the history of the Indians ; every page and every year has its dark stain.   The story of one tribe is the story of all, varied only by differences of time and place ; but neither time nor place makes any difference in the main facts.   Colorado is as greedy and unjust in 1880 as was Georgia in 1830, and Ohio

in 1795 ; and the United States Government breaks promises
now as deftly as then, and with an added ingenuity from long
practice.

One of its strongest supports in so doing is the wide-spread
sentiment among the people of dislike to the Indian, of impatience with his presence as a "barrier to civilization," and distrust of it as a possible danger. The old tales of the frontier
life, with its horrors of Indian warfare, have gradually, by two
or three generations' telling, produced in the average mind
something like an hereditary instinct of unquestioning and unreasoning aversion which it is almost impossible to dislodge or
soften.

There are hundreds of pages of unimpeachable testimony on
the side of the Indian ; but it goes for nothing, is set down as
sentimentalism or partisanship, tossed aside and forgotten.

President after president has appointed commission after
commission to inquire into and report upon Indian affairs, and
to make suggestions as to the best methods of managing them.
The reports are filled with eloquent statements of wrongs done
to the Indians, of perfidies on the part of the Government ;
they counsel, as earnestly as words can, a trial of the simple
and unperplexing expedients of telling truth, keeping promises, making fair bargains, dealing justly in all ways and all
things. These reports are bound up with the Government's Annual Reports, and that is the end of them. It would probably
be no exaggeration to say that not one American citizen out of
ten thousand ever sees them or knows that they exist, and yet
any one of them, circulated throughout the country, read by
the right-thinking, right-feeling men and women of this land,
would be of itself a "campaign document" that would ini-
tiate a revolution which would not subside until the Indians'
wrongs were, so far as is now left possible, righted.

In 1869 President Grant appointed a commission of nine
men, representing the influence and philanthropy of six leading

States, to visit the different Indian reservations, and to "examine all matters appertaining to Indian affairs."

In the report of this commission are such paragraphs as the following: "To assert that 'the Indian will not work' is as true as it would be to say that the white man will not work.

"Why should the Indian be expected to plant corn, fence lands, build houses, or do anything but get food from day to day, when experience has taught him that the product of his labor will be seized by the white man to-morrow? The most industrious white man would become a drone under similar circumstances. Nevertheless, many of the Indians" (the commissioners might more forcibly have said 130,000 of the Indians) "are already at work, and furnish ample refutation of the assertion that 'the Indian will not work.' There is no escape from the inexorable logic of facts.

"The history of the Government connections with the Indians is a shameful record of broken treaties and unfulfilled promises. The history of the border white man's connection with the Indians is a sickening record of murder, outrage, robbery, and wrongs committed by the former, as the rule, and occasional savage outbreaks and unspeakably barbarous deeds of retaliation by the latter, as the exception.

"Taught by the Government that they had rights entitled to respect, when those rights have been assailed by the rapacity of the white man, the arm which should have been raised to protect them has ever been ready to sustain the aggressor.

"The testimony of some of the highest military officers of the United States is on record to the effect that, in our Indian wars, almost without exception, the first aggressions have been made by the white man; and the assertion is supported by every civilian of reputation who has studied the subject. In addition to the class of robbers and outlaws who find impunity in their nefarious pursuits on the frontiers, there is a large class of professedly reputable men who use every means in their power to bring on Indian wars for the sake of the profit to be realized from the presence of troops and the expenditure of Government funds in their midst. They proclaim death to the Indians at all times in words and publications, making no distinction between the innocent and the guilty. They irate the lowest class of men to the perpetration of the darkest deeds against their victims, and as judges and jurymen shield them from the justice due to their crimes. Every crime committed by a white man against an Indian is concealed or palliated. Every offence committed by an Indian against a white man is borne on the wings of the post or the telegraph to the remotest corner of the land, clothed with all the horrors which the reality or imagination can throw around it. Against such influences as these the people of the United States need to be warned."

To assume that it would be easy, or by any one sudden stroke of legislative policy possible, to undo the mischief and hurt of the long past, set the Indian policy of the country right for the future, and make the Indians at once safe and happy, is the blunder of a hasty and uninformed judgment. The notion which seems to be growing more prevalent, that simply to make all Indians at once citizens of the United States would be a sovereign and instantaneous panacea for all their ills and all the Government's perplexities, is a very inconsiderate one. To administer complete citizenship of a sudden, all round, to all Indians, barbarous and civilized alike, would be as grotesque a blunder as to dose them all round with any one medicine, irrespective of the symptoms and needs of their diseases. It would kill more than it would cure. Nevertheless, it is true, as was well stated by one of the superintendents of Indian Affairs in 1857, that, "so long as they are not citizens of the United States, their rights of property must remain insecure against invasion. The doors of the federal tribunals being barred against them while wards and dependents, they can only partially exercise the rights of free government, or give to those who make, execute, and construe the few laws they are allowed to enact, dignity sufficient to make them respectable. While they continue individually to gather the crumbs that fall from the table of the United States, idleness, improvidence, and indebtedness will be the rule, and industry, thrift, and freedom from debt the exception. The utter absence of individual title to particular lands deprives every one among them of the chief incentive to labor and exertion—the very mainspring on which the prosperity of a people depends."

All judicious plans and measures for their safety and salvation must embody provisions for their becoming citizens as fast as they are fit, and must protect them till then in every right and particular in which our laws protect other "persons" who are not citizens.

There is a disposition in a certain class of minds to be impatient with any protestation against wrong which is unaccompanied or unprepared with a quick and exact scheme of remedy. This is illogical. When pioneers in a new country find a tract of poisonous and swampy wilderness to be reclaimed, they do not withhold their hands from fire and axe till they see clearly which way roads should run, where good water will spring, and what crops will best grow on the redeemed land. They first clear the swamp. So with this poisonous and baffling part of the domain of our national affairs—let us first "clear the swamp."

However great perplexity and difficulty there may be in the details of any and every plan possible for doing at this late day anything like justice to the Indian, however hard it may be for good statesmen and good men to agree upon the things that ought to be done, there certainly is, or ought to be, no perplexity whatever, no difficulty whatever, in agreeing upon certain things that ought not to be done, and which must cease to be done before the first steps can be taken toward righting the wrongs, curing the ills, and wiping out the disgrace to us of the present condition of our Indians.

Cheating, robbing, breaking promises—these three are clearly things which must cease to be done. One more thing, also, and that is the refusal of the protection of the law to the Indian's rights of property, "of life, liberty, and the pursuit of happiness."

When these four things have ceased to be done, time, statesmanship, philanthropy, and Christianity can slowly and surely do the rest. Till these four things have ceased to be done, statesmanship and philanthropy alike must work in vain, and even Christianity can reap but small harvest.

APPENDIX.

I.

THE SAND CREEK MASSACRE.

THE following letters were printed in the *New York Tribune* in the winter of 1879. They are of interest, not only as giving a minute account of one of the most atrocious massacres ever perpetrated, but also as showing the sense of justice which is to be found in the frontiersman's mind to-day. That men, exasperated by atrocities and outrages, should have avenged themselves with hot haste and cruelty, was, perhaps, only human; but that men should be found, fifteen years later, apologizing for, nay, justifying the cruel deed, is indeed a matter of marvel.

LETTER I.

In June, 1864, Governor Evans, of Colorado, sent out a circular to the Indians of the Plains, inviting all friendly Indians to come into the neighborhood of the forts, and be protected by the United States troops. Hostilities and depredations had been committed by some bands of Indians, and the Government was about to make war upon them. This circular says:

"In some instances they (the Indians) have attacked and killed soldiers, and murdered peaceable citizens. For this the Great Father is angry, and will certainly hunt them out and punish them; but he does not want to injure those who remain friendly to the whites. He desires to protect and take care of them. For this purpose I direct that all friendly Indians keep away from those who are at war, and go to places of safety. Friendly Arapahoes and Cheyennes belonging to the Arkansas River will go to Major Colby, United States Agent at Fort Lyon, who will give them provisions and show them a place of safety."

In consequence of this proclamation of the governor, a band of

Cheyennes, several hundred in number, came in and settled down near Fort Lyon. After a time they were requested to move to Sand Creek, about forty miles from Fort Lyon, where they were still guaranteed " perfect safety " and the protection of the Government. Rations of food were issued to them from time to time. On the 27th of November, Colonel J. M. Chivington, a member of the Methodist Episcopal Church in Denver, and Colonel of the First Colorado Cavalry, led his regiment by a forced march to Fort Lyon, induced some of the United States troops to join him, and fell upon this camp of friendly Indians at daybreak. The chief, White Antelope, always known as friendly to the whites, came running toward the soldiers, holding up his hands and crying " Stop! stop! " in English. When he saw that there was no mistake, that it was a deliberate attack, he folded his arms and waited till he was shot down. The United States flag was floating over the lodge of Black Kettle, the head chief of the tribe; below it was tied also a small white flag as additional security—a precaution Black Kettle had been advised by United States officers to take if he met troops on the Plains. In Major Wynkoop's testimony, given before the committee appointed by Congress to investigate this massacre, is the following passage:

" Women and children were killed and scalped, children shot at their mothers' breasts, and all the bodies mutilated in the most horrible manner. * * * The dead bodies of females profaned in such a manner that the recital is sickening, Colonel J. M. Chivington all the time inciting his troops to their diabolical outrages."

Another man testified as to what he saw on the 30th of November, three days after the battle, as follows :

" I saw a man dismount from his horse and cut the ear from the body of an Indian, and the scalp from the head of another. I saw a number of children killed ; they had bullet-holes in them ; one child had been cut with some sharp instrument across its side. I saw another that both ears had been cut off. * * * I saw several of the Third Regiment cut off fingers to get the rings off them. I saw Major Sayre scalp a dead Indian. The scalp had a long tail of silver hanging to it."

Robert Bent testified :

" I saw one squaw lying on the bank, whose leg had been broken. A soldier came up to her with a drawn sabre. She raised her arm to protect herself ; he struck, breaking her arm. She rolled over, and raised her other arm; he struck, breaking that, and then left her without killing her. I saw one squaw cut open, with an unborn child lying by her side."

Major Anthony testified :

" There was one little child, probably three years old, just big enough to walk through the sand. The Indians had gone ahead, and this little child was behind, following after them. The little fellow was perfectly naked, travelling in the sand. I saw one man get off his horse at a distance of about seventy-five yards and draw up his rifle and fire. He missed the child. Another man came up and said, ' Let me try the son of a b—. I can hit him.' He got down off his horse, kneeled down, and fired at the little child, but he missed him. A third man came up, and made a similar remark, and fired, and the little fellow dropped."

The Indians were not able to make much resistance, as only a part of them were armed, the United States officers having required them to give up their guns. Luckily they had kept a few.

When this Colorado regiment of demons returned to Denver they were greeted with an ovation. *The Denver News* said : " All acquitted themselves well. Colorado soldiers have again covered themselves with glory; " and at a theatrical performance given in the city, these scalps taken from Indians were held up and exhibited to the audience, which applauded rapturously.

After listening, day after day, to such testimonies as these I have quoted, and others so much worse that I may not write and *The Tribune* could not print the words needful to tell them, the committee reported: " It is difficult to believe that beings in the form of men, and disgracing the uniform of United States soldiers and officers, could commit or countenance the commission of such acts of cruelty and barbarity; " and of Colonel Chivington: " He deliberately planned and executed a foul and dastardly massacre, which would have disgraced the veriest savage among those who were the victims of his cruelty."

This was just fifteen years ago, no more. Shall we apply the same rule of judgment to the white men of Colorado that the Government is now applying to the Utes? There are 130,000 inhabitants of Colorado; hundreds of them had a hand in this massacre, and thousands in cool blood applauded it when it was done. There are 4000 Utes in Colorado. Twelve of them, desperate, guilty men, have committed murder and rape, and three or four hundred of them did, in the convenient phrase of our diplomacy, " go to war against the Government; " *i. e.*, they attempted, by force of arms, to restrain the entrance upon their own lands—lands bought, owned and paid for—of soldiers that the Government had sent there, to be ready to make war upon them, in case the agent thought it best to do so! This is the plain English of it. This is the plain, naked truth of it.

And now the Secretary of the Interior has stopped the issue of rations to 1000 of these helpless creatures; rations, be it understood, which are not, and never were, a charity, but are the Utes' rightful dues, on account of lands by them sold; dues which the Government promised to pay "annually forever." Will the American people justify this? There is such a thing as the conscience of a nation—as a nation's sense of justice. Can it not be roused to speak now? Shall we sit still, warm and well fed, in our homes, while five hundred women and little children are being slowly starved in the bleak, barren wildernesses of Colorado? Starved, not because storm, or blight, or drouth has visited their country and cut off their crops; not because pestilence has laid its hand on them and slain the hunters who brought them meat, but because it lies within the promise of one man, by one word, to deprive them of one-half their necessary food for as long a term of years as he may please; and " the Secretary of the Interior cannot consistently feed a tribe that has gone to war against the Government."

We read in the statutes of the United States that certain things may be done by " executive order " of the President. Is it not time for a President to interfere when hundreds of women and children are being starved in his Republic by the order of one man ? Colonel J. M. Chivington's method was less inhuman by far. To be shot dead is a mercy, and a grace for which we would all sue, if to be starved to death were our only other alternative.

New York, Jan. 31st, 1880.   H. H.

This letter drew from the former editor of the *Rocky Mountain News*, a Denver newspaper, the following reply :

LETTER II.

To the Editor of the Tribune:

Sir,—In your edition of yesterday appears an article, under the above caption, which arraigns the people of Colorado as a community of barbarous murderers, and finally elevates them above the present Secretary of the Interior, thereby placing the latter gentleman in a most unenviable light if the charges averred be true. " The Sand Creek Massacre " of 1864 is made the text and burden of the article; its application is to the present condition of the White River band of Utes in Colorado. Quotations are given from the testimony gathered, and the report made thereon by a committee of Congress charged with a so-called investigation of the Sand Creek affair. That investigation was made for a certain selfish purpose. It was to break down and ruin certain men. Evidence was taken upon one side only. It was largely false, and infamously partial. There was no answer for the defence.

The Cheyenne and Arapahoe Indians assembled at Sand Creek were not under the protection of a United States fort. A few of them had been encamped about Fort Lyon and drawing supplies therefrom, but they had gradually disappeared and joined the main camp on Dry Sandy, forty miles from the fort, separated from it by a waterless desert, and entirely beyond the limit of its control or observation. While some of the occupants were still, no doubt, occasional visitors at the fort, and applicants for supplies and ammunition, most of the warriors were engaged in raiding the great Platte River Road, seventy-five miles farther north, robbing and burning trains, stealing cattle and horses, robbing and destroying the United States mails, and killing white people. During the summer and fall they had murdered over fifty of the citizens of Colorado. They had stolen and destroyed provisions and merchandise, and driven away stock worth hundreds of thousands of dollars. They had interrupted the mails, and for thirty-two consecutive days none were allowed to pass their lines. When satiated with murder and arson, and loaded with plunder, they would retire to their sacred refuge on Sand Creek to rest and refresh themselves, recruit their wasted supplies of ammunition from Fort Lyon—begged under the garb of gentle, peaceful savages—and then return to the road to relieve their tired comrades, and riot again in carnage and robbery. These are facts; and when the "robbers' roost" was cleaned out, on that sad but glorious 27th day of November, 1864, they were sufficiently proven. Scalps of white men not yet dried; letters and photographs stolen from the mails; bills of lading and invoices of goods; bales and bolts of the goods themselves, addressed to merchants in Denver; half-worn clothing of white women and children, and many other articles of like character, were found in that poetical Indian camp, and recovered by the Colorado soldiers. They were brought to Denver, and those were the scalps exhibited in the theatre of that city. There was also an Indian saddle-blanket entirely fringed around the edges with white women's scalps, with the long, fair hair attached. There was an Indian saddle over the pommel of which was stretched skin stripped from the body of a white woman. Is it any wonder that soldiers flushed with victory, after one of the hardest campaigns ever endured by men, should indulge — some of them — in unwarranted atrocities after finding such evidence of barbarism, and while more than forty of their comrades were weltering in their own blood upon the field?

If "H. H." had been in Denver in the early part of that summer, when the bloated, festering bodies of the Hungate family—father, mother, and two babes—were drawn through the streets naked in an ox-wagon, cut, mutilated, and scalped—the work of those same red fiends who were so justly punished at Sand Creek; if, later, "H. H." had seen an upright and most estimable business man go crazy over the news of his son's being tortured to death a hundred miles down the Platte, as I did; if "H. H." had seen one-half the Colorado homes made desolate that fateful season, and a tithe of the tears that were caused to flow, I think there would have been one little word of excuse for the people of Colorado—more than a doubtful comparison with an inefficient and culpable Indian policy. Bear in mind that Colorado had no railroads then. Her supplies reached her by only one road—along the Platte—in wagons drawn by oxen, mules, or horses. That line was in full possession of the enemy. Starvation stared us in the face. Hardly a party went or came without some persons being killed. In some instances whole trains were cut off and destroyed. Sand Creek saved Colorado, and taught the Indians the most salutary lesson they had ever learned. And now, after fifteen years, and here in the shadow of the Nation's Capitol, with the spectre of "H. H.'s" condemnation staring me in the face, I am neither afraid nor ashamed to repeat the language then used by *The Denver News:* "All acquitted themselves well. Colorado soldiers have again covered themselves with glory."

Thus much of history is gone over by "H. H." to present in true dramatic form the deplorable condition of the White River Utes, 1000 in number, who are now suffering the pangs of hunger and the discomfort of cold in the wilds of Western Colorado, without any kind agent to issue rations, provide blankets, or build fires for them. It is really too bad. A painful dispensation of Providence has deprived them of their best friend, and they are desolate and bereaved. He placed his life and its best efforts, his unbounded enthusiasm for their good, his great Christian heart—all at their service. But an accident befell him, and he is no more. The coroner's jury that sat upon his remains found that his dead body had a barrel stave driven into his mouth, a log-chain around his neck, by which it had been dragged about like a dead hog, and sundry bullet-holes through his body. The presumption was that from the effect of some one of these accidents he died; and, alas! he is no longer to serve out weekly rations to his flock of gentle Utes. There is no sorrow over his death or the desolation it wrought, but there is pity, oceans of pity, for the Indians who are hungry and cold. True, at the time he died they took the flour, the pork, and salt, and coffee, and sugar, and tobacco, and blankets, and all the other supplies that he would have issued to them through all this long winter had he lived. With his care these would have lasted until spring, and been sufficient for their wants; but, without it, "H. H." is suspicious that they are all gone, and yet it is but just past the middle of winter. Can "H. H." tell why this is thus? It is also true that they drove away the large herd of cattle from the increase of which that same unfortunate agent and his predecessors had supplied them with beef for eleven years past, and yet the consumption did not keep pace with the natural increase. They took them all, and are presumed to have them now. True, again, they had at the beginning of winter, or at the period of the melancholy loss of their best friend, about 4000 horses that were rolling fat, and three acres of dogs—not bad food in an emergency, or for an Indian thanksgiving feast—some of which should still remain.

THE WHOLE WHITE RIVER BAND GUILTY.

But "H. H." intimates that there is an alleged excuse for withholding rations from these poor, persecuted red angels. "Twelve" of them have been bad, and the tyrant at the head of the Interior Department is systematically starving all of the 1000 who constitute the band, and their 4000 horses, and 1800 cattle, and three acres of dogs, and six months' supplies, because those twelve bad Indians cannot conscientiously pick themselves out and be offered up as a burnt-offering and a sacrifice to appease the wrath of an outraged and partly civilized nation. This is the present indictment, and the Secretary and the President are commanded to stand up and plead "Guilty or not guilty, but you know you are guilty, d—n you." Now I challenge and defy "H. H.," or any

other person living, to pick out or name twelve White River male
Utes, over sixteen years of age, who were *not* guilty, directly or
indirectly, as principals or accomplices before the fact, in the
Thornburgh attack or in the Agency massacre. I know these
Indians well enough to know that these attacks were perfectly
understood and deliberately planned. I cannot be made to believe that a single one of them, of common-sense and intelligence,
was ignorant of what was to take place, and that knowledge extended far beyond the White River band. There were plenty of
recruits from both the Los Pinos and the Uintah bands. In withholding supplies from the White River Utes the Secretary of the
Interior is simply obeying the law. He cannot, except upon his
own personal responsibility, issue supplies to a hostile Indian
tribe, and the country will hold him accountable for a departure
from his line of duty. Inferentially the Indians are justified by
"H. H." in their attack upon Thornburgh's command. Their
object was to defend "their own lands—lands bought, owned,
and paid for." Bought of whom, pray ? Paid for by whom ?
To whom was payment made? The soldiers were making no
attack; they contemplated none. The agent had no authority
to order an attack. He could not proclaim war. He could have
no control whatever over the troops. But his life was in danger.
The honor of his family was at stake. He asked for protection.
"H. H." says he had no right to it. His life and the honor of
his aged wife and of his virgin daughter are gone, and "H. H."
is the champion of fiends who wrought the ruin.

WM. N. BYERS.

Washington, D. C., Feb. 6th, 1880.

The most fitting reply to the assertions in this extraordinary
document was by still further citations from the sworn testimony
given before the Congressional committees—evidence with which
volumes could have been filled.

LETTER III.

To the Editor of the Tribune:

SIR,—In reply to the letter in Sunday's *Tribune*, headed "The
Starving Utes," I would like to place before the readers of *The
Tribune* some extracts from sworn testimony taken in Colorado
on the subject of the Sand Creek massacre. The writer of this
letter says:

"The Cheyenne and Arapahoe Indians assembled at Sand
Creek were not under the protection of a United States fort."

The following testimony is that of Lieutenant Craven, Senate Document, vol. ii., 1866–67, p. 46:

"I had some conversation with Major Downing, Lieutenant Maynard, and Colonel Chivington. I stated to them my feelings in regard to the matter—that I believed it to be murder—and stated the obligations that we of Major Wynkoop's command were under to those Indians.

"To Colonel Chivington I know I stated that Major Wynkoop had pledged his word as an officer and man to those Indians, and that all officers under him were indirectly pledged in the same manner that he was, and that I felt that it was placing us in very embarrassing circumstances to fight the same Indians that had saved our lives, as we all felt that they had.

"Colonel Chivington's reply was that he believed it to be right and honorable to use any means under God's heaven to kill Indians that would kill women and children; and, 'damn any one that was in sympathy with Indians;' and, 'such men as Major Wynkoop and myself had better get out of the United States service.'"

This conversation was testified to by other witnesses. Major Wynkoop, it will be remembered, was the officer in command at Fort Lyon when this band of Cheyennes and Arapahoes came in there to claim protection, in consequence of the governor's proclamation, saying that,

"All friendly Arapahoes and Cheyennes, belonging on the Arkansas River, will go to Major Colby, United States Indian Agent at Fort Lyon, who will give them provisions and show them a place of safety."

Major Wynkoop was succeeded in the command of Fort Lyon by Major Anthony, who continued for a time to issue rations to these Indians, as Major Wynkoop had done; but after a time he called them together and told them he could not feed them any longer; they would better go where they could hunt. *He selected the place to which they were to move on Sandy Creek.* They obeyed, and he gave back to them some of the arms which had been taken away. They were moved to Sandy Creek, about forty miles from Fort Lyon, partly "for fear of some conflict between them and the soldiers or emigrants," Fort Lyon being on a thoroughfare of travel. One of the chiefs—One Eye—was hired by Major Anthony at $125 a month "to obtain information for the use of the military authorities. Several times he brought news to the fort of proposed movements of hostile Indians." This chief was killed in the massacre.

This is the testimony of Captain Soule, First Colorado Cavalry:

" Did you protest against attacking those Indians? "

" I did."

" Who was your commanding officer? "

" Major Anthony."

" Did you inform Major Anthony of the relations existing with Black Kettle? "

" I did. He knew the relations. I frequently talked to him about it."

" What answer did Major Anthony make to your protests ? "

" He said that we were going to fight the hostile Indians at Smoky Hill. He also said that he was in for killing all Indians, and that he had only been acting friendly with them until he could get a force large enough to go out and kill all of them."

This is the testimony of S. E. Brown:

" Colonel Chivington in a public speech said his policy was to kill and scalp all, little and big: nits made lice."

Governor Hunt testified as follows: [Governor Hunt was one of the earliest settlers in Colorado. He was United States Marshal, Delegate to Congress, and afterward Governor of the Territory.]

" We have always regarded Black Kettle and White Antelope as the special friends of the white man ever since I have been in this country."

" Do you know of any acts of hostility committed by them or with their consent? "

" No, sir, I do not."

" Did you ever hear any acts of hostility attributed to them by any one? "

" No, sir." * * *

The following extract is:

" The regiment, when they marched into Denver, exhibited Indian scalps."

This is from the official report of Major Wynkoop, major commanding Fort Lyon.

" In conclusion, allow me to say that, from the time I held the consultation with the Indian chiefs on the head-waters of Smoky Hill up to the date of this massacre by Colonel Chivington, not one single depredation had been committed by the Cheyenne and Arapahoe Indians. The settlers of the Arkansas Valley had returned to their ranches, from which they had fled, had taken in their crops, and had been resting in perfect security under assurances from myself that they would be in no danger for the present. Since this last horrible murder by Colonel Chivington the country presents a scene of desolation. All communication is cut off with the States, except by sending large bodies of troops, and already over a hundred whites have fallen victims to the fearful vengeance of these betrayed Indians."

January 15th, 1865.

The writer of this letter says, in regard to the investigation of the Sand Creek massacre by the Congressional committee, that "evidence was taken upon one side only," and "there was no answer for the defence."

A large part of the testimony is sworn evidence, given by the Governor of Colorado, by Colonel J. M. Chivington himself, who planned and executed the massacre, and by Major Anthony, who accompanied him with troops from Fort Lyon. The writer of this article says that "the investigation was made for a certain selfish purpose, * * * to break down and ruin certain men."

The names of Senator Foster, Senator Doolittle, and "honest Ben Wade" are the best refutation of this statement. It will be hard to impeach the trustworthiness of reports signed by these names, and one of these reports says:

"It is difficult to believe that beings in the form of men, and disgracing the uniform of United States soldiers and officers, could commit or countenance the commission of such acts of cruelty and barbarity."

Of Colonel Chivington, it says:

"He deliberately planned and executed a foul and dastardly massacre, which would have disgraced the veriest savage among those who were the victims of his cruelty."

And of Major Anthony:

"The testimony of Major Anthony, who succeeded an officer disposed to treat these Indians with justice and humanity, is sufficient of itself to show how unprovoked and unwarranted was this massacre. He testifies that he found these Indians camped near Fort Lyon when he assumed command of that fort; that they professed their friendliness to the whites, and their willingness to do whatever he demanded of them; that they delivered their arms up to him; that they went to and encamped on the place designated by him; that they gave him information from time to time of acts of hostility which were meditated by other hostile bands, and in every way conducted themselves properly and peaceably;

and yet he says it was fear and not principle which prevented his killing them while they were completely in his power; and, when Colonel Chivington appeared at Fort Lyon on his mission of murder and barbarity, Major Anthony made haste to accompany him with men and artillery.''

The writer of this letter says that the evidence given in this "so-called investigation" was "largely false and infamously partial." If this were the case, why did not all persons so "infamously" slandered see to it that before the year ended their own version of the affair should reach, if not the general public, at least the Department of the Interior? Why did they leave it possible for the Secretary of the Interior to incorporate in his Annual Report for 1865—to be read by all the American people—these paragraphs?

" No official account has ever reached this office from its own proper sources of the most disastrous and shameful occurrence, the massacre of a large number of men, women, and children of the Indians of this agency (the Upper Arkansas) by the troops under the command of Colonel Chivington of the United States Volunteer Cavalry of Colorado. * * *

" When several hundred of them had come into a place designated by Governor Evans as a rendezvous for those who would separate themselves from the hostile parties, these Indians were set upon and butchered in cold blood by troops in the service of the United States. The few who escaped to the northward told a story which effectually prevented any more advances toward peace by such of the bands as were well disposed."

And why did the Government of the United States empower General Sanborn, in the Council held October 12th, 1865, with the Arapahoes and Cheyennes, including the remnants of bands that had escaped from the Sand Creek massacre, to formally and officially repudiate the action of the United States soldiers in that massacre? General Sanborn said, in this council:

" We all feel disgraced and ashamed when we see our officers or soldiers oppressing the weak, or making war on those who are at peace with us. * * * We are willing, as representatives of the President, to restore all the property lost at Sand Creek, or its value. * * * He has sent out his commissioners to make reparation, as far as we can. * * * So heartily do we repudiate the actions of our soldiers that we are willing to give to the chiefs in their own right 320 acres of land each, to hold as his own forever, and to each of the children and squaws who lost husbands or parents;

we are also willing to give 160 acres of land as their own, to keep as long as they live."

The writer of this letter, quoting the statement from a previous article in *The Tribune*, that the White River Utes, in their attack on Major Thornburgh's command, fought "to defend their own lands—lands bought, owned, and paid for," asks:

"Bought of whom, pray? Paid for by whom? To whom was payment made?"

"Bought" of the United States Government, thereby recognizing the United States Government's right to "the sovereignty of the soil" as superior to the Indians' "right of occupancy."

"Paid for" by the Ute Indians, by repeated "relinquishments" of said "right of occupancy" in large tracts of valuable lands; notably by the "relinquishment," according to the Brunot Treaty of 1873, of 4,000,000 acres of valuable lands, "unquestionably rich in mineral deposits."—*Annual Report of the Secretary of the Interior for* 1873, p. 464.

"To whom was payment made?"

To the United States Government, which has accepted and ratified such exchanges of "right of occupancy" for "right of sovereignty," and such sales of "right of occupancy" for large sums of money by repeated and reiterated treaties.

The Secretary of the Interior has incorporated in his Annual Report for 1879 (in the report on Indian Affairs, p. 36) the following paragraphs:

"Let it be fully understood that the Ute Indians have a good and sufficient title to 12,000,000 acres of land in Colorado, and that these Indians did not thrust themselves in the way of the white people, but that they were originally and rightfully possessors of the soil, and that the land they occupy has been acknowledged to be theirs by solemn treaties made with them by the United States.

"It will not do to say that a treaty with an Indian means nothing. It means even more than the pledge of the Government to pay a bond. It is the most solemn declaration that any government of any people ever enters into. Neither will it do to say that treaties never ought to have been made with Indians. That question is now not in order, as the treaties have been made, and must be lived up to whether convenient or otherwise.

"By beginning at the outset with the full acknowledgment of the absolute and indefeasible right of these Indians to 12,000,000

acres in Colorado, we can properly consider what is the best
method of extinguishing the Indian title thereto without injustice to the Indians, and without violating the plighted faith of
the Government of the United States."

The writer of this letter says:

"In withholding supplies from the White River Utes, the
Secretary of the Interior is simply obeying the law. He cannot,
except upon his own personal responsibility, issue supplies to a
hostile Indian tribe."

Secretary Schurz has published, in the Annual Report of the
Department of the Interior for 1879, the following paragraph in
regard to this case of the White River Utes:

"The atrocity of the crimes committed should not prevent
those individuals who are innocent from being treated as such,
according to Article 17 of the treaty, viz. : *Provided*, that if any
chief of either of the confederated bands make war against the
United States, or in any manner violate this treaty in any essential part, said chief shall forfeit his position as chief, and all rights
to any of the benefits of this treaty ; but, *provided further*, any
Indian of either of these confederated bands who shall remain at
peace, and abide by the terms of this treaty in all its essentials,
shall be entitled to its benefits and provisions, notwithstanding
his particular chief and band have forfeited their rights thereto."

The writer of this letter says, in allusion to the murders and
outrages committed by some of the White River Utes, that "H. H.
is the champion of the fiends who wrought the ruin." Have the
readers of *The Tribune* so understood my protests against the
injustice of punishing the innocent for the crimes of the guilty ?

H. H.

New York, Feb. 22d, 1880.

This letter was followed by a card from Mr. Byers, reiterating
some of his assertions; and by a second short letter, which closed
the discussion.

To the Editor of the Tribune:

SIR,—I ask only a little space for reference to the communication of " H. H." in to-day's *Tribune*. It is asked, " If the investigation of the Sand Creek affair was so unfair, why did not the
people of Colorado correct the false impression by presenting
their own version of the case?" The answer is that the case
was prejudged, and we were denied a hearing in our defence.

The inference is conveyed in to-day's article that Indian hostilities on the plains were provoked by and followed after the Sand Creek massacre. We, who were so unfortunate as to be citizens of Colorado at the time, know that a very great majority of the savage atrocities of that period occurred before the battle of Sand Creek. We know that the Sand Creek Indian camp was the common rendezvous of the hostile bands who were committing those atrocities. We know that comparatively few occurred afterward. No amount of special pleading, no reiteration of partial statements, and withholding of more important truths, will change the facts so well known to the earlier settlers of Colorado.

I deny that the Utes have either bought or paid for any land. They have relinquished for a consideration a certain portion of the land they formerly claimed, and still retain the other portion. I deny, also, that only twelve of the White River Utes are guilty and the great mass of them innocent. The contrary is the fact.

WM. N. BYERS.

New York, Feb. 24th, 1880.

To the Editor of the Tribune:

SIR,—In reply to the assertion that the perpetrators of the Sand Creek massacre were "denied a hearing in their defence," I wish to state to the readers of *The Tribune* that, in addition to the Congressional committees from whose reports I have already quoted, there was appointed a Military Commission to investigate that massacre. This commission sat seventy-three days, in Denver and at Fort Lyon. Colonel J. M. Chivington called before it, in his "defence," all the witnesses he chose, and gave notice on the seventy-third day of the commission's sitting that he did not "wish to introduce any more witnesses for the defence." He also had (and used) the privilege of cross-examining every witness called by the commission. The evidence given before this commission occupies over two hundred pages of Volume II., Senate Documents for 1866-'67.

In reply to the assertion that "a great majority of the savage atrocities of that period occurred before" the massacre at Sand Creek, and that "comparatively few occurred after," I will give to the readers of *The Tribune* one extract from the report of the Indian Peace Commission of 1868. Alluding to the Sand Creek massacre, the report says:

"It scarcely has its parallel in the records of Indian barbarity. Fleeing women, holding up their hands and praying for mercy, were shot down ; infants were killed and scalped in derision ; men were tortured and mutilated in a manner that would put to shame the savages of interior Africa. No one will be astonished that a war ensued which cost the Government $30,000,000, and carried conflagration and death into the border settlements. During the spring and summer of 1865 no less than 8000 troops were withdrawn from the effective forces engaged in the Rebellion to meet this Indian war."

The Commissioners who made this report were N. J. Taylor, President; J. B. Henderson, John B. Sanborn, William T. Sherman, Lieutenant-general; William S. Harvey, Brevet Major-general; Alfred H. Terry, Brevet Major-general; C. C. Augur, Brevet Major-general; S. F. Tappan.

In reply to the assertion that the Utes have not " either bought or paid for any land," I will ask such of *The Tribune* readers as are interested in the subject to read the "Brunot Treaty," made September 13th, 1873, " between Felix R. Brunot, Commissioner for the United States, and the chiefs, headmen, and men " of the seven confederated bands of Utes. It is to be found in the report of the Department of the Interior for 1873, p. 454.

In conclusion of the discussion as to the Sand Creek massacre, I will relate one more incident of that terrible day. It has not been recorded in any of the reports. It was told in Colorado, to one of the members of the Senate Committee at the time of their investigation : One of the squaws had escaped from the village, and was crouching behind some low sage brush. A frightened horse came running toward her hiding-place, its owner in hot pursuit. Seeing that the horse was making directly for her shelter, and that she would inevitably be seen, and thinking that possibly if she caught the horse, and gave him back to the owner, she might thus save her life, she ran after the horse, caught it, and stood holding it till the soldier came up. Remembering that with her blanket rolled tight around her she might possibly be taken for a man, as she put into the soldier's hand the horse's bridle, with the other hand she threw open her blanket enough to show her bosom, that he might see that she was a woman. He put the muzzle of his pistol between her breasts and shot her dead; and afterward was " not ashamed " to boast of the act. It was by such deeds as this that "the Colorado soldiers acquitted themselves well, and covered themselves with glory." H. H.

New York, Feb. 28th, 1880.

II.

THE PONCA CASE.

Extract from Treaty with the Poncas, giving them Dakota Lands.

"ART. II.—In consideration of the cession or release of that portion of the reservation above described by the Ponca tribe of Indians to the Government of the United States, the Government of the United States, by way of rewarding them for their constant fidelity to the Government thereof, and with a view of returning to the said tribe of Ponca Indians their old burying-grounds and cornfields, hereby cede and relinquish to the tribe of Ponca Indians the following described fractional townships, to wit, township thirty-one (31), north range, seven (7) west; also fractional township thirty-two (32), north ranges, six (6), seven (7). eight (8), nine (9), and ten (10) west; also fractional township thirty-three (33), north ranges, seven (7) and eight (8) west; and also all that portion of township thirty-three (33), north ranges, nine (9) and ten (10) west, lying south of Ponca Creek; and also all the islands in the Niobrara or Running Water River lying in front of lands or townships above ceded by the United States to the Ponca tribe of Indians."

A correspondence which was held with the Secretary of the Interior in the winter of 1879, in regard to the Poncas, is so excellent an illustration of the methods and policy of the Interior Department that it is worth while to give it at length here.

FIRST LETTER.

MRS. JACKSON TO SECRETARY SCHURZ.

New York, Friday, Jan. 9th, 1880.

To the Secretary of the Interior :

DEAR SIR,—I have received from a Boston lady a letter which has so important a bearing on the interests of the Poncas that I take the liberty of asking you to read and reply to the following extracts. I send them to you with the writer's permission:

" In Boston most of those who are likely to give most largely and feel most strongly for the Indians have confidence in Secretary Schurz. They think that so far he has shown himself their friend, and they feel unprepared to help any plan with regard to the Indians which he opposes. The greatest service which could be rendered to the Indian cause at present would be given, therefore, by some one sufficiently interested to obtain an answer who would write to Secretary Schurz, and request him, on the part of the Indians, either to aid them by publicly and cordially endorsing this effort of the Poncas to secure their legal rights in the courts, or else to give his reasons against this attempt, in so clear a form that one could understand them. If there are good reasons, there can be no ground for keeping them secret, and the public has a right to know them. If not, no man can call himself a friend of the Indians who throws cold water on the present interest of the public in this matter.

"Secretary Schurz has already stated that it was not worth while to sue for the Ponca lands, as the Poncas are better off where they now are; but Secretary Schurz cannot deny that it is worth ten times $10,000 to prove that if the Government seizes land given to the Indians forever by solemn compact, the latter can by the courts recover it. Secretary Schurz has also said that a bill to give the Indians land in severalty is already before Congress. If he wishes that bill to pass he must know that it is only by help of the people that the ignorance, apathy, and greed which are accountable for the shameful record of the past can be overcome; and that, whatever his sentiments toward these particular Poncas, he cannot afford to throw aside the interest they have excited.

"For a hundred years the Indians have been the victims of fraud and oppression on the part of the Government. Will anything put an end to it but to give the Indians the legal right to protect themselves? Promises and plans will not do it, for who can assure their performance? Secretary Schurz's position is a strange one, and the public are waiting and watching to see what it means. Is it possible that he is satisfied to have 250,000 human beings, with valuable possessions (however uncivilized), held as absolute slaves, with no rights, and at the mercy of a government like ours, whose constant changes, to say the least, render most improbable the wise, equitable, and humane treatment he recommends in his report—and when the distance of the Indian from the personal interests of all but those States which have a personal interest in possessing his lands makes the assistance of Congress in such treatment still more unlikely? I cannot but believe that he has allowed himself to be driven into an opposition he does not really feel; and that he will yet have the magnanimity to forget any criticism on his own acts, and take the lead with those who would try to give the Indians a permanent defence against the vicissitudes of party and the greed of men.

"I will not forget to add that if the three thousand and odd hundreds of dollars needed to complete the ten thousand required to pay the costs of the Ponca suits cannot be raised in the great city of New York, I will myself guarantee to raise it in Boston in twenty-four hours if Secretary Schurz will openly endorse the plan."

The matter stands, therefore, in this shape: If you can say that you approve of the Poncas bringing the suits they wish to bring for the recovery of their lands, all the money for which they ask can be placed in their hands immediately. The writer of the above letter assured me that she would herself give the entire sum if there were any difficulty in raising it. If you do not approve of the Poncas bringing these suits, or making an effort to bring them, are you willing to give the reasons of your disapproval? It would be a great satisfaction to those Boston friends of yours whose action in this matter turns solely on your decision, if these reasons could be stated in clear and explicit form.

Yours respectfully, HELEN JACKSON.

SECRETARY SCHURZ TO MRS. JACKSON.

Department of the Interior, Office of the Secretary, Jan. 17th, 1880.

DEAR MADAM,—I should certainly have answered your letter of the 9th instant more promptly had I not been somewhat overburdened with official business during the past week. I hope you will kindly pardon the involuntary delay.

As I understand the matter, money is being collected for the purpose of engaging counsel to appear for the Poncas in the courts of the United States, partly to represent them in the case of an appeal from Judge Dundy's *habeas corpus* decision, and partly to procure a decision for the recovery of their old reservation on the Missouri River. I believe that the collection of money for these purposes is useless. An appeal from Judge Dundy's *habeas corpus* decision can proceed only from the Government, not from the Poncas, for the simple reason that the decision was in favor of the latter. An appeal was, indeed, entered by the United States District-attorney at Omaha immediately after the decision had been announced. Some time ago his brief was submitted to me. On examining it, I concluded at once to advise the attorney-general of my opinion that it should be dropped, as I could not approve the principles upon which the argument was based. The attorney-general consented to instruct the district-attorney accordingly, and thus Judge Dundy's decision stands without further question on the part of the Government. Had an appeal been prosecuted, and had Judge Dundy's decision been sustained by the court above, the general principles involved in it would simply have been affirmed without any other practical effect than that already obtained. This matter is therefore ended.

As to the right of the Poncas to their old reservation on the Missouri, the Supreme Court has repeatedly decided that an Indian tribe cannot sue the United States or a State in the federal courts. The decisions are clear and uniform on this point. Among lawyers with whom I discussed this matter, I have not found a single one who entertained a different view; but I did find among them serious doubts as to whether a decision, even if the Poncas could bring suits, would be in their favor, considering the facts in the case. But, inasmuch as such a suit cannot be brought at all, this is not the question. It is evidently idle to collect money and to fee attorneys for the purpose of doing a thing which cannot be done. Had the disinterested friends of the Indians who are engaged in this work first consulted lawyers on the question of possibility, they would no doubt have come to the same conclusion.

The study I have given to the Indian question in its various aspects, past and present, has produced in my mind the firm conviction that the only certain way to secure the Indians in their possessions, and to prevent them from becoming forever a race of homeless paupers and vagabonds, is to transform their tribal title into individual title, inalienable for a certain period; in other words, to settle them in severalty, and give them by patent an individual fee-simple in their lands. Then they will hold their lands by the same title by which white men hold theirs, and they will, as a matter of course, have the same standing in the courts, and the same legal protection of their property. As long as they hold large tracts in the shape of reservations, only small parts of which they can make useful to themselves and to others, the whole being held by the tribe in common, their tenure will always be insecure. It will grow more and more so as our population increases, and the quantity of available land diminishes. We may call this an ugly and deplorable fact, but it is a fact for all that. Long experience shows that the protests of good people in the name of justice and humanity have availed but very little against this tendency, and it is useless to disguise and unwise to overlook it, if we mean to do a real service to the Indians.

For this reason I attach much more importance to the passage of legislation providing for the settlement of the Indians in severalty, and giving them individual title in fee-simple, the residue of their lands not occupied by them to be disposed of for their benefit, than to all the efforts, however well intended, to procure judicial decisions which, as I have shown, cannot be had. I am glad to say that the conversations I have had with senators and representatives in Congress on the policy of settling the Indians in severalty have greatly encouraged my hope of the success of the " severalty bill " during the present session.

I need not repeat here what I said in a letter to Mr. Edward Atkinson, which you may possibly have seen some time ago in the Boston papers, about the necessity of educating Indian children. You undoubtedly understand that as well as I do, and I hope you will concur in my recommendation that the money collected for taking the Ponca case into the courts, which is impossible of accomplishment, and as much more as can be added, be devoted to the support and enlargement of our Indian schools, such as those at Hampton and Carlisle. Thus a movement which undoubtedly has the hearty sympathy of many good men and women, but which at present seems in danger of being wasted on the unattainable, may be directed into a practical channel, and confer a real and lasting benefit on the Indian race.

Very respectfully yours,
C. Schurz.

Mrs. Helen Jackson, New York.

MRS. JACKSON'S SECOND LETTER.

Brevoort House, New York, Thursday, Jan. 22d, 1880.

Hon. Carl Schurz:

Dear Sir,—Your letter of the 17th instant is at hand. If I understand this letter correctly, the position which you take is as follows : That there is in your opinion, and in the opinion of the lawyers whom you have consulted on the subject, no way of bringing before the courts the suits for the prosecution of which money has been and is being contributed by the friends of the Poncas; that the reason you do not approve of this movement is that " it is evidently idle to collect money and to fee attorneys for the purpose of doing a thing which cannot be done." This is

the sole reason which I understand you to give for discountenanc-
ing the collection of money for these suits. Am I correct in this?
And are we to infer that it is on this ground and no other that
you oppose the collection of money for this purpose? Are we to
understand that you would be in favor of the Poncas recovering
their lands by process of law, provided it were practicable?

You say, also, that you hope I will "concur" in your "recommendation that the money collected for taking the Ponca case
into the courts shall be devoted to the support and enlargement
of our Indian schools." May I ask how it would be, in your opinion, possible to take money given by thousands of people for one
specific purpose and use it for another different purpose? You
say, "Had the friends of the Indians who are engaged in this
work first consulted lawyers on the question of possibility, they
would, no doubt, have come to the same conclusion." Had the
friends of the Indians engaged in this work, and initiated this
movement without having consulted lawyers, it would have been
indeed foolish. But this was not the case. Lawyers of skill and
standing were found ready to undertake the case; and the matter stands therefore to-day precisely as it stood when I wrote to
you on the 17th instant. All the money which is thought to be
needed for carrying the Ponca case before the courts can be raised
in twenty-four hours in Boston, if you can say that you approve
of the suits being brought. If your only objection to the movement is the one objection which you have stated, namely, that it
would be futile, can you not say that, if lawyers of standing are
ready to undertake the case, you would be glad to see the attempt made in the courts, and the question settled? If it is, as
you think, a futile effort, it will be shown to be so. If it is, as the
friends and lawyers of the Poncas think, a practicable thing, a
great wrong will be righted.

You say that "to settle them (the Indians) in severalty, and
give them by patent an individual fee-simple in their lands," will
enable them to "hold their lands by the same title by which white
men hold theirs," and that "then they will, as a matter of course,
have the same standing in the courts and the same legal protection of their property." May I ask you if any bill has been
brought before Congress which is so worded as to secure these
ends? My only apology for troubling you again is my deep interest in the Indians, and in the Ponca case especially.

Yours truly,

HELEN JACKSON.

Washington, D. C., Jan. 26th, 1880.

DEAR MADAM,—In reply to your letter of the 22d instant, I beg leave to say that if an Indian tribe could maintain an action in the courts of the United States to assert its rights, I should object to it just as little as I would object to the exercise of the same privilege on the part of white men. What I do object to is the collection of money from philanthropic and public-spirited persons, ostensibly for the benefit of the Indians, but in fact for the benefit of attorneys and others who are to be paid for again testing a question which has been tested more than once, and has been decided by the Supreme Court so clearly and comprehensively that further testing seems utterly futile. You say that there are lawyers of skill and standing ready to undertake the case. Of course there are such. You can find lawyers of skill and standing to undertake for a good fee any case, however hopeless: that is their business. But I am by no means of your opinion that, whether it be futile or not, the experiment should be tried once more, and for this purpose the collection of money should be further encouraged. It cannot be said in this case that if the attempt will not help it will not hurt. There seems to be now a genuine and active interest in the Indian question springing up. Many sincere friends of the Indian are willing to spend time and money for the promotion of their welfare. Such a movement can do great good if wisely guided in the direction of attainable objects; but if it be so conducted that it can result only in putting money into the pockets of private individuals, without any benefit to the Indians, the collapse will be as hurtful as it seems to be inevitable It will not only be apt to end a movement which, if well directed, might have become very useful, but it will also deter the sincere friends of the Indians who contributed their means in the hope of accomplishing something from further efforts of that kind, so that we may find it very difficult, for a long time at least, to engage this active sympathy again. Confidence once abused does not revive very quickly. This is my view of the case. You ask me " how it would be possible to take money given by thousands of people for one specific purpose, and use it for another and different purpose," meaning the support of Indian schools. It would, in my opinion, be far better to lay the matter in its true aspect frankly before the contributors, and to ask them for their consent to the change of purpose, than to throw away the money for a purpose which cannot be accomplished.

In reply to your inquiry whether any bill has been brought before Congress providing for the settlement of the Indians in severalty, and for conferring upon the individual title in fee-simple to the lands allotted to them, I am glad to say that several bills of this kind have been introduced in both the Senate and the House, and are now before the respective committees on Indian affairs for consideration. If such a bill passes, of which there is great hope, the Indian, having a fee title by patent to the piece of land which he individually, not as a member of a tribe, holds as his own, will stand in the eye of the law just like any other owner of property in his individual right, and, as a matter of course, will have the same standing in court. This will do more in securing the Indian in the practical enjoyment of his property than anything else I can think of, and it has long been my endeavor to bring about just this result. I trust we shall obtain the desired legislation during the present session of Congress.

Very respectfully yours,   C. SCHURZ.

Mrs. HELEN JACKSON, New York.

The evasive and inconclusive character of these replies of the Secretary provoked much comment, and gave rise to a very widespread and natural impression that he was for some reason or other averse to the restoration to the Poncas of their old homes. The letters were reviewed by one of the editors of the *New York Times* in a paper so admirable that the letters ought not to be printed without it.

CIVIL RIGHTS IN ACRES.

(From the New York Times, February 21st, 1880.)

" As most of the readers of the *Times* already know, friends of the Ponca Indians are endeavoring to have the tribe restored to their old reservation in Dakota. Or, more strictly speaking, it is proposed that their reservation shall be restored to them. The lands occupied by the Poncas were ceded to them by the United States by solemn treaty. By a cruel and wicked blunder, which no man has attempted to explain, those lands were ceded to the Sioux. But the Sioux did not want the lands, and they have never occupied them unto this day. To this robbery of the tribe was added the destruction of their houses, movable property, and farms. A citizen of the United States would have redress in the courts for such an outrage as this. An Indian has no legal status. He is merely a live and particularly troublesome animal, in the eye of the law. But, while the Poncas were trying to get back on their lands, they were arrested by order of the Secretary of the Interior, on the charge of running away from the agency to which they had been sent by the Government when their lands were taken from them. It is not necessary to add words to intensify this accumulation of criminal folly and wrong. Certain citizens of Nebraska, hearing of the injustice which was being perpetrated on the Poncas, raised funds, and had the chiefs brought before United States District Judge Dundy on a writ of *habeas corpus*, to inquire why they were thus restrained of their liberty. Judge Dundy decided that an Indian was 'a person' within the meaning of the *Habeas Corpus* Act, and that these persons were unlawfully held in duress.

" It was thought that the United States would appeal from this dictum, but no appeal was taken, much to the disappointment of the friends of the Indians, as it was hoped that a decision could be reached to show whether the Indian was or was not so far clothed with the privilege of a citizen that he could have a standing in the courts of law. Accordingly, the public-spirited and philanthropic persons who had espoused the cause of the Poncas resolved to make up a case, which, carried to the United States Supreme Court, should determine once and forever this moot point. To this end money has been raised by subscription, by special gift, and by contributions taken at public meetings in various parts of the country. A lady residing in Boston, moved by the pitiful condition of the Indians, who tried to struggle toward civilization, offered to supply all the money which was lacking toward the expenses of the suit, provided Secretary Schurz would give some public assurances that he favored this manner of determining the case, or would give his reasons against this attempt. The lady's proposition was sent to Mrs. Helen Hunt Jackson, whose disinterested and efficient labors in behalf of the deeply-wronged Poncas had already attracted attention. Mrs. Jackson forwarded to Secretary Schurz the whole statement. Thereupon an interesting correspondence ensued. This correspondence has been printed in the Boston papers, presumably by direction of Secretary Schurz.

" In reply to the request to say whether he approves of the movement to carry the Ponca case to the Supreme Court, in order that the tribe may recover their old reservation, the Secretary says that this would be useless, as the courts have repeatedly decided that an Indian tribe cannot sue the United States. Unfortunately, Mr. Schurz does not cite these cases, but we must take it for granted that he knows what he is talking about. He adds that he has taken the advice of lawyers, who coincide with him in this opinion. As a suit cannot be brought at all, according to the Secretary and his legal advisers, it would be idle to collect money for this purpose; and the Secretary suggests that, if the disinterested friends of the Indians had consulted lawyers before they began their work, they would be of his opinion as to the futility of the attempt. This, of course, leaves the impression that the Secretary withholds his approval of the movement to secure legal rights for the Poncas, though he does not say so in express terms. His reason for not approving the attempt is that it will do no good. His solution to the Indian problem, as it is vaguely called, is to settle the Indians in severalty, breaking up their tribal organization, and giving to each individual his lands in fee-simple. This, the Secretary thinks, will enable them to hold their lands by the same title as that by which white men hold theirs, and, 'as a matter of course, they will have the same standing in the courts' as white men. It is to be regretted that the Secretary did not pause here long enough to show how the giving to an Indian of 160 acres of land can clothe him with civil rights which he does not now possess, and which the Secretary thinks that the courts cannot give him. For this reason, however, Mr. Schurz is greatly in favor of legislation providing for the settlement of the Indians in severalty, various bills to accomplish which, he says, are in preparation. As for the money raised already, the Secretary suggests that since, in his opinion, it would be misspent in obtaining judicial decision, it might be used in the education of Indian children.

"Replying to this, Mrs. Jackson asks if the Secretary would be in favor of the Poncas recovering their lands by process of law, provided that could be done. To this direct and very important inquiry we regret to notice that the Secretary finds himself unable to reply, although, in a letter immediately following this, he does say that if an Indian tribe could maintain an action at law in the courts to assert its rights, he would no more object to it than he would to a white man's doing the same thing. As to the suggestion that the money collected for the expenses of legal proceedings be used for educational purposes, Mrs. Jackson asks the Secretary how it would be possible to take money given for one specific purpose and use it for another and wholly different purpose. Mr. Schurz rejoins that the consent of the donors may first be obtained; but he forgets that it would be impossible to canvass the country to ascertain the wishes of thousands of unknown givers to this fund. Referring to the intimation that the friends of the Indians had not taken legal counsel in this matter, and that the Secretary had, Mrs. Jackson observes that they did take such counsel, and that an omission to do so would have been indeed foolish.

"It will be observed that the Secretary's objection to the attempt to secure civil rights is its futility; and, in answer to Mrs. Jackson's statement that the friends of the Indians have sought the opinions of lawyers in this case, he replies that one ' can find lawyers of skill and standing to undertake, for a good fee, any case, however hopeless.' To those who might think that this is unjustly severe on the legal profession, it should be said that Mr Schurz has been by profession a lawyer, and should know what he is talking about. And we must presume that Mr. Schurz's profound knowledge of the law, which is fortified by the opinions of eminent legal men, induces him to consider the whole case closed in advance of its submission to the courts. It would be interesting, however, to know if the Secretary's lawyers of skill and standing are less easily influenced by the prospect of a ' good fee' than the lawyers of skill and standing consulted by the friends of the Poncas. The exceedingly able opinion of Secretary Schurz, we find, is that it is useless to give the Indian a standing in the courts through judicial decisions, as he can readily secure this by accepting from the Government of the United States a deed of 160 acres of land."

CONDITION OF THE PONCAS IN THE SUMMER OF 1880.

Standing Bear and his party, after their release by the decision of Judge Dundy, settled on an island in the Niobrara River, which was a part of their old reservation, and had fortunately been overlooked when the United States Government took forcible possession of the rest of their land and presented it to the Sioux. Here they were joined by other fugitives of their tribe till the number reached about one hundred and thirty. A committee which had been organized in Omaha for their relief supplied them with farming implements, and they went industriously to work. This committee published in July, 1880, a report containing the following paragraphs:

" We consider the treatment of the Ponca Indians as one of the most heart-sickening chapters in our national record of Indian wrongs, and we are determined to spare no effort to restore to them their stolen homes and rights, and to relieve the American people of the stigma of this terrible wrong.

" The Senate of the United States during the past winter appointed a select committee 'to ascertain and report the circumstances of the removal of the Ponca Indians from their reservation, and whether the said Indians are not entitled to be restored thereto.' This Senate Committee devoted a long time to a thorough and patient investigation of this whole Ponca case, and reported that the Poncas had been 'forced, without authority of law, from their homes to the Indian Territory,' and reported also a bill for their restoration to their former reservation, and recommending 'that $50,000 be appropriated for the purpose of taking the Poncas back, and restoring their now dilapidated homes.'

"This able report of the United States Senate says that 'in dealing with one of the most peaceable and orderly and well-disposed of all the tribes of Indians, the Government has violated in the most flagrant manner their rights of property, and disregarded their appeals to the honor and justice of the United States, and the dictates of humanity.'"

The report also says that " the committee can find no language sufficiently strong to condemn the whole proceeding, and trace to it all the troubles which have come upon the Poncas, and the hardships and sufferings which have followed them since they were taken from their old reservation and placed in their present position in the Indian Territory."

The Omaha Ponca Relief Committee need no better vindication of their action in behalf of this distressed and outraged people than these strong and weighty words of a committee of United States Senators, composed of representative men of both political parties.

The Omaha Committee consisted of Bishop Clarkson, of Nebraska, chairman; Rev. A. F. Sherrill, Rev. W. I. Harsha, Leavitt Burnham, W. M. Yates, and P. L. Perine.

At the request of this committee, Mr. T. H. Tibbles in June went to the Indian Territory to visit the Poncas (of whom only about 400 were left alive). He was authorized "to assure them of the interest and efforts of humane people all over the country in their behalf, and to notify them that the Omaha Committee were ready to assist them in any practical way to return to their old homes, from which they had been unjustly and inhumanly ejected."

Mr. Tibbles succeeded in visiting the Poncas, although the Government agent interfered with him in many ways, and finally arrested him by author.ty of an order from Washington to arrest any member of the Omaha Committee who came upon the reservation. He was insulted by the agent, taken by force out of the reservation, and threatened with much more severe treatment if he ever returned.

This high-handed outrage on a free citizen of the United States aroused indignation throughout the country. The comments of the Press on the occurrence showed that people were at last waking up to a sense of the tyrannical injustice of the Indian Department. The *New York Tribune* said, editorially:

" The Indian Department may as well understand at once that the Ponca case has passed out of their control. It is a matter of simple justice which the people are determined to see righted. * * * No petty Indian agent has the legal right to imprison, maltreat, and threaten the life of any citizen totally guiltless of offence beyond that of working to give these serfs of the Government the standing of human beings. * * * It is the Government of this great Republic, where all men are free and equal, that holds these Poncas prisoners on a tract where to remain is death. They are innocent of any crime except that they have been robbed of their land, and that they ask to bring suit, as a black man or convict could do, in the courts for its recovery."

Mr. Tibbles reported the condition of the Poncas in Indian Territory as " deplorable in the extreme. They live in constant dread and fear, and are as much imprisoned as if they were in a penitentiary." They seem " to have lost all hope, are brokenhearted and disconsolate. With one or two exceptions, they are making no effort to help themselves. Their so-called farms are miserable little patches, to which they pay very little attention. One of them said to me, ' If the Government forces me to stay here, it can feed me. I had a good farm back at our old home, and if I was back there I would farm again ; I have no heart to work here.' The one hundred and fifteen who are back on the old reservation have a much larger amount of land under cultivation than the whole four hundred who are in Indian Territory. They have kept their crops in good condition, and are full of energy and hope."

The Government Agency for the Poncas having been transferred to the Indian Territory, the annuities due the tribe were of course paid there, and that portion of the tribe which had fled back to Dakota received nothing. Moreover, the Indian Bureau issued an order forbidding any Ponca who should leave the Indian Territory to take with him any kind of property whatsoever, under penalty of being arrested for stealing. As they could not take their families on the long, hard journey to Dakota without food or means of transportation, this order kept them imprisoned in Indian Territory as effectually as a military guard could have done.

The Government employés in charge of them reported, meanwhile, that they had " made up their minds to live and die where they are. * * * There exists a feeling of contentment in the tribe that will make it very difficult for any one to induce them to leave their present home," says a general press despatch, presumably dictated by the Indian Bureau, and sent throughout the country on July 15th.

It seems an insult to people's common-sense to suppose that this statement would be believed, close on the heels of the general order for the arrest of all fleeing Poncas who should dare to take with them out of the Indian Territory one dollar's worth of property. A very superfluous piece of legislation, surely, for a community so "contented" that it would be " difficult for any one to induce them to leave their homes."

THE LEGAL ASPECT OF THE CASE.

The chivalric and disinterested attorneys who had had the charge of the Ponca case from the outset, were not to be intimidated by the threats nor outwitted by the expedients of the Indian Bureau. The ingenious devices practised by the Department of the Interior to hinder the getting service of summons upon the defendants in the suits necessary to recover the Poncas' lands, make by themselves a shameful chapter, which will some day be written out. But on the 13th of July the attorneys were able to report to the Omaha Committee as follows :

REPORT OF THE ATTORNEYS.

Omaha, July 13th, 1880.

To Omaha Ponca Indian Committee :

In response to the inquiry of one of your members as to the condition of the suits instituted by us to liberate Standing Bear and his associate from the custody of the military, and to recover possession of the Ponca reservation, we make the following statement:

On April 8th, 1879, was filed by us the petition in the case of United States *ex rel.* Ma-chu-nah-zha (Standing Bear) *et al. vs.* George Crook, a Brigadier-general of the Army of the United States and Commander of the Department of the Platte, in the U.S. District Court for the District of Nebraska, for a writ of *habeas corpus* for the release of Standing Bear and his companions. This cause was tried about the first of May, 1879, and Standing Bear and his companions were restored to their liberty. Thereupon the U. S. District-attorney took the case to the United States Circuit Court for this District by appeal, and about May 19th, upon hearing before Mr. Justice Miller, Associate Justice of the Supreme Court of the United States, was there continued, and on January 5th, 1880, the appeal was dismissed on the motion of the U. S. District-attorney.

On April 3d, 1880, was commenced by us the case of Ponca tribe of Indians *vs.* Makh-pi-ah-lu-ta, or Red Cloud, in his own behalf, and in behalf of the Sioux nation of Indians, in the U. S. Circuit Court for the District of Nebraska, and on May 18th, 1880, we commenced in the same court the case of Ponca tribe of Indians *vs.* Sioux nation of Indians. These cases were commenced, and are being prosecuted by us, to recover possession of and establish the title of the Ponca tribe of Indians to so much of their old reservation as lies within the limits of Nebraska. Great delay was made necessary in the commencement of these cases, and the ones subsequently commenced in Dakota, of which we below make mention, owing to difficulties in getting service of summons upon the defendants. On May 22d, 1880, service of summons was had on the defendants in both cases, and some action will be taken therein at the next term of the court.

About the 20th of May, 1880, there were commenced in Dakota other suits in the name of the Ponca tribe of Indians, and against the Sioux nation of Indians, and against certain of their chiefs, to settle and establish the title of the Ponca tribe of Indians to so much of their old reservation as lies within the limits of Dakota. Service has been had in these cases, and the several suits mentioned will be prosecuted by us with all convenient speed.

We might add that we also have in charge the case of John Elk *vs.* Charles Wilkins, in the U. S. Circuit Court for this District, which is being prosecuted by us to determine the rights of

Indians under the Fourteenth Amendment of the Constitution of the United States. Respectfully submitted,

A. J. POPPLETON,
JNO. L. WEBSTER.

III.

TESTIMONIES TO INDIAN CHARACTER.

" EARLY in 1800 the Governor of the North-west Territory, in his message to the assembly, invited their attention to the condition of the Indians. He observed that, irrespective of the principles of religion and justice, it was the interest and should be the policy of the United States to be at peace with them; but that could not continue to be the case if the treaties existing between them and the Government were broken with impunity by the inhabitants of the Territory. He referred to the well-known fact that while the white men loudly complained of every injury committed by the Indians, however trifling, and demanded immediate reparation, they were daily perpetrating against them injuries and wrongs of the most provoking and atrocious nature, for which the perpetrators had not been brought to justice.* * * He stated that the number of those unfortunate people who had been murdered since the peace of Greenville was sufficient to produce serious alarm for the consequences. He added, further, that a late attempt to bring to punishment a white man, who was clearly proved to have killed two adult Indians and wounded two of their children, had proved abortive."—BURNET's *Notes on North-west Territory.*

CHARACTER OF NORTH-WESTERN INDIANS.

" Among other falsehoods it has been asserted confidently, but without a shadow of argument or fact to sustain the assertion, that they cannot be brought to a state of civilization, or be induced to form communities and engage in the pursuits of agriculture and the arts, in consequence of some physical difference between them and the Anglo-Saxon race. This hypothesis is contradicted by experience, which has abundantly shown that the two races, when placed in the same situation, and acted upon by the same causes, have invariably resorted to the same expedients and pursued the same policy.

" This averment is sustained by a reference to the white people who have been taken prisoners in childhood and brought up among the Indians. In every such case the child of civilization has become the ferocious adult of the forest, manifesting all the peculiarities, tastes, and preferences of the native Indian. His manners, habits, propensities, and pursuits have been the same, so that the most astute philosophical observer has not been able to discover any difference between them, except in the color of the skin, and in some instances even this has been removed by long exposure to the elements, and the free use of oils and paints."

The many instances which there are on record of cases in which persons taken captive by the Indians, while young, have utterly refused in later life to return to their relatives and homes, go to confirm this statement of Judge Burnet's.

On the other hand, he says: " The attempts that have been made at different times to improve the minds and cultivate the morals of these people have always been attended by success.

" On an unprejudiced comparison between the civilized educated white man and the civilized educated Indian, all this theory of an organic constitutional difference between the European and the native Indian vanishes.

" In what respect have Ross, Boudinot, Hicks, Ridge, and others differed from the educated men of our own race? Inasmuch then as the reclaimed educated Indian becomes assimilated to the white man, and the European brought up from infancy among the Indians becomes identified with them, this alleged difference cannot be real, it must be imaginary.

" The fact is, the difficulty of civilizing the natives of this continent is neither greater nor less than that which retarded the improvement of the barbarous nations of Europe two thousand years ago. * * * Men uncivilized have always delighted in the chase, and had a propensity to roam; both history and experience prove that nothing but necessity, arising from such an increase of population as destroys the game, has ever induced men to settle in communities, and rely on the cultivation of the earth for subsistence. In the progress of civilization the chase has given way to the pastoral state, and that has yielded to agriculture as the increase of numbers has rendered it necessary.

" As soon as the Cherokees and the Wyandots were surrounded by a white population, and their territory was so contracted as to cut off their dependence on hunting and fishing, they became farmers, and manifested a strong desire to cultivate the arts; and this would have been the choice of the whole Indian race if the policy of the Government had permitted it!

" It is not just to consider the natives of this country as a distinct and inferior race because they do not generally imitate us, when we not only remove every consideration that could induce them to do so, but in fact render it impossible. What motive of ambition was there to stimulate them to effort, when they were made to feel that they held their country as tenants at will, liable to be driven off at the pleasure of their oppressors?

" As soon as they were brought to a situation in which necessity prompted them to industry, and induced them to begin to adopt our manners and habits of life, the covetous eye of the white man was fixed on their incipient improvements, and they received the chilling notice that they must look elsewhere for permanent homes.

" At the time our settlements were commencing north-west of the Ohio, the Indians were its acknowledged owners and sovereigns; the Government claimed no right either of occupancy or soil, except as they obtained it by purchase."

(On the 31st of July, 1793, the United States Commissioners said to the assembled chiefs of the North-western tribes, in a council held at the home of one Captain Elliott, on the Detroit River: " By the express authority of the President of the United States, we acknowledge the property, or right of soil to the great country above described, to be in the Indian nations as long as they desire to occupy it; we claim only the tracts before particularly mentioned, and the right of pre-emption granted by the King, as before explained.")

" The entire country from Pennsylvania to the Mississippi was admitted to be theirs, and a more delightful, fertile valley cannot be found on the earth. * * *

" Unconscious of the ruinous consequences that were to follow their intimacy with white men, they ceded to the American Government large and valuable portions of the country at nominal prices. Those lands were rapidly settled by Americans, in whose purity and friendship the unsuspecting natives had great confidence; nor did they awake from that delusion till their habits of sobriety and morality had been undermined, and the vices engendered by intemperance and idleness had contaminated every tribe. * * *

" Their subsistence became precarious; their health declined; their self-respect, their dignity of character, and the heroism inherited from their ancestors were lost. They became in their own estimation a degraded, dependent race. The Government, availing itself of their weakness and want of energy, succeeded by bribes and menaces in obtaining the best portions of their country, and eventually in driving them from the land of their birth to a distant home in an unknown region.

" This distressing chapter of aboriginal history began at the treaty of Greenville, in 1795, and terminated in less than fifty years. The writer of these notes witnessed its commencement, progress, and close."—BURNET'S *Notes on North-west Territory.*

NES PERCÉS AND FLAT-HEADS IN THEIR OWN COUNTRY.

" They were friendly in their dispositions, and honest to the most scrupulous degree in their intercourse with the white men. * * * Simply to call these people religious would convey but a faint idea of the deep hue of piety and devotion which pervades the whole of their conduct. Their honesty is immaculate; and their purity of purpose and their observance of the rites of their religion are most uniform and remarkable. They are certainly more like a nation of saints than a horde of savages."—CAPTAIN BONNEVILLE'S *Narrative, revised by* W. IRVING.

" I fearlessly assert to the world, and I defy contradiction, that the North American Indian is everywhere in his native state a highly moral and religious being, endowed by his Maker with an intuitive knowledge of some great Author of his being and the universe—in dread of whose displeasure he constantly lives with the apprehension before him of a future state, when he expects to be rewarded or punished according to the merits he has gained or forfeited in this world.

" I never saw any other people who spend so much of their lives in humbling themselves before and worshipping the Great Spirit as these tribes do, nor any whom I would not as soon suspect of insincerity and hypocrisy.

" Self-denial and self-torture, and almost self-immolation, are continual modes of appealing to the Great Spirit for his countenance and forgiveness.

" To each other I have found these people kind and honorable, and endowed with every feeling of parental, filial, and conjugal affection that is met with in more enlightened communities."—CATLIN'S *North American Indians.*

Mr. Catlin spent eight years among the Indians more than forty years ago. He travelled among the wildest of them, lived with them in the freest intimacy, and this is his verdict as to their native traits, when uncontaminated by white men and whiskey.

As long ago as 1724, the Jesuit Father Lafitau wrote of the Indians, and stated that to his own experience he added that of Father Garnier, who had lived sixty years among them: "They are possessed," says he, "of sound judgment, lively imagination, ready conception, and wonderful memory. All the tribes retain at least some trace of an ancient religion, handed down to them from their ancestors, and a form of government. They reflect justly upon their affairs, and better than the mass of the people among ourselves. They prosecute their ends by sure means; they evince a degree of coolness and composure which would exceed our patience; they never permit themselves to indulge in passion, but always, from a sense of honor and greatness of soul, appear masters of themselves. They are high-minded and proud; possess a courage equal to every trial, an intrepid valor, the most heroic constancy under torments, and an equanimity which neither misfortunes nor reverses can shake. Toward each other they behave with a natural politeness and attention, entertaining a high respect for the aged, and a consideration for their equals which appears scarcely reconcilable with that freedom and independence of which they are so jealous. They make few professions of kindness, but y t are affable and generous. Toward strangers and the unfortunate they exercise a degree of hospitality and charity which might put the inhabitants of Europe to the blush."

Father Lafitau does not disguise the fact that the Indians have great faults. He says they are "suspicious and vindictive, cruel to their enemies."

Père Lallemant, a missionary among the Hurons, says: "In point of intellect they are not at all inferior to the natives of Europe; I could not have believed that, without instruction, nature could have produced such ready and vigorous eloquence, or such a sound judgment in their affairs as that which I have so much admired among the Hurons. I admit that their habits and customs are barbarous in a thousand ways; but, after all, in matters which they consider as wrong, and which their public condemns, we observe among them less criminality than in France, although here the only punishment of a crime is the shame of having committed it."

In a history of New France, published in 1618, it is stated of the Indians that "they are valorous, faithful, generous, and humane; their hospitality is so great that they extend it to every one who is not their enemy. They speak with much judgment and reason, and, when they have any important enterprise to undertake, the chief is attentively listened to for two or three hours together, and he is answered point to point, as the subject may require."

In 1656 the Jesuit missionaries among the Iroquois reported: " Among many faults caused by their blindness and barbarous education, we meet with virtues enough to cause shame among the most of Christians. Hospitals for the poor would be useless among them, because there are no beggars; those who have are so liberal to those who are in want, that everything is enjoyed in common. The whole village must be in distress before any individual is left in necessity."

Captain Carver, who travelled in 1766 among the wildest tribes, describes them as " cruel, barbarous, and revengeful in war, persevering and inflexible in pursuit of an enemy, sanguinary in their treatment of prisoners, and sparing neither age nor sex." On the other hand, he found them temperate in their mode of living, patient of hunger and fatigue, sociable and humane to all whom they looked on as friends, and ready to share with them the last morsel of food they possessed, or to expose their lives in their defence. In their public character he describes them as " possessing an attachment to their nation unknown to the inhabitants of any other country, combining as if actuated by one soul against a common enemy, never swayed in their councils by selfish or party views, but sacrificing everything to the honor and advantage of their tribe, in support of which they fear no danger, and are affected by no sufferings. They are not only affectionately attached, indeed, to their own offspring, but are extremely fond of children in general. They instruct them carefully in their own principles, and train them up with attention in the maxims and habits of their nation. Their system consists chiefly in the influence of example, and impressing on them the traditionary histories of their ancestors. When the children act wrong, their parents remonstrate and reprimand but never chastise them."— HALKETT's *Hist. Notes.*

The very idea of corporal punishment of little children seems to have been peculiarly obnoxious to the native North American. In the " Relation de Nouvelle France," published in 1633, there is a curious story of an incident which took place at Quebec. A party of Indians, watching a French drummer-boy beat his drum, pressed more closely around him than he liked, and he struck one of the Indians in the face with his drum-stick so sharply that the blow drew blood. The Indians, much offended, went to the interpreter and demanded apologies and a present, according to their custom. " No," said the interpreter, " our custom is to punish the offender; we will punish the boy in your presence." When the Indians saw the child stripped for the flogging they began immediately to beg for his pardon; but as the soldiers continued their preparations for whipping the lad, one of the Indians suddenly stripped himself and threw his robe over the boy, crying out, " Scourge me, if you choose, but do not strike the boy ! " The good Father Le Jeune, who tells this story, adds that this unwillingness of the Indians to see any child chastised " will probably occasion trouble to us in the design we have to instruct their youth."

As far back as 1587 we find evidence that the Indians were not without religion. Thomas Hariot, an employé of Sir Walter Raleigh's, writing from the Virginia colony, says of the Virginia Indians: " Theye beleeve that there are many gods, which theye call Mantaoc, but of different sorts and degrees; one onely chief and Great God, which hath been from all eternitie; who, as theye affirme, when hee proposed to make the world, made first other gods of a principall order, to bee as means and instruments to bee used in the creation and government to folow; and after the sunne, moone, and starres as pettie gods, and the instruments of the other order more principall."

" In general," says Hunter, " a day seldom passes with an elderly Indian, or others who are esteemed wise and good, in which a blessing is not asked, or thanks returned to the Giver of Life, sometimes audibly, but more generally in the devotional language of the heart."

All the employés of the North-west Fur Company bear the same testimony to the fidelity and honesty of the Indians.

General H. Sibley once said to Bishop Whipple that for thirty years it had been the uniform boast of the Sioux in every council that they had never taken the life of a white man.

IV.

OUTRAGES COMMITTED ON INDIANS BY WHITES.

In Captain Bonneville's narrative of five years spent in the Rocky Mountains are many instances of cruel outrages committed by whites upon Indians.

"One morning one of his trappers, discovering that his traps had been carried off in the night, took a horrid oath that he would kill the first Indian he should meet, innocent or guilty. As he was returning with his comrades to camp, he beheld two unfortunate Root Diggers seated on the bank, fishing; advancing upon them, he levelled his rifle, shot one on the spot, and flung his bleeding body into the stream.

"A short time afterward, when this party of trappers were about to cross Ogden's River, a great number of Shoshokies, or Root Diggers, were posted on the opposite bank, when they imagined they were there with hostile intent; they advanced upon them, levelled their rifles, and killed twenty-five of them on the spot. The rest fled to a short distance, then halted and turned about, howling and whining like wolves, and uttering most piteous wailings. The trappers chased them in every direction. The poor wretches made no defence, but fled in terror; nor does it appear from the accounts of the boasted victors that a weapon had been wielded by the Indians throughout the affair."

There seemed to be an emulation among these trappers which could inflict the greatest outrages on the natives. They chased them at full speed, lassoed them like cattle, and dragged them till they were dead.

At one time, when some horses had been stolen by the Riccarees, this same party of trappers took two Riccaree Indians prisoners, and declared that, unless the tribe restored every horse that had been stolen, these two Indians, who had strayed into the trappers' camp without any knowledge of the offence committed, should be burnt to death.

"To give force to their threat, a pyre of logs and fagots was heaped up and kindled into a blaze. The Riccarees released one horse and then another; but, finding that nothing but the relinquishment of all their spoils would purchase the lives of the captives, they abandoned them to their fate, moving off with many parting words and howlings, when the prisoners were dragged to the blazing pyre and burnt to death in sight of their retreating comrades.

" Such are the acts that lead to terrible recriminations on the part of the Indians. Individual cases of the kind dwell in the recollections of whole tribes, and it is a point of honor and conscience to avenge them.

" The records of the wars between the early settlers of Virginia and New England and the natives exhibit cruelties on both sides that make one shudder. * * * When the Indian would tear the scalp from the crown of the scarcely yet dead victim, and mutilate the body, could he be expected to reform those cruelties when he saw the white man in his turn cut off the heads of his people, and mutilate and quarter their bodies, as was done with King Philip's, whose head, after being cut off, was sent to Plymouth and hung up there on a gibbet, where it remained twenty years, while one of his hands was sent to Boston as a trophy, his body being quartered and hung upon four trees? "—M'FORLEY'S *History and Travels.*

FROM REPORT OF THE INDIAN BUREAU FOR 1854.

" Port Orford, Oregon Territory, February 5th, 1854.

" I grieve to report to you that a most horrid massacre, or rather an out-and-out barbarous murder, was perpetrated on a portion of the Nason tribe, residing at the mouth of the Coquille River, on the morning of the 28th of January last, by a party of forty miners. Before giving you the result of my examination and my own conclusions, I will give you the reasons which that party assign in justification of their acts.

" They avow that, for some time past, the Indians at the mouth of the Coquille have been insolent; that they have been in the habit of riding the horses of white men without permission; that of late they have committed many thefts, such as stealing paddles and many other articles the property of white men; that one of their number recently discharged his gun at the ferry-house; and that but a few days prior to the attack on the Indians, the chief, on leaving the ferry-house, where he had just been fed, fired his gun at a party of four white men standing near the door of the house. They further state that, on the 27th of January, they sent for the chief to come in for a talk; that he not only refused to come in, but sent back word that he would kill white men if they came to his home; that he meant to kill all the white men he could; that he was determined to drive the white men out of his country; that he would kill the men at the ferry, and burn their houses. Immediately after this conversation with the chief, the white men at and near the ferry-house assembled, and deliberated on the necessity of an immediate attack on the Indians.

" The result of their deliberation, with the full proceedings of their meeting, is herein enclosed. At the conclusion, a courier was despatched to the upper mines for assistance. A party of about twenty responded to the call, and arrived at the ferry-house on the evening preceding the morning of the massacre. On the arrival of this re-enforcement the proceedings of the meeting first held were reconsidered, and unanimously approved.

" At the dawn of day on the morning of the 28th of January the party of the ferry, joined by about twenty men from the upper mines, organized, and, in three detachments, marched upon the Indian ranches, and consummated a most inhuman slaughter. A full account of what they term ' a fight ' you will find in the report which their captain, George H. Abbott, forwarded to me on the day of the massacre.

" The Indians were roused from sleep to meet their death, with but feeble show of resistance. They were shot down as they were attempting to escape from their houses; fifteen men and one squaw killed; two squaws badly wounded. On the part of the white men, not even the slightest wound was received. The houses of the Indians, with but one exception, were fired, and entirely destroyed. Thus was committed a massacre too inhuman to be readily believed. Now for my examination of this horrid affair.

" On the morning of the 29th of January I left Port Orford for the Coquille. We arrived at the ferry-house early in the evening of that day. Early in the morning of the day after my arrival I sent for the chief, who immediately came in, attended by about thirty of his people. The chief, as well as his people, was so greatly alarmed—apparently apprehensive that the white men would kill them even in my presence—that it was with a good deal of difficulty that I could induce him to express his mind freely. He seemed only anxious to stipulate for peace and the future safety of his people; and to procure this he was willing to accept any terms that I might dictate. The chief was evidently afraid to complain of or censure the slaughterers of his tribe, and for a time replied to all the charges made against him with hesitancy. After repeated assurances of protection, he finally answered to the point every interrogatory. I asked him if he had at any time fired at the man at the ferry-house. 'No!' was his prompt reply. At the time he was said to have fired at the white man, he declared with great earnestness that he shot at a duck in the river, at a distance of some two hundred yards from the ferry-house, when on his way home, and possibly the ball of his gun might have bounded from the water. My subsequent observation of the course of the river, and the point from which he was said to have fired, convinced me that his statement was entitled to the fullest credit. His statement is confirmed by the doubt expressed by one of the party at whom he was said to have fired.

" The white men making the accusation only heard the whizzing of a bullet. This was the only evidence adduced in proof of the chief having fired at them. I asked the chief if he, or if to his knowledge any of his people, had ever fired at the ferry-house. To this he answered, 'No.' He most emphatically denied ever sending threatening language to the men at the ferry, but admitted that some of his people had. He also admitted that some of his tribe had stolen from white men, and that they had used their horses without permission. He did not deny that his heart had been bad toward white men, and that he had hoped they would leave his country. He promised to do all I required of him. If I desired, he said he would leave the home of his fathers and take his people to the mountains; but, with my permission and protection, he would prefer remaining in the present home of his people.

" Everything I asked or required of him he readily assented to, promising most solemnly to maintain on his part permanent friendly relations with white men. My interview with the tribe occupied about two hours. During the entire council they listened with most profound attention, evidently being determined to fasten on their minds all that fell from my lips. At the conclusion of the council I requested the chief to send for all the guns and pistols in the possession of his men. You will be surprised when I tell you that all the guns and pistols in the hands of the Indians at the ranches amounted to just five pieces, two of which were unserviceable; as to powder and ball, I do not believe they had five rounds. Does this look like being prepared for war? Can any sane man believe those Indians, numbering not over seventy-five, all told, including women and children, had concocted a plan to expel from their country some three hundred whites? Such a conclusion is too preposterous to be entertained for a moment. There was no necessity for resorting to such extreme measures. I regard the murder of those Indians as one of the most barbarous acts ever perpetrated by civilized men. But what can be done? The leaders of the party cannot be arrested, though justice loudly demands their punishment. Here we have not even a justice of the peace ; and as to the military force garrisoned at Fort Orford, it consists of four men. If such murderous assaults are to be continued, there will be no end of Indian war in Oregon."—F. M. SMITH, *Sub-Agent*.

The Simon Kenton referred to in the following narrative was an experienced Indian fighter, and commanded a regiment in the war of 1812.

"In the course of the war of 1812 a plan was formed by some of the militia stationed at Urbana, Ohio, to attack an encampment of friendly Indians, who had been threatened by the hostile tribes, and were invited to remove with their families within our frontier settlements as a place of safety, under an assurance that they should be protected. Kenton remonstrated against the movement as being not only mutinous, but treacherous and cowardly. He vindicated the Indian character against the false charges which were alleged in justification of the outrage they were about to perpetrate, and warned them against the infamy they would incur by destroying a defenceless band of men, women, and children, who had been induced to place themselves in their power by a solemn promise of protection.

" He appealed to their humanity, their honor, and their duty as soldiers. He contrasted his knowledge of the character of those unfortunate people with their ignorance of it. He told them that he had endured suffering and torture at their hands again and again, but that it was in time of war, when they were defending their wives and children, and when he was seeking to destroy and exterminate them; and that, under those circumstances, he had no right to complain, and never did complain. But, said he, in time of peace they have always been kind, faithful friends, and generous, trustworthy men.

" Having exhausted the means of persuasion without effect, and finding them still resolved on executing their purpose, he took a rifle and called on them to proceed at once to the execution of the foul deed—declaring with great firmness that he would accompany them to the encampment, and shoot down the first man who attempted to molest it. ' My life,' said he, ' is drawing to a close: what remains of it is not worth much;' but, much or little, he was resolved that, if they entered the Indian camp, it should be done by passing over his corpse. Knowing that the old veteran would fulfil his promise, their hearts failed them; not one ventured to take the lead; their purpose was abandoned, and the Indians were saved."—BURNET *on the North-west Territory.*

V.

EXTRACTS

FROM THE REPORT OF THE COMMISSION SENT TO TREAT WITH THE SIOUX CHIEF, SITTING BULL, IN CANADA.

THE commission consisted of Brigadier-general Terry, Hon. A. G. Lawrence, and Colonel Corbin, secretary. After one month's journey, *via* Omaha, Nebraska, Helena, Montana, and Fort Benton, these gentlemen were met on the Canadian boundary by a Canadian officer with a mounted escort, who conducted them to Fort Walsh, when they were met by Sitting Bull and the other chiefs.

General Terry recapitulated to them the advantages of being at peace with the United States, the kindly treatment that all surrendered prisoners had received, and said: " The President invites you to come to the boundary of his and your country, and there give up your arms and ammunition, and thence to go to the agencies to which he will assign you, and there give up your horses, excepting those which are required for peace purposes. Your arms and horses will then be sold, and with all the money obtained for them cows will be bought and sent to you."

It is mortifying to think that representatives of the United States should have been compelled gravely to submit in a formal council proposals so ludicrous as these. The Indians must have been totally without sense of humor if they could have listened to them without laughter. Sitting Bull's reply is worthy of being put on record among the notable protests of Indian chiefs against the oppressions of their race.

He said: "For sixty-four years you have kept me and my people, and treated us bad. What have we done that you should want us to stop? We have done nothing. It is all the people on your side that have started us to do all these depredations. We could not go anywhere else, and so we took refuge in this country. * * * I would like to know why you came here. In the first place I did not give you the country; but you followed me from one place to another, so I had to leave and come over to this country, * * * You have got ears, and you have got eyes to see with them, and you see how I live with these people. You see me. Here I am. If you think I am a fool, you are a bigger fool than I am. This house is a medicine house. You come here to tell us lies, but we don't want to hear them. I don't wish any such language used to me—that is, to tell me lies in my Great Mother's house. This country is mine, and I intend to stay here and to raise this country full of grown people. See these people here. We were raised with them " (again shaking hands with the British officers). " That is enough, so no more. * * * The part of the country you gave me you ran me out of. * * * I wish you to go back, and to take it easy going back."

The-one-that-runs-the-Ree, a Santee chief, said: " You did n't treat us well, and I don't like you at all. * * * I will be at peace with these people as long as I live. This country is ours. We did not give it to you. You stole it away from us. You have come over here to tell us lies, and I don't propose to talk much, and that is all I have to say. I want you to take it easy going home. Don't go in a rush."

Nine, a Yankton, said: " Sixty-four years ago you got our country, and you promised to take good care of us and keep us. You ran from one place to another killing us and fighting us.* * * You did not treat us right over there, so we came back over here. * * * I come in to these people here, *and they give me permission to trade with the traders. That is the way I make my living.* Everything I get I buy from the traders. I don't steal anything.* * * I am going to live with these people here."

So profound a contempt did the Indians feel for this commission that they allowed a squaw to address it.

A squaw, named The-one-that-speaks-once, wife of The-man-that-scatters-the-bear, said: " I was over at your country. I wanted to raise my children there, but you did not give me any time. I came over to this country to raise my children, and have a little peace " (shaking hands with the British officers); " that is all I have to say to you. I want you to go back where you came from. These are the people that I am going to stay with and raise my children with."

The Indians having risen, being apparently about to leave the room, the interpreter was directed to ask the following questions: " Shall I say to the President that you refuse the offers that he has made to you ? Are we to understand that you refuse those offers ? " Sitting Bull answered: " I could tell you more, but that is all I have to tell. If we told you more, you would not pay any attention to it. This part of the country does not belong to your people. You belong on the other side, this side belongs to us."

The Crow, shaking hands, and embracing Colonel McLeod, and shaking hands with the other British officers, said : " This is the way I will live in this part of the country. * * * *These people that don't hide anything*, they are all the people I like. * * * Sixty-four years ago I shook hands with the soldiers, and ever since that I have had hardships. I made peace with them; and ever since then I have been running from one place to another to keep out of their way. * * * Go to where you were born, and stay there. I came over to this country, and my Great Mother knows all about it. She knows I came over here, and she don't wish anything of me. We think, and all the women in the camp think, we are going to have the country full of people. * * * I have come back in this part of the country again to have plenty more people, to live in peace, and raise children."

The Indians then inquired whether the commission had anything more to say, and the commission answered that they had nothing more to say, and the conference closed.

The commission, with a naïve lack of comprehension of the true situation of the case, go on to say that " they are convinced that Sitting Bull and the bands under him will not seek to return to this country at present. It is believed that they are restrained from returning," partly by their recollection of the severe handling they had by the military forces of the United States in the last winter and spring, and partly " by their belief that, for some reason which they cannot fathom, the Government of the United States earnestly desires that they shall return. * * * In their intense hostility to our Government, they are determined to contravene its wishes to the best of their ability." It would seem so—even to the extent of foregoing all the privileges offered them on their return—the giving up of all weapons—the exchanging of their horses for cows—and the priceless privilege of being shut up on reservations, off which they could not go without being pursued, arrested, and brought back by troops. What a depth of malignity must be in the breasts of these Indians, that to gratify it they will voluntarily relinquish all these benefits, and continue to remain in a country where they must continue to hunt, and make their own living on the unjust plan of free trade in open markets !

VI.

ACCOUNT OF SOME OF THE OLD GRIEVANCES OF THE SIOUX.

INTERVIEW BETWEEN RED IRON, CHIEF OF THE SISSETON SIOUX, AND GOVERNOR RAMSEY, IN DECEMBER, 1852.

CLAIMS had been set up by the Indian traders for $400,000 of the money promised to the Sioux by the treaties of 1851 and 1852. The Indians declared that they did not owe so much. Governor Ramsey endeavored to compel Red Iron to sign a receipt for it; he refused. He said his tribe had never had the goods. He asked the governor to appoint arbitrators—two white men and one Indian; it was refused. He then said that he would accept three white men as arbitrators, if they were honest men: this was refused.

An eye-witness has sketched the appearance of the chief on that occasion, and the interview between him and the governor : The council was crowded with Indians and white men when Red Iron was brought in, guarded by soldiers. He was about forty years old, tall and athletic; about six feet high in his moccasins, with a large, well-developed head, aquiline nose, thin compressed lips, and physiognomy beaming with intelligence and resolution. He was clad in the half-military, half-Indian costume of the Dakota chiefs. He was seated in the council-room without greeting or salutation from any one. In a few minutes the governor, turning to the chief in the midst of a breathless silence, by the aid of an interpreter, opened the council.

Governor Ramsey asked : " What excuse have you for not coming to the council when I sent for you ? "

The chief rose to his feet with native grace and dignity, his blanket falling from his shoulders, and purposely dropping the pipe of peace, he stood erect before the governor with his arms folded, and right hand pressed on the sheath of his scalping-knife; with firm voice he replied :

" I started to come, but your braves drove me back."

Gov. " What excuse have you for not coming the second time I sent for you ? "

Red Iron. " No other excuse than I have given you."

Gov. " At the treaty I thought you a good man, but since you have acted badly, and I am disposed to break you. I do break you."

Red Iron. "You break me! My people made me a chief. My people love me. I will still be their chief. I have done nothing wrong."

Gov. "Why did you get your braves together and march around here for the purpose of intimidating other chiefs, and prevent their coming to the council ?"

Red Iron. "I did not get my braves together, they got together themselves to prevent boys going to council to be made chiefs, to sign papers, and to prevent single chiefs going to council at night, to be bribed to sign papers for money we have never got. We have heard how the Medewakantons were served at Mendota; that by secret councils you got their names on paper, and took away their money. We don't want to be served so. My braves wanted to come to council in the daytime, when the sun shines, and we want no councils in the dark. We want all our people to go to council together, so that we can all know what is done."

Gov. "Why did you attempt to come to council with your braves, when I had forbidden your braves coming to council?"

Red Iron. "You invited the chiefs only, and would not let the braves come too. This is not the way we have been treated before; this is not according to our customs, for among Dakotas chiefs and braves go to council together. When you first sent for us, there were two or three chiefs here, and we wanted to wait till the rest would come, that we might all be in council together and know what was done, and so that we might all understand the papers, and know what we were signing. When we signed the treaty the traders threw a blanket over our faces and darkened our eyes, and made us sign papers which we did not understand, and which were not explained or read to us. We want our Great Father at Washington to know what has been done."

Gov. "Your Great Father has sent me to represent him, and what I say is what he says. He wants you to pay your old debts, in accordance with the paper you signed when the treaty was made, and to leave that money in my hands to pay these debts. If you refuse to do that I will take the money back."

Red Iron. "You can take the money back. We sold our land to you, and you promised to pay us. If you don't give us the money I will be glad, and all our people will be glad, for we will have our land back if you don't give us the money. That paper was not interpreted or explained to us. We are told it gives about 300 boxes ($300,000) of our money to some of the traders. We don't think we owe them so much. We want to pay all our debts. We want our Great Father to send three good men here to tell us how much we do owe, and whatever they say we will pay; and that's what all these braves say. Our chiefs and all our people say this." All the Indians present responded, "Ho! ho!"

Gov. "That can't be done. You owe more than your money will pay, and I am ready now to pay your annuity, and no more; and when you are ready to receive it, the agent will pay you."

Red Iron. "We will receive our annuity, but we will sign no papers for anything else. The snow is on the ground, and we have been waiting a long time to get our money. We are poor; you have plenty. Your fires are warm. Your tepees keep out the cold. We have nothing to eat. We have been waiting a long time for our moneys. Our hunting-season is past. A great many of our people are sick, for being hungry. We may die because you won't pay us. We may die, but if we do we will leave our bones on the ground, that our Great Father may see where his Dakota children died. We are very poor. We have sold our hunting-grounds and the graves of our fathers. We have sold our own graves. We have no place to bury our dead, and you will not pay us the money for our lands."

The council was broken up, and Red Iron was sent to the guard-house, where he was kept till next day. Between thirty and forty of the braves of Red Iron's band were present during this arrangement before the governor. When he was led away, they departed in sullen silence, headed by Lean Bear, to a spot a quarter of a mile from the council-house, where they uttered a succession of yells—the gathering signal of the Dakotas. Ere the echoes died away, Indians were hurrying from their tepees toward them, prepared for battle. They proceeded to the eminence near the camp, where mouldered the bones of many warriors. It was the memorable battle-ground, where their ancestors had fought, in a conflict like Waterloo, the warlike Sacs and Foxes, thereby preserving their lands and nationality. Upon this field stood two hundred resolute warriors ready to do battle for their hereditary chief. Lean Bear, the principal brave of Red Iron's band, was a large, resolute man, about thirty-five years of age, and had great influence in his nation.

Here, on their old battle-ground, Lean Bear recounted the brave deeds of Red Iron, the long list of wrongs inflicted on the

Indians by the white men, and proposed to the braves that they should make a general attack on the whites. By the influence of some of the half-breeds, and of white men who were known to be friendly to them, Lean Bear was induced to abandon his scheme; and finally, the tribe, being starving, consented to give up their lands and accept the sum of money offered to them.

" Over $55,000 of this treaty money, paid for debts of the Indians, went to one Hugh Tyler, a stranger in the country, 'for getting the treaties through the Senate, and for necessary disbursements in securing the assent of the chiefs.' "

Five years later another trader, under the pretence that he was going to get back for them some of this stolen treaty money, obtained their signature to vouchers, by means of which he cheated them out of $12,000 more. At this same time he obtained a payment of $4,500 for goods he said they had stolen from him. Another man was allowed a claim of $5,000 for horses he said they had stolen from him.

" In 1858 the chiefs were taken to Washington, and agreed to the treaties for the cession of all their reservation north of the Minnesota River, under which, as ratified by the Senate, they were to have $166,000; but of this amount they never received one penny till four years afterward, when $15,000 in goods were sent to the Lower Sioux, and these were deducted out of what was due them under former treaties."—*History of the Sioux War,* by ISAAC V. D. HEARD.

This paragraph gives the causes of the fearful Minnesota massacre, in which eight hundred people lost their lives.

The treaty expressly provided that no claims against the Indians should be paid unless approved by the Indians in open council. No such council was held. A secret council was held with a few chiefs, but the body of the Indians were ignorant of it. There was a clause in this treaty that the Secretary of the Interior might use any funds of the Indians for such purposes of civilization as his judgment should dictate. Under this clause the avails of over six hundred thousand acres of land were taken for claims against the Indians. Of the vast amount due to the Lower Sioux, only a little over $800 was left to their credit in Washington at the time of the outbreak. Moreover, a portion of their annual annuity was also taken for claims.

REMOVAL OF THE SIOUX AND WINNEBAGOES FROM MINNESOTA IN 1863.

" The guard that accompanied these Indians consisted of four commissioned officers, one hundred and thirty-five soldiers, and one laundress; in all, one hundred and forty persons. The number of Santee Sioux transported was thirteen hundred and eighteen. For the transportation and subsistence of these Indians and the guard there was paid the sum of $36,322.10.

" The number of Winnebagoes transported was nineteen hundred and forty-five; for their transportation and subsistence there was paid the farther sum of $56,042.60—making the whole amount paid the contractors $92,364.70.

" The Sioux were transported from Fort Snelling to Hannibal, Missouri, on two steamboats. One of the boats stopped there, and the Indians on it crossed over to St. Joseph, on the Missouri River, by rail. The other boat continued to the junction of the Mississippi and Missouri rivers, and thence up the latter to St. Joseph; and here the Indians that crossed over by rail were put upon the boat, and from thence to Crow Creek all of them were on one boat. They were very much crowded from St. Joseph to Crow Creek. Sixteen died on the way, being without attention or medical supplies. All the Indians were excluded from the cabin of the boat, and confined to the lower and upper decks. It was in May, and to go among them on the lower deck was suffocating. They were fed on hard bread and mess pork, much of it not cooked, there being no opportunity to cook it only at night when the boat laid up. They had no sugar, coffee, or vegetables. Confinement on the boat in such a mass, and want of proper food, created much sickness, such as diarrhœa and fevers. For weeks after they arrived at Crow Creek the Indians died at the rate of from three to four per day. In a few weeks one hundred and fifty had died, mainly on account of the treatment they had received after leaving Fort Snelling."—MANEYPENNY, *Our Indian Wards.*

FOOD OF THE INDIANS AT CROW CREEK, DAKOTA, IN THE WINTER OF 1864.

" During the summer the Indians were fed on flour and pork; they got no beef till fall. They suffered for want of fresh beef as well as for medical supplies. In the fall their ration began to fail; and the issue was gradually reduced; and the Indians complained bitterly. * * * The beef furnished was from the cattle that hauled the supplies from Minnesota. These cattle had travelled over three hundred miles, hauling the train, with nothing to eat but the dry prairie grass, there being no settlements on the route they came. The cattle were very poor. Some died or gave out on the trip, and such were slaughtered, and the meat brought in on the train for food for the Indians. About the 1st of January, 1864, near four hundred of the cattle were slaughtered. Except the dry prairie grass, which the frost had killed, these cattle had no food from the time they came to Crow Creek until they were slaughtered. A part of the beef thus made was piled up in the warehouse in snow, and the remainder in like manner packed in snow outside. This beef was to keep the Indians until the coming June. The beef was black, and very poor—the greater part only skin and bone. Shortly after the arrival of the train from Minnesota the contractors for supplying the Indians with flour took about one hundred head of the oxen, selecting the best of them, yoked them up, and sent them with wagons to Sioux City, some two hundred and forty miles, to haul up flour. This train returned in February, and these oxen were then slaughtered, and fed to the Indians.

"In January the issue of soup to the Indians commenced. It was made in a large cotton-wood vat, being cooked by steam carried from the boiler of the saw-mill in a pipe to the vat. The vat was partly filled with water, then several quarters of beef chopped up were thrown into it, and a few sacks of flour added. The hearts, lights. and entrails were added to the compound, and in the beginning a few beans were put into the vat; but this luxury did not continue long. This soup was issued every other day—to the Santee Sioux one day, the alternate day to the Winnebagoes. It was very unpalatable. On the day the Indians received the soup they had no other food issued to them. They were very much dissatisfied, and said they could not live on the soup, when those in charge told them if they could live elsewhere they had better go, but that they must not go to the white settlements. Many of them did leave the agency, some going to Fort Sully, others to Fort Randall, in search of food. From a description of this nauseous mess called soup, given by Samuel C. Haynes, then at Fort Randall, and assistant-surgeon in the military service, it is seen that the Indians had good cause to leave Crow Creek. He states that there were thrown into the vat 'beef, beef-heads, entrails of the beeves, some beans, flour, and pork. I think there were put into the vat two barrels of flour each time, which was not oftener than once in twenty-four hours. This mass was then cooked by the steam from the boiler passing through the pipe into the vat. When that was done, all the Indians were ordered to come with their pails and get it. It was dipped out to the Indians with a long-handled dipper made for the purpose. I cannot say the quantity given to each. It was about the consistency of very thin gruel. The Indians would pour off the thinner portion and eat that which settled at the bottom. As it was dipped out of the vat, some of the Indians would get the thinner portions and some would get some meat. I passed there frequently when it was cooking, and was often there when it was being issued. It had a very offensive odor. It had the odor of the contents of the entrails of the beeves. I have seen the settlings of the vat after they were through issuing it to the Indians, when they were cleaning the vat, and the settlings smelled like carrion—like decomposed meat. Some of the Indians refused to eat it, saying they could not, it made them sick.' "—MANEYPENNY, *Our Indian Wards.*

VII.

LETTER FROM SARAH WINNEMUCCA,

AN EDUCATED PAH-UTE WOMAN.

To Major H. Douglas, U. S. Army:

SIR,—I learn from the commanding officer at this post that you desire full information in regard to the Indians around this place, with a view, if possible, of bettering their condition by sending them on the Truckee River Reservation. All the Indians from here to Carson City belong to the Pah-Ute tribe. My father, whose name is Winnemucca, is the head chief of the whole tribe; but he is now getting too old, and has not energy enough to command, nor to impress on their minds the necessity of their being sent on the reservation. In fact, I think he is entirely opposed to it. He, myself, and most of the Humboldt and Queen's River Indians were on the Truckee Reservation at one time; but if we had stayed there, it would be only to starve. I think that if they had received what they were entitled to from the agents, they would never have left them. So far as their knowledge of agriculture extends, they are quite ignorant, as they have never had the opportunity of learning; but I think, if proper pains were taken, that they would willingly make the effort to maintain themselves by their own labor, providing they could be made to believe that the products were their own, for their own use and comfort. It is needless for me to enter into details as to how we were treated on the reservation while there. It is enough to say that we were confined to the reserve, and had to live on what fish we might be able to catch in the river. If this is the kind of civilization awaiting us on the reserves, God grant that we may never be compelled to go on one, as it is much preferable to live in the mountains and drag out an existence in our native manner. So far as living is concerned, the Indians at all military posts get enough to eat and considerable cast-off clothing.

But how long is this to continue? What is the object of the Government in regard to Indians? Is it enough that we are at peace? Remove all the Indians from the military posts and place them on reservations such as the Truckee and Walker River Reservations (as they were conducted), and it will require a greater military force stationed round to keep them within the limits than it now does to keep them in subjection. On the other hand, if the Indians have any guarantee that they can secure a permanent home on their own native soil, and that our white neighbors can be kept from encroaching on our rights, after having a reasonable share of ground allotted to us as our own, and giving us the required advantages of learning, I warrant that the savage (as he is called to-day) will be a thrifty and law-abiding member of the community fifteen or twenty years hence.

Sir, if at any future time you should require information regarding the Indians here, I will be happy to furnish the same if I can.

SARAH WINNEMUCCA.

Camp McDermitt, Nevada, April 4th, 1870.

VIII.

LAWS OF THE DELAWARE NATION OF INDIANS.

[Adopted July 21st, A.D. 1866.]

THE chiefs and councillors of the Delaware tribe of Indians convened at their council-house, on the reservation of said tribe, adopted July 21st, 1866, the following laws, to be amended as they think proper:

ARTICLE I.

Section 1. A national jail shall be built on the public grounds, upon which the council-house is now situated.

Sec. 2. Any person who shall steal any horse, mule, ass, or cattle of any kind, shall be punished as follows: For the first offence the property of the offender shall be sold by the sheriff, to pay the owner of the animal stolen the price of said animal, and all costs he may sustain in consequence of such theft. But if the offender has no property, or if his property be insufficient to pay for the animal stolen, so much of his annuity shall be retained as may be necessary to pay the owner of said animal, as above directed, and no relative of said offender shall be permitted to assist him in paying the penalties of said theft. For the second offence the thief shall be sent to jail for thirty-five days, and shall pay all costs and damages the owner may sustain on account of said theft. For the third offence the thief shall be confined in jail three months, and shall pay all costs and damages, as above provided.

Sec. 3. If any person shall steal a horse beyond the limits of the reserve, and bring it within the limits thereof, it shall be lawful for the owner to pursue and reclaim the same upon presenting satisfactory proof of ownership, and, if necessary, receive the assistance of the officers of the Delaware nation. *And it is further provided,* that such officials as may from time to time be clothed with power by the United States agent may pursue such offender either within or without the limits of the reserve.

Sec. 4. Whoever shall ride any horse without the consent of the owner thereof shall, for the first offence, pay the sum of ten dollars for each day and night that he may keep the said animal; and for the second offence shall be confined in jail for the term of twenty-one days, besides paying a fine of ten dollars.

Sec. 5. Whoever shall reclaim and return any such animal to the rightful owner, other than the wrong-doer, as in the last section mentioned, shall receive therefor the sum of two and fifty-hundredths dollars.

Sec. 6. In all cases of theft, the person or persons convicted of such theft shall be adjudged to pay all costs and damages resulting therefrom; and in case of the final loss of any animal stolen, then the offender shall pay the price thereof in addition to the costs and damages, as provided in a previous section.

Sec. 7. Whoever shall steal any swine or sheep shall, for the first offence, be fined the sum of fifteen dollars; ten of which shall be paid to the owner of the sheep or swine taken, and five dollars to the witness of the theft; for the second offence the thief shall, in addition to the above penalty, be confined in jail for twenty-eight days; and for the third offence the thief shall be confined four weeks in jail, and then receive a trial, and bear such punishment as may be adjudged upon such trial.

Sec. 8. Whoever shall steal a fowl of any description shall, for the first offence, pay to the owner of such animal the sum of five dollars; for the second offence, in addition to the above penalty, the thief shall be confined in jail for twenty-one days. The witness by whom such theft shall be proven shall be entitled to receive such reasonable compensation as may be allowed to him, to be paid by the offender.

Sec. 9. A lawful fence shall be eight rails high, well staked and ridered. If any animal shall break through or over a lawful fence, as above defined, and do any damage, the owner of the enclosure shall give notice thereof to the owner of such animal, without injury to the animal. The owner of such animal shall therefore take care of the same, and prevent his doing damage; but should he neglect or refuse so to do, the animal itself shall be sold to pay for the damage it may have done. But if the premises be not enclosed by a lawful fence, as above defined, the owner of the enclosure shall receive no damages; but should he injure any animal getting into such enclosure, shall pay for any damage he may do such animal.

Sec. 10. Every owner of stock shall have his or her brand or mark put on such stock, and a description of the brand or mark of every person in the tribe shall be recorded by the national clerk.

ARTICLE II.

Sec. 1. Whoever shall maliciously set fire to a house shall, for the first offence, pay to the owner of such house all damages which he may sustain in consequence of such fire; and, in addition thereto, for the second offence shall be confined in jail for the term of twenty-one days.

Sec. 2. Should human life be sacrificed in consequence of any such fire, the person setting fire as aforesaid shall suffer death by hanging.

Sec. 3. It shall be unlawful for any person to set on fire any woods or prairie, except for the purpose of protecting property, and then only at such times as shall permit the person so setting the fire to extinguish the same.

Sec. 4. Whoever shall violate the provisions of the last preceding section shall, for the first offence, be fined the sum of five dollars, and pay the full value of all property thereby destroyed; for the second offence, in addition to the penalty above described, the offender shall be confined in jail for the term of thirty-five days; and for the third offence the same punishment, except that the confinement in jail shall be for the period of three months.

Sec. 5. Any person living outside of the reserve cutting hay upon the land of one living on the reserve, shall pay to the owner of such land the sum of one dollar per acre, or one-half of the hay so cut.

Sec. 6. No person shall sell any wood on the reserve, except said wood be first cut and corded.

ARTICLE III.

Sec. 1. Whoever shall find any lost article shall forthwith return the same to the owner, if he can be found, under the penalty imposed for stealing such article, for a neglect of such duty.

Sec. 2. Whoever shall take any article of property without permission of its owner shall pay the price of the article so taken, and receive such punishment as the judge in his discretion may impose.

ARTICLE IV.

Sec. 1. Whoever shall take up any animal on the reserve as a stray shall, within one week, have the description of such animal recorded in the stray-book kept by the council.

Sec. 2. If the owner of said stray shall claim the same within one year from the day on which the description was recorded, he shall be entitled to take it, after duly proving his property, and paying at the rate of five dollars per month for the keeping of such animal.

Sec. 3. The title to any stray, duly recorded, and not claimed within one year from the date of such record, shall rest absolutely in the person taking up and recording the same.

Sec. 4. Whoever shall take up a stray, and refuse or neglect to record a description of the same, as provided in Section 1 of this Article, shall be deemed to have stolen such animal, if the same be found in his possession, and shall suffer the penalties inflicted for stealing like animals. The stray shall be taken from him, and remain at the disposal of the council, and a description of the same shall be recorded in the stray-book.

ARTICLE V.

Sec. 1. If a person commit murder in the first degree, he shall, upon conviction, suffer the penalty of death; but if the evidence against him be insufficient, or if the killing be done in self-defence, the person doing the killing shall be released.

Sec. 2. Whoever shall, by violence, do bodily harm to the person of another shall be arrested, and suffer such punishment as may on trial be adjudged against him; and should death result from such bodily harm done to the person of another, the offender shall be arrested, and suffer such punishment as may be adjudged against him.

Sec. 3. Whoever shall wilfully slander an innocent party shall be punished for such slander at the discretion of the judge.

Sec. 4. Whoever, being intoxicated or under the influence of liquor, shall display at the house of another, in a dangerous or threatening manner, any deadly weapons, and refuse to desist therefrom, being commanded so to do, and put up such weapons, either by the owner of the house or by any other person, shall for the first offence be fined the sum of five dollars, and pay all damages which may accrue; for the second offence shall be confined in jail twenty-one days, and pay a fine of ten dollars, and pay all damages which may accrue; and for the third offence shall be imprisoned in the jail for thirty-five days, be fined twenty dollars, and pay all damages as aforesaid.

Sec. 5. Officers shall be appointed to appraise all damages accruing under the last preceding section, who shall hear all the evidence, and render judgment according to the law and the evidence.

Sec. 6. Whoever shall, being under the influence of liquor, attend public worship or any other public meeting, shall first be commanded peaceably to depart; and if he refuses, it shall be the duty of the sheriff to arrest and confine such person until he becomes sober; and the offender shall pay a fine of five dollars.

Sec. 7. It shall be the duty of the sheriff to attend all meetings for public worship.

Sec. 8. No member of the Delaware nation shall be held liable for any debts contracted in the purchase of intoxicating liquors.

Sec. 9. The United States Agent and the chiefs shall have power to grant license to bring merchandise to the national payment ground for sale to so many traders as they may think proper for the interest of the nation.

Sec. 10. It shall be unlawful for any one person to bring any kind of drinks, except coffee, on the payment ground ; and any person who shall offend against this section shall forfeit his drinkables and his right to remain on the payment ground.

Sec. 11. It shall be unlawful for any one person to bring within the reserve more than one pint of spirituous liquors at any one time. For the first offence against this section the offender shall forfeit his liquors, and pay a fine of five dollars; for the second offence he shall forfeit his liquors, and pay a fine of ten dollars ; and for the third offence he shall forfeit his liquors, and be fined the sum of twenty-five dollars.

Sec. 12. Any person who shall find another in possession of more than one pint of liquor at one time upon the reserve may lawfully spill and destroy the same, and shall use such force as may be necessary for such purpose. Should the owner resist, and endeavor to commit bodily harm upon the person engaged in spilling or destroying said liquor, he shall be taken into custody by the sheriff, and be punished as an offender against the law.

Sec. 13. The sheriff may lawfully compel any man or any number of men, ministers of the Gospel excepted, to assist in capturing any person who shall violate these laws.

Sec. 14. Whoever shall offer resistance to any capture or arrest for violating any of the provisions of these laws shall be punished, not only for the original offence for which he was arrested, but also for resisting an officer.

ARTICLE VI.

Sec. 1. All business affecting the general interest of the nation shall be transacted by the council in regular sessions.

Sec. 2. All personal acts of chiefs, councillors, or private individuals, in such matters as affect the general interest of the nation, shall be considered null and void.

Sec. 3. Whoever shall violate the last preceding section by undertaking, in a private capacity and manner, to transact public and national business, shall be imprisoned in the national jail for a period not less than six months nor more than one year, and shall forfeit his place of office or position in the nation; which place or position shall be filled by the appointment of other suitable persons.

Sec. 4. Councillors shall be appointed who shall take an oath faithfully to perform their duties to the nation, and for neglect of such duties others shall be appointed to fill their places.

Sec. 5. Should a councillor go on a journey, so that it is impossible for him to attend the meetings of the council regularly, he may appoint a substitute who shall act for him in his absence.

Sec. 6. Certain days shall be set apart for council and court days.

Sec. 7. The chiefs and councillors shall appoint three sheriffs, at a salary of one hundred and fifty dollars per annum each; one clerk, at one hundred dollars per annum; and one jailer, at a salary of one hundred dollars per annum, whose salary shall be due and payable half-yearly; and in case either of the above officers shall neglect or refuse to perform any of the duties of his office, he shall forfeit his salary, and his office shall be declared vacant, and another shall be appointed to fill the office.

Sec. 8. The chiefs and councillors shall semi-annually, in April and October, make an appropriation for national expenses, which appropriation shall be taken from the trust fund, or any other due the Delawares, and paid to the treasury.

Sec. 9. There shall be a treasurer appointed annually, on the first day of April, whose duty it shall be to receive and disburse all moneys to be used for national purposes ; but the treasurer shall pay out money only on order of chiefs and councillors, and for his services shall be paid five per cent. on the amount disbursed.

ARTICLE VII.

Sec. 1. It shall be lawful for any person, before his or her death, to make a will, and thereby dispose of his or her property as he or she may desire.

Sec. 2. If a man dies, leaving no will to show the disposal of his property, and leaves a widow and children, one-fourth of his property shall be set aside for the payment of his debts. Should the property so set aside be insufficient to pay all his debts in full, it shall be divided among his creditors *pro rata*, which *pro rata* payment shall be received by his creditors in full satisfaction of all claims and demands whatever.

Sec. 3. If the property so set apart for the payment of debts is more than sufficient to pay all debts, the remainder shall be equally divided among the children.

Sec. 4. The widow shall be entitled to one-third of the property not set aside for the payment of debts.

Sec. 5. If a man dies, leaving no widow or children, his debts shall first be paid out of the proceeds of his personal property, and the remainder, if any, with the real estate, shall be given to the nearest relative.

Sec. 6. Whoever shall take or receive any portion of the property belonging to the widow and orphans, shall be punished as if he had stolen the property.

Sec. 7. The council shall appoint guardians for orphan children when they deem it expedient so to do.

Article VIII.

Sec. 1. If a white man marry a member of the nation, and accumulate property by such marriage, said property shall belong to his wife and children; nor shall he be allowed to remove any portion of such property beyond the limits of the reserve.

Sec. 2. Should such white man lose his wife, all the property shall belong to the children, and no subsequent wife shall claim any portion of such property.

Sec. 3. Should such white man die in the nation, leaving no children, all his property shall belong to his wife, after paying his debts.

Sec. 4. Should such white man lose his wife, and have no children, one-half of the personal property shall belong to him, and the other half shall belong to his wife's nearest relatives.

Sec. 5. Should such white man be expelled from the reserve, and the wife choose to follow her husband, she shall forfeit all her right and interest in the reserve.

Article IX.

Sec. 1. No member of the nation shall lease any grounds to persons not members of the nation.

Sec. 2. Should a white man seek employment of any member of the nation, he shall first give his name to the United States Agent, and furnish him with a certificate of good moral character, and also a statement of the time for which he is employed, and the name of his employer.

Sec. 3. The employed shall pay all hired help according to agreement.

Sec. 4. Any person or persons violating any of the provisions of these laws on the reserve shall be punished as therein provided.

Sec. 5. All white men on the reserve disregarding these laws shall also be expelled from the reserve.

ARTICLE X.

Sec. 1. Whoever shall forcibly compel any woman to commit adultery, or who shall commit a rape upon a woman, shall, for the first offence, be fined the sum of fifty dollars, and be imprisoned in jail for thirty-five days; for the second offence he shall be fined one hundred dollars, and be confined three months in the national jail; and for the third offence he shall be punished as the court shall see proper.

IX.

ACCOUNT OF THE CHEROKEE WHO INVENTED THE CHEROKEE ALPHABET.

"SEQUOYAH, a Cherokee Indian, instead of joining the rude sports of Indian boys while a child, took great delight in exercising his ingenuity by various mechanical labors. He also assisted in the management of his mother's property, consisting of a farm and cattle and horses. In his intercourse with the whites he became aware that they possessed an art by which a name impressed upon a hard substance might be understood at a glance by any one acquainted with the art. He requested an educated half-breed, named Charles Hicks, to write his name; which being done, he made a die containing a fac-simile of the word, which he stamped upon all the articles fabricated by his mechanical ingenuity. From this he proceeded to the art of drawing, in which he made rapid progress before he had the opportunity of seeing a picture or engraving. These accomplishments made the young man very popular among his associates, and particularly among the red ladies; but it was long before incessant adulation produced any evil effect upon his character. At length, however, he was prevailed upon to join his companions, and share in the carouse which had been supplied by his own industry. But he soon wearied of an idle and dissipated life, suddenly resolved to give up drinking, and learned the trade of a blacksmith by his own unaided efforts. In the year 1820, while on a visit to some friends in a Cherokee village, he listened to a conversation on the art of writing, which seems always to have been the subject of great curiosity among the Indians. Sequoyah remarked that he did not regard the art as so very extraordinary, and believed he could invent a plan by which the red man might do the same thing. The company were incredulous; but the matter had long been the subject of his reflections, and he had come to the conclusion that letters represented words or ideas, and being always uniform, would always convey the same meaning. His first plan was to invent signs for words; but upon trial he was speedily satisfied that this would be too cumbrous and laborious, and he soon contrived the plan of an alphabet which should represent sounds, each character standing for a syllable. He persevered in carrying out his intention, and attained his object by forming eighty-six characters.

" While thus employed he incurred the ridicule of his neighbors, and was entreated to desist by his friends. The invention, however, was completely successful, and the Cherokee dialect is now a written language; a result entirely due to the extraordinary genius of Sequoyah. After teaching many to read and write, he left the Cherokee nation in 1822 on a visit to Arkansas, and introduced the art among the Cherokees who had emigrated to that country; and, after his return home, a correspondence was opened in the Cherokee language between the two branches of the nation. In the autumn of 1823 the General Council bestowed upon him a silver medal in honor of his genius, and as an expression of gratitude for his eminent public services."—*North American Review.*

" We may remark, with reference to the above, that as each letter of this alphabet represents one of eighty-six sounds, of which in various transpositions the language is composed, a Cherokee can read as soon as he has learned his alphabet. It is said that a clever boy may thus be taught to read in a single day."—*The Saturday Magazine*, London, April, 1842.

X.

PRICES PAID BY WHITE MEN FOR SCALPS.

" In the wars between France and England and their colonies, their Indian allies were entitled to a premium for every scalp of an enemy. In the war preceding 1703 the Government of Massachusetts gave twelve pounds for every Indian scalp. In 1722 it was augmented to one hundred pounds—a sum sufficient to purchase a considerable extent of American land. On the 25th of February, 1745, an act was passed by the American colonial legislature, entitled ' An Act for giving a reward for scalps.' "—*Sketches of the History, Manners, and Customs of the North American Indians, by* JAMES BUCHANAN, 1824.

"There was a constant rivalry between the Governments of Great Britain, France, and the United States as to which of them should secure the services of the barbarians to scalp their white enemies, while each in turn was the loudest to denounce the shocking barbarities of such tribes as they failed to secure in their own service; and the civilized world, aghast at these horrid recitals, ignores the fact that nearly every important massacre in the history of North America was organized and directed by agents of some one of these Governments."—GALE, *Upper Mississippi.*

XI.

EXTRACT FROM TREATY WITH CHEYENNES, IN 1865.

ART. 6th of the treaty of Oct. 14th, 1865, between the United States and the chiefs and headmen representing the confederated tribes of the Arapahoe and Cheyenne Indians:

"The United States being desirous to express its condemnation of, and as far as may be repudiate the gross and wanton outrages perpetrated against certain bands of Cheyenne and Arapahoe Indians by Colonel J. M. Chivington, in command of United States troops, on the 29th day of November, 1864, at Sand Creek, in Colorado Territory, while the said Indians were at peace with the United States and under its flag, whose protection they had by lawful authority been promised and induced to seek, and the Government, being desirous to make some suitable reparation for the injuries thus done, will grant 320 acres of land by patent to each of the following named chiefs of said bands, * * * and will in like manner grant to each other person of said bands made a widow, or who lost a parent on that occasion, 160 acres of land. * * * The United States will also pay in United States securities, animals, goods, provisions, or such other useful articles as may in the discretion of the Secretary of the Interior be deemed best adapted to the respective wants and conditions of the persons named in the schedule hereto annexed, they being present and members of the bands who suffered at Sand Creek on the occasion aforesaid, the sums set opposite their names respectively, as a compensation for property belonging to them, and then and there destroyed or taken from them by the United States troops aforesaid."

One of the Senate amendments to this treaty struck out the words "by Colonel J. M. Chivington, in command of United States troops." If this were done with a view of relieving "Colonel J. M. Chivington" of obloquy, or of screening the fact that "United States troops" were the instruments by which the murders were committed, is not clear. But in either case the device was a futile one. The massacre will be known as "The Chivington Massacre" as long as history lasts, and the United States must bear its share of the infamy of it.

XII.

WOOD-CUTTING BY INDIANS IN DAKOTA.

In his report for 1877 the Superintendent of Indian Affairs in Dakota says: "Orders have been received to stop cutting of wood by Indians, to pay them for what they have already cut, to take possession of it and sell it. This I am advised is under a recent decision which deprives Indians of any ownership in the wood until the land is taken by them in severalty. If agents do not enforce these orders, they lay themselves liable. If they do enforce them, the Indians are deprived of what little motive they have for labor. In the mean time, aliens of all nations cut wood on Indian lands, sell to steamboats, fill contracts for the army and for Indian agencies at high prices. * * * Cutting wood is one of the very few things an Indian can do in Dakota at this time."

XIII.

SEQUEL TO THE WALLA WALLA MASSACRE.

[This narrative was written by a well-known army officer, correspondent of the *Army and Navy Journal*, and appeared in that paper Nov. 1st, 1879.]

The history of that affair (the Walla Walla Massacre) was never written, we believe; or, if it was, the absolute facts in the case were never given by any unprejudiced person, and it may be interesting to not a few to give them here. The story, as told by our Washington correspondent, "Ebbitt," who was a witness of the scenes narrated, is as follows:

" The first settlements in Oregon, some thirty years ago, were

made by a colony of Methodists. One of the principal men
among them was the late Mr. or Governor Abernethy, as he was
called, as he was for a short time the prominent Governor of Oregon. He was the father-in-law of our genial Deputy Quartermas-
ter-general Henry C. Hodges, an excellent man, and he must not
be remembered as one of those who were responsible for the shocking proceedings which we are about to relate. A minister by the
name of Whitman, we believe, had gone up to the Walla Walla
region, where he was kindly received by the Cayuse and other
friendly Indians, who, while they did not particularly desire to
be converted to the Christian faith as expounded by one of Wesley's followers, saw no special objection to the presence of the
missionary. So they lived quietly along for a year or two; then
the measles broke out among the Indians, and a large number of
them were carried off. They were told by their medicine men
that the disease was owing to the presence of the whites, and Mr.
Whitman was notified that he must leave their country. Filled
with zeal for the cause, and not having sense enough to grasp the
situation, he refused to go.

" At this time the people of the Hudson's Bay Company had
great influence with all the Indians in that region, and the good
old Governor Peter Skeen Ogden was the chief factor of the Company at Fort Vancouver. He was apprised of the state of feeling
among the Indians near the mission by the Indians themselves,
and he was entreated by them to urge Whitman to go away, for
if he did not he would surely be killed. The governor wrote up
to the mission advising them to leave, for a while at least, until
the Indians should become quiet, which they would do as soon
as the measles had run its course among them. His efforts were
useless, and sure enough one day in 1847, we believe, the mission
was cleaned out, the missionary and nearly all of those connected
with it being killed.

" An Indian war follows. This was carried on for some months,
and with little damage, but sufficient for a claim by the territory
upon the General Government for untold amounts of money. Two
or three years later, when the country had commenced to fill up
with emigration, and after the regiment of Mounted Riflemen and
two companies of the First Artillery had taken post in Oregon,
the people began to think that it would be well to stir up the
matter of the murder of the Whitman family. General Joseph
Lane had been sent out as governor in 1849, and he doubtless
thought it would be a good thing for him politically to humor

the people of the territory. Lane was a vigorous, resolute, Western man, who had been a general officer during the Mexican war, and he then had Presidential aspirations. So the governor came to Fort Vancouver, where the head-quarters of the department were established, under Colonel Loring, of the Mounted Rifles, and procured a small escort, with which he proceeded to hunt up the Indians concerned in the massacre, and demand their surrender. By this time the Indians had begun to comprehend the power of the Government; and when the governor found them, and explained the nature of his mission, they went into council to decide what was to be done. After due deliberation, they were convinced that if they were to refuse to come to any terms they would be attacked by the soldiers, of whom they then had deadly fear, and obliged to abandon their country forever. So they met the governor, and the head chief said that they had heard what he had to say. It was true that his people had killed the whites at the mission, but that they did so for the reason that they really thought that a terrible disease had been brought among them by the whites; that they had begged them to go away from them, for they did not wish to kill them, and that they only killed them to save their own lives, as they thought. He said that for this the whites from down the Columbia had made war upon them, and killed many more of their people than had been killed at the mission, and they thought they ought to be satisfied. As they were not, three of their principal men had volunteered to go back with the governor to Oregon City to be tried for the murder. This satisfied the governor, and the men bid farewell to their wives and little ones and to all their tribe, for they very well knew that they would never see them again. They knew that they were going among those who thirsted for their blood, and that they were going to their death, and that death the most ignominious that can be accorded to the red man, as they were to be hung like dogs.

" The governor and his party left. The victims gave one long last look at the shore as they took the little boat on the Columbia, but no word of complaint ever came from their lips. When they arrived at Fort Vancouver we had charge of these Indians. They were not restrained in any way—no guard was ever kept over them, for there was no power on earth that could have made them falter in their determination to go down to Oregon City, and die like men for the salvation of their tribe.

" At Oregon City these men walked with their heads erect, and with the bearing of senators, from the little boat, amidst the jibes and jeers of a brutal crowd, to the jail which was to be the last covering they would ever have over their heads.

" The trial came on, the jury was empanelled, and Captain Claiborne, of the Mounted Rifles, volunteered to defend the Indians, who were told that they were to have a fair trial, and that they would not be punished unless they were found guilty. To all this they paid no heed. They said it was all right, but they did not understand a word of what they were compelled to listen to for several days, and they cared nothing for the forms of the law. They had come to die, and when some witnesses swore that they recognized them as the very Indians who killed Whitman— all of which was explained to them—not a muscle of their faces changed, although it was more than suspected that the witnesses were never near the mission at the time of the massacre. The trial was over, and, of course, the Indians were condemned to be hanged. Without a murmur or sigh of regret, and with a dignity that would have impressed a Zulu with profound pity, these men walked to the gallows and were hung, while a crowd of civilized Americans—men, women, and children of the nineteenth century—looked on and laughed at their last convulsive twitches.

" We have read of heroes of all times, but never did we read of or believe that such heroism as these Indians exhibited could exist. They knew that to be accused was to be condemned, and they would be executed in the civilized town of Oregon City just as surely as would a poor woman accused of being a witch have been executed in the civilized and Christian town of Salem, in the good State of Massachusetts, two hundred years ago.

" A generation has passed away since the execution or murder of these Indians at Oregon City. Governor Lane still lives, not as ex-President, but as a poor but vigorous old man down in the Rogue River Valley. The little nasty town of Oregon City was the scene of a self-immolation as great as any of which we read in history, and there were not three persons there who appreciated it. The accursed town is, we hear, still nastier than ever, and the intelligent jury—no man of whom dared to have a word of pity or admiration for those poor Indians—with the spectators of that horrid scene, are either dead and damned, or they are sunk in the oblivion that is the fate of those who are born without souls."

XIV.

AN ACCOUNT

OF THE NUMBERS, LOCATION, AND SOCIAL AND INDUSTRIAL
CONDITION OF EACH IMPORTANT TRIBE AND BAND OF IN-
DIANS WITHIN THE UNITED STATES, WITH THE EXCEPTION
OF THOSE DESCRIBED IN THE PREVIOUS PAGES.

[From the Report of Francis A. Walker, United States Commissioner of Indian
Affairs for the year 1872.]

THE Indians within the limits of the United States, exclusive
of those in Alaska, number, approximately, 300,000.

They may be divided, according to their geographical location
or range, into five grand divisions, as follows: in Minnesota, and
States east of the Mississippi River, about 32,500; in Nebraska,
Kansas, and the Indian Territory, 70,650; in the Territories of
Dakota, Montana, Wyoming, and Idaho, 65,000; in Nevada, and
the Territories of Colorado, New Mexico, Utah, and Arizona,
84,000; and on the Pacific slope, 48,000. * * * As regards their
means of support and methods of subsistence, they may be divided as follows: those who support themselves upon their own
reservations, receiving nothing from the Government except interest on their own moneys, or annuities granted them in consideration of the cession of their lands to the United States, number
about 130,000; those who are entirely subsisted by the Government, about 31,000; those in part subsisted, 84,000,—together,
about 115,000; those who subsist by hunting and fishing, upon
roots, nuts, berries, etc., or by begging and stealing, about 55,000.

TRIBES EAST OF THE MISSISSIPPI RIVER.

NEW YORK.

The Indians of New York, remnants of the once powerful
"Six Nations," number 5070. They occupy six reservations in
the State, containing in the aggregate 68,668 acres. Two of
these reservations, viz., the Alleghany and Cattaraugus, belonged
originally to the Colony of Massachusetts; but, by sale and assignment, passed into the hands of a company, the Indians holding a
perpetual right of occupancy, and the company referred to, or
the individual members thereof, owning the ultimate fee. The
same state of facts formerly existed in regard to the Tonawanda

reserve; but the Indians who occupy it have purchased the ultimate fee of a portion of the reserve, which is now held in trust for them by the Secretary of the Interior. The State of New York exercises sovereignty over these reservations. The reservations occupied by the Oneidas, Onondagas, and Tuscaroras have been provided for by treaty stipulations between the Indians and the State of New York. All six reserves are held and occupied by the Indians in common. While the Indian tribes of the continent, with few exceptions, have been steadily decreasing in numbers, those of New York have of late more than held their own, as is shown by an increase of 100 in the present reports over the reported number in 1871, and of 1300 over the number embraced in the United States census of 1860. On the New York reservations are twenty-eight schools; the attendance during some portions of the past year exceeding 1100; the daily average attendance being 608. Of the teachers employed, fifteen are Indians, as fully competent for this position as their white associates. An indication of what is to be accomplished in the future, in an educational point of view, is found in the successful effort, made in August last, to establish a teacher's institute on the Cattaraugus Reservation for the education of teachers specially for Indian schools. Thirty-eight applicants attended, and twenty-six are now under training. The statistics of individual wealth and of the aggregate product of agricultural and other industry are, in general, favorable; and a considerable increase in these regards is observed from year to year. Twenty thousand acres are under cultivation; the cereal crops are good; while noticeable success has been achieved in the raising of fruit.

MICHIGAN.

The bands or tribes residing in Michigan are the Chippewas of Saginaw, Swan Creek, and Black River; the Ottawas and Chippewas; the Pottawattomies of Huron; and the L'Anse band of Chippewas.

The Chippewas of Saginaw, Swan Creek, and Black River, numbering 1630, and the Ottawas and Chippewas, 6039, are indigenous to the country. They are well advanced in civilization; have, with few exceptions, been allotted lands under treaty provisions, for which they have received patents; and are now entitled to all the privileges and benefits of citizens of the United States. Those to whom no allotments have been made can secure homesteads under the provisions of the Act of June 10th, 1872. All treaty stipulations with these Indians have expired. They now have no money or other annuities paid to them by the United States Government. The three tribes first named have in all four schools, with 115 scholars; and the last, two schools, with 152 scholars.

The Pottawattomies of Huron number about fifty.

The L'Anse band of Chippewas, numbering 1195, belong with the other bands of the Chippewas of Lake Superior. They occupy a reservation of about 48,300 acres, situated on Lake Superior, in the extreme northern part of the State. But few of them are engaged in agriculture, most of them depending for their subsistence on hunting and fishing. They have two schools, with an attendance of fifty-six scholars.

The progress of the Indians of Michigan in civilization and industry has been greatly hindered in the past by a feeling of uncertainty in regard to their permanent possession and enjoyment of their homes. Since the allotment of land, and the distribution of either patents or homestead certificates to these Indians (the L'Anse or Lake Superior Chippewas, a people of hunting and fishing habits, excepted), a marked improvement has been manifested on their part in regard to breaking land and building houses. The aggregate quantity of land cultivated by the several tribes is 11,620 acres—corn, oats, and wheat being the chief products. The dwellings occupied consist of 244 frame and 835 log-houses. The aggregate population of the several tribes named (including the confederated "Chippewas, Ottawas, and Pottawattomies," about 250 souls, with whom the Government made a final settlement in 1866 of its treaty obligations) is, by the report of their agent for the current year, 9117—an increase over the number reported for 1871 of 402; due, however, perhaps as much to the return of absent Indians as to the excess of births over deaths. In educational matters these Indians have, of late, most unfortunately, fallen short of the results of former years; for the reason mainly that, their treaties expiring, the provisions previously existing for educational uses failed.

WISCONSIN.

The bands or tribes in Wisconsin are the Chippewas of Lake Superior, the Menomonees, the Stockbridges, and Munsees, the Oneidas, and certain stray bands (so-called) of Winnebagoes, Pottawattomies, and Chippewas.

The Chippewas of Lake Superior (under which head are included the following bands: Fond du Lac, Boise Forte, Grand

Portage, Red Cliff, Bad River, Lac de Flambeau, and Lac Court
D'Oreille) number about 5150.   They constitute a part of the
Ojibways (anglicized in the term Chippewas), formerly one of the
most powerful and warlike nations in the north-west, embracing
many bands, and ranging over an immense territory, extending
along the shores of Lakes Huron, Michigan, and Superior to the
steppes of the Upper Mississippi.   Of this great nation large numbers are still found in Minnesota, many in Michigan, and a fragment in Kansas.

The bands above mentioned by name are at present located on
several small reservations set apart for them by treaties of September 30th, 1854, and April 7th, 1866, in Wisconsin and Minnesota, comprising in all about 695,290 acres.   By Act of Congress
of May 29th, 1872, provision was made for the sale, with the consent of the Indians, of three of these reservations, *viz.*, the Lac de
Flambeau and Lac Court D'Oreille in Wisconsin, and the Fond
du Lac in Minnesota; and for the removal of the Indians located
thereon to the Bad River Reservation, where there is plenty of
good arable land, and where they can be properly cared for, and
instructed in agriculture and mechanics.

The greater part of these Indians at present lead a somewhat
roving life, finding their subsistence chiefly in game hunted by
them, in the rice gathered in its wild state, and in the fish afforded
by waters conveniently near.   Comparatively little is done in
the way of cultivating the soil.   Certain bands have of late been
greatly demoralized by contact with persons employed in the construction of the Northern Pacific Railroad, the line of which runs
near one (the Fond du Lac) of their reservations.   Portions of
this people, however, especially those situated at the Bad River
Reservation, have begun to evince an earnest desire for self-im-
provement.   Many live in houses of rude construction, and raise
small crops of grain and vegetables ; others labor among the
whites; and a number find employment in cutting rails, fence-
posts, and saw-logs for the Government.   In regard to the efforts
made to instruct the children in letters, it may be said that, without being altogether fruitless, the results have been thus far meagre and somewhat discouraging.   The majority of the parents profess to wish to have their children educated, and ask for schools;
but when the means are provided and the work undertaken, the
difficulties in the way of success to any considerable extent appear
in the undisciplined character of the scholars, which has to be
overcome by the teacher without parental co-operation, and in

the great irregularity of attendance at school, especially on the part of those who are obliged to accompany their parents to the rice-fields, the sugar-camps, or the fishing-grounds.

The Menomonees number 1362, and are located on a reservation of 230,400 acres in the north-eastern part of Wisconsin. They formerly owned most of the eastern portion of the State, and, by treaty entered into with the Government on the 18th of October, 1848, ceded the same for a home in Minnesota upon lands that had been obtained by the United States from the Chippewas ; but, becoming dissatisfied with the arrangement, as not having accorded them what they claimed to be rightfully due, subsequently protested, and manifested great unwillingness to remove. In view of this condition of affairs, they were, by the President, permitted to remain in Wisconsin, and temporarily located upon the lands they now occupy, which were secured to them by a subsequent treaty made with the tribe on the 12th of May, 1854. This reservation is well watered by lakes and streams, the latter affording excellent power and facilities for moving logs and lumber to market ; the most of their country abounding with valuable pine timber. A considerable portion of the Menomonees have made real and substantial advancement in civilization; numbers of them are engaged in agriculture ; others find remunerative employment in the lumbering camp established upon their reservation, under the management of the Government Agent, while a few still return at times to their old pursuits of hunting and fishing.

Under the plan adopted by the Department in 1871, in regard to cutting and selling the pine timber belonging to these Indians, 2.000.000 feet have been cut and driven, realizing $23,731, of which individual Indians received for their labor over $3000, the treasury of the tribe deriving a net profit of five dollars per thousand feet. The agent estimates that, for labor done by the Indians upon the reservation, at lumbering, and for work outside on railroads, during the past year, about $20,000 has been earned and received, exclusive of the labor rendered in building houses, raising crops, making sugar. gathering rice, and hunting for peltries. The work of education upon the reservations has been of late quite unsatisfactory, but one small school being now in operation, with seventy scholars, the average attendance being fifty.

The Stockbridges and Munsees, numbering 250, occupy a reservation of 60,800 acres adjoining the Menomonees. The Stockbridges came originally from Massachusetts and New York. After several removals, they, with the Munsees, finally located on their present reservation. Under the provisions of the Act of February 6th, 1871, steps are now being taken to dispose of all of their reservation, with the exception of eighteen sections best adapted for agricultural purposes, which are reserved for their future use. They have no treaty stipulations with the United States at the present time ; nor do they receive any annuities of any kind from the Government. These tribes—indeed it may be said this tribe (the Stockbridges), for of the Munsees there probably remain not more than half a dozen souls—were formerly an intelligent, prosperous people, not a whit behind the most advanced of the race, possessed of good farms, well instructed, and industrious. Unfortunately for them, though much to the advantage of the Government, which acquired thereby a valuable tract of country for white settlement, they removed, in 1857, to their present place of abode. The change has proved highly detrimental to their interests and prospects. Their new reservation, the greater part poor in soil and seriously affected by wet seasons and frequent frosts, has never yielded them more than a meagre subsistence. Many have for this reason left the tribe, and have been for years endeavoring to obtain a livelihood among the whites, maintaining but little intercourse with those remaining on the reservation, yet still holding their rights in the tribal property. The result has been bickerings and faction quarrels, prejudicial to the peace and advancement of the community. More than one-half of the present membership of the tribe, from both the " citizen " and the " Indian " parties, into which it has been long divided, are reported by the agent as having decided to avail themselves of the enrolment provisions in the Act of Congress of February, 1871, before referred to, by which they will finally receive their share of the tribal property, and become citizens of the United States. Those who desire to retain their tribal relation under the protection of the United States may, under the act adverted to, if they so elect by their council, procure a new location for their future home. The school interests and religious care of this people are under the superintendence of Mr. Jeremiah Slingerland, a Stockbridge of much repute for his intelligence, and his success in the cause of the moral and educational improvement of his people.

The Oneidas, numbering 1259, have a reservation of 60,800 acres near Green Bay. They constitute the greater portion of the tribe of that name (derived from Lake Oneida, where the tribe then resided), formerly one of the " Six Nations." * * *

The Indians residing within the limits of Minnesota, as in the case of those of the same name living in Wisconsin, heretofore noticed, constitute a portion of the Ojibway or Chippewa nation, and comprise the following bands: Mississippi, Pillager, Winnebagoshish, Pembina, Red Lake, Boise Forte, Fond du Lac, and Grand Portage. The last three bands, being attached to the agency for the Chippewas of Lake Superior, have been treated of in connection with the Indians of Wisconsin. The five first-named bands number in the aggregate about 6455 souls, and occupy, or rather it is intended they shall ultimately occupy, ample reservations in the central and northern portion of the State, known as the White Earth, Leech Lake, and Red Lake reservations, containing altogether about 4,672,000 acres—a portion of which is very valuable for its pine timber. * * *

Mississippi Bands.—These Indians reside in different localities. Most of them are on their reservation at White Earth; others are at Mille Lac, Gull Lake, and some at White Oak Point reservations. Upon the first-named reservation operations have been quite extensive in the erection of school-buildings, dwelling-houses, shops, and mills, and in breaking ground. At one time during the past summer there was a prospect of an abundant yield from 300 acres sown in cereals; but, unfortunately, the grasshoppers swept away the entire crop; and a second crop of buckwheat and turnips proved a failure. The Indians on this reservation are well-behaved, and inclined to be industrious. Many of them are engaged in tilling the soil, while others are learning the mechanical arts; and they may, as a body, be said to be making considerable progress in the pursuits of civilized life. About one-half of the Indians at Gull Lake have been removed to White Earth: the remainder are opposed to removal, and will, in their present feeling, rather forfeit their annuities than change their location. The Mille Lac Chippewas, who continue to occupy the lands ceded by them in 1863, with reservation of the right to live thereon during good behavior, are indisposed to leave their old home for the new one designed for them on the White Earth Reservation. Only about twenty-five have thus far been induced to remove. Their present reservation is rich in pine lands, the envy of lumber dealers; and there is a strong pressure on all sides for their early removal. They should have help from the Government, whether they remain or remove;

and this could be afforded to a sufficient extent by the sale for their benefit of the timber upon the lands now occupied by them. Probably the Government could provide for them in no better way.

The White Oak Point Chippewas were formerly known as Sandy Lake Indians. They were removed in 1867 from Sandy Lake and Rabbit Lake to White Oak Point, on the Mississippi, near the eastern part of the Leech Lake Reservation. This location is unfavorable to their moral improvement and material progress, from its proximity to the lumber camps of the whites. Thus far the effort made to better their condition, by placing them on farming land, has proved a failure. The ground broken for them has gone back into grass, and their log-houses are in ruins, the former occupants betaking themselves to their wonted haunts. It would be well if these Indians could be induced to remove to the White Earth Reservation.

At Red Lake the Indians have had a prosperous year: good crops of corn and potatoes have been raised, and a number of houses built. This band would be in much better circumstances were they possessed of a greater quantity of arable lands. That to which they are at present limited allows but five acres, suitable for that use, to each family. It is proposed to sell their timber, and with the proceeds clear lands, purchase stock, and establish a manual-labor school.

The Pembina bands reside in Dakota Territory, but are here noticed in connection with the Minnesota Indians, because of their being attached to the same agency. They have no reservation, having ceded their lands by treaty made in 1863, but claim title to Turtle Mountain in Dakota, on which some of them resided at the time of the treaty, and which lies west of the line of the cession then made. They number, the full-bloods about 350, and the half-breeds about 100. They lead a somewhat nomadic life, depending upon the chase for a precarious subsistence, in connection with an annuity from the Government of the United States.

The Chippewas of Minnesota have had but few educational advantages; but with the facilities now being afforded, and with the earnest endeavors that are now being put forth by their agent and the teachers employed, especially at White Earth, it is expected that their interests in this regard will be greatly promoted. At White Earth school operations have been quite successful; so much so, that it will require additional accommodations to meet the demands of the Indians for the education of their children.

The only other school in operation is that at Red Lake, under the auspices of the American Indian Mission Association.

INDIANA.

There are now in Indiana about 345 Miamis, who did not go to Kansas when the tribe moved to that section under the treaty of 1840. They are good citizens, many being thrifty farmers, giving no trouble either to their white neighbors or to the Government. There is also a small band called the Eel River band of Miamis, residing in this State and in Michigan.

NORTH CAROLINA, TENNESSEE, AND GEORGIA.

Cherokees.—There are residing in these States probably about 1700 Cherokees, who elected to remain, under the provisions respecting Cherokees averse to removal, contained in the twelfth article of the treaty with the Cherokees of 1835. Under the Act of July 29th, 1848, a *per capita* transportation and subsistence fund of $53 33 was created and set apart for their benefit, in accordance with a census-roll made under the provisions of said act; the interest on which fund, until such time as they shall individually remove to the Indian country, is the only money to which those named in said roll, who are living, or the heirs of those who have deceased, are entitled. This interest is too small to be of any benefit; and some action should be taken by Congress, with a view of having all business matters between these Indians and the Government settled, by removing such of them west as now desire to go, and paying those who decline to remove the *per capita* fund referred to. The Government has no agent residing with these Indians. In accordance with their earnestly expressed desire to be brought under the immediate charge of the Government, as its wards, Congress, by law approved July 27th, 1868, directed that the Secretary of the Interior should cause the Commissioner of Indian Affairs to take the same supervisory charge of them as of other tribes of Indians; but this practically amounts to nothing, in the absence of means to carry out the intention of the law with any beneficial result to the Indians. The condition of this people is represented to be deplorable. Before the late Rebellion they were living in good circumstances, engaged, with all the success which could be expected, in farming, and in various minor industrial pursuits. Like all other inhabitants of this section, they suffered much during the war, and are now, from this and other causes, much impoverished.

FLORIDA.

Seminoles.—There are a few Seminoles, supposed to number about 300, still residing in Florida—being those, or the descendants of those, who refused to accompany the tribe when it removed to the West many years ago. But little is known of their condition and temper.

NEBRASKA, KANSAS, AND THE INDIAN TERRITORY.

The tribes residing in Nebraska, Kansas, and the Indian Territory are divided as follows: in Nebraska, about 6485; in Kansas, 1500; in the Indian Territory, 62,465.

NEBRASKA.

The Indians in Nebraska are the Santee Sioux, Winnebagoes, Omahas, Pawnees, Sacs and Foxes of the Missouri, Iowas, and the Otoes and Missourias. * * *

Omahas.—The Omahas, a peaceable and inoffensive people, numbering 969, a decrease since 1871 of fifteen, are native to the country now occupied by them, and occupy a reservation of 345,600 acres adjoining the Winnebagoes. They have lands allotted to them in severalty, and have made considerable advancement in agriculture and civilization, though they still follow the chase to some extent. Under the provisions of the Act of June 10th, 1872, steps are being taken to sell 50,000 acres of the western part of their reservation. The proceeds of the sale of these lands will enable them to improve and stock their farms, build houses, etc., and, with proper care and industry, to become in a few years entirely self-sustaining. A few cottages are to be found upon this reservation. There are at present three schools in operation on this reservation, with an attendance of 120 scholars.

Pawnees.—The Pawnees, a warlike people, number 2447, an increase for the past year of eighty-three. They are located on a reservation of 288,000 acres, in the central part of the State. They are native to the country now occupied by them, and have for years been loyal to the Government, having frequently furnished scouts for the army in operations against hostile tribes or marauding bands. Their location, so near the frontier, and almost in constant contact with the Indians of the plains, with whom they have been always more or less at war, has tended to retard their advancement in the arts of civilization. They are, however, gradually becoming more habituated to the customs of the whites, are giving some attention to agriculture, and, with the disappearance of the buffalo from their section of the country, will doubtless settle down to farming and to the practice of mechanical arts in earnest. The Act of June 10th, 1872, heretofore referred to, provides also for the sale of 50,000 acres belonging to the Pawnees, the same to be taken from that part of their reservation lying south of Loup Fork. These lands are now being surveyed; and it is believed that, with the proceeds of this sale, such improvements, in the way of building houses and opening and stocking farms, can be made for the Pawnees as will at an early day induce them to give their entire time and attention to industrial pursuits. There are two schools in operation on the reservation— one a manual-labor boarding-school, the other a day-school, with an attendance at both of 118 scholars. Provision was also made by Congress, at its last session, for the erection of two additional school-houses for the use of this tribe.

Sacs and Foxes of the Missouri.—These Indians, formerly a portion of the same tribe with the Indians now known as the Sacs and Foxes of the Mississippi, emigrated many years ago from Iowa, and settled near the tribe of Iowas, hereafter to be mentioned. They number at the present time but eighty-eight, having been steadily diminishing for years. They have a reservation of about 16,000 acres, lying in the south-eastern part of Nebraska and the north-eastern part of Kansas, purchased for them from the Iowas. Most of it is excellent land; but they have never, to any considerable extent, made use of it for tillage, being almost hopelessly disinclined to engage in labor of any kind, and depending principally for their subsistence, a very poor one, upon their annuity, which is secured to them by the treaty of October 31st, 1837, and amounts to $7870. By Act of June 10th, 1872, provision was made for the sale of a portion or all of their reservation, the proceeds of such sale to be expended for their immediate use, or for their removal to the Indian Territory or elsewhere. They have consented to the sale of their entire reservation; and, so soon as funds shall have been received from that source, steps will be taken to have them removed to the Indian Territory south of Kansas.

Iowas.—These Indians, numbering at present 225, emigrated years ago from Iowa and North-western Missouri, and now have a reservation adjoining the Sacs and Foxes of the Missouri, containing about 16,000 acres. They belong to a much better class of Indians than their neighbors the Sacs and Foxes, being temperate, frugal, industrious, and interested in the education of their children. They were thoroughly loyal during the late rebellion, and furnished a number of soldiers to the Union army. Many of them are good farmers; and as a tribe they are generally extending their agricultural operations, improving their dwellings, and adding to their comforts. A large majority of the tribe are anxious to have their reservation allotted in severalty; and, inasmuch as they are not inclined to remove to another locality, it would seem desirable that their wishes in this respect should be complied with. One school is in operation on the reservation, with an attendance of sixty-eight scholars, besides an industrial home for orphans, supported by the Indians themselves.

Otoes and Missourias. — These Indians, numbering 464, an increase of fourteen over last year, were removed from Iowa and Missouri to their present beautiful and fertile reservation, comprising 160,000 acres, and situated in the southern part of Nebraska. Until quite recently they have evinced but little disposition to labor for a support, or in any way to better their miserable condition; yet cut off from their wonted source of subsistence, the buffalo, by their fear of the wild tribes which have taken possession of their old hunting-grounds, they have gradually been more and more forced to work for a living. Within the last three years many of them have opened farms and built themselves houses. A school has also been established, having an attendance of ninety-five scholars.

KANSAS.

The Indians still remaining in Kansas are the Kickapoos, Pottawattomies (Prairie band), Chippewas and Munsees, Miamis, and the Kansas or Kaws.

Kickapoos. — The Kickapoos emigrated from Illinois, and are now located, to the number of 290, on a reservation of 19,200 acres, in the north-eastern part of the State. During the late war a party of about one hundred, dissatisfied with the treaty made with the tribe in 1863, went to Mexico, upon representations made to them by certain of their kinsmen living in that republic that they would be welcomed and protected by the Mexican Government; but, finding themselves deceived, attempted to return to the United States. Only a few, however, succeeded in reaching the Kickapoo Agency. The Kickapoos now remaining in Mexico separated from the tribe more than twenty years ago, and settled among the southern Indians in the Indian Territory, on or near the Washita River, whence they went to Mexico, where they still live, notwithstanding the efforts of the Government of late to arrange with Mexico for their removal to the Indian Territory, and location upon some suitable reservation. Their raids across the border have been a sore affliction to the people of Texas; and it is important that the first promising occasion should be taken to secure their return to the United States, and their establishment where they may be carefully watched, and restrained from their depredatory habits, or summarily punished if they persist in them. The Kickapoos remaining in Kansas are peaceable and industrious, continuing to make commendable progress in the cultivation of their farms, and showing much interest in the education of their children. Under the provisions of the treaty of June 28th, 1862, a few of these Indians have received lands in severalty, for which patents have been issued, and are now citizens of the United States. Two schools are in operation among these Indians, with a daily average attendance of thirty-nine scholars.

Pottawattomies.—The Prairie band is all of this tribe remaining in Kansas, the rest having become citizens and removed, or most of them, to the Indian Territory. The tribe, excepting those in Wisconsin heretofore noticed, formerly resided in Michigan and Indiana, and removed to Kansas under the provisions of the treaty of 1846. The Prairie band numbers, as nearly as ascertained, about 400, and is located on a reserve of 77,357 acres, fourteen miles north of Topeka. Notwithstanding many efforts to educate and civilize these Indians, most of them still cling tenaciously to the habits and customs of their fathers. Some, however, have recently turned their attention to agricultural pursuits, and are now raising stock, and most of the varieties of grain produced by their white neighbors. They are also showing more interest in education than formerly—one school being in operation on the reservation, with an attendance of eighty-four scholars.

Chippewas and Munsees.—Certain of the Chippewas of Saginaw, Swan Creek, and Black River, removed from Michigan under the treaty of 1836; and certain Munsees, or Christian Indians, from Wisconsin under the treaty of 1839. These were united by the terms of the treaty concluded with them July 16th, 1859. The united bands now number only fifty-six. They own 4760 acres of land in Franklin County, about forty miles south of the town of Lawrence, holding the same in severalty, are considerably advanced in the arts of life, and earn a decent living, principally by agriculture. They have one school in operation, with an attendance of sixteen scholars. These Indians at present have no treaty with the United States; nor do they receive any assistance from the Government.

Miamis.—The Miamis of Kansas formerly resided in Indiana, forming one tribe with the Miamis still remaining in that State, but removed in 1846 to their present location, under the provisions of the treaty of 1840.

Owing to the secession of a considerable number who have allied themselves with the Peorias in the Indian Territory, and also to the ravages of disease consequent on vicious indulgences, especially in the use of intoxicating drinks, this band, which on its removal from Indiana embraced about five hundred, at present numbers but ninety-five. These have a reservation of 10,240 acres in Linn and Miami Counties, in the south-eastern part of Kansas, the larger part of which is held in severalty by them.

The Superintendent of Indian Affairs, in immediate charge, in his report for this year says the Miamis remaining in Kansas are greatly demoralized, their school has been abandoned, and their youth left destitute of educational advantages. Considerable trouble has been for years caused by white settlers locating aggressively on lands belonging to these Indians, no effort for their extrusion having been thus far successful.

Kansas or Kaws.—These Indians are native to the country they occupy. They number at present 593; in 1860 they numbered 803. Although they have a reservation of 80,640 acres of good land in the eastern part of the State, they are poor and improvident, and have in late years suffered much for want of the actual necessaries of life. They never were much disposed to labor, depending upon the chase for a living, in connection with the annuities due from the Government. They have been growing steadily poorer; and even now, in their straitened circumstances, and under the pressure of want, they show but little inclination to engage in agricultural pursuits, all attempts to induce them to work having measurably proved failures. Until quite recently they could not even be prevailed upon to have their children educated. One school is now in operation, with an attendance of about forty-five scholars. By the Act of May 8th, 1872, provision was made for the sale of all the lands owned by these Indians in Kansas, and for their removal to the Indian Territory. Provision was also made, by the Act of June 5th, 1872, for their settlement within the limits of a tract of land therein provided to be set apart for the Osages. Their lands in Kansas are now being appraised by commissioners appointed for the purpose, preparatory to their sale.

INDIAN TERRITORY.

The Indians at present located in the Indian Territory—an extensive district, bounded north by Kansas, east by Missouri and Arkansas, south by Texas, and west by the one hundredth meridian, designated by the commissioners appointed under Act of Congress, July 20th, 1867, to establish peace with certain hostile tribes, as one of two great Territories (the other being, in the main, the present Territory of Dakota, west of the Missouri) upon which might be concentrated the great body of all the Indians east of the Rocky Mountains—are the Cherokees, Choctaws, Chickasaws, Creeks, Seminoles, Senecas, Shawnees, Quapaws, Ottawas of Blanchard's Fork and Roche de Bœuf, Peorias, and confederated Kaskaskias, Weas and Piankeshaws, Wyandottes, Pottawattomies, Sacs and Foxes of the Mississippi, Osages, Kiowas, Comanches, the Arapahoes and Cheyennes of the south, the Wichitas and other affiliated bands, and a small band of Apaches long confederated with the Kiowas and Comanches. * * *

Choctaws and Chickasaws.—These tribes are for certain national purposes confederated. The Choctaws, numbering 16,000—an increase of 1000 on the enumeration for 1871—have a reservation of 6,688,000 acres in the south-eastern part of the Territory; and the Chickasaws, numbering 6000, own a tract containing 4,377,600 acres adjoining the Choctaws on the west. These tribes originally inhabited the section of country now embraced within the State of Mississippi, and were removed to their present location in accordance with the terms of the treaties concluded with them, respectively, in 1820 and 1832. The remarks made respecting the language, laws, educational advantages, industrial pursuits, and advancement in the arts and customs of civilized life of the Cherokees will apply in the main to the Choctaws and Chickasaws. The Choctaws have thirty-six schools in operation, with an attendance of 819 scholars; the Chickasaws eleven, with 379 scholars. The Choctaws, under the treaties of November 16th, 1805, October 18th, 1820, January 20th, 1825, and June 22d, 1855, receive permanent annuities as follows: in money, $3000; for support of government, education, and other beneficial purposes, $25,512 89; for support of light-horsemen, $600; and for iron and steel, $320. They also have United States and State stocks, held in trust for them by the Secretary of the Interior, to the amount of $506,427 20, divided as follows: on account of "Choctaw general fund," $454,000; of "Choctaw school fund," $52,427 20. The interest on these funds, and the annuities, etc., are turned over to the treasurer of the nation, and expended under the direction of the National Council in the manner and for the objects indicated in each case. The Chickasaws, under Act of February 25th, 1799, and treaty of April 28th, 1866, have a permanent annuity of $3000. They also have United States and State stocks, held in trust for them by the Secretary of the Interior, to the amount of $1,185,947 03⅔—$183,947 03⅔ thereof being a "national fund," and $2000 a fund for "incompetents." The interest on these sums, and the item of $3000 first referred to, are paid over to the treasurer of the nation, and disbursed by him under the direction of the National Council, and for such objects as that body may determine.

Creeks.—The Creeks came originally from Alabama and Georgia. They numbered at the latest date of enumeration 12,295, and have a reservation of 3,215,495 acres in the eastern and central part of the territory. They are not generally so far advanced as the Cherokees, Choctaws, and Chickasaws, but are making rapid progress, and will doubtless in a few years rank in all respects with their neighbors, the three tribes just named. The Creeks, by the latest reports, have thirty-three schools in operation; one of which is under the management of the Methodist Mission Society, and another supported by the Presbyterians. The number of scholars in all the schools is 760. These Indians have, under treaties of August 7th, 1790, June 16th, 1802, January 24th, 1826, August 7th, 1856, and June 14th, 1866, permanent annuities and interest on moneys uninvested as follows: in money, $68,258 40; for pay of blacksmiths and assistants, wagon-maker, wheelwright, iron and steel, $3250; for assistance in agricultural operations, $2000; and for education, $1000. The Secretary of the Interior holds in trust for certain members of the tribe, known as "orphans," United States and State bonds to the amount of $76,999 66, the interest on which sum is paid to those of said orphans who are alive, and to the representatives of those who have deceased.

Seminoles.—The Seminoles, numbering 2398, an increase of 190 over the census of 1871, have a reservation of 200,000 acres adjoining the Creeks on the west. This tribe formerly inhabited the section of country now embraced in the State of Florida. Some of them removed to their present location under the provisions of the treaties of 1832 and 1833. The remainder of the tribe, instigated by the former chief, Osceola, repudiated the treaties, refused to remove, and soon after commenced depredating upon the whites. In 1835 these depredations resulted in war, which continued seven years, with immense cost of blood and treasure. The Indians were at last rendered powerless to do further injury, and, after efforts repeated through several years, were finally, with the exception of a few who fled to the everglades, removed to a reservation in the now Indian territory. In 1866 they ceded to the United States, by treaty, the reservation then owned by them, and purchased the tract they at present occupy. They are not so far advanced in the arts of civilized life as the Cherokees, Choctaws, Chickasaws, and Creeks, but are making rapid progress in that direction, and will, it is confidently believed, soon rank with the tribes named. They cultivate 7600 acres; upon which they raised during the past year 300,000 bushels of corn, and 6000 bushels of potatoes. They live in log-houses, and own large stocks of cattle, horses, and hogs. The schools of the Seminoles number four, with an attendance of 169 scholars.

They receive, under treaties made with them August 7th, 1856, and March 21st, 1866, annuities, etc., as follows: interest on $500,000, amounting to $25,000 annually, which is paid to them as annuity; interest on $50,000, amounting to $2500 annually, for support of schools; and $1000, the interest on $20,000, for the support of their government.

Senecas and Shawnees.—The Senecas, numbering 214, and the Shawnees, numbering ninety, at the present time, removed, some thirty-five or forty years ago, from Ohio to their present location in the north-eastern corner of the territory. They suffered severely during the Rebellion, being obliged to leave their homes and fly to the north, their country being devastated by troops of both armies. Under the provisions of the treaty of 1867, made with these and other tribes, the Senecas, who were then confederated with the Shawnees, dissolved their connection with that tribe, sold to the United States their half of the reservation owned by them in common with the Shawnees, and connected themselves with those Senecas who then owned a separate reservation. The Shawnees now have a reservation of 24,960 acres, and the united Senecas one of 44,000 acres. These tribes are engaged in agriculture to a considerable extent. They are peaceable and industrious. Many are thrifty farmers, and in comfortable circumstances. They have one school in operation, with an attendance of thirty-six scholars, which includes some children of the Wyandottes, which tribe has no schools.

Quapaws.—These Indians number at the present time about 240. They are native to the country, and occupy a reservation of 104,000 acres in the extreme north-east corner of the territory. They do not appear to have advanced much within the past few years. In common with other tribes in that section, they suffered greatly by the late war, and were rendered very destitute. Their proximity to the border towns of Kansas, and the facilities thereby afforded for obtaining whiskey, have tended to retard their progress; but there has recently been manifested a strong desire for improvement; and with the funds derived from the sale of a part of their lands, and with the proposed opening of a school among them, better things are hoped for in the future.

Ottawas.—The Ottawas of Blanchard's Fork and Roche de Bœuf number, at the present time, 150. They were originally located in Western Ohio and Southern Michigan, and were removed, in accordance with the terms of the treaty concluded with them in 1831, to a reservation within the present limits of Kansas. Under the treaty of 1867 they obtained a reservation of 24,960 acres, lying immediately north of the western portion of the Shawnee Reservation. They have paid considerable attention to education, are well advanced in civilization, and many of them are industrious and prosperous farmers. They have one school, attended by fifty-two scholars. The relation of this small band to the Government is somewhat anomalous, inasmuch as, agreeably to provisions contained in the treaties of 1862 and 1867, they have become citizens of the United States, and yet reside in the Indian country, possess a reservation there, and maintain a purely tribal organization. They removed from Franklin Co., Kansas, in 1870.

Peorias, etc.—The Peorias, Kaskaskias, Weas, and Piankeshaws, who were confederated in 1854, and at that time had a total population of 259, now number 160. They occupy a reservation of 72,000 acres, adjoining the Quapaw Reservation on the south and west. Under treaties made with these tribes in 1832, they removed to a tract within the present limits of Kansas, where they remained until after the treaty of 1867 was concluded with them, in which treaty provision was made whereby they obtained their present reservation. These Indians are generally intelligent, well advanced in civilization, and, to judge from the statistical reports of their agent, are very successful in their agricultural operations, raising crops ample for their own support. With the Peorias are about forty Miamis from Kansas. They have one school in operation, with an attendance of twenty-nine scholars.

Wyandottes.—The Wyandottes number at the present time 222 souls. Ten years ago there were 435. They occupy a reservation of 20,000 acres, lying between the Seneca and Shawnee reservations. This tribe was located for many years in North-western Ohio, whence they removed, pursuant to the terms of the treaty made with them in 1842, to a reservation within the present limits of Kansas. By the treaty made with them in 1867 their present reservation was set apart for those members of the tribe who desired to maintain their tribal organization, instead of becoming citizens, as provided in the treaty of 1855. They are poor, and, having no annuities and but little force of character, are making slight progress in industry or civilization. They have been lately joined by members of the tribe, who, under the treaty, accepted citizenship. These, desiring to resume their relations with their people, have been again adopted into the tribe.

Pottawattomies.—These Indians, who formerly resided in Michigan and Indiana, whence they removed to Kansas, before going down into the Indian Territory numbered about 1600. They have, under the provisions of the treaty of 1861 made with the tribe, then residing in Kansas, become citizens of the United States. By the terms of said treaty they received allotments of land, and their proportion of the tribal funds, with the exception of their share of certain non-paying State stocks, amounting to $67,000, held in trust by the Secretary of the Interior for the Pottawattomies. Having disposed of their lands, they removed to the Indian Territory, where a reservation thirty miles square, adjoining the Seminole Reservation on the west, had been, by the treaty of 1867, provided for such as should elect to maintain their tribal organization. It having been decided, however, by the Department that, as they had all become citizens, there was consequently no part of the tribe remaining which could lay claim, under treaty stipulations, to the reservation in the Indian Territory, legislation was had by Congress at its last session — Act approved May 23d, 1872 — by which these citizen Pottawattomies were allowed allotments of land within the tract originally assigned for their use as a tribe, to the extent of 160 acres to each head of family, and to each other person twenty-one years of age, and of eighty acres to each minor. Most if not all of them are capable of taking care of themselves; and many of them are well-educated, intelligent, and thrifty farmers.

Absentee Shawnees.—These Indians, numbering 663, separated about thirty years ago from the main tribe, then located in Kansas, and settled in the Indian Territory, principally within the limits of the thirty miles square tract heretofore referred to in the remarks relative to the Pottawattomies, where they engaged in farming, and have since supported themselves without assistance from the Government.

Sacs and Foxes.—The Sacs and Foxes of the Mississippi number at the present time 463. In 1846 they numbered 2478. They have a reservation of 483,340 acres, adjoining the Creeks on the west, and between the North Fork of the Canadian and the Red Fork of the Arkansas Rivers. They formerly occupied large tracts of country in Wisconsin, Iowa, and Missouri, whence they removed, by virtue of treaty stipulations, to a reservation within the present limits of Kansas. By the terms of the treaties of 1859 and 1868 all their lands in Kansas were ceded to the United States, and they were given in lieu thereof their present reservation. These Indians, once famous for their prowess in war, have not, for some years, made any marked improvement upon their former condition. Still they have accomplished a little, under highly adverse circumstances and influences, in the way of opening small farms and in building houses, and are beginning to show some regard for their women by relieving them of the burdens and labors heretofore required of them. There is hope of their further improvement, although they are still but one degree removed from the Blanket or Breech-clout Indians. They have one school in operation, with an attendance of only about twelve scholars. Three hundred and seventeen members of these tribes, after their removal to Kansas, returned to Iowa, where they were permitted to remain, and are now, under the Act of March 2d, 1867, receiving their share of the tribal funds. They have purchased 419 acres of land in Tama County, part of which they are cultivating. They are not much disposed to work, however, on lands of their own, preferring to labor for the white farmers in their vicinity, and are still much given to roving and hunting.

Osages.—The Osages, numbering 3956, are native to the general section of the country where they now live. Their reservation is bounded on the north by the south line of Kansas, east by the ninety-sixth degree of west longitude, and south and west by the Arkansas River, and contains approximately 1,760,000 acres. They still follow the chase, the buffalo being their main dependence for food. Their wealth consists in horses (of which they own not less than 12,000) and in cattle.

Kiowas, Comanches, and Apaches.—These tribes, confederated under present treaty stipulations, formerly ranged over an extensive country lying between the Rio Grande and the Red River. As nearly as can be ascertained, they number as follows: Kiowas, 1930; Comanches, 3180; and Apaches, 380. They are now located upon a reservation secured to them by treaty made in 1867, comprising 3,549,440 acres in the south-western part of the Indian Territory, west of and adjoining the Chickasaw country. Wild and intractable, these Indians, even the best of them, have given small signs of improvement in the arts of life; and, substantially, the whole dealing of the Government with them thus far has been in the way of supplying their necessities for food and clothing, with a view to keeping them upon their reservation, and preventing their raiding into Texas, with the citizens of which State they were for many years before their present establishment on terms of mutual hatred and injury. Some individuals and bands have remained quiet and peaceable upon their reservation, evincing a disposition to learn the arts of life, to engage in agriculture, and to have their children instructed in letters. To these every inducement is being held out to take up land, and actively commence tilling it. Thus far they have under cultivation but 100 acres, which have produced the past year a good crop of corn and potatoes. The wealth of these tribes consists in horses and mules, of which they own to the number, as reported by their agent, of 16,500, a great proportion of the animals notoriously having been stolen in Texas.

However, it may be said, in a word, of these Indians, that their civilization must follow their submission to the Government, and that the first necessity in respect to them is a wholesome example, which shall inspire fear and command obedience. So long as four-fifths of these tribes take turns at raiding into Texas, openly and boastfully bringing back scalps and spoils to their reservation, efforts to inspire very high ideas of social and industrial life among the communities of which the raiders form so large a part will presumably result in failure.

Arapahoes and Cheyennes of the South.—These tribes are native to the section of country now inhabited by them. The Arapahoes number at the present time 1500, and the Cheyennes 2000. By the treaty of 1867, made with these Indians, a large reservation was provided for them, bounded on the north by Kansas, on the east by the Arkansas River, and on the south and west by the Red Fork of the Arkansas. They have, however, persisted in a refusal to locate on this reservation; and another tract, containing 4,011,500 acres, north of and adjoining the Kiowa and Comanche Reservation, was set apart for them by Executive order of August 10th, 1869. By Act of May 29th, 1872, the Secretary of the Interior was authorized to negotiate with these Indians for the relinquishment of their claim to the lands ceded to them by the said treaty, and to give them in lieu thereof a "sufficient and permanent location" upon lands ceded to the United States by the Creeks and Seminoles in treaties made with them in 1866. Negotiations to the end proposed were duly entered into with these tribes unitedly; but, in the course of such negotiations, it has become the view of this office that the tribes should no longer be associated in the occupation of a reservation. The Arapahoes are manifesting an increasing disinclination to follow farther the fortunes of the Cheyennes, and crave a location of their own. Inasmuch as the conduct of the Arapahoes is uniformly good, and their disposition to make industrial improvement very decided, it is thought that they should now be separated from the more turbulent Cheyennes, and given a place where they may carry out their better intentions without interruption, and without the access of influences tending to draw their young men away to folly and mischief. With this view a contract, made subject to the action of Congress, was entered into between the Commissioner of Indian Affairs and the delegation of the Arapahoe tribe which visited Washington during the present season (the delegation being fully empowered thereto by the tribe), by which the Arapahoes relinquish all their interest in the reservation granted them by the treaty of 1867, in consideration of the grant of a reservation between the North Fork of the Canadian River and the Red Fork of the Arkansas River, and extending from a point ten miles east of the ninety-eighth to near the ninety-ninth meridian of west longitude. Should this adjustment of the question, so far as the Arapahoes are concerned, meet the approval of Congress, separate negotiations will be entered into with the Cheyennes, with a view to obtaining their relinquishment of the reservation of 1867, and their location on some vacant tract within the same general section of the Indian Territory.

A considerable number of the Arapahoes are already engaged in agriculture, though at a disadvantage; and, when the question of their reservation shall have been settled, it is confidently believed that substantially the whole body of this tribe will turn their attention to the cultivation of the soil. Two schools are conducted for their benefit at the agency, having an attendance of thirty-five scholars. Of the Cheyennes confederated with the Arapahoes, the reports are less favorable as to progress made in industry, or disposition to improve their condition. Until 1867 both these tribes, in common with the Kiowas and Comanches, were engaged in hostilities against the white settlers in Western Kansas; but since the treaty made with them in that year they have, with the exception of one small band of the Cheyennes, remained friendly, and have committed no depredations.

Wichitas, etc. — The Wichitas and other affiliated bands of Keechies, Wacoes, Towoccaroes, Caddoes, Ionies, and Delawares, number 1250, divided approximately as follows: Wichitas, 299; Keechies, 126; Wacoes, 140; Towoccaroes, 127; Caddoes, 392; Ionies, 85; Delawares, 81. These Indians, fragments of once important tribes originally belonging in Louisiana, Texas, Kansas, and the Indian Territory, were all, excepting the Wichitas and Delawares, removed by the Government from Texas, in 1859, to the " leased district," then belonging to the Choctaws and Chickasaws, where they have since resided, at a point on the Washita River near old Fort Cobb. They have no treaty relations with the Government, nor have they any defined reservation. They have always, or at least for many years, been friendly to the whites, although in close and constant contact with the Kiowas and Comanches. A few of them, chiefly Caddoes and Delawares, are engaged in agriculture, and are disposed to be industrious. Of the other Indians at this agency some cultivate small patches in corn and vegetables, the work being done mainly by women; but the most are content to live upon the Government. The Caddoes rank among the best Indians of the continent, and set an example to the other bands affiliated with them worthy of being more generally followed than it is. In physique, and in the virtues of chastity, temperance, and industry, they are the equals of many white communities.

A permanent reservation should be set aside for the Indians of this agency; and, with proper assistance, they would doubtless in a few years become entirely self-sustaining. But one school is in operation, with an attendance of eighteen scholars. These Indians have no annuities; but an annual appropriation of $50,000 has for several years been made for their benefit. This money is expended for goods and agricultural implements, and for assistance and instruction in farming, etc.

DAKOTA, MONTANA, WYOMING, AND IDAHO.

The tribes residing in Dakota, Montana, Wyoming, and Idaho are divided as follows: in Dakota, about 28,000; Montana, 30,000; Wyoming, 2000; and Idaho, 5000. The present temporary location of the Red Cloud Agency has, however, drawn just within the limits of Wyoming a body of Indians varying from 8000 to 9000, who are here, and usually reckoned as belonging to Dakota.

DAKOTA.

The Indians within the limits of Dakota Territory are the Sioux, the Poncas, and the Arickarees, Gros Ventres, and Mandans. * * *

Arickarees, Gros Ventres, and Mandans. — These tribes number 2200, and have a reservation set apart for their occupancy by Executive order of April 12th, 1870, comprising 8,640,000 acres, situated in the north-western part of Dakota and the eastern part of Montana, extending to the Yellowstone and Powder rivers. They have no treaty with the Government, are now and have always been friendly to the whites, are exceptionally known to the officers of the army and to frontiersmen as "good Indians," and are engaged to some extent in agriculture. Owing to the shortness of the agricultural season, the rigor of the climate, and the periodical ravages of grasshoppers, their efforts in this direction, though made with a degree of patience and perseverance not usual in the Indian character, have met with frequent and distressing reverses; and it has from time to time been found necessary to furnish them with more or less subsistence to prevent starvation. They are traditional enemies of the Sioux; and the petty warfare maintained between them and the Sioux of the Grand River and Cheyenne River Agencies — while, like most warfare confined to Indians alone, it causes wonderfully little loss of life — serves to disturb the condition of these agencies, and to retard the progress of all the parties concerned. These Indians should be moved to the Indian Territory, south of Kansas, where the mildness of the climate and the fertility of the soil would repay their labors, and where, it is thought, from their willingness to labor and their docility under the control of the Government, they would in a few years become wholly self-supporting. The question of their removal has been submitted to them, and they seem inclined to favor the project, but have expressed a desire to send a delegation of their chiefs to the Indian Territory, with a view of satisfying themselves as to the desirableness of the location. Their wishes in this respect should be granted early next season, that their removal and settlement may be effected during the coming year. Notwithstanding their willingness to labor, they have shown but little interest in education. Congress makes an appropriation of $75,000 annually for goods and provisions, for their instruction in agricultural and mechanical pursuits, for salaries of employés, and for the education of their children, etc.

MONTANA.

The Indian tribes residing within the limits of Montana are the Blackfeet, Bloods, and Piegans, the Gros Ventres of the Prairie, the Assinaboines, the Yanktonais, Santee and Teton (so-called) Sioux, a portion of the Northern Arapahoes and Cheyennes, the River Crows, the Mountain Crows, the Flat-heads, Pend d'Oreilles and Kootenays, and a few Shoshones, Bannocks, and Sheep-eaters, numbering in the aggregate about 32,412. They are all, or nearly all, native to the regions now occupied by them respectively.

The following table will exhibit the population of each of these tribes, as nearly as the same can be ascertained:

Blackfeet, Bloods, and Piegans	7500
Assinaboines	4790
Gros Ventres	1100
Santee, Yanktonais, Uncpapa, and Cut-head Sioux, at Milk River Agency	2625
River Crows	1240
Mountain Crows	2700
Flat-heads	460
Pend d'Oreilles	1000
Kootenays	320
Shoshones, Bannocks, and Sheep-eaters	677
Roving Sioux, commonly called Teton Sioux, including those gathered during 1872 at and near Fort Peck (largely estimated)	8000
Estimated total	30,412

The number of Northern Cheyennes and Arapahoes roaming in Montana, who, it is believed, have co-operated with the Sioux under Sitting Bull, in their depredations, is not known: it is probably less than 1000.

The Blackfeet, Bloods, and Piegans (located at the Blackfeet Agency, on the Teton River, about seventy-five miles from Fort Benton), the Gros Ventres, Assinaboines, the River Crows, about 1000 of the Northern Arapahoes and Cheyennes, and the Santee and Yankton Sioux (located at the Milk River Agency, on the Milk River, about one hundred miles from its mouth), occupy

jointly a reservation in the extreme northern part of the Territory, set apart by treaties (not ratified) made in 1868 with most
of the tribes named, and containing about 17,408,000 acres. The
Blackfeet, Bloods, and Piegans, particularly the last-named band,
have been, until within about two years, engaged in depredating
upon the white settlers. The Indians at the Milk River Agency,
with the exception of the Sioux, are now, and have been for several years, quiet and peaceable. The Sioux at this agency, or
most of them, were engaged in the outbreak in Minnesota in
1862. On the suppression of hostilities they fled to the northern
part of Dakota, where they continued roaming until, in the fall
of 1871, they went to their present location, with the avowed intention of remaining there. Although they had been at war for
years with the Indians properly belonging to the Milk River Agency, yet, by judicious management on the part of the agent of the
Government stationed there, and the influence of some of the most
powerful chiefs, the former feuds and difficulties were amicably
arranged; and all parties have remained friendly to each other
during the year past. The Indians at neither the Blackfeet nor
the Milk River Agency show any disposition to engage in farming; nor have they thus far manifested any desire for the education of their children. They rely entirely upon the chase and
upon the bounty of the Government for their support. They,
however, quite scrupulously respect their obligation to preserve
the peace; and no considerable difficulty has of late been experienced, or is anticipated, in keeping them in order. The Blackfeet, Bloods, and Piegans have an annual appropriation of $50,000
made for their benefit; the Assinaboines, $30,000; the Gros Ven-
tres of the Prairie, $35,000; the River Crows, $30,000. These
funds are used in furnishing the respective tribes with goods and
subsistence, and generally for such other objects as may be deemed necessary to keep the Indians quiet.

Mountain Crows.—These Indians have a reservation of 6,272,000
acres, lying in the southern part of the Territory, between the Yellowstone River and the north line of Wyoming Territory. They
have always been friendly to the whites, but are inveterate enemies of the Sioux, with whom they have for years been at war.
By the treaty of 1868—by the terms of which their present reservation was set apart for their occupancy—they are liberally supplied with goods, clothing, and subsistence. But few of them
are engaged in farming, the main body relying upon their success
in hunting, and upon the supplies furnished by the Government

for their support. They have one school in operation, with an attendance, however, of only nine scholars. By the treaty of May 7th, 1868, provision is made by which they are to receive for a limited number of years the following annuities, etc., viz.: in clothing and goods, $22,723 (twenty - six instalments due); in beneficial objects, $25,000 (six instalments due); in subsistence, $131,400 (one instalment due). Blacksmiths, teachers, physician, carpenter, miller, engineer, and farmer are also furnished for their benefit, at an expense to the Government of $11,600.

Flat-heads, etc.—The Flat-heads, Pend d'Oreilles, and Kootenays have a reservation of 1,433,600 acres in the Jocko Valley, situated in the north-western part of the Territory, and secured to them by treaty of 1855. This treaty also provided for a reservation in the Bitter-root Valley, should the President of the United States deem it advisable to set apart another for their use. The Flat-heads have remained in the last-named valley; but under the provisions of the Act of June 5th, 1872, steps are being taken for their removal to the Jocko Reservation. Many of these Indians are engaged in agriculture; but, as they receive little assistance from the Government, their progress in this direction is slow. They have one school in operation, with an attendance of twenty-seven scholars.

Shoshones, etc.—The Shoshones, Bannocks, and Sheep-eaters are at present located about twenty miles above the mouth of the Lemhi Fork of the Salmon River, near the western boundary of the Territory. They have shown considerable interest in agriculture, and many of them are quite successful as farmers. They have no reservation set apart for them, either by treaty or by Executive order. They are so few in number that it would probably be better to remove them, with their consent, to the Fort Hall Reservation in Idaho, where their brethren are located, than to provide them with a separate reservation. They have no schools in operation. An annual appropriation of $25,000 is made for these Indians, which sum is expended for their benefit in the purchase of clothing, subsistence, agricultural implements, etc.

WYOMING.

The Indians in this Territory, with the exception of the Sioux and Northern Arapahoes and Cheyennes, mentioned under the heads of Dakota and Montana, respectively, are the eastern band of Shoshones, numbering about 1000. The Shoshones are native to the country. Their reservation in the Wind River Valley, containing 2,688,000 acres, was set apart for them by treaty of 1868.

But little advancement in civilization has been made by these Indians, owing to their indisposition to labor for a living, and to the incessant incursions into their country of the Sioux and the Northern Arapahoes and Cheyennes, with which tribes they have for many years been at war. The losses sustained from these incursions, and the dread which they inspire, tend to make the Shoshones unsettled and unwilling to remain continuously on the reservation. They therefore spend most of the year in roaming and hunting, when they should be at work tilling the soil and improving their lands. There is one school at the agency, having an attendance of ten scholars, in charge of an Episcopal missionary as teacher.

IDAHO.

The Indian tribes in Idaho are the Nez Percés, the Boisé and Bruneau Shoshones, and Bannocks, the Cœur d'Alênes, and Spokanes, with several other small bands, numbering in the aggregate about 5800 souls. * * *

Shoshones and Bannocks.—These Indians, numbering 1037—the former 516 and the latter 521—occupy a reservation in the southeastern part of the Territory, near Fort Hall, formerly a military post. This reservation was set apart by treaty of 1868 and Executive order of July 30th, 1869, and contains 1,568,000 acres. The Shoshones on this reservation have no treaty with the Government. Both bands are generally quiet and peaceable, and cause but little trouble; are not disposed to engage in agriculture, and, with some assistance from the Government, depend upon hunting and fishing for subsistence. There is no school in operation on the reservation.

Cœur d'Alênes, etc.—The Cœur d'Alênes, Spokanes, Kootenays, and Pend d'Oreilles, numbering about 2000, have no treaty with the United States, but have a reservation of 256,000 acres set apart for their occupancy by Executive order of June 14th, 1867, lying thirty or forty miles north of the Nez Percés Reservation. They are peaceable, have no annuities, receive no assistance from the Government, and are wholly self-sustaining. These Indians have never been collected upon a reservation, nor brought under the immediate supervision of an agent. So long as their country shall remain unoccupied, and not in demand for settlement by the whites, it will scarcely be desirable to make a change in their location; but the construction of the Northern Pacific Railroad, which will probably pass through or near their range, may make it expedient to concentrate them. At present they are largely under the influence of Catholic missionaries of the Cœur d'Alêne Mission.

***

COLORADO, NEW MEXICO, UTAH, ARIZONA, AND NEVADA.

The tribes residing in Colorado, New Mexico, Utah, Arizona, and Nevada are divided as follows: in Colorado, about 3800; New Mexico, 19,000; Utah, 10,000; Arizona, 25,000; and Nevada, 13,000.

COLORADO.

The Indians residing in Colorado Territory are the Tabequache band of Utes, at the Los Pinos Agency, numbering 3000, and the Yampa, Grand River, and Uintah bands of the White River Agency, numbering 800. They are native to the section which they now inhabit, and have a reservation of 14,784,000 acres in the western part of the Territory, set apart for their occupancy by treaty made with them in 1868. The two agencies above named are established on this reservation, the White River Agency being in the northern part, on the river of that name, and the other in the south-eastern part. This reservation is much larger than is necessary for the number of Indians located within its limits; and, as valuable gold and silver mines have been, or are alleged to have been, discovered in the southern part of it, the discoveries being followed by the inevitable prospecting parties and miners, Congress, by Act of April 23d, 1872, authorized the Secretary of the Interior to enter into negotiations with the Utes for the extinguishment of their right to the south part of it.

A few of these Indians, who have declined to remove to and remain upon the reservation, still roam in the eastern part of the Territory, frequently visiting Denver and its vicinity, and causing some annoyance to the settlers by their presence, but committing no acts of violence or extensive depredations. The Indians of Colorado have thus far shown but little interest in the pursuits of civilized life or in the education of their children. A school is in operation at the Northern or White River Agency, with an attendance of forty scholars. Steps are also being taken to open one at the southern or Los Pinos Agency.

NEW MEXICO.

The tribes residing and roaming within the limits of New Mexico are the Navajoes; the Mescalero, Gila, and Jicarilla bands of

Apaches; the Muache, Capote, and Weeminuche bands of Utes; and the Pueblos.

Navajoes.—The Navajoes now number 9114, an increase of 880 over last year's enumeration. Superintendent Pope considers this increase to be mainly due to the return, during the year, of a number who had been held in captivity by the Mexicans. They have a reservation of 3,328,000 acres in the north-western part of New Mexico and north-eastern part of Arizona, set apart for them by treaty of 1868. These Indians are natives of the section of the country where they are now located. Prior to 1864 no less than seven treaties had been made with these tribes, which were successively broken on their part, and that, with but one exception, before the Senate could take action on the question of their ratification. In 1864 the Navajoes were made captives by the military, and taken to the Bosque Redondo Reservation, which had been set apart for the Mescalero Apaches, where they were for a time held as prisoners of war, and then turned over to this Department. After the treaty of 1868 had been concluded, they were removed to their present location, where they have, as a tribe, remained quiet and peaceable, many of them being engaged in agriculture and in raising sheep and goats. Of these they have large flocks, numbering 130,000 head, which supply them not only with subsistence, but also with material from which they manufacture the celebrated, and for warmth and durability unequalled, Navajo blanket. They also have a stock of 10,000 horses. These Indians are industrious, attend faithfully to their crops, and even put in a second crop when the first, as frequently happens, is destroyed by drought or frost. One school is in operation on the reservation, with an attendance of forty scholars.

Mescalero Apaches.—These Indians, numbering about 830, are at present located—not, however, upon a defined reservation secured to them—near Fort Stanton, in the eastern part of the Territory, and range generally south of that point. Prior to 1864 they were located on the Bosque Redondo Reservation, where they were quiet and peaceable until the Navajoes were removed to that place. Being unable to live in harmony with the new-comers, they fled from the reservation, and until quite recently have been more or less hostile. They are now living at peace with the whites, and conducting themselves measurably well. They have no schools, care nothing apparently about the education of their children, and are not to any noticeable extent engaged in farming, or in any pursuit of an industrial character.

These Indians have no treaty with the United States; nor do they receive any annuities. They are, however, subsisted in part by the Government, and are supplied with a limited quantity of clothing when necessary. In addition to the Mescaleros proper, Agent Curtis reports as being embraced in his agency other Indians, called by him Aguas Nuevos, 440; Lipans, 350 (probably from Texas); and Southern Apaches, 310, whose proper home is no doubt upon the Tularosa Reservation. These Indians, the agent remarks, came from the Comanche country to his agency at various dates during the past year.

Gila (sometimes called Southern) Apaches.—This tribe is composed of two bands, the Mimbres and Mogollons, and number about 1200. They are warlike, and have for years been generally unfriendly to the Government. The citizens of Southern New Mexico, having long suffered from their depredatory acts, loudly demanded that they be removed; and to comply with the wish of the people, as well as to prevent serious difficulties and possibly war, it was a year or two since decided to provide the Indians with a reservation distant from their old home, and there establish them. With a view to that end a considerable number of them were collected early last year at Cañada Alamosa. Subsequently, by Executive order dated November 9th, 1871, a reservation was set apart for them with other roving bands of Apaches in the Tularosa Valley, to which place 450 of them are reported to have been removed during the present year by United States troops. These Indians, although removed against their will, were at first pleased with the change, but, after a short experience of their new home, became dissatisfied; and no small portion left the reservation to roam outside, disregarding the system of passes established. They bitterly object to the location as unhealthy, the climate being severe and the water bad. There is undoubtedly much truth in these complaints. They ask to be taken back to Cañada Alamosa, their own home, promising there to be peaceable and quiet. Of course nothing can be said of them favorable to the interests of education and labor. Such of these Indians as remain on the reservation are being fed by the Government. They have no treaty with the United States; nor do they receive annuities of any kind.

Jicarilla Apaches.—These Indians, numbering about 850, have for several years been located with the Muache Utes, about 650 in number, at the Cimarron Agency, upon what is called "Maxwell's Grant," in North-eastern New Mexico. They have no treaty relations with the Government; nor have they any reservation set apart for them. Efforts were made some years ago to have them, with the Utes referred to, remove to the large Ute Reservation in Colorado, but without success. The Cimarron Agency, however, has lately been discontinued; and these Apaches will, if it can be effected without actual conflict, be removed to the Mescalero Agency at Fort Stanton. Four hundred Jicarilla Apaches are also reported as being at the Tierra Amarilla Agency.

Muache, Weeminuche, and Capote Utes.—These bands—the Muache band, numbering about 650, heretofore at the Cimarron Agency, and the other two bands, numbering 870, at the Abiquiu Agency—are all parties to the treaty made with the several bands of Utes in 1868. It has been desired to have these Indians remove to their proper reservation in Colorado; but all efforts to this end have thus far proved futile. The discontinuance of the Cimarron Agency may have the effect to cause the Muaches to remove either to that reservation or to the Abiquiu Agency, now located at Tierra Amarilla, in the north-western part of the territory. These three bands have generally been peaceable, and friendly to the whites. Recently, however, some of them have shown a disposition to be troublesome; but no serious difficulty is apprehended. None of them appear disposed to work for a subsistence, preferring to live by the chase and on the bounty of the Government; nor do they show any inclination or desire to have their children educated, and taught the habits and customs of civilized life. Declining to remove to and locate permanently upon the reservation set apart for the Utes in Colorado, they receive no annuities, and participate in none of the benefits provided in the treaties of 1863 and 1868 with the several bands of Ute Indians referred to under the head of " Colorado."

Pueblos.—The Pueblos, so named because they live in villages, number 7683. They have 439,664 acres of land confirmed to them by Act of Congress of December 22d, 1858, the same consisting of approved claims under old Spanish grants. They have no treaty with the United States, and receive but little aid from the Government. During the past two years efforts have been made, and are still being continued, to secure the establishment of schools in all the villages of the Pueblos, for the instruction of their children in the English language. Five such schools are now being conducted for their benefit.

The history of the Pueblos is an interesting one. They are the remains of a once powerful people, and in habits and modes of life are still clearly distinguished from all other aborigines of the continent. The Spanish invaders found them living generally in towns and cities. They are so described by Spanish historians as far back as 1540. They early revolted, though without success, against Spanish rule; and in the struggle many of their towns were burnt, and much loss of life and property occasioned. It would seem, however, that, in addition to the villagers, there were others at that time living dispersed, whose reduction to Pueblos was determined upon and made the subject of a decree by Charles V. of Spain, in 1546, in order chiefly, as declared, to their being instructed in the Catholic faith. Under the Spanish Government schools were established at the villages; the Christian religion was introduced, and impressed upon the people, and the rights of property thoroughly protected. By all these means a high degree of civilization was secured, which was maintained until after the establishment of Mexican independence; when, from want of Government care and support, decay followed, and the Pueblos measurably deteriorated, down to the time when the authority of the United States was extended over that country: still they are a remarkable people, noted for their sobriety, industry, and docility. They have few wants, and are simple in their habits and moral in their lives. They are, indeed, scarcely to be considered Indians, in the sense traditionally attached to that word, and, but for their residence upon reservations patented to these bands in confirmation of ancient Spanish grants, and their continued tribal organization, might be regarded as a part of the ordinary population of the country. There are now nineteen villages of these Indians in New Mexico. Each village has a distinct and organized government, with its governor and other officers, all of whom are elected annually by the people, except the *cacique*, a sort of high-priest, who holds his office during life. Though nominally Catholics in religion, it is thought that their real beliefs are those of their ancestors in the days of Montezuma.

UTAH.

The tribes residing wholly or in part within the limits of Utah are the North-western, Western, and Goship bands of Shoshones; the Weber, Yampa, Elk Mountain, and Uintah bands of Utes; the Timpanagos, the San Pitches, the Pah-Vents, the Piedes, and She-be-rechers—all, with the exception of the Shoshones, speaking the Ute language, and being native to the country inhabited by them.

North-western, Western, and Goship Shoshones.—These three bands of Shoshones, numbering together about 3000, have treaties made with the Government in 1863. No reservations were provided to be set apart for them by the terms of said treaties, the only provision for their benefit being the agreement on the part of the United States to furnish them with articles, to a limited extent and for a limited term, suitable to their wants as hunters or herdsmen. Having no reservations, but little can be done for their advancement. They live in North-western Utah and North-eastern Nevada, and are generally inclined to be industrious, many of them gaining a livelihood by working for the white settlers, while others cultivate small tracts of land on their own account.

The Weber Utes, numbering about 300, live in the vicinity of Salt Lake City, and subsist by hunting, fishing, and begging. The Timpanagos, numbering about 500, live south of Salt Lake City, and live by hunting and fishing. The San Pitches, numbering about 300, live, with the exception of some who have gone to the Uintah Valley Reservation, in the country south and east of the Timpanagos, and subsist by hunting and fishing. The Pah-Vents number about 1200, and occupy the Territory south of the Goships, cultivate small patches of ground, but live principally by hunting and fishing. The Yampa Utes, Piedes, Piutes, Elk Mountain Utes, and She-be-rechers live in the eastern and southern parts of the Territory. They number, as nearly as can be estimated, 5200; do not cultivate the soil, but subsist by hunting and fishing, and at times by depredating in a small way upon the white settlers. They are warlike and migratory in their habits, carrying on a petty warfare pretty much all the time with the southern Indians. These bands of Utes have no treaties with the United States: they receive no annuities, and but very little assistance from the Government.

The Uintah Utes, numbering 800, are now residing upon a reservation of 2,039,040 acres in Uintah Valley, in the north-eastern corner of the Territory, set apart for the occupancy of the Indians in Utah by Executive order of October 3d, 1861, and by Act of Congress of May 5th, 1864. This reservation comprises some of the best farming land in Utah, and is of sufficient extent to maintain all the Indians in the Territory. Some of the Indians located here show a disposition to engage in agriculture, though most of them still prefer the chase to labor. No steps have yet been taken to open a school on the reservation. The Uintah Utes have no treaty with the United States; but an appropriation averaging about $10,000 has been annually made for their civilization and improvement since 1863.

ARIZONA.

The tribes residing in the Territory of Arizona are the Pimas and Maricopas, Papagoes, Mohaves, Moquis, and Orivas Pueblos, Yumas, Yavapais, Hualapais, and different bands of the Apaches. All are native to the districts occupied by them, respectively.

Pimas and Maricopas.—These, said to have been in former years "Village" or "Pueblo" Indians, number 4342, and occupy a reservation of 64,000 acres, set apart for them under the Act of February 28th, 1859, and located in the central part of the Territory, on the Gila River. They are, and always have been, peaceful and loyal to the Government; are considerably advanced, according to a rude form of civilization, and being industrious, and engaged quite successfully, whenever the conditions of soil and climate are favorable, in farming operations, are nearly self-sustaining. The relations of these bands with the neighboring whites are, however, very unfavorable to their interests; and the condition of affairs is fast growing worse. The difficulty arises out of the fact of the use, and probably the improvident use, by the whites above them, of the water of the Gila River, by which they are deprived of all means of irrigating their lands. Much dissatisfaction is manifested on this account; and the result is, so far, that many of the Indians have left the reservation, and gone to Salt River Valley, where they are making a living by tilling the soil, not, however, without getting into trouble at this point also with the settlers.

The Pimas and Maricopas are greatly interested in the education of their children. Two schools are in operation on the reservation, with an attendance of 105 scholars. These tribes have no treaty with the United States, and receive but little assistance from the Government.

Papagoes.—These Indians, numbering about 5000, are of the same class, in some respects, as the Pueblos in New Mexico, living in villages, cultivating the soil, and raising stock for a support. They have no reservation set apart for their occupancy, but inhabit the south-eastern part of the Territory. Many of them have embraced Christianity; and they are generally well-behaved, quiet, and peaceable. They manifest a strong desire to have their children educated; and steps to this end have been taken by the Department. These Indians have no treaty relations with the

United States, and receive no assistance from the Government. The expediency of assigning to the Papagoes a reservation, and concentrating them where they can be brought within the direct care and control of the Government, is under consideration by the Department. There seems to be no reason to doubt that, if so established, and once supplied with implements and stock, they would become in a short time not only self-sustaining but prosperous.

Mohaves.—These Indians have a reservation of 75,000 acres, located on the Colorado River, and set apart for them and other tribes in the vicinity of said river, under the Act of March 3d, 1865. The Mohaves number about 4000, of whom only 828 are on the reservation, the rest either roaming at large or being fed at other reservations in the Territory. An irrigating canal has been built for them at great expense; but farming operations have not as yet proved very successful. Over 1100 acres, however, are being cultivated by the Indians. The crops consist of corn, melons, and pumpkins. These Indians show but little progress in civilization. The parents objecting to the education of their children, no schools have been put in operation on the reservation, as they could be conducted only on a compulsory system. The Mohaves have no treaty stipulations with the United States; but they are partly subsisted, and are largely assisted in their farming operations, from the general incidental fund of the Territory.

Yumas.—These Indians number probably 2000. They inhabit the country near the mouth of the Colorado River, but belong to the reservation occupied by the Mohaves. They refuse, however, to remove to the reservation, and gain a scanty subsistence by planting, and by cutting wood for steamers plying on the river. Many of them remain about Arizona City, performing menial services for the whites, and gratifying their inveterate passion for gambling. They have no treaty with the United States, and receive but little assistance from the Government.

Hualapais.—These Indians, numbering about 1500, inhabit the country near the Colorado River, north of the Mohaves, ranging a considerable distance into the interior. They have been, and still are, more or less hostile. Those who are quiet and peaceable are, with members of other bands of Indians, being fed by the Government at Camps McDowell, Beal's Spring, and Date Creek.

Yavapais and Apaches.—These Indians are estimated to number from 8000 to 12,000, the lower estimate being the more reasonable. Their ranging-grounds are in the central, northern, and eastern parts of the Territory. Most of them have long been hostile to the Government, committing numerous robberies and murders. Earnest efforts have been made during the past year to settle them on reservations, three of which, viz., Camp Apache, Camp Grant, and Camp Verde, were set apart for their occupancy by Executive order dated November 9th, 1871. These efforts, however, have not resulted very successfully; the Indians occasionally coming upon the reservations in large numbers, but leaving without permission, and, indeed, defiantly, whenever so disposed, oftentimes renewing their depredations before their supplies of government rations are exhausted. Many of the bands of this tribe (if it can be called a tribe; habits, physical structure, and language all pointing to a great diversity in origin among the several bands) are seemingly incorrigible, and will hardly be brought to cease their depredations and massacres except by the application of military force.

NEVADA.

The tribes residing in Nevada are Pah-Utes, Piutes, Washoes, Shoshones, and Bannocks, and are native to the districts inhabited by them respectively.

Pah-Utes.—These Indians, numbering about 6000, inhabit the western part of the State. Two reservations have been set apart for them—one known as the Walker River, the other as the Pyramid Lake Reservation, containing each 320,000 acres. These Indians are quiet, and friendly to the whites—are very poor, and live chiefly upon fish, game, seeds, and nuts, with such assistance as the Government from time to time renders them. They show considerable disposition to labor; and those on the reservations, especially the Walker River Reservation, are cultivating small patches of ground. The Pyramid Lake Reservation affords, in addition, excellent fishing, and the surrounding settlements a ready market for the catch over and above what the Indians require for their own consumption. No schools have been established for these Indians. They have no treaty relations with the Government, and receive no annuities.

Piutes. — The Piutes, numbering probably 2500, inhabit the south-eastern part of the State. They have no reservation set apart for them; nor have they any treaty with the United States. They roam about at will, are very destitute, and obtain a living principally by pilfering from the whites, although a few of them are engaged in a small way in farming. But very little can be

done for these Indians by the Government in their present unsettled condition. They should be brought upon one of the reservations set apart for the Indians in Nevada, or upon the Uintah Reservation in Utah, where they could receive suitable care and proper instruction in the arts of civilized life.

Washoes.—These Indians, numbering about 500, are a poor, miserable, and debauched people, and spend most of their time among
the white settlements, where they gain some supplies of food and
clothing by menial services. They have no reservation and no
treaty, are not in charge of any agent of the Government; and
vice and disease are rapidly carrying them away.

Shoshones.—The Shoshones are a portion of the North-western,
Western, and Goship bands, referred to under the head of " Utah."
Those roaming or residing in the eastern part of Nevada number
about 2000. The remarks made respecting their brethren in Utah
will equally apply to them.

Bannocks.—The Bannocks, roaming in the north-eastern part of
the State, number, probably, 1500, and are doubtless a portion of
the people of that name ranging in Eastern Oregon and Southern
Idaho. They have no treaty with the Government, nor any reservation set apart for them, and are not in charge of any United
States agent. They should, if possible, be located upon the Fort
Hall Reservation in Idaho, where some steps could be taken to
advance them in civilization.

THE PACIFIC SLOPE.

The Indians on the Pacific slope are divided as follows: in
Washington Territory, about 14,000; in Oregon, 12,000; in California, 22,000.

WASHINGTON TERRITORY.

The tribes residing in Washington Territory are the Nisqually,
Puyallup, and other confederate tribes; the D'Wamish and other
allied bands; the Makahs, the S'Klallams, the Qui-nai-elts and
Qui-leh-utes, the Yakamas, the Chehalis, and other allied tribes,
and the Colville, Spokanes, Cœur d'Alênes, Okanagans, and others.

Nisqually, Puyallup, and others. — These Indians, numbering
about 1200, have three reservations, containing, as per treaty of
1854, 26,776 acres, situated on the Nisqually and Puyallup Rivers,
and on an island in Puget Sound. Some of these Indians are en-

gaged in farming, and raise considerable wheat, also potatoes and other vegetables. Many are employed by the farmers in their vicinity; while others still are idle and shiftless, spending their time wandering from place to place. One school is in operation on the Puyallup Reservation, with an attendance of eleven scholars.

D'Wamish and others.—The D'Wamish and other allied tribes number 3600, and have five reservations, containing in all 41,716 acres, set apart by treaty made with them in 1855, and located at as many points on Puget Sound. Many of these Indians, particularly those residing on the Lummi Reservation, are industrious farmers, raising all the produce necessary for their support, and owning a large number of cattle, horses, hogs, etc.; while others are either employed by the neighboring white farmers or engaged in lumbering on their own account. They are generally Christianized, most of them members of the Catholic Church. One school, with fifty-seven scholars, is in operation on the Tulalip Reservation, where all the Government buildings are located. This school has had a remarkable degree of success, as reported by the agent and by disinterested visitors.

Makahs.—These Indians number 604, and have a reservation of 12,800 acres, set apart by treaty made with them in 1855, and located at the extreme north-west corner of the Territory. They are a bold, hardy race, not inclined to till the soil for a support, but depending principally upon fishing and the taking of fur-seal for their livelihood. One school is in operation among them, with an attendance of sixteen scholars.

S'Klallams.—These Indians, numbering 919, have a reservation of 4000 acres, set apart by treaty made with them in 1855, and located on what is known as "Hood's Canal." Some of them are engaged, in a small way, in farming; and others are employed in logging for the neighboring saw-mills. Their condition generally is such that their advancement in civilization must necessarily be slow. A school has been established on the reservation, and is attended by twenty-two scholars.

Qui-nai-elts, Qui-leh-utes, Hohs, and Quits.—These Indians number 520, and have a reservation of 25,600 acres, in the extreme eastern part of the Territory, and almost wholly isolated from white settlements, set apart under a treaty made with them July 1st, 1855. But one of the four tribes mentioned, the Qui-nai-elts, live upon the reservation: the others reside at different points along the coast, northward from the reservation. These declare that they never agreed to sell their country, and that they never knowingly signed any treaty disposing of their right to it. The bottom land on the reservation is heavily timbered, and a great deal of labor is required to clear it; but, when cleared, it produces good crops. Many of the Indians, though in the main fish-eaters (the Qui-nai-elt River furnishing them with salmon in great abundance), are cultivating small patches, and raise sufficient vegetables for their own use. One school is in operation on the reservation, with an attendance of fifteen scholars.

Yakamas.—The Yakamas number 3000, and have a reservation in the southern part of the Territory, containing 783,360 acres, set apart for them by treaty of June 9th, 1855. These Indians belong to numerous bands, confederated under the title of Yakamas. Many of them, under the able management of their present agent, have become noticeably advanced in civilization, and are good farmers or skilled mechanics. The manual-labor school at the Yakama Agency has been a complete success, and of incalculable benefit in imparting to the children a practical knowledge of farming and of the different mechanical arts. Their principal wealth is in horses, of which they own 12,000. The fact that the reservation for these Indians is located east of the Cascade Mountains, away from all contact with the whites, has doubtless tended, in a great measure, to make this what it is—the model agency on the Pacific slope: though to this result the energy and devotion of Agent Wilbur have greatly contributed. Churches have been built on the reservation, which are well attended, the services being conducted by native preachers. There are at present two schools, with an attendance of forty-four scholars.

Chehalis and others, Remnants of Tribes, and Parties to no Treaty with the Government.—These Indians number about 600, and have a reservation of 4322 acres in the eastern part of the territory, set apart for them by Executive order of July 8th, 1864. A considerable portion of the land in this reservation is excellent for agricultural purposes; and quite extensive crops are being raised by the Indians of the Chehalis tribe. None of the other tribes for whom the reservation was intended reside upon it, declining to do so for the reason that they do not recognize it as their own, and fear to prejudice their claims to other lands by so doing.

All these Indians have horses and cattle in abundance. They are industrious; and, being good field-hands, those of them who do not farm on their own account find ready employment from the surrounding farmers, their services always commanding the highest wages. Having no treaty relations with the Government, no direct appropriations are made for their benefit. They, however, receive some assistance from the general incidental fund of the Territory. The Indians herein referred to as not living upon the reservation are of the Cowlitz, Chinook, Shoalwater Bay, and Humboldt tribes. They profess to desire a home at the mouth of the Humboldt and Coinoose rivers, where they originated.

Colville and other Tribes.—These Indians, numbering 3349, occupy the north-eastern portion of the territory. They have no treaty relations with the Government, and, until the present year, have had no reservation set apart for them. They are now, however, to be established, under an order of the President of July 2d, 1872, in the general section of the Territory where they now are, upon a tract which is bounded on the south and east by the Columbia River, on the west by the Okinakane River, and on the north by British Columbia. The tribes for whom this reservation is designed are known as Colvilles, Okinakanes, San Poels, Lake Spokanes, Cœur d'Alênes, Calispells, and Methows. Some of these Indians, however, have settled upon valuable tracts of land, and have made extensive improvements, while others, to a considerable number, have begun farming in a small way at various points within the district from which it is proposed to remove their respective tribes. It is doubtful whether these individuals will voluntarily remove to the reservation referred to, which is some distance west of their present location. It is proposed, therefore, to allow such as are engaged in farming to remain where they are, if they so desire. Owing to the influx of whites into the country thus claimed or occupied by these Indians, many of them have been crowded out; and some of them have had their own unquestionable improvements forcibly wrested from them. This for a time during the past summer caused considerable trouble, and serious difficulties were apprehended; but thus far peace has been preserved by a liberal distribution among them of agricultural implements, seeds, blankets, etc. No funds are appropriated specially for these Indians, such supplies and presents as are given them being furnished from the general incidental fund of the Territory.

OREGON.

The tribes residing in Oregon are the Umatillas, Cayuses, Walla-Wallas, Wascoes, Molels, Chasta Scotans, Coosas, Alseas, Klamath, Modocs, and Wal-pah-pee Snakes, besides numerous other small bands. They are all native to the country. On account of the great number of small tribes and bands in this State—the number of tribes and bands parties to the same treaty being in some cases as high as ten or fifteen—these Indians will be treated of, and the remarks concerning them will be made, under the heads of the agencies at which they are respectively located.

Umatilla Agency.—The tribes located at this agency are the Umatillas, Cayuses, and a portion of the Walla-Wallas, and number 837. They have a reservation of 512,000 acres, situated in the north-eastern part of the State, set apart for them by treaty of June 9th, 1855. This reservation is very fertile, and, as usual in such cases, has attracted the cupidity of the whites. A proposition was made last year, under the authority of Congress, to have the Indians take land in severalty, or sell and remove to some other reservation. The Indians, however, in the exercise of their treaty rights, refused to accede to this proposition. These Indians are successfully engaged in agricultural operations, are nearly self-supporting, and may be considered, comparatively speaking, wealthy. It is gratifying to state that the introduction of whiskey by whites upon this reservation, and its sale to the Indians, has, during the last year, received a decided check through the vigilance of Agent Cornoyer in causing the arrest and trial of four citizens for a violation of the law in this respect. All the parties charged were convicted, and are now in prison. This is especially worthy of note, from the fact that it is always exceedingly difficult to obtain convictions for such dealing with Indians in any section of the country. There is one school in operation on the reservation, with an attendance of twenty-seven scholars.

Warm Spring Agency.—The Indians at this agency, known as the "Confederated Tribes and Bands of Indians in Middle Oregon," comprise seven bands of the Walla-Walla and Wasco tribes, numbering 626. They have a reservation of 1,024,000 acres, located in the central part of the State, set apart for them by the treaty of June 25th, 1855. Though there is but little really good land in this reservation, many of the Indians, by reason of their industry, have succeeded measurably in their farming operations, and may be considered as self-sustaining. In morals they have greatly improved; so that polygamy, the buying and selling of wives, gambling, and drunkenness have ceased to be common among them, as in the past. There are some, however, who are disposed to wander off the reservation and lead a vagabond life. But little advancement has been made in education among these

Indians. One school is in operation at the agency, with an attendance of fifty-one scholars.

Grand Ronde Agency.—The Indians at this agency comprise the Molalla, Clackama, Calapooia, Molel, Umpqua, Rogue River, and other bands, seventeen in all, with a total population of 870. The reservation upon which these bands are located is in the northwestern part of the State. It contains 69,120 acres, and was set apart for their occupation by treaty of January 22d, 1855, with the Molallas, Clackamas, etc., and by Executive order of June 30th, 1857. Some portions of this reservation are well adapted to grain-raising, though much of it is rough and heavily timbered. An allotment of land in severalty has been directed to be made, much to the gratification and encouragement of the tribes. These Indians are inclined to industry, and show commendable zeal in cultivating their farms, growing crops which compare favorably with those of their white neighbors. Their customs and habits of life also exhibit a marked improvement. One school is in operation, with an attendance of fifty scholars.

Siletz Agency.—The Indians at this agency are the Chasta Scotans and fragments of fourteen other bands, called, generally, coast-tribes, numbering altogether about 2500. These Indians, including those at the Alsea Sub-agency, have a reservation of 1,100,800 acres set apart for them by treaty of August 11th, 1855; which treaty, however, has never been ratified, although the reservation is occupied by the Indians. They were for a long time much averse to labor for a support; but recently they have shown more disposition to follow agriculture, although traditionally accustomed to rely chiefly upon fish for food. Many already have their farms well fenced and stocked, with good, comfortable dwellings and out-houses erected thereon. There is no reason why they should not, in time, become a thoroughly prosperous people. The failure to make allotments of land in severalty, for which surveys were commenced in 1871, has been a source of much uneasiness to the Indians, and has tended to weaken their confidence in the good intentions of the Government. One school is in operation on the reservation, with an attendance of twenty scholars. None of the tribes or bands at this agency have any treaty relations with the United States, unless it may be a few members of the Rogue River band, referred to under the head of the Grand Ronde Agency.

Alsea Sub-agency.—The Indians at this sub-agency are the Alseas, Coosas, Sinselans, and a band of Umpquas, numbering in all

300, located within the limits of the reservation referred to under the head of the Siletz Agency. The remarks made about the Indians at the Siletz Agency will generally apply to the Indians of this sub-agency. The Coosas, Sinselans, and Umpquas are making considerable advancement in agriculture, and, had they advantages of instruction, would rapidly acquire a proficiency in the simpler mechanical branches of industry. The Alseas are not so tractable, and exhibit but little desire for improvement. All the assistance they receive from the Government is supplied out of the limited amount appropriated for the general incidental expenses of the service in Oregon.

Klamath Agency.—The Indians belonging to this agency are the Klamaths and Modocs, and the Yahooskin and Wal-pah-pee bands of Snakes, numbering altogether about 4000, of whom only 1018 are reported at the agency. They have a reservation containing 768,000 acres, set apart for them by the treaty of October 14th, 1864, and by Executive order of March 14th, 1871, situated in the extreme southern portion of the State. This reservation is not well adapted to agriculture. The climate is cold and uncertain; and the crops are consequently liable to be destroyed by frosts. It is, however, a good grazing country. Although this reservation is, comparatively speaking, a new one, the Indians located upon it are making commendable progress, both in farming operations and in lumbering. A part of the Modocs, who belong by treaty to this agency, and who were at one time located upon the reservation, have, on account of their troubles with the Klamaths—due principally to the overbearing disposition of the latter—left the agency, and refuse to return to it. They desire to locate upon a small reservation by themselves. Under the circumstances they should be permitted to do this, or else be allowed to select a tract on the Malheur Reservation. There is no school at present in operation for these Indians.

Malheur Reservation.—This reservation, set apart by Executive order of September 12th, 1872, is situated in the south-eastern part of the State. Upon this it is the intention of the Department eventually to locate all the roving and straggling bands, in Eastern and South-eastern Oregon, which can be induced to settle there. As no funds are at the disposal of the Department with which to make the necessary improvements, and to provide temporary subsistence for Indians removed, the work has not yet been fairly commenced. The Indians who should be collected upon this reservation are now a constant source of annoyance to the white settlers. They hang about the settlements and military posts, begging and stealing; and, unless some prompt measures be taken to bring them under the care and control of an agent of the Government, serious trouble may result at any time. Congress should make the necessary appropriation during the coming session to maintain an agent for these Indians, to erect the agency buildings, and to provide subsistence for such as may be collected and may remain upon the reservation.

Indians not upon Reservations.—There are a number of Indians, probably not less than 3000, "renegades," and others of roving habits, who have no treaty relations with the Government, and are not in charge of any agent. The tribal names of some of these are the Clatsops, Nestucals, Tillamooks, Nehalims, Snakes, and Nez Percés. The "renegades," such in fact, and so called, roam on the Columbia River, and are of considerable annoyance to the agents at Warm Springs and Umatilla: others, the Snakes, 200 in number, are upon the edge of the Grand Ronde Reservation. These live by hunting and fishing, and profess to desire to have lands allotted to them, and a school provided for their children. The Nez Percés, belonging in Idaho, to the estimated number of 200, are found in Wallowa Valley, in the eastern part of the State. They claim that they were not parties to the treaty with the Nez Percé tribe years ago; that the valley in which they live has always belonged to them; and they strenuously oppose its settlement by the whites.

CALIFORNIA.

The tribes in California are the Ukie, Pitt River, Wylackie, Concon, Redwood, Humboldt, Hoonsolton, Miscott, Siah, Tule, Tejon, Coahuila, King's River, and various other bands and tribes, including the "Mission Indians," all being native to the country.

Round Valley Agency.—The Indians belonging to this agency are the Ukies, Concons, Pitt Rivers, Wylackies, and Redwoods, numbering in all 1700. The number has been increased during the past year by bringing in 1040 Indians collected in Little Lake and other valleys. A reservation containing 31,683 acres has been set apart, per Act of April 8th, 1864, and Executive order of March 30th, 1870, in the western and northern part of the State, for these Indians, and for such others as may be induced to locate thereon. The lands in the reservation are very fertile; and the climate admits of a widely varied growth of crops. More produce being raised than is necessary for the subsistence of the Indians, the proceeds derived from the sale of the surplus are used in purchasing stock and work animals, and for the further improvement of the reservation. Several of the Indians are engaged in cultivating gardens, while others work as many as twenty-five or thirty acres on their own account.

The Indians on this reservation are uniformly quiet and peaceable, notwithstanding that they are much disturbed by the white trespassers. Suits, by direction of the Department, were commenced against such trespassers, but without definite results as yet; the Attorney-general having directed the United States District-attorney to suspend proceedings. Of this reservation the Indian Department has in actual possession and under fence only about 4000 acres; the remainder being in the possession of settlers, all clamorous for breaking up the reservation and driving the Indians out.

The Indians at this reservation have shown no especial disposition to have their children educated; and no steps were taken to that end until in the summer of 1871, when a school was commenced. There is now one school in operation, with an attendance of 110 scholars. These Indians have no treaties with the Government; and such assistance as is rendered them in the shape of clothing, etc., is from the money appropriated for the general incidental expenses of the Indian service in the State.

Hoopa Valley Agency.—The Indians belonging to this agency are the Humboldts, Hoonsoltons, Miscotts, Siahs, and several other bands, numbering 725.

A reservation was set apart, per Act of April 8th, 1864, for these and such other Indians in the northern part of the State as might be induced to settle thereon. This reservation is situated in the north-western part of the State, on both sides of the Trinity River, and contains 38,400 acres. As a rule, sufficient is raised on the reservation to supply the wants of the Indians. These Indians are quiet and peaceable, and are not disposed to labor on the reservation in common, but will work industriously when allowed to do so on their own individual account. One school is in operation on the reservation, with an attendance of seventy-four scholars. Having no treaty relations with the United States, and, consequently, no regular annuities appropriated for their benefit, the general incidental fund of the State is used so far as may be necessary, and so far as the amount appropriated will admit, to furnish assistance in the shape of clothing, agricultural implements, seeds, etc. Besides these, their agent has a general supervisory control of certain

Klamath Indians, who live adjacent to the reservation and along the banks of the Klamath River. These formerly belonged to a reservation bearing their name, which was, years ago, abandoned in consequence of the total destruction by flood of agency buildings and improvements. They now support themselves chiefly by hunting and fishing, and by cultivating small patches in grain and vegetables.

Tule River Farm, or Agency.—The Indians located at this point are the Tules and Manaches, numbering 374. These Indians are gradually improving, are quite proficient in all kinds of farmwork, and show a good disposition to cultivate the soil on their own account. There is one school in operation at the Tule River Farm, with an attendance of thirty-seven scholars. About sixty miles from the agency reside several hundred King's River Indians, who are in a wretched and destitute condition. They desire to be attached to the agency, and have in the past received occasional supplies of food from it.

Indians not on Reservations.—In addition to the Indians located at the three agencies named, there are probably not less than 20,000, including the Mission Indians (so called), the Coahuilas, Owen's River, and others, in the southern part of the State; and those on the Klamath, Trinity, Scott, and Salmon rivers, in the northern part. The Mission Indians, having been for the past century under the Catholic missions established on the California coast, are tolerably well advanced in agriculture, and compare favorably with the most highly civilized tribes of the east. The Coahuilas, and others inhabiting the south-eastern and eastern portions of the State, and those in the north, support themselves by working for white settlers, or by hunting, fishing, begging, and stealing, except, it may be, a few of the northern Indians, who go occasionally to the reservations and the military posts in that section for assistance in the way of food.

There are also about 4000 Owen's River and Manache Indians east of the Sierras, whom the settlers would gladly see removed to a reservation, and brought under the care of an agent. The Department has under consideration the propriety of establishing a new reservation, upon which shall be concentrated these and numerous other Indians, in which event the Tule River Agency could advantageously be discontinued.

XV.

REPORT

ON THE CONDITION AND NEEDS OF THE MISSION INDIANS OF CALIFORNIA, MADE BY SPECIAL AGENTS HELEN JACKSON AND ABBOT KINNEY, TO THE COMMISSIONER OF INDIAN AFFAIRS.

Colorado Springs, Col., July 13th, 1883.

SIR, — In compliance with our instructions bearing dates November 28th, 1882, and January 12th, 1883, we have the honor to submit to you the following report on the subject of the Mission Indians in Southern California.

The term " Mission Indians " dates back over one hundred years, to the time of the Franciscan missions in California. It then included all Indians who lived in the mission establishments, or were under the care of the Franciscan Fathers. Very naturally the term has continued to be applied to the descendants of those Indians. In the classification of the Indian Bureau, however, it is now used in a somewhat restricted sense, embracing only those Indians living in the three southernmost counties of California, and known as Serranos, Cahuillas, San Luisenos, and Dieguinos; the last two names having evidently come from the names of the southernmost two missions, San Luis Rey and San Diego. A census taken in 1880, of these bands, gives their number as follows:

Serranos	381
Cahuillas	675
San Luisenos	1,120
Dieguinos	731
Total	2,907

This estimate probably falls considerably short of the real numbers, as there are no doubt in hiding, so to speak, in remote and inaccessible spots, many individuals, families, or even villages, that have never been counted. These Indians are living for the most part in small and isolated villages; some on reservations set apart for them by Executive order; some on Government land not reserved, and some upon lands included within the boundaries of confirmed Mexican grants.

Considerable numbers of these Indians are also to be found on the outskirts of white settlements, as at Riverside, San Bernardino, or in the colonies in the San Gabriel Valley, where they live like gypsies in brush huts, here to-day, gone to-morrow, eking out a miserable existence by days' works, the wages of which are too often spent for whiskey in the village saloons. Travellers in Southern California, who have formed their impressions of the Mission Indians from these wretched wayside creatures, would be greatly surprised at the sight of some of the Indian villages in the mountain valleys, where, freer from the contaminating influence of the white race, are industrious, peaceable communities, cultivating ground, keeping stock, carrying on their own simple manufactures of pottery, mats, baskets, &c., and making their living, —a very poor living, it is true; but they are independent and self-respecting in it, and ask nothing at the hands of the United States Government now, except that it will protect them in the ownership of their lands,—lands which, in many instances, have been in continuous occupation and cultivation by their ancestors for over one hundred years.

From tract after tract of such lands they have been driven out, year by year, by the white settlers of the country, until they can retreat no farther; some of their villages being literally in the last tillable spot on the desert's edge or in mountain fastnesses. Yet there are in Southern California to-day many fertile valleys, which only thirty years ago were like garden spots with these same Indians' wheat-fields, orchards, and vineyards. Now, there is left in these valleys no trace of the Indians' occupation, except the ruins of their adobe houses; in some instances these houses, still standing, are occupied by the robber whites who drove them out. The responsibility for this wrong rests, perhaps, equally divided between the United States Government, which permitted lands thus occupied by peaceful agricultural communities to be put "in market," and the white men who were not restrained either by humanity or by a sense of justice, from "filing" homestead claims on lands which had been fenced, irrigated, tilled, and lived on by Indians for many generations. The Government cannot justify this neglect on the plea of ignorance. Repeatedly, in the course of the last thirty years, both the regular agents in charge of the Mission Indians and special agents sent out to investigate their condition have made to the Indian Bureau full reports setting forth these facts.

In 1873 one of these special agents, giving an account of the

San Pasquale Indians, mentioned the fact that a white man had just pre-empted the land on which the greater part of the village was situated. He had paid the price of the land to the register of the district land office, and was daily expecting his patent from Washington. "He owned," the agent says, "that it was hard to wrest from these well-disposed and industrious creatures the homes they had built up; but," said he, "if I had not done it, somebody else would; for all agree that the Indian has no right to public lands." This San Pasquale village was a regularly organized Indian pueblo, formed by about one hundred neophytes of the San Luis Rey Mission, under and in accordance with the provisions of the Secularization ⌐ct in 1834. The record of its founding is preserved in the Mexican archives at San Francisco. These Indians had herds of cattle, horses, and sheep; they raised grains, and had orchards and vineyards. The whole valley in which this village lay was at one time set off by Executive order as a reservation, but by the efforts of designing men the order was speedily revoked; and no sooner has this been done than the process of dispossessing the Indians began. There is now, on the site of that old Indian pueblo, a white settlement numbering 35 voters. The Indians are all gone,—some to other villages; some living near by in cañons and nooks in the hills, from which, on the occasional visits of the priest, they gather and hold services in the half-ruined adobe chapel built by them in the days of their prosperity.

This story of the San Pasquale Indians is only a fair showing of the experiences of the Mission Indians during the past fifty years. Almost without exception they have been submissive and peaceable through it all, and have retreated again and again to new refuges. In a few instances there have been slight insurrections among them, and threatenings of retaliation; but in the main their history has been one of almost incredible long suffering and patience under wrongs.

In 1851 one of the San Luiseno bands, the Aqua Caliente Indians, in the north part of San Diego County, made an attack on the house of a white settler, and there was for a time great fear of a general uprising of all the Indians in the country. It is probable that this was instigated by the Mexicans, and that there was a concerted plan for driving the Americans out of the country. The outbreak was easily quelled, however; four of the chiefs were tried by court-martial and shot by order of General Heintzelman, and in January of the following year a treaty was made with the San Luiseno and Dieguino Indians, setting off for them large tracts of land. This treaty was made by a United States commissioner, Dr. Wozencraft, and Lieutenant Hamilton, representing the Army, and Col. J. J. Warner, the settler whose house had been attacked. The greater part of the lands which were by this treaty assigned to the Indians are now within the boundaries of grants confirmed and patented since that time; but there are many Indian villages still remaining on them, and all Indians living on such lands are supposed to be there solely on the tolerance and at the mercy of the owners of said ranches, and to be liable to ejectment by law. Whether this be so or not is a point which it would seem to be wise to test before the courts. It is certain that in the case of all these Mission Indians the rights involved are quite different from and superior to the mere "occupancy" right of the wild and uncivilized Indian.

At the time of the surrender of California to the United States these Mission Indians had been for over seventy years the subjects, first of the Spanish Government, secondly of the Mexican. They came under the jurisdiction of the United States by treaty provisions, — the treaty of Guadalupe Hidalgo, between the United States and Mexico, in 1848. At this time they were so far civilized that they had become the chief dependence of the Mexican and white settlers for all service indoors and out. In the admirable report upon these Indians made to the Interior Department in 1853, by the Hon. B. D. Wilson, of Los Angeles, are the following statements: —

" These same Indians had built all the houses in the country, planted all the fields and vineyards. Under the Missions there were masons, carpenters, plasterers, soap-makers, tanners, shoe-makers, blacksmiths, millers, bakers, cooks, brick-makers, carters and cart-makers, weavers and spinners, saddlers, shepherds, agriculturalists, horticulturalists, vineros, vaqueros; in a word, they filled all the laborious occupations known to civilized society."

The intentions of the Mexican Government toward these Indians were wise and humane. At this distance of time, and in face of the melancholy facts of the Indians' subsequent history, it is painful to go over the details of the plans devised one short half-century ago for their benefit. In 1830 there were in the twenty-one missions in California some 20,000 or 30,000 Indians, living comfortable and industrious lives under the control of the Franciscan Fathers. The Spanish colonization plan had, from the outset, contemplated the turning of these mission establishments into pueblos as soon as the Indians should have become sufficiently civilized to make this feasible. The Mexican Government, carrying out the same general plan, issued in 1833 an act, called the Secularization Act, decreeing that this change should be made. This act provided that the Indians should have assigned to them cattle, horses, and sheep from the mission herds; also, lands for cultivation. One article of Governor Figueroa's regulations for the carrying out of the Secularization Act provided that there should be given to every head of a family, and to all above twenty-one years of age, though they had no family, a lot of land not exceeding 400 varas square, nor less than 100. There was also to be given to them in common, enough land for pasturing and watering their cattle. Another article provided that one-half the cattle of each mission school should be divided among the Indians of that mission in a proportionable and equitable manner; also one-half of the chattels, instruments, seeds, &c. Restrictions were to be placed on the disposition of this property. The Indians were forbidden " to sell, burden, or alienate under any pretext the lands given them. Neither can they sell the cattle." The commissioners charged with the carrying out of these provisions were ordered to " explain all the arrangements to the Indians with suavity and patience; " to tell them that the lands and property will be divided among them so that each one may " work, maintain, and govern himself without dependence on any one." It was also provided that the rancherias (villages) situated at a distance from the missions, and containing over twenty-five families, might, if they chose, form separate pueblos, and the distribution of lands and property to them should take place in the same manner provided for those living near the missions.

These provisions were in no case faithfully carried out. The administration of the Missions' vast estates and property was too great a temptation for human nature, especially in a time of revolution and misrule. The history of the thirteen years between the passing of the Secularization Act and the conquest of California is a record of shameful fraud and pillage, of which the Indians were the most hapless victims. Instead of being permitted each one to work, maintain, and govern himself without dependence on any one, as they had been promised, their rights to their plats of land were in the majority of cases ignored; they were forced to labor on the mission lands like slaves; in many instances they were hired out in gangs to cruel masters. From these cruelties and oppressions they fled by hundreds, returning to their old wilderness homes. Those who remained in the neighborhood of the pueblos became constantly more and more demoralized, and were subjected to every form of outrage. By a decree of the Los Angeles aqumiento, about the time of our taking possession of California, all Indians found without passes, either from the alcalde of the pueblos in which they lived, or from their "masters [significant phrase], were to be treated as horse-thieves and enemies." At this time there were, according to Mr. Wilson's report, whole streets in Los Angeles where every other house was a grog-shop for Indians ; and every Saturday night the town was filled with Indians in every stage of intoxication. Those who were helpless and insensible were carried to the jail, locked up, and on Monday morning bound out to the highest bidders at the jail gates. " The Indian has a quick sense of justice," says Mr. Wilson ; " he can never see why he is sold out to service for an indefinite period for intemperance, while the white man goes unpunished for the same thing, and the very richest and best men, to his eye, are such as tempt him to drink, and sometimes will pay him for his labor in no other way." Even the sober and industrious and best skilled among them could earn but little; it having become a custom to pay an Indian only half the wages of a white man.

From this brief and necessarily fragmentary sketch of the position and state of the Mission Indians under the Mexican Government, at the time of the surrender of California to the United States, it will be seen that our Government received by the treaty of Guadalupe Hidalgo a legacy of a singularly helpless race in a singularly anomalous position. It would have been very difficult, even at the outset, to devise practicable methods of dealing justly with these people, and preserving to them their rights. But with every year of our neglect the difficulties have increased and the wrongs have been multiplied, until now it is, humanly speaking, impossible to render to them full measure of justice. All that is left in our power is to make them some atonement. Fortunately for them, their numbers have greatly diminished. Suffering, hunger, disease, and vice have cut down more than half of their numbers in the last thirty years; but the remnant is worth saving. Setting aside all question of their claim as a matter of atonement for injustice done, they are deserving of help on their own merits. No one can visit their settlements, such as Aqua Caliente, Saboba, Cahuilla Valley, Santa Ysabel, without having a sentiment of respect and profound sympathy for men who, friendless, poor, without protection from the law, have still continued to work, planting, fencing, irrigating, building houses on lands from which long experience has taught them that the white man can drive them off any day he chooses. That drunkenness, gambling, and other immoralities are sadly prevalent among them, cannot be denied; but the only wonder is that so many remain honest and virtuous under conditions which make practically null and void for them most of the motives which keep white men honest and virtuous.

Having thus given as brief a presentation as possible of the general situation and nature of these Indians, we will proceed to state what, to the best of our judgment, are the steps which ought to be taken by the United States Government in their behalf. The descriptions of the most important villages we visited, and the detailed accounts of circumstances and situations on which our suggestions are based, are given for convenience of reference in separate exhibits.

1st. The first and most essential step, without which there is no possibility of protecting these Indians or doing anything intelligently for them, is the determining, resurveying, rounding out, and distinctly marking, their reservations already existing. The only way of having this done accurately and honestly, is to have it done by a surveyor who is under the orders and constant supervision of an intelligent and honest commissioner; not by an independent surveyor who runs or " floats " reservation lines where he and his friends or interested parties choose, instead of where the purpose of the United States Government, looking to the Indians' interests, had intended. There have been too many surveys of Indian reservations in Southern California of this sort. (See Exhibits C, H, I, J, L.) All the reservations made in 1876— and that comprises nearly all now existing—were laid off by guess, by the surveyor in San Diego, on an imperfect county map. These sections, thus guessed at by the surveyor, were reported by the commissioner to the Interior Department, set aside by Executive order, and ordered to be surveyed. When the actual survey came to be made, it was discovered that in the majority of cases the Indian villages intended to be provided for were outside the reservation lines, and that the greater part of the lands set apart were wholly worthless. The plats of these reservations are in the surveyor-general's office at San Francisco. On each of them was marked by the surveyor an additional line in color, showing what tracts ought to be added to take in the Indian villages and fields. So far as we could learn, no action was taken in regard to these proposed additions.

The reservation lines, when thus defined, should be marked plainly and conspicuously by monuments and stakes, leaving no room for doubt. A plat of each reservation should then be given to the Indians living on it. It was pathetic, in our visits to village after village, to hear the Indians' request reiterated for this thing, —" a paper to show to the white men where their lands were." Every fragment of writing they had ever received, which could by any possibility bear on their title to their lands, they had carefully preserved; old tattered orders from Army officers thirty years back, orders from justices of the peace, &c., all worthless of course, but brought forward with touching earnestness to show us. In no single instance had the reservation lines ever been pointed out to them. One band, the Sequan Indians, who had never seen any agent, said they had been told that they were on a reservation, but they did not know if it were true or not. They had been obliged to give up keeping stock, because they could not find any place where the whites would let them pasture cattle. (See Exhibit J.)

There are some settlements of Indians on Government lands not set off as reservations, in some instances not surveyed. These tracts should all be surveyed, their boundaries marked, and the lands withdrawn from market to be permanently set aside for the Indians' use. We use the term "rounding out" in regard to these reservations chiefly on account of the complication which results from their being in some cases within the limit of railroad grants, and made subsequent to those grants. Some are actually within the limits of the Southern Pacific Railroad grant; others will be within the limits of the Texas Pacific grant, should that be confirmed. The odd sections thus belonging to the railroads should be secured to the Indians. There are also a few claims to lands within reservation boundaries, which are legal on account of their having been made before the reservations were set off. These should be extinguished. (See Exhibit O.)

2d. All white settlers now on reservations should be removed. For the last four years stray settlers have been going in upon reservation tracts. This is owing to the lack of boundary definitions and marks as aforesaid, also to the failure of the surveys to locate the reservations so as to take in all the ground actually occupied by Indian villages. Thus, in many instances, the Indians' fields and settlements have been wrested from them, and they in their turn have not known where they could or could not go. There is not a single reservation of any size which is free from white settlers. It would seem that agents in charge of these Indians should have been authoritatively instructed in no case to allow squatters to settle on lands known to be within reservation lines, whether they were occupied by Indians or not. (See Exhibits H, I, O.)

The amount of land set off in Indian reservations in Southern California appears by the record to be very large, but the proportion of it which is really available is very small. San Diego County itself is four-fifths desert and mountain, and it is no exaggeration to say that the proportion of desert and mountain in the reservation is even larger than this. By thus resurveying, rounding out, and freeing from white settlers the present reservations, adding to them all Government lands now actually in occupation by Indians, there will be, according to the best of our judgment, nearly land enough for the accommodation of all the Mission Indians except those whose settlements are on grants.

3d. In regard to this latter class, *i. e.*, those whose villages are now within the boundaries of confirmed grants, the Government has to choose between two courses of action,—either to remove them and make other provision for them, or to uphold and defend their right to remain where they are. In support of the latter course we believe a strong case could be made out, and we have secured from one of the ablest firms in Southern California a written legal opinion on this point. (See Exhibit A.) It seems clear that this contest should be made by the Government itself. It is impossible for these poverty-stricken and ignorant people to undertake on their own account and at their own expense the legal settlement of this matter. It would be foolish to advise it; inhuman to expect it. A test case could be made which would settle the question for all. (See Exhibit B.) In case the decision be favorable to the Indians remaining, the ranch owners should then be called on to mark off the boundaries of the Indians' lands according to the California State law covering such cases. (See Exhibit R.) Whether the lands thus reverting to the Indians could properly be considered as Government lands or not, would be a question to be determined. Probably the surest way of securing them for the Indians' permanent use would be to consider them as such and have them defined as reservations by act of Congress.

4th. And this brings us to our fourth recommendation, which is, that all these Indians' reservations, those already set off by

Executive order, and all new ones made for them, whether of Government lands now in their occupation, or of lands which may be hereafter by legal process reclaimed for them from the grant lands on which they are now living, be patented to the several bands occupying them; the United States to hold the patent in trust for the period of twenty-five years; at the expiration of that time the United States to convey the same by patent to said Indians, as has been done for the Omaha Indians. The insecurity of reservations made merely by Executive order is apparent, and is already sadly illustrated in Southern California by the history of the San Pasquale Reservation, that of Aqua Caliente, and others. The insecurity of reservations set apart by act of Congress is only a degree less. The moment it becomes the interest and purpose of white men in any section of the country to have such reservation tracts restored to the public domain, the question of its being done is only a question of influence and time. It is sure to be done. The future of these industrious, peaceable, agricultural communities ought not to be left a single day longer than is necessary, dependent on such chances; chances which are always against and never for Indians' interests in the matter of holding lands. The best way and time of allotting these Indians' lands to them in severalty must be left to the decision of the Government, a provision being incorporated in their patent to provide for such allotments from time to time as may seem desirable, and agents and commissioners being instructed to keep the advantages of this system constantly before the Indians' minds. Some of them are fit for it now, and earnestly desire it, but the majority are not ready for it. The communal system, on which those now living in villages use their lands, satisfies them, and is apparently administered without difficulty. It is precisely the same system as that on which the pueblo lands were cultivated by the early Spanish settlers in Southern California. They agree among themselves to respect each other's right of occupancy; a man's right to a field this year depending on his having cultivated it last year, and so on. It seems not to occur to these Indians that land is a thing to be quarrelled over.

In the village of Aqua Caliente, one of the most intelligent of the young men was so anxious to show us his fields that we went with him a little distance outside the village limits to see them. He had some eight acres in grain, vine, and fruit trees. Pointing first in one direction, then in another, he indicated the places where his ground joined other men's ground. There was no line of demarcation whatever, except it chanced to be a difference of crops. We said to him, "Alessandro, how do you know which is your land and which is theirs?" He seemed perplexed, and replied, "This was my mother's land. We have always had it." "But," we persisted, "suppose one of these other men should want more land and should take a piece of yours?" "He couldn't," was all the reply we could get from Alessandro, and it was plain that he was greatly puzzled by the suggestion of the possibility of neighbors trespassing on each other's cultivated fields.

5th. We recommend the establishment of more schools. At least two more are immediately needed, one at the Rincon, and one at Santa Ysabel. (See Exhibits G, L.) As the reservations are gradually cleared, defined and assured for the Indians' occupancy, hundreds of Indians who are now roving from place to place, without fixed homes, will undoubtedly settle down in the villages, and more schools will be needed. It is to be hoped, also, that some of the smaller bands will unite with the larger ones, for the sake of the advantages of the school and other advantages of a larger community. The isolated situation of many of the smaller settlements is now an insuperable difficulty in the way of providing education for all the children. These Indians are all keenly alive to the value of education. In every village that we visited we were urged to ask the Government to give them a school. In one they insisted upon ranging the children all in rows, that we might see for ourselves that there were children enough to justify the establishing of a school.

In this connection we would suggest that if a boarding and industrial school, similar to those at Hampton and Carlisle, could be established in Southern California, it would be of inestimable value, and would provide opportunities for many children who, owing to the isolation of their homes, could not be reached in any other way.

We would further suggest that, in our judgment, only women teachers should be employed in these isolated Indian villages. There is a great laxity of morals among these Indians; and in the wild regions where their villages lie, the unwritten law of public sentiment, which in more civilized communities does so much to keep men virtuous, hardly exists. Therefore the post of teacher in these schools is one full of temptations and danger to a man. (See Exhibit M.) Moreover, women have more courage and self-denying missionary spirit, sufficient to undertake such a life, and have an invaluable influence outside their school-rooms. They go familiarly into the homes, and are really educating the parents as well as the children in a way which is not within the power of any man, however earnest and devoted he may be.

We would also suggest that great good might be accomplished among these Indians by some form of itinerary religious and educational labor among them. In the list of assignments of Indian agencies to different religious denominations, as given in the report of the Indian Bureau for 1882, the Mission Agency is assigned to the Evangelical Lutheran; but we could not learn that this denomination had done any work among them. So far as the Mission Indians have any religion at all they are Catholics. In many of the villages are adobe chapels, built in the time of the missions, where are still preserved many relics of the mission days, such as saints' images, holy-water kettles, &c. In these chapels on the occasions of the priest's visits the Indians gather in great numbers, women sometimes walking two days' journey, bringing their babies on their backs to have them baptized. There are also in several of the villages old Indians, formerly trained at the missions, who officiate with Catholic rites at funerals, and on Sundays repeat parts of the Mass. As these Indians are now situated in isolated settlements so far apart, and so remote from civilized centres, the only practicable method of reaching them all would be by some form of itinerary labor. A fervent religious and practical teacher, who should spend his time in going from village to village, remaining in each a few days or weeks, as the case might be, would sow seed which would not cease to grow during the intervals of his absence. If he were a man of sound common-sense and knowledge of laws of life, fitted to instruct the Indians in matters of hygiene, cleanliness, ventilation, &c., and in a few of the simple mechanical arts, as well as in the doctrines of religion and morality, he would do more for the real good of these people at present than can be accomplished by schools.

6th. The suggestion of the value of itinerary labor among the Indians leads to our next recommendation, which we consider of great importance, viz., that it should be made the duty of any Government agent in charge of the Mission Indians to make a round of inspection at least twice a year, visiting each village or settlement however small. In no other way can anything like a proper supervision of these Indians' interests be attained. This proof of the Government's intention to keep a sharp eye on all that might occur in relation to the Indians would have a salutary moral effect, not only on the Indians, but on the white settlers in their neighborhood. It would also afford the means of dealing with comparative promptitude with the difficulties and troubles continually arising. As it is now, it is not to be wondered at that the Indians feel themselves unprotected and neglected, and the white settlers feel themselves safe in trespassing on Indians' property or persons. In some of the villages, where pre-emption claims have been located within the last four years, no agent has ever been. It is safe to say, that had an agent been on the ground each year, with the proper authority to take efficient measures, much of the present suffering and confusion would have been prevented. In the case, for instance, of the Los Coyotes village, filed on a few months ago (see Exhibit F), there was no reason why those lands should not have been set apart for the Indians long ago, had their situation been understood; so in the San Ysidro case, and others. The whole situation of an agent in regard to the Mission Indians is totally different from that of ordinary agency on a reservation. The duties of an Indian agent on a reservation may be onerous, but they are in a sense simple. His Indians are all together, within comparatively narrow limits, and, so to speak, under his hand, and dependent largely on the Government. The Mission Indians, on the contrary, are scattered in isolated settlements thirty, forty, a hundred miles away from the agency headquarters, many of them in regions difficult of access. Moreover, the Indians are in the main self-supporting and independent. Protection or oversight worth anything to them can only be given by a systematic method of frequent visitation.

What is true in this respect of the agent's work is, if possible, still truer of the physician's. If there is to be an agency physician for the Mission Indians at all, he should be a young, strong, energetic man, who is both able and willing to make at least four circuits a year through the villages, and who will hold himself bound to go when called in all cases of epidemics, serious illness, or accidents occurring among Indians within one day's journey of the agency headquarters. Whatever salary it is necessary to pay to secure such service as this should be paid, or else the office of agency physician to the Mission Indians should be abolished. Anything less than this is a farce and a fraud.

7th. We recommend that there be secured the appointment of a lawyer, or a law firm in Los Angeles, to act as special United States attorney in all cases affecting the interests of these Indians.

They have been so long without any protection from the law that outrages and depredations upon them have become the practice in all white communities near which they live. Indians' stock is seized, corraled and held for fines, sometimes shot, even on the Indians' own reservations or in the public domain. In seasons of dearth roving stockmen and shepherds drive their herds and flocks into Indians' grain-fields, destroying their subsistence for a whole year. Lands occupied by Indians or by Indian villages are filed on for homestead entry precisely as if they were vacant lands. This has been more than once done without the Indians receiving any warning until the sheriff arrived with the writ for their ejectment. The Indians' own lives are in continual danger, it being a safe thing to shoot an Indian at any time when only Indian witnesses are present. (See Exhibits C, E.) It is plain that all such cases as these should be promptly dealt with by equal means. One of the greatest difficulties in the position of the Mission Indians' agent is, that in all such cases he is power-less to act except through the at best slow and hitherto unsatis-factory channel of reporting to the Interior Department. He is in the embarrassing position of a guardian of wards with prop-erty and property rights, for the defence of which he is unable to call in prompt legal assistance. In instances in which the In-dians themselves have endeavored to get redress through the courts, they have in the majority of cases—to the shame of the Southern California bar be it spoken—been egregiously cheated. They are as helpless as children in the hands of dishonest, un-scrupulous men. We believe that the mere fact of there being such a United States legal authority near at hand to act for the Indians would in a short time, after a few effective illustrations of its power, do away with the greater proportion of the troubles demanding legal interference.

The question of the rights of Indians living on grant lands to remain there will, if the Department decides to test it by law, involve some litigation, as it will no doubt be contested by the ranch owners; but this point once settled, and the Indians secured in the ownership of their lands, a very few years will see the end of any special need of litigation in their behalf. We recommend in this connection and for this office the firm of Brunson & Wells, of Los Angeles. We have obtained from this firm a clear and admirable opinion on these Indians' right to their present homes (see Exhibit A), and we know them to be of high standing at the bar and to have a humane sympathy for Indians.

8th. We recommend that there should be a judicious distribution of agricultural implements among these Indians. No village should be omitted. Wagons, harness, ploughs, spades, and hoes are greatly needed. It is surprising to see what some of these villages have accomplished with next to no implements. In the Santa Ysabel village the Indians had three hundred acres in wheat; there were but three old broken ploughs in the village, no harness, and no wagon. (See Exhibit G.) There is at present much, and not unfounded, sore feeling in some of the villages which have thus far received no help of this kind, while others of the villages have been supplied with all that was needed.

9th. There should always be provided for the Mission Indians' agency a small fund for the purchase of food and clothing for the very old and sick in times of especial destitution. The Mission Indians as a class do not beg. They are proud-spirited, and choose to earn their living. They will endure a great deal before they will ask for help. But in seasons of drought or when their little crops have, for any cause, failed, there is sometimes great distress in the villages. Last winter the Cahuillas, in the Cahuilla Valley (see Exhibit C), were for many weeks without sufficient food. The teacher of their school repeatedly begged them to let her write to the agent for help, but they refused. At last one night the captain and two of the head men came to her room and said she might write. They could no longer subdue the hunger. She wrote the letter; the next morning at daylight the Indians were at her door again. They had reconsidered it, they said, and they would not beg. They would rather starve, and they would not permit her to send the letter.

10th. The second and third special points on which we were instructed to report to the Department were, whether there still remains in Southern California any Government land suitable for an Indian reservation, and if not, in case lands must be bought for that purpose, what lands can be most advantageously purchased. There is no Government land remaining in Southern California in blocks of any size suitable for either white or Indian occupancy. The reason that the isolated little settlements of Indians are being now so infringed upon and seized, even at the desert's edge and in stony fastnesses of mountains, is that all the good lands—*i. e.*, lands with water or upon which water can be developed—are taken up.

We recommend two purchases of land,—one positively, the other contingently. The first is the Pauma Ranch, now owned by Bishop Mora, of Los Angeles. (See Exhibit P.) This ranch, lying as it does between the Rincon and Pala Reservations on the north and south, and adjoining the La Jolla Reservation, affords an admirable opportunity to consolidate a large block of land for Indian occupancy. It is now, in our opinion, a desirable tract. While it is largely hilly and mountainous, there is considerable good sheep and cattle pasturing on it, and a fair amount of bottom land for cultivation along the river. The price asked for it is, as lands are now selling in Southern California, low. If the already existing reservations are cleared of whites, unified, and made ready for Indian occupancy, and the Government lands now in actual occupation by Indians be assured to them, the addition of this Pauma Ranch will be, in our opinion, all that will be required to make comfortable provision for all the Indians, except those living within the boundaries of confirmed grants.

Should the Department decide to remove all these and provide them with new homes, we recommend the purchase of the Santa Ysabel ranch. (See Exhibit Q.) The purchase of this ranch for an Indian reservation was recommended to the Government some years ago, but it was rejected on account of the excessive price asked for it. It is now offered to the Government for $95,000. During the past ten years the value of lands in Southern California has in many places quadrupled; in some it is worth more than twenty times what it was then. We have no hesitation in saying that it is not now possible to buy an equally suitable tract for any less money. The ranch contains 17,719.40 acres; is within the rain belt of San Diego County, is well watered, and, although it is largely mountainous, has good pasture, some meadow land, and some oak timber. It is, moreover, in the region to which the greater proportion of these Indians are warmly attached and in the vicinity of which most of them are now living. One large Indian village is on the ranch. (See Exhibit G.) Father Ubach, the Catholic priest of San Diego, who has known these Indians for seventeen years, says of it, " it is the only tract to which human power can force these Indians to remove." We recommend this purchase only as a last resort in the event of the Department's being compelled to provide new homes for all the Indians now living within the boundaries of confirmed grants.

In conclusion, we would make the suggestion that there are several small bands of Mission Indians north of the boundaries of the so-called Mission Indians' agency, for whom it would seem to be the duty of the Government to care as well as for those already enumerated. One of these is the San Carlos Indians, living near the old San Carlos Mission at Monterey. There are nearly one hundred of these, and they are living on lands which were given to them before the Secularization Act in 1834. These lands are close to the boundaries of the ranch San Francisquito of Monterey. These boundaries have been three times extended, each time taking in a few more acres of the Indians' lands, until now they have only ten or twelve acres left. There are also some very destitute Indians living in the neighborhood of the San Antonio Mission, some sixty miles south of Monterey, and of San Miguel, forty miles farther south, and of Santa Juez near Santa Barbara. These Indians should not be overlooked in arrangements made for the final establishing of the Mission Indians in Southern California.

Hoping that these recommendations may be approved by the Department, we are,

Very respectfully yours,

HELEN JACKSON.
ABBOT KINNEY.

Hon. H. PRICE, Commissioner of Indian Affairs.

INDEX OF EXHIBITS.

Exhibit A.

Los Angeles, Cal., May 12th, 1883.

Sir,—In response to your verbal request asking our opinion as to the following questions, *viz.* : —

1st, Have civilized Indians and those who are engaged in agriculture or labor of any kind, and also those who are known as Pueblos or Rancheros Indians in California, a right to occupy and possess lands which they and their predecessors had continuously occupied, possessed, and enjoyed while said lands were under the jurisdiction of the Mexican Government, up to and at the date of the ratification of the treaty Guadalupe Hidalgo between the United States and the Mexican Republic, March, 1848, notwithstanding that said lands so occupied and enjoyed by the Indians aforesaid had been while they were so occupying and possessing the same, by the proper Spanish and Mexican authorities before the ratification of said treaty granted to certain Spanish and Mexican citizens, and since the acquisition by the United States of the territory embracing said lands so granted been by the United States confirmed, surveyed, and patented to the grantees or their legal representatives ?

2d. Has the United States Government the right to condemn lands within the State of California for the purpose of giving Indians homes thereon?

We have the honor to submit the following as our reply and answer to the above interrogatories. Before and at the date of the treaty of Guadalupe Hidalgo, all the territory now known as California was a part of and under the jurisdiction of the Mexican Republic. We do not regard it as necessary, in order to answer the questions propounded, to give a history of the land-laws of Spain and Mexico, nor the method of acquiring land prior to August 18th, 1824.

On August 18th, 1824, the Mexican Congress enacted a general colonization law, prescribing the mode of granting lands throughout the Mexican territory. This law was limited and defined by a series of regulations ordained by the Mexican Government, November 21st, 1828. By these laws and regulations, which have ever since continued in force, the governors of Territories were authorized to grant, with certain specified exceptions, vacant land. By the fundamental laws of 1824, the regulations of 1824, and the regulations of the departmental legislature consistent therewith, all Mexican grants in California have been determined; and by this has been determined the validity of every grant of land in California. (Lesse & Vallejo *vs.* Clark, 3 Cal. 17.) The limitations, as well as the fundamental laws mentioned, provided that in making grants or distribution of land (such as are now known as Mexican grants), —

1st. It must be vacant land, and, if occupied by Indians, then without prejudice to them.

2d. That such land as would be granted to the damage and injury of the Indians should be returned to the rightful owners.

The Mexican Government reserved from private grant all lands occupied and possessed by the Indians. Great care was taken to make strict reservation of such land; and by law no valid grant of land occupied or possessed by Indians could be made so as to dispossess them. When California was ceded to the United States, the rights of property of its citizens remained unchanged. By the law of nations those rights were sacred and inviolable, and the obligations passed to the new government to protect and maintain them. The term property, as applied to lands, embraces all titles, legal or equitable, perfect or imperfect. (Teschemacher *vs.* Thompson, 18 Cal. 12.) The United States never had, and does not now possess, any power under or by virtue of said treaty whereby it could or can confer upon a citizen holding and claiming property granted by the Mexican Government other or different property rights than those conferred by such Government, and such as were possessed, enjoyed, and held by him while under the jurisdiction of such government. It cannot abridge or enlarge the right to enjoy and to possess property held by virtue of Mexican law at the date of said treaty, nor can it deprive persons of any right to property which belonged to them at the date of said treaty.

A mere grant of land by the Mexican governor without compliance by the grantee with the further requisitions of the Mexican laws forms but an inchoate title, and the land passed to the United States, which hold it subject to the trust imposed by the treaty and the equities of the grantee. *The execution of the trust is a political power.* (Lesse *vs.* Clark, 3 Cal. 17.)

By the fundamental laws of 1824, the regulation of 1828, and the regulation of the departmental legislature, one condition was that in making private grants of lands the lands granted must be vacant lands. Lands occupied by and in possession of Indians were not such vacant lands; for by the same laws and regulations it was provided that such grants must be without prejudice or damage to the Indians, and that such land granted to the damage and injury of the Indians should be returned to the rightful owners. (New Code, law 9, title 12, book 4.)

The Mexican authorities recognized the rights of Indians to hold, enjoy, and possess lands, and there are of record a number of grants made by the Mexican authorities to Indians. They not only had the right to receive grants of land under the Mexican laws, but also to convey the lands so granted. (United States *vs.* Sinnol, Hoffman's Reports, 110.)

It will be observed that at the date when private grants of land were made with some regard for law, the limitation and conditions required by law to be observed were inserted in such grants, *viz.*: L. C., No. 342–6,

S. D., 398; L. C., No. 254–219, S. D., 228–407; L. C., No. 740–372, N. D., 208; L. C., No. 326–359, N. D., 389; Hoffman's Report Land Cases, pp. 35 *et seq.*; Surveyor-General's letter, dated San Francisco, March 14, 1883, and addressed to Mrs. William S. Jackson.

The Indians and their descendants, who occupied and now occupy lands within the grants above named, as well as grants containing claims of a similar character, are in our opinion possessed and seized of the lands which were and have been and now are in their possession; and they can hold the same against persons claiming the same by virtue of a United States patent, issued upon a confirmed Mexican grant. This leaves to be answered the following question : Can the Indians hold lands for which a United States patent has issued conditioned as set out in the first question, provided no conditions or limitations are contained or expressed in the grant? This is a question beset and surrounded by many difficulties ; nor do we deem it necessary to do more than refer to restrictions and limitations contained in the laws of Mexico concerning private grants of lands upon which Indians were residing,—lands which were occupied by them. It is certain that if such lands were granted by a Mexican official, and the authorities omitted to recite the conditions and limitations required by law, and reserve from the operation of such grant such lands as the law conditioned could not be conveyed by such grant, such a grant would and could not take it out of the operation of the law. It could not defeat the rights of those whose rights attached by reason of law. If the officers of the Mexican Government to whom was confided the trust exceeded their authority as regulated by the solemnities and formalities of the law, the courts are bound to take notice of it, and cannot shield those claiming under such title from the necessary consequence of ignorance, carelessness, or arbitrary assumption of power. (Lesse & Vallejo *vs.* Clark, 3 Cal. 17.)

It is now necessary to inquire how far and to what extent will the issuance to the grantee of the United States patent change or modify this rule. We shall not discuss, as we do not deem it necessary, the decision of the United States Supreme Court, that " a United States patent cannot be attached collaterally, but may be by a direct proceeding," as we did not regard these decisions as in any way affecting the question submitted and now before us.

In 1851, March 3d, Congress passed an act entitled " An act to ascertain and settle the private land-claims in the State of California." By said statute it was enacted " that it shall be the duty of the commission herein provided for to ascertain and report to the Secretary of the Interior the tenure by which the Mission lands are held, and those held by civilized Indians, and those who are engaged in agriculture or labor of any *kind*, and also those which are *occupied* and cultivated by Pueblos or Rancheros Indians." (U. S. Statutes at Large, vol. ix. p. 634, sec. 16, Little & Brown's ed.) We have no means of ascertaining whether such a report was made, or, if made, its contents. We have no doubt the commission did their duty and complied with the law, and that their report will be found on file in the Department of the Interior. This report, if in our hands, would greatly aid us in reaching a correct conclusion. By the same act it is further provided that the patent of the United States issued to parties holding Mexican grants are conclusive between the United States and the said claimants only, and shall not affect the interest of that person. (*Ib.* p. 634.) If the report of the commission established the fact that the Indians were residing upon and occupying lands within the boundaries of claimed grants, which grants have no conditions or limitation inserted therein, that they claimed such lands by virtue of the laws of Mexico, this evidence, with such other evidence as we understand can be furnished, is in our opinion enough to establish under the law, as we regard it, a right in the Indians to hold and occupy such lands against the confirmee or patentee. If, however, no such report has been made, we are of the opinion, if conclusive evidence can be furnished proving that these Indians were in possession of these lands at the time these grants were made by the Mexican authorities, that they continued in possession, and were in possession at the date of the treaty, and have since continued in possession, the law will entitle them to hold such land against all persons claiming under the patent.

We answer the second question propounded as follows : —

By the fifth amendment to the Constitution of the United States it is provided : * * * "Nor shall private property be taken for public use without just compensation." Would the taking of lands belonging to citizens for the purpose of giving the same to Indians be such a public use as is contemplated by the Constitution? We are of the opinion it would not. (Walther *vs.* Warner, 25 Mo. 277 ; Board of Education *vs.* Hockman, 48 Mo. 243 ; Buffalo & New York Railroad Company *vs.* Brannan, 9 N. Y. 100 ; Bradley *vs.* New York, &c. Railroad Company, 21 Conn. 294 ; Fisher *vs.* Horicon Iron Work, &c. Company, 10 Wis. 354 ; New Orleans & Railroad Company *vs.* Railroad Company, 53 Ala. 211 ; Conn *vs.* Horrigan, 2 Allen, 159 ; Chambers *vs.* Sattuler, 40 Cal. 497 ; Railroad Company *vs.* City of Stockton, 41 Cal. 149 ; Channel Company *vs.* Railroad Company, 51 Cal. 269 ; Gilmer *vs.* Lime Point, 18 Cal. 229 ; Conn *vs.* Tewksbury, 11 Metcalf, 55 ; Manufacturing Company *vs.* Head, 56 N. H. 386 ; Olmstead *vs.* Camp, 33 Conn. 532 ; Buckman *vs.* Saratoga Railroad Company, 3 Paige Ch. 45 ; Memphis Freight Company *vs.* Memphis, 4 Cold. 419 ; Enfield Toll Bridge Company *vs.* Hartford Railroad Company, 17 Conn. 42.)

We are, very respectfully,

BRUNSON & WELLS, Attorneys-at-Law.

ABBOT KINNEY, Esq., Los Angeles, Cal.

Exhibit B.

SABOBA.

Saboba is the name of a village of Indians of the Serrano tribe, one hundred and fifty-seven in number, living in the San Jacinto Valley, at the base of the San Jacinto Mountains, in San Diego County. The village is within the boundaries of a Mexican grant, patented to the heirs of J. Estudillo, January 17th, 1880. The greater part of the grant has been sold to a company which, in dividing up its lands, allotted the tract where the Saboba village lies to one M. R. Byrnes, of San Bernardino, who proposes to eject the Indians unless the United States Government will buy his whole tract of seven hundred acres at an exorbitant price. The Saboba village occupies about two hundred acres, the best part of Mr. Byrnes's tract. The Indians have lived in the place for over a hundred years. They have adobe houses, fenced fields and orchards, and irrigating ditches. There is in the village a never-failing spring, with a flow of about twenty-five miner's inches. It is claimed by the Indians that the first surveys did not take in their village. This is probably true; the resurveying of grants and "floating" their lines so as to take in lands newly discovered to be of value, and leave out others discovered to be worthless, being a common practice in California. In a country where water is gold, such a spring as these Saboba Indians owned could not long escape notice or be left long in the undisturbed possession of Indians. These Indians support themselves now, and have always done so, by farming, and by going out in organized bands as sheep-shearers and vintagers. They are industrious and peaceable, and make in good seasons a fairly comfortable living. They formerly kept stock, but since the new occupancy, allotting and fencing of the valley, have been obliged to give it up. There is a Government school in this village, numbering from thirty to forty pupils, who have made remarkable progress in their studies. The school is taught by a Pennsylvania lady, formerly a teacher of the freedmen. Her gentleness and refinement have exerted an influence all through the village, and her self-denying labors among the people in times of sickness and suffering have been the work of a missionary rather than of a teacher. The following letters were written by two of the children in this school, both under fourteen years of age. They were written without the teacher's knowledge or aid, and brought to her with the request that she would send them. The handwritings are clear and good : —

To the President of the United States:

Mr. President: Dear Sir,—I wish to write a letter for you, and I will try to tell you some things. The white people call San Jacinto rancho their land,

and I don't want them to do it. We think it is ours, for God gave it to us first. Now I think you will tell me what is right, for you have been so good to us, giving us a school and helping us. Will you not come to San Jacinto some time to see us, the school, and the people of Saboba village? Many of the people are sick, and some have died. We are so poor that we have not enough good food for the sick, and sometimes I am afraid that we are all going to die. Will you please tell what is good about our ranches, and come soon to see us?

Your friend,

RAMON CAVAVI.

Mrs. Jackson:

MY DEAR FRIEND,—I wish to write you a letter about the American people that want to drive us away from our own village of Saboba. I don't know what they can be about. I don't know why they do so. My teacher told me she was very sorry about the town, and then my teacher said, I think they will find a good place for you if you have to go; but I do hope they will not drive you away. Then it will be very good for all the people of Saboba. It is a very good town for the people. They have all the work done on their gardens, and they are very sorry about the work that is done. My work is very nicely done also. The people are making one big fence to keep the cows and the horses off their garden.

Your true friend,

ANTONIO LEON.

These Saboba Indians are greatly dispirited and disheartened at the prospect of being driven out of their homes, and feel that the Government ought to protect them. The captain of the village, a very sensible and clear-headed man, said, "If the Government says we must go, we must; but we would rather die right here than move." The right of these Indians to the tract they have so long occupied and cultivated is beyond question. That this right could be successfully maintained in the courts is the opinion of the law firm of Brunson & Wells, whose admirable paper covering all cases of this kind is given herewith. (See exhibit.)

We found three miles from this village on Government land a narrow cañon called Indian Cañon, in which half a dozen Indian families were living. The cañon is but five or six miles long and very narrow; but it has a small, never-failing brook in it, and some good bottom land, on which the Indians had excellent wheat crops growing. The sides of it are moderately well wooded. It was surprising that so desirable a nook had been overlooked or omitted by the surveyors of the San Jacinto Ranch. We wrote to the Department immediately, recommending its being set aside for Indians' use. In another beautiful cañon, also with a never-failing stream running through it, we found living the old chief, Victoriano, nearly one hundred years old. The spot was an oasis of green, oak and willow trees, a wheat field, and apricot orchard and vineyard, the latter planted by Victoriano's father.

This place has been given by Victoriano to his grandson, who we were told is taking steps to secure it to himself under the Indian Homestead Act.

Exhibit C.

THE CAHUILLA RESERVATION.

The Cahuilla Valley is about forty miles from Saboba, high up among the peaks and spurs of the San Jacinto Mountains; a wild, barren, inaccessible spot. The Cahuilla village, situated here, was one of the most interesting that we visited, and the Indians seemed a clear-headed, more individual and independent people than any other we saw. This is partly due to their native qualities, the tribe having been originally one of the most warlike and powerful in the country, as is indicated by their name, which signifies " master." The isolation of this village has also tended to keep these Indians self-respecting and independent. There is no white settlement within ten miles, there being comparatively little to tempt white men into these mountain-fastnesses. The population of the village numbers from one hundred and fifty to two hundred. The houses are of adobe, thatched with reeds; three of the houses have shingled roofs, and one has the luxury of a floor. These Indians make the greater part of their living by stock-raising. They also send out a sheep-shearing band each year. They have sixteen fields, large and small, under cultivation, and said they would have had many more except for the lack of ploughs, there being but one plough for the whole village. They raise wheat, barley, corn, squashes, and watermelons. Sometimes the frost kills the corn, and occasionally the grasshoppers descend on the valley, but aside from these accidents their crops do well. All through the village were to be seen their curious outdoor granaries—huge baskets made of twisted and woven twigs and set up on poles. The women were neatly dressed, the children especially so, and the faces of all, men, women, and children, had an animation and look of intellectual keenness very uncommon among the Southern California Indians. On the outskirts of the village is a never-failing hot spring. In this water the Indians, old and young, are said to be continually bathing. It was the Indians' impression that the lines of their reservation ran directly through the centre of this hot spring. They had been told so by some white men, but they know nothing certainly. The lines had never been shown to them. On subsequent examination at the surveyor-general's office in San Francisco we discovered that this spring and the village itself are entirely outside the reservation lines; also that another Indian settlement called Duasno, a few miles distant, and intended to have been included in the reservation, is outside the lines. The Cahuilla Reservation stands recorded as containing twenty-six sections of land; so far as we could judge of the region, it seemed to us a generous estimate to say that there might be possibly five hundred acres of cultivatable land in it. In good years there would be considerable pasturage on the sides of the mountains; but far the greater part of the tract is absolutely worthless, being bare and stony mountains. The Cahuillas, however, are satisfied with it. They love the country, and would not exchange it for fertile valleys below. They said that they would be perfectly contented if the Government would only mark their land off for them, and set up boundaries so that they could know where they might keep their own stock and keep the white men's stock out. All they asked for in addition to this was some harnesses, wagons, and agricultural implements, especially ploughs. Of these last the captain reiterated, and was not satisfied till he saw the figures written down, that ten was the smallest number that would be sufficient for the village.

A few rods from the hot spring there stood a good adobe house, shut up, unoccupied. The history of this house is worth telling, as an illustration of the sort of troubles to which Indians in these remote regions, unprotected by the Government, and unable to protect themselves, are exposed. Some eight years ago the Cahuillas rented a tract of their land as pasture to two Mexicans named Machado. These Machados, by permission of the Indians, built this adobe house, and lived in it when looking after their stock. At the expiration of the lease the house was to be the property of the Indians. When the Machados left they said to the Cahuilla captain, "Here is your house." The next year another man named Thomas rented a pasture tract from the Indians and also rented this house, paying for the use of it for two years six bulls, and putting into it a man named Cushman, who was his overseer. At the end of the two years Thomas said to the Cahuillas, "Here is your house; I now take my cattle away." But the man Cushman refused to move out of the house; said it was on railroad land which he had bought of the railroad company. In spite of the Indians' remonstrances he lived on there for three or four years. Finally he died. After his death his old employer, Thomas, who had once rented this very house from the Indians, came forward, claimed it as his own, and has now sold it to a man named Parks. Through all this time the Indians committed no violence on the trespassers. They journeyed to Los Angeles to find out from the railroad company whether Cushman owned the land as he said, and were told that he did not. They laid the matter before their agent, but he was unable to do anything about it. It would seem of the greatest importance in the case of this reservation, and of all others similarly placed, that the odd section claimed or owned by the railroad companies should be secured and added to the permanent reservation. Much further trouble will in this way be saved.

An incident which had occurred on the boundaries of the Cahuilla Reservation a few weeks before our arrival there is of importance as an illustration of the need of some legal protection for the Indians in Southern California. A Cahuilla Indian named Juan Diego had built for himself a house and cultivated a small patch of ground on a high mountain ledge a few miles north of the village. Here he lived alone with his wife and baby. He had been for some years what the Indians call a "locoed" Indian, being at times crazy; never dangerous, but yet certainly insane for longer or shorter periods. His condition was known to the agent, who told us that he had feared he would be obliged to shut Juan up if he did not get better. It was also well known throughout the neighboring country, as we found on repeated inquiry. Everybody knew that Juan Diego was "locoed." (This expression comes from the effect a weed of that name has upon horses, making them wild and unmanageable.) Juan Diego had been off to find work at sheep-shearing. He came home at night riding a strange horse. His wife exclaimed, "Why, whose horse is that?" Juan looked at the horse, and replied confusedly, "Where is my horse, then?" The woman, much frightened, said, "You must take that horse right back; they will say you stole it." Juan replied that he would as soon as he had rested; threw himself down and fell asleep. From this sleep he was awakened by the barking of the dogs, and ran out of the house to see what it meant. The woman followed, and was the only witness of what then occurred. A white man, named Temple, the owner of the horse which Juan had ridden home, rode up, and on seeing Juan poured out a volley of oaths, levelled his gun and shot him dead. After Juan had fallen on the ground Temple rode closer and fired three more shots in the body, one in the forehead, one in the cheek, and one in the wrist, the woman looking on. He then took his horse, which was standing tied in front of the house, and rode away. The woman, with her baby on her back, ran to the Cahuilla village and told what had happened. This was in the night. At dawn the Indians went over to the place, brought the murdered man's body to the village, and buried it. The excitement was intense. The teacher, in giving us an account of the affair, said that for a few days she feared she would be obliged to close her school and leave the village. The murderer went to the nearest justice of the peace and gave himself up, saying that he had in self-defence shot an Indian. He swore that the Indian ran towards him with a knife. A jury of twelve men was summoned, who visited the spot, listened to Temple's story, pronounced him guiltless, and the judge so decided. The woman's testimony was not taken. It would have been worthless if it had been, so far as influencing that jury's minds was concerned. Her statement was positive that Juan had no knife, nor weapon of any kind ; sprang up from his sleep and ran out hastily to see what had happened, and was shot almost as soon as he had crossed the threshold of the door. The district attorney in San Diego, on being informed by us of the facts in the case, reluctantly admitted that there would be no use whatever in bringing a white man to trial for murder of an Indian under such circumstances, with only Indian testimony to convict him. This was corroborated, and the general animus of public feeling vividly illustrated to us by a conversation we had later with one of the jurors in the case, a fine, open-hearted, manly young fellow, far superior in education and social standing to the average Southern California ranchman. He not only justified Temple's killing the Indian, but said he would have done the same thing himself. " I don't care whether the Indian had a knife or not," he said ; " that didn't cut any figure at all the way I looked at it. Any man that'd take a horse of mine and ride him up that mountain trail, I'd shoot him whenever I found him. Stockmen have just got to protect themselves in this country." The fact that Juan had left his own horse, a well-known one, in the corral from which he had taken Temple's ; that he had ridden the straight trail to his own door, and left the horse tied in front of it, thus making it certain that he would be tracked and caught, weighed nothing in this young man's mind. The utmost concession that he would make was finally to say, " Well, I'll agree that Temple was to blame for firin' into him after he was dead. That was mean, I'll allow."

The account of our visit to the Cahuilla Reservation would be incomplete without a brief description of the school there. It numbers from forty to fifty scholars, and is taught by a widow who, with her little daughter ten years of age, lives in one small room built on at the end of the school-house. Part of the room is curtained off into a recess holding bed, washstand, and bureau. The rest of the room is a sitting-room, kitchen, store-room, and barely holds the cooking-stove, table, and chairs. Here alone, with her little daughter, in a village of near two hundred Indians, ten miles from any white man's home, this brave woman has lived more than a year, doing a work of which the hours spent in the school-room are the smallest part. The Indians come to her with every perplexity and trouble ; call on her for nursing when they are ill, for food when they are destitute. If she would allow it her little room could always be crowded with women, and men also, eager to watch and learn. The Cahuillas have good brains, are keen, quick, and persevering. The progress that these children have made in the comparatively short time since their school was opened was far beyond that ordinarily made by white children in the same length of time. Children who two years ago did not know a letter, read intelligently in the second and third readers, spelled promptly and with remarkable accuracy, and wrote clear and legible hands, their copy-books being absolutely free from blots or erasures ; some of the older pupils went creditably through a mental arithmetic examination, in which the questions were by no means easy to follow. They sang songs in fair tune and time, and with great spirit, evidently enjoying this part of the exercises more than all the rest. We had carried to them a parcel of illustrated story-books, very kindly contributed by some of the leading publishers in New York and Boston, and the expression of the rows of bright dark eyes as the teacher held up book after book was long to be remembered. The strain on the nervous system of teachers in such positions as this can hardly be estimated by ordinary standards. The absolute isolation, the ceaseless demand, the lack, not only of the comforts, but of many of the necessities of life, all mount up into a burden which it would seem no woman could long endure. Last winter there was a snow-storm in the Cahuilla Valley lasting two days and nights. A fierce wind drove the dry snow in at every crevice of the poorly built adobe house, like sand in a sand-storm. The first day of the storm the school had to be closed early in the day, as the snow fell so fast on books and slates nothing could be done. The last night of the storm the teacher and her little girl spent the entire night in shovelling snow out of the room. They would pile it in a blanket, open the door, empty the blanket, and then resume shovelling. They worked hard all night to keep pace with the storm. When the snowing stopped the school-room was drifted full, and for many days after was wet and damp. It would seem as if the school term in such places as this ought not to be over eight months in the year. The salaries, however, should not be reduced, for they are barely living salaries now, every necessary of life being procured at a great disadvantage in these wild regions. One of these teachers told us she had been obliged to give an Indian $1 to ride to the nearest store and bring her one dollar's worth of sugar. It was the opinion of the Cahuilla teacher (a teacher of experience at the East before her marriage) that the Indians would accomplish more in eight months than in the nine. The strain upon them also is too great—of the unwonted confinement and continuous brain work. Should this change be made the vacation should be so arranged as to be taken at the sheep-shearing season, at which times all the schools are much broken up by the absence of the elder boys.

Exhibit D.

THE WARNER'S RANCH INDIANS.

The tract known as Warner's Ranch lies in the northern part of San Diego County, about forty miles from the Cahuilla Valley. It contains two grants, the San José del Valle and the Valle de San José; the first containing between 26,000 and 27,000 acres, confirmed to J. J. Warner, patented January 16th, 1880; the second, containing between 17,000 and 18,000 acres, confirmed to one Portilla, patented January 10th, 1880. The whole property is now in the possession of Governor Downey, of Los Angeles. There are said to be several conflicting claims yet unsettled. The ranch is now used as a sheep and stock ranch, and is of great value. It is a beautiful region, well watered and wooded. There are within its boundaries five Indian villages, of San Luisenos and Diegmons—Aqua Caliente, Puerta de la Cruz, Puerta de San José, San José, and Mataguay. The last four are very small, but Aqua Caliente has long been the most flourishing and influential village in the country. It was formerly set apart as a reservation, but the executive order was cancelled January 17th, 1880, immediately after the patenting of the San José del Valle Ranch, within the boundaries of which it was then claimed that the village lay, although to the best information we could get the first three surveys of that ranch did not take the village in. The aged captain of the Aqua Caliente Indians still preserves a paper giving a memorandum of the setting off of this reservation of about 1,120 acres for this people. It was by executive order, 1875. He also treasures several other equally worthless papers—a certificate from a San Diego judge that the Indians are entitled to their lands; a memorandum of a promise from General Kearney, who assured them that in consideration of their friendliness and assistance to him they should retain their homes without molestation, "although the whole State should fill with white men." It is not to be wondered at that these Aqua Caliente Indians find it difficult to-day to put any faith in white men's promises.

It will be seen from the above brief statement of the situation that they have an exceedingly strong claim on the Government for protection in their right to their lands. Since the restoration of their village and fields "to the public domain," the patenting of the ranches and their sale to Governor Downey, the Indians have been in constant anxiety and terror. Governor Downey has been considerate and humane in his course toward them, and toward all the Indians on his estate. And his superintendent also is friendly in his treatment of them, permitting them all the liberty he can consistently with his duty to the ranch. He finds their labor invaluable at sheep-shearing time, and is able throughout the year to give them occasional employment. But the Indians know very well that according to the usual course of things in San Diego County they are liable any day to be ejected by process of law; and it is astonishing that under the circumstances they have so persevered in their industries of one sort and another. They have a good number of fields under cultivation. They also make saddle mats and hats out of fibrous plants; the women make baskets and lace. It is said to be the most industrious village in the county; the old captain dealing severely with any Indian found idle. They have also a small revenue from the hot springs, from which the village takes its name. These bubble up in a succession of curious stone basins in the heart of the village. They are much resorted to in summer by rheumatic and other patients, who rent the Indians' little adobe houses and pay them a small tax for the use of the waters. The Indians themselves at these times move into bush huts in a valley or cañon some two miles above the village, where their chief cultivated fields lie. They were very earnest to know from us if we would advise their planting more of this ground. They said they would have planted it all except that they were afraid of being driven away. This upper valley and these planting fields were said to be on Government land; but on examination of the surveyor's plats in the Los Angeles land office, we could find no field notes to indicate their location. These Indians have in use another valley called Lost Valley, some fifteen miles from their village high up in the mountains, and reached only by one very steep trail. Here they keep their stock, being no longer able to pasture it below. They were touchingly anxious to have us write down the numbers of cattle, horses, sheep, each man had, and report to Washington, that the President might see how they were all trying to work. There are probably from one hundred and twenty-five to one hundred and fifty head of cattle owned in the village, about fifty horses, and one hundred sheep.

There is here a Government school, taught by a young German lady of excellent education and much enthusiasm in her work. At great cost and risk she has carried her piano up into these wilds, and finds it an invaluable assistance in training and influencing her pupils. It was a scene not to be forgotten, when after their exercises in reading, arithmetic, &c., in all of which they showed a really wonderful proficiency, the children crowded into the teacher's little room and sang their songs to the piano accompaniment, played by her with spirit and feeling. "My country, 'tis of thee, sweet land of liberty," was the song they seemed to like best; all unaware how little applicable to their own situation were its strains of exultant joy and freedom. In this one tiny room adjoining the school-room this young lady lives, sleeps, prepares her own food, frequently having a "cooking class" of Indian women, whom she is teaching to make soups, bread, &c., and to do fine washing. It is impossible to put too much appreciative sympathy on these women teachers in Indian schools in Southern California. Their situation and their work are unique in isolation and difficulty.

The other Indian villages on Warner's Ranch do not demand separate description, consisting of not more than half a dozen houses each, and numbering only from fifteen to thirty Indians. Each village, however, has its own captain, and its cultivated fields, orchards, &c., to which the Indians are profoundly attached, and from which it would be very hard to induce them to move, spite of their poverty, and the difficulty of making a living, as they are now placed.

During our stay at Warner's Ranch, the captain of the San José village had an experience which will illustrate the helplessness of these Indian farmers in Southern California. He had on a piece of Government land, a short distance from his village, a fenced wheat-field of some fifty acres; it was his chief dependence for his year's support. Going away one day, he left his aged father in charge at home; the old man wandered away, and during his absence one of the roving sheep-herders, of whom the country is full, broke down the fence, turned in his flock, and when Domingo came home at night the whole field was eaten close to the ground. Hearing of our being at the superintendent's house, Domingo came over to ask if we could help him in the matter. The quiet, matter-of-course way in which he told the story was more impressive than any loudness of complaint would have been. He said very simply, "What can I do for food this winter?" Mr. Kinney rode over to the village, saw the field, and after some trouble found the herder, who, much frightened, said he did it by his master's orders. This master, an Italian, lived some twenty miles away; the nearest justice of the peace, sixteen miles. On seeing the justice we found that nothing could be done in the way of securing damages from the sheep-owner until two white men, residents of the county, should inspect the premises and estimate the damages. Domingo rode sixteen miles in the night in a fierce storm of sleet and rain, with letters from us to white men on the ranch, asking them to do this. He was back again at daylight with a note from one of them, saying that he could not induce a man to go with him. Finally, the justice, at our request, hired two men at days' wages to go and inspect the Indian's field. They estimated the damages at about one-tenth of the real amount, and thus we were obliged to leave the matter. We afterwards received a letter from the Italian stating that he had settled with Domingo, but not mentioning the sum paid. It was plain that except for our taking hold of the affair the Indian would never have recovered a cent. This is by no means an exceptional instance.

Exhibit E.

THE SAN YSIDRO INDIANS.

In the San Ysidro Cañon, about eight miles from Warner's Ranch, has been living from time immemorial a band of San Luiseno Indians, numbering from fifty to seventy-five, and called by the name of their cañon. We first saw the captain of these Indians in Los Angeles, in the office of the United States Court Commissioner, Mr. H. T. Lee, of whose kindness and humane sympathy in dealing with all Indian matters which come under his notice it is not out of place here to make grateful mention. This Captain Pablo, with two of his head men, had walked a three days' journey to Los Angeles to see if he could get any help in the matter of lands which had been wrested from his people. His story was a pitiful one. Some six years ago a white man named Chatham Helm had come in at the head of their cañon, three miles above the site of their village, taken up a homestead claim there, cutting off the greater part of their water supply, and taking some of their cultivated fields, and leaving them restricted room for their stock. Since that time they had been growing poorer and poorer, but had managed to live by cultivating lands below the village near the mouth of the cañon, where there was another small stream. But now a new squatter had appeared below them, and filed on all the remaining lands, including the site of the village itself. The man Helm, above them, had patented his lands, built a good house, and was keeping considerable stock. The Indians could have no water except what he permitted to come down the cañon. Three years ago one of their number had been shot dead by Helm, who was set free on the usual plea of self-defence. Since then the Indians had been in continual terror. The new squatter had threatened them with the same fate if they came near his enclosures. Between these two squatters the Indian village was completely hemmed in and cut off, and starvation stared them in the face. In fact, in the course of the last winter one little girl had actually died for want of food. Their countenances corroborated the tale. They were gaunt with hunger and full of despair. It would exceed the limits of this paper to give a full report of the interview with these Indians. It will not soon be forgotten by any one taking part in it,—the solemn tones in which the Indians replied to the interpreter's questions, the intent and imploring gaze with which they studied all our faces and listened to all the words unintelligible to them in which we spoke with one another.

It was finally decided to forward to the Interior Department the affidavits of these Indians, setting forth the manner in which they had been robbed of their lands, and requesting that Cloos's entry be held for cancellation, and that Helm's patent be reopened. It was found, on looking the matter up in Washington, that several years ago this cañon had been withdrawn from market with a view to having it set off as a reservation for the Indians living in it, but the matter had slipped everybody's mind. On visiting the San Ysidro Cañon ourselves a few weeks later, we found that Cloos, taking time by the forelock, had sold out his homestead claim, his house, and what he was pleased to call his "improvements," for $600 to a poor old widow, Mrs. Pamela Hagar by name. We found Mrs. Hagar, with her son, on the ground, preparing to go into the bee business. She appeared very little surprised at hearing that the claim she had bought was a questionable one, remarking: " Well, I mistrusted something was wrong; Cloos seemed in such a hurry to get his money." This woman appeared nearly as helpless as the Indians themselves. The deed she had taken from Cloos was not acknowledged; she had not got it recorded; her name was misspelled in it; and the enumeration of the sections, &c., in it did not agree with the list in the land office certificate. She begged us to ask the Government to refund to her the sum she had paid to Cloos, and signed by her mark a paper saying she would accept it It is a small sum, and as the poor old woman made the transaction in good faith, knowing nothing about the Indians' presence on the place, it would seem not unreasonable that she should be paid. The next morning Cloos himself appeared on the scene, very angry and resentful. He said he had " a perfect right to file on that land; " that " Indians were not citizens " and " had no right to public lands," and that " the stockmen of San Diego County were not going to stand the Indians' killing their stock much longer; " that " the Government ought to put the Indians all together somewhere and take care of them," and that " there'd be a big fight with Indians in San Diego County before long, we might rest assured of that; " and much more of the same sort, which would not be worth repeating, except that it is a good illustration of the animus of the greater portion of Southern California ranchmen towards Indians. A few days after this we were gladdened by the news from Washington that Cloos's filing was held for cancellation, and that the Attorney-General had ordered proceedings to be begun in San Francisco for the vacating of Chatham Helm's patent. A few instances of such promptitude as this would change the whole status of the South California Indians, giving courage to them, and, what is still more important, making it clear to the perception of white men that the Indians' rights are no longer to be disregarded as they have been.

Exhibit F.

THE LOS COYOTES.

Five miles up from the head of the San Ysidro Cañon, to be reached only by a steep and narrow trail, lies a small valley on the desert side of the mountains. It is little more than a pocket on a ledge. From its rim one looks down directly into the desert. Few white men have ever penetrated to it, and the Indians occupying it have been hitherto safe, by reason of the poverty and inaccessibility of their home. No agent has ever visited them; they have supported themselves by keeping stock and cultivating their few acres of land. There are not more than eighty acres all told in the valley. About three weeks before our arrival at Warner's Ranch a man named Jim Fane, a comrade of Helm, who had usurped the San Ysidro Cañon, having, no doubt, learned through Helm of the existence of the Los Coyotes Valley, appeared in the village and offered the Indians $200 for their place. They refused to sell, upon which he told them that he had filed on the land, should stay in any event, and proceeded to cut down trees and build a corral. It seems a marvellous forbearance on the part of a community numbering twenty-six able-bodied men and twenty-one women not to take any forcible measures to repel such an intruder as this. But the South California Indians have learned by long experience that in any contest with white men they are sure to be found in the wrong. Not an Indian laid violent hands on Fane. He seems to have gone about as safely in the heart of this Indian village, which he was avowedly making ready to steal, as if he had been in an empty wilderness. Mr. Kinney found him there, hard at work, his belt full of cartridges and pistols. He was a rough fellow, at first disposed to be defiant and blustering, but on being informed of the Department's action in the case of Cloos's filing, he took a milder tone, and signed a paper saying that he would take $75 for his "improvements." Later in the day, after consulting with his friend Helm, he withdrew the paper and announced his determination to stay in the valley. On inquiry at the land office at Los Angeles we found that his filing had been returned to him for correction of errors. We were therefore in time to secure the stopping of all further proceedings on his part through the land office. Nothing, however, but authorized and authoritative action on the part of the agent representing the Interior Department will stop his proceedings on the ground. Just before leaving California we received an urgent letter from the Los Coyotes' captain, saying that Fane was still there—still cutting down their trees and building corrals.

The Indians of this band are robust, active, and finely made, more nearly in the native health and strength of the race than any other band in the country. The large proportion of children also bore testimony to their healthful condition, there being thirty-five children to twenty-one women and twenty-six men. The captain had the lists of his people kept by three lines of notches on a stick, a new notch being made for each birth and crossed out for each death. They could count only up to five. Everything beyond that was "many." Their houses were good, built of hewn pine timber with thatched roofs made from some tough fibrous plant, probably the yucca. Each house had a thatched bower in front of it and stood in a fenced enclosure. These Indians raise beans, pumpkins, wheat, barley, and corn. They have twenty-five head of cattle and more horses. They say they have lived in this valley always, and never desire to leave it. The only things they asked for were a harness, chain, coulter, and five ploughs. They have now one plough.

This village is one of the best illustrations of our remarks on the need of itinerary labor among the Mission Indians. Here is a village of eighty-four souls living in a mountain fastness which they so love they would rather die than leave it, but where the ordinary agencies and influences of civilization will never reach, no matter how thickly settled the regions below may come. A fervent religious and practical teacher spending a few weeks each year among these Indians might sow seed that would never cease growing during the intervals of his absence.

Exhibit G.

THE SANTA YSABEL RANCH.

The Santa Ysabel Ranch is adjoining to Warner's Ranch. It is a well-wooded, well-watered, beautiful country, much broken by steep and stony mountains. The original grant of this ranch was confirmed March 17th, 1858, to one José Ortego and the heirs of Edward Stokes. The patent was issued May 14th, 1872. It is now owned by a Captain Wilcox, who has thus far not only left undisturbed the Indian village within the boundaries of his estate, but has endeavored to protect the Indians by allowing to the ranch lessee a rebate of $200 yearly on the rent on account of the Indians' occupancy. There is in the original grant of this ranch the following clause : "The grantees will leave free and undisturbed the agricultural lands which the Indians of San Diego are actually occupying."

We found on arriving at the Santa Ysabel village that an intelligent young Indian living there had recently been elected as general over the Dieguino Indians in the neighborhood. He showed to us his papers and begged us to wait till he could have all his captains gathered to meet us. Eight villages he reported as being under his control,—Santa Ysabel, Mesa Grande, Mesa Chilquita, San José, Mataguay, La Puerta, Laguna, and Anaha. He was full of interest and inquiry and enthusiasm about his people. "I want know American way," he said in his broken English. "I want make all my people like American people. How I find out American laws ? When white men lose cow, lose pig, they come here with pistol and say we must find or give up man that stole. How we know ? Is that American law? We all alone out here. We got nobody show us. Heap things I want ask about. I make all my people work. We can't work like American people ; we ain't got work with ; we ain't got wagon, harness ; three old broked ploughs for all these people. What we want, some man right here to go to. While you here white man very good ; when you go away trouble same as before."

There are one hundred and seventy-one Indians in this village. They are very poor. Many of their houses are of tule or brush, their clothes were scanty and ragged, some of the older men wearing but a single garment. That they had not been idle their big wheat-field proved; between three and four hundred acres fenced and the wheat well up. "How do you divide the crops?" we asked. "Every man knows his own piece," was the reply. They sell all of this wheat that they can spare to a storekeeper some three miles away. Having no wagon they draw the wheat there on a sort of sledge or wood triangle, about four feet long, with slats across it. A rope is tied to the apex of this, then fastened to the horn of a saddle on a horse ridden by a man, who steers the sledge as best he may. The Indians brought this sledge to show us, to prove how sorely they needed wagons. They also made the women bring out all the children and arrange them in rows, to show that they had enough for a school, repeating over and over that they had many more, but they were all out digging wild roots and vegetables. "If there was not great many them, my people die hungry," said the general; "them most what we got eat." It is a sore grievance to these Santa Ysabel Indians that the Aqua Caliente Indians, only twenty miles away, have received from the Government a school, ploughs, wagons, &c., while nothing whatever has deen done for them. "Them Aqua Caliente Indians got everything," said the general; "got hot springs too; make money on them hot springs; my people got no chance make money."

On the second day of our stay in this region we saw four of the young general's captains, those of Puerta San Felipe, San José, Anaha, and Laguna. In Puerta San Felipe are sixty-four people. This village is on a confirmed grant, the "Valle de San Felipe," confirmed to Felipe Castillo. The ranch is now leased to a Frenchman, who is taking away the water from the Indian village, and tells the captain that the whole village belongs to him, and that if anybody so much as hunts a rabbit on the place he will put him in prison. These people are in great destitution and trouble, being deprived of most of their previous means of support. The Anaha captain reported fifty-three people in his village. White men had come in and fenced up land on both sides of him. "When he plants his wheat and grain the white men run their hogs into the fields;" and "when the white men find anything dead they come to him to make him tell everything about it, and he has not got anything to tell." The San José captain had a similar story. The Laguna captain was a tall, swarthy, well-to-do-looking Indian, so unlike all the rest that we wondered what there could have been in his life to produce such a difference. He said nobody troubled him. He had good land, plenty of water, raised grain and vegetables, everything he wanted except watermelons. His village contained eleven persons; was to be reached only by a steep trail, the last four miles. We expressed our pleasure at finding one Indian captain and village that were in no trouble and wanted for nothing. He smiled mysteriously, as we afterward recalled, and reiterated that nobody troubled him. The mystery was explained later, when we discovered accidentally in San Diego that this Laguna village had not escaped, as we supposed, the inroads of white men, and that the only reason that the Laguna Indians were not in trouble was that they had peaceably surrendered half their lands to a white man, who was living amicably among them under a sort of contract or lease.

Exhibit H.

MESA GRANDE.

Mesa Grande lies high up above the Santa Ysabel village and fifteen miles west of it. The tract adjoins the Santa Ysabel Ranch, and is, as its name indicates, a large table-land. There was set off here in 1876 a large reservation, intended to include the Mesa Grande Indian village, and also a smaller one of Mesa Chilquita; but, as usual, the villages were outside of the lines, and the lands reserved were chiefly worthless. One of the settlers in the neighborhood told us he would not take the whole reservation as a gift and pay the taxes on it. The situation of the Indians here is exceedingly unfortunate and growing more and more so daily. The good Mesa Grande lands, which they once owned and occupied, and which should have been secured to them, have been fast taken up by whites, the Indians driven off, and, as the young general said, "all bunched up till they haven't got any room." Both the Mesa Chilquita and Mesa Grande plateaus are now well under cultivation by whites, who have good houses and large tracts fenced in.

They have built a good school-house, which we chanced to pass at the hour of recess, and noting Indian faces among the children, stopped to inquire about them. There were, out of twenty-seven scholars, fifteen Indians or half-breeds, some of them the children of Indians who had taken up homesteads. We asked the teacher what was the relative brightness of the Indian and white children. Supposing that we shared the usual prejudice against Indians, the teacher answered in a judiciously deprecating tone, "Well, really there isn't so much difference between them as you would suppose." "In favor of which race?" we asked. Thus suddenly enlightened as to our animus in the matter, the teacher changed his tone, and said he found the Indian children full as bright as the whites; in fact, the brightest scholar he had was a half-breed girl.

On the census list taken of Indians in 1880 Mesa Grande and Mesa Chilquita are reported as having, the first one hundred and three Indians, the second twenty-three. There are probably not so many now, the Mesa Chilquita tract being almost wholly in possession of the whites. The Mesa Grande village has a beautiful site on a small stream, in a sort of hill basin, surrounded by higher hills. The houses are chiefly adobe, and there is on one of the slopes a neat little adobe chapel, with a shingled roof nearly done, of which the Indians were very proud. There were many fields of grain and a few fruit orchards. The women gathered around our carriage in eager groups, insisting on shaking hands, and holding up their little children to shake hands also. They have but once seen an agent of the Government, and any evidence of real interest in them and their welfare touches them deeply.

The condition of the Indians in this district is too full of complications and troubles to be written out here in detail. A verbatim copy of a few of our notes taken on the spot will give a good picture of the situation.

Chrysanto, an Indian, put off his farm two months ago by white man named Jim Angel, with certificate of homestead from Los Angeles land office. Antonio Douro, another, put off in same way from his farm near school-house. He had built good wooden house ; the white man took that and half his land. He was ploughing when the white man came and said, "Get out! I have bought this land." They have been to the agent. They have been ten times, till they are tired to go. Another American named Hardy ran an Indian off his farm, built a house on it ; then he sold it to Johnson, and Johnson took a little more land ; and Johnson sold it to Stone, and he took still more. They used to be well fixed, had plenty of stock and hundreds of horses. Now they are all penned up, and have had to pay such fines they have got poor. Whites take their horses and cattle and corral them and make them pay 25 cents, 50 cents to get them out. "Is that American law ?" they asked ; "and if it is law for Indians' horses, is it not same for white men's horses ?" But one Indian shut up some of the white men's horses that came on his land, and the constable came and took them all away and made the Indian pay money. The Americans so thick now they want all the Indians away ; so, to make them go, they keep accusing them of stealing.

This is a small tithe of what we were told. It was pitiful to see the hope die out of the Indians' faces as they laid grievance after grievance before us, and we were obliged to tell them we could do nothing, except to "tell the Government." On our way back to Santa Ysabel we were waylaid by several Indians, some of them very aged, each with the same story of having been driven off or being in imminent danger of being driven off his lands.

On the following day we had a long interview with one of the white settlers of Mesa Grande, and learned some particulars as to a combination into which the Mesa Grande whites had entered to protect themselves against cattle and horse thieves. The young Indian general was present at this interview. His boots were toeless; he wore an old gingham shirt and ragged waistcoat, but his bearing was full of dignity. According to the white man's story, this combination was not a vigilance committee at all. It was called "The Protective League of Mesa Grande," and had no special reference to Indians in any way. According to the Indian general's story it was a vigilance committee, and all the Indians knew very well that their lives were in danger from it. The white man protested against this, and reiterated his former statements. To our inquiry why, if the league were for the mutual protection of all cattle-owners in the region, the captains of the Indian villages were not invited to join it, he replied that he himself would have been in favor of that, but that to the average white settler in the region such a suggestion would be like a red rag to a bull; that he himself, however, was a warm friend to the Indians. "How long you been friend to Indians?" asked the boy-general, with quiet sarcasm. We afterwards learned by inquiry of one of the most influential citizens of a neighboring town, that this protective league was in fact nothing more or less than a vigilance committee, and that it meant short shrift to Indians; but being betrayed by one of its members it had come to an untimely end, to the great relief of all law-abiding people in the vicinity. He also added that the greater part of the cattle and horse stealing in the region was done by Mexicans and whites, not by Indians.

Whether it is possible for the Government to put these Mesa Grande Indians into a position to protect themselves, and have anything like a fair chance to make their living in their present situation, is a question; but that it ought to be done, if possible, is beyond question. It is grievous to think that this fine tract of land so long owned and occupied by these Indians, and in good faith intended by the Government to be set aside for their use, has thus passed into other hands. Even if the reservation tract, some three hundred acres, has been by fraudulent representations restored to the public domain, and now occupied by a man named Clelland, who has taken steps to patent it, the tract by proper investigation and action could probably be reclaimed for the Indians' use.

Exhibit I.

CAPITAN GRANDE.

Capitan Grande is the name of the cañon through which the San Diego River comes down from the Cuyumaca Mountains, where it takes its rise. The cañon is thirty-five miles from the city of San

Diego ; is fifteen miles long, and has narrow bottom lands along the river, in some places widening out into good meadows. It is in parts beautifully wooded and full of luxuriant growths of shrubs and vines and flowering plants. In 1853 a band of Dieguino Indians were, by the order of Lieutenant Magruder, moved from San Diego to this cañon (see Paper No. 1, appended hereto). These Indians have continued ever since to live there, although latterly they have been so much pressed upon by white settlers that their numbers have been reduced. A large reservation, showing on the record nineteen full sections, was set off here, in 1876, for these Indians. It is nearly all on the bare sides of the mountain walls of the cañon. As usual, the village site was not taken in by the lines. Therefore white settlers have come in and the Indians been driven away. We were informed that a petition was in circulation for the restoration to the public domain of a part of this reservation. We could not succeed in finding a copy of this petition ; but it goes without saying that any such petition means the taking away from the Indians the few remaining bits of good land in their possession. There are now only about sixty Indians left in this cañon. Sixteen years ago there were from one hundred and fifty to two hundred—a flourishing community with large herds of cattle and horses and good cultivated fields. It is not too late for the Government to reclaim the greater part of this cañon for its rightful owners' use. The appended affidavits, which we forwarded to Washington, will show the grounds on which we earnestly recommended such a course.

PAPER No. 1.

Copy of Colonel Magruder's order locating the Indians in Capitan Grande.

Mission San Diego, February 1st, 1853.

Permission is hereby given to Patricio and Leandro, alcalde and captain, to cultivate and live at the place called Capitan Grande, about four leagues to the south and east of Santa Ysabel, as it is with extreme difficulty that these Indians can gain a subsistence on the lands near the mission in consequence of the want of sufficient water for irrigation. It is understood that this spot, called, as above, Capitan Grande, is a part of the public domain. All persons are hereby warned against disturbing or interfering with the said Indians, or their people, in the occupation or cultivation of said lands. Any complaints in reference to said cultivation or to the right of occupancy must be laid before the commanding officer of this post, in the absence of the Indian agent for this part of the country.

(Signed by Colonel Magruder.)

PAPER No. 2.

Copy of affidavit of the captain of Capitan Grande Indians and one of his head men.

State of California, County of San Diego:

In the application of Daniel C. Isham, James Meade, Mary A. Taylor, and Charles Hensley.

Ignacio Curo and Marcellino, being duly sworn by me through an interpreter, and the words being interpreted to each and every one of them, each for himself deposes and says:

I am an Indian belonging to that portion of the Dieguino Indians under the captainship of Ignacio Curo, and residing in the rancheria of Capitan Grande, being also a part and portion of the Indian people known as Mission Indians; our said rancheria was located at Capitan Grande, where we all now reside in A. D. 1853, by an order issued by Colonel Magruder, of the United States Army, located at the post of San Diego on February 1st of said year, 1853. That since that time we and our families have resided on and possessed said lands. That said lands are included in township 14 south, range 2 east, of San Bernardino meridian in San Diego County, State of California.

That affiants are informed and believe that Daniel C. Isham, James Meade, Mary A. Taylor, and Charles Hensley have each of them filed in the land office of Los Angeles their application for pre-emption or homestead of lands included in the lands heretofore possessed by affiants, and now occupied by the rancheria of affiants as a home for themselves and families. That said affiants and their tribe have constantly occupied and partly cultivated the land so claimed by said Isham, Meade, Taylor, and Hensley since the year 1853. That they nor their tribe have ever signed any writing yielding possession or abandoning their rights to said lands; but that said parties heretofore mentioned are attempting by deceit, fraud, and violence to obtain said lands from affiants and the Government of the United States. Affiants therefore pray that the land officers of the United States Government will protect them in their right, and stay all proceedings on the part of said claimants until the matter is thoroughly investigated and the rights of the respective parties adjudicated.

IGNACIO CURO, his + mark.
MARCELLINO, his + mark.

Witness: M. A. LUCE.

PAPER No. 3.

Copy of affidavit of Anthony D. Ubach, in regard to Capitan Grande Indians, and in the matter of the application of Daniel Isham, James Meade, Mary A. Taylor, and Charles Hensley.

Anthony D. Ubach, being first duly sworn, on oath deposes and says: I am now, and have been continuously for the last seventeen years, Catholic pastor at San Diego, and have frequently made official visitations to the various Indian villages or rancherias in said county; that I have frequently during said time visited the Capitan Grande Rancheria, on the San Diego River, in said county of San Diego; that when I first visited said rancheria, some seventeen years ago, the Indians belonging to the rancheria cultivated the valley below the falls on the San Diego River and herded and kept their stock as far up as said falls; that I know the place now occupied and claimed by the above-named applicants, and each of them, and also the place occupied and claimed by Dr. D. W. Strong; that from the time I first visited said rancheria until the lands were occupied by the aforesaid white men said lands were occupied, cultivated, and used by the Indians of Capitan Grande Rancheria as a part of their rancheria; that upon one occasion I actéd as interpreter for Capitan Ignacio Curo in a negotiation between said Capitan Ignacio and D. W. Strong, and that said Strong at that time rented from said Ignacio a portion of the rancheria lands for bee pasture; I also know that Capt. A. P. Knowles and A. S. Grant also rented the lands from the Indians of the rancheria when they first located there.

Anthony D. Ubaoh.

San Diego, State of California.

Paper No. 4.

Copy of the deposition of J. S. Manasse in the matter of the Capitan Grande Indians and the application of Daniel Isham, James Meade, Mary A. Taylor, and Charles Hensley.

State of California, San Diego County:

J. S. Manasse, being first duly sworn, on oath deposes and says: I am now, and have been continuously since the year 1853, a resident of said county of San Diego; that I have known these certain premises on the San Diego River, said county, known as the Capitan Grande Rancheria, since the year 1856; that at that time and for many years thereafter the Indians belonging to said Capitan Grande Rancheria occupied and cultivated their fields as far up as the falls on the San Diego River; that the premises now occupied by the above-named applicants were so occupied and cultivated by the Indians belonging to said rancheria during the time aforesaid; I know that about one year ago Capt. A. P. Knowles paid rent to Ignacio Curo for a portion of the land now claimed by the above-named applicant, Charles Hensley; also that when I first knew of the rancheria and for many years thereafter the Indians of that rancheria owned and kept there a considerable number of cattle, horses, and sheep.

J. S. Manasse.

The lands above referred to as claimed by Dr. D. W. Strong were patented by him September 15th, 1882. They include all the lands formerly cultivated by the Indians and used for stock pasturage at the head of the cañon. When, at the expiration of his first year's lease of the tract for bee pasturage, the Indians asked if he wished to renew the lease he informed them that he should stay and file on the land. His lines are as follows: N. E. $\frac{1}{4}$ of N. E. $\frac{1}{4}$, S. $\frac{1}{2}$ of N. E. $\frac{1}{4}$, and N. W. $\frac{1}{4}$ of S. E. $\frac{1}{4}$, Sec. 2, T. 14 S., R. 2 E., S. B. M., Home. No. 969.

Charles Hensley's homestead entry is as follows: No. 986, March 29th, 1882. S. ½ of N. W. ¼ and W. ½ of S. W. ¼, Sec. 22, T. 14 S., R. 2 E., S. B. M. This is on the original site of the Indian village, and Hensley is living in Capitan Ignacio Curo's house, for which, after being informed that he had to leave it at any rate and might as well get a little money for it, Ignacio took a small sum of money.

James Meade's entry, which included Mary Taylor's interest, is as follows: No. 987, March 29th, 1882. N. ½ of N. W. ¼ and N. ½ of N. E. ¼, Sec. 22, T. 14 S., R. 2 E., S. B. M. Captain Knowles's lines we did not ascertain. He claims and in one way or another occupies several tracts in the cañon.

Exhibit J.

THE SEQUAN INDIANS.

The Sequan Indians are a small band of Dieguino Indians living in a rift of the hills on one side of the Sweetwater Cañon, about twenty miles from San Diego. There are less than fifty of them all told. They are badly off, having for the last ten years been more and more encroached on by white settlers, until now they can keep no cattle, and have little cultivable land left. There is a small reservation of one section set off for them, but the lines were never pointed out to them, and they said to us they did not know whether it were true that they had a reservation or not. They had heard also that there was an agent for the Indians, but they did not know whether that were true or not. As nearly as we could determine, this village is within the reservation lines; and if it is, some of the fields which have been recently taken away from the Indians by the whites must be also. They had the usual bundle of tattered "papers" to show, some of which were so old they were hardly legible. One of them was a certificate from a justice of the peace in San Diego, setting forth that this justice, by virtue of power in him vested by the California State law, did —

"permit hereby all these Indians to occupy peaceably and without disturbance all the certain land and premises heretofore occupied and held by these Indians aforesaid, including all their right and title to all other necessary privileges thereto belonging, mainly the water necessary for the irrigation of their lands."

These Indians are much dispirited and demoralized, and wretchedly poor. Probably the best thing for them would be, in case the Capitan Grande Cañon is cleared of whites and assured to the Indians, to remove there and join the Capitan Grande band.

Exhibit K.

THE CONEJOS.

The Conejos are of the Dieguino tribe. Their village is said to be partly on the Capitan Grande Reservation. One man familiar with the region told us that the reservation line ran through the centre of the Conejos village. The village is reached only by a nine-miles horse-back trail, and we did not visit it. The captain came to San Diego to see us, and we also learned many particulars of the village from an intelligent ranchwoman who has spent eleven summers in its vicinity. There are thirty-two men, twenty-six women, and twenty-two children in the band. They have good fields of wheat, and raise corn, squashes, and beans; yet there is not a plough in the village. The captain is very strenuous in his efforts to make all his Indians work. When strange Indians come to the village to visit, they also are set to work. No one is allowed to remain longer than three days without lending a hand at the village labor. They are a strong and robust band. They say they have always lived in their present place. The captain asked for ploughs, harnesses, and " all things to work with," also for some clothes for his very old men and women. He also begged to be " told all the things he ought to know ; " said no agent had ever visited them, and " no one ever told them anything."

In many of their perplexities they are in the habit of consulting Mrs. Gregory, and she often mounts her horse and rides nine miles to be present at one of their councils. Not long ago one of their number, a very young Indian, having stabbed a white man living near Julian, was arrested, put in jail, and in imminent danger of being lynched by the Julian mob. They were finally persuaded, however, to give him up to his tribe to be tried and punished by them. Mrs. Gregory was sent for to be present at the trial. The facts in the case were, that the Irishman had attempted to take the young Indian's wife by force. The husband interfering, the Irishman, who was drunk, fired at him, upon which the Indian drew his knife and stabbed the Irishman. Mrs. Gregory found the young Indian tied up in the snow, a circle of Indians sitting around him. Recounting the facts, the captain said to Mrs. Gregory, "Now, what do you think I ought to do?" "Would you think he deserved punishment if it were an Indian he had stabbed under the same circumstances?" asked Mrs. Gregory. "Certainly not," was the reply, "we should say he did just right." "I think so too," said Mrs. Gregory; "the Irishman deserved to be killed." But the captain said the white people would be angry with him if no punishment were inflicted on the young man; so they whipped him and banished him from the rancheria for one year. Mrs. Gregory said that during the eleven years that they had kept their cattle ranch in the neighborhood of this village, but one cow had ever been stolen by the Indians ; and in that instance the Indians themselves assisted in track-ing the thief, and punished him severely.

Exhibit L.

PALA AND ITS NEIGHBORHOOD.

In the days of the prosperity of the San Luis Rey Mission, Pala was one of its chief appanages. It lies an easy day's journey from San Luis Rey, in the valley of the San Luis Rey River. It has also a little stream of its own, the Pala Creek. It is a beautiful spot, sur-rounded by high hills, with wooded spars, and green bits of meadow here and there. The ruins of the old mission buildings are still stand-ing, and services are held several times a year in the dilapidated chapel. It has always been a favorite spot with the San Luis Rey Indians, some five or six hundred of whom are living in the region. The chief settlements are Pala, Pauma, Apeche, La Jolla, and Rincon. At Pala, La Jolla, and Rincon are reservations. Of the Pala Reservation some tracts have been restored to the public domain, to be patented to whites. The remainder of this reservation, so far as we could learn its location, contains very little good land, the greater part of it being in the wash of the creek. The Rincon Reservation is better, being at the head of the valley, directly on the river, walled in to the south by high moun-tains. It is, as its name signifies, in a corner. Here is a village of nearly two hundred Indians ; their fields are fenced, well irrigated, and under good cultivation in grains and vegetables. They have stock —cattle, horses, and sheep. As we drove into the village, an Indian boy was on hand with his hoe to instantly repair the break in the em-bankment of the ditches across which we were obliged to drive. These Indians have been reported to us as being antagonistic and troublesome, having refused to have a Government school established there. Upon inquiry of them we found that the latter fact was true. They said they wanted a title to their lands, and till they had that they did not wish to accept anything from the Government ; that the agent had promised it to them again and again, but that they had now lost faith in ever getting it. The captain said : "The commissioners come one day and tell us we own the lands and fields ; the next day comes some-body and measures, and then we are out of our houses and fields, and have to live like dogs." On the outskirts of this village is living a half-breed, Andrew Scott, who claims some of the Indians' fields and cuts off part of their water supply. He is reported as selling whiskey to them, and in this and other ways doing them great harm. It is not improbable that he would be found to be within the reservation lines.

Between the Rincon and Pala lies the Pauma village. It is on the Pauma Ranch, the purchase of which for Indian occupancy we have recommended to the Government. This ranch is now rented, and the Indians are much interfered with by the lessee, who is naturally reluctant to lose the profit off a single acre of the land. There is in the original grant of the Pauma Ranch the following clause : " They shall have free the arable lands now occupied by the Indians who are established thereon, as also the lands they may need for their small quantity of live stock."

The La Jolla region we were unable to visit. The Indian village is said to be outside the reservation lines. There is a claim against this tract, and the La Jolla captain told us that the parties representing it had said to him that they were coming in with sheep next year, and would drive all the Indians out. Upon inquiry at the surveyor-general's office in San Francisco in regard to the La Jolla tract, we learned that there is a record on file in the archives of that department purporting to show that there was a grant made in favor of the Indians of San Luis Rey, Pablo, and José Apis, for a tract of land named La Jolla, in the immediate vicinity of the Valle de San José, dated November 7th, 1845, signed by Pio Pico ; deposited in the archives January 31st, 1878. From Mr. Chauncey M. Hayes, a resident of San Luis Rey, the agent of the Pauma Ranch, we received the following letter on the subject of La Jolla :

"La Jolla was granted November 7th, 1845, by the Mexican Government to José and Pablo Apis Indians, Expediente No. 242, and is recorded in the surveyor-general's office, in book No. 4, p. 17. It was not presented to the land commissioner in 1858, and remained without any action being taken. Col. Cave J. Couts, now deceased, bought the interest of the grantees, and a contract was afterwards made between Judge E. D. Sawyer, of San Francisco, and himself to secure its approval by a special act of Congress. About three years ago an act was passed approving the grant for about 8,848 acres, reserving therefrom all lands then occupied. If this included Indians, there would not be much of La Jolla left."

It is evident that this is a claim which should be closely investigated. The probabilities are that it would not bear such investigation. In Pala some of the Indians had been ejected from their homes under circumstances of great cruelty and injustice ; affidavits setting forth the facts in their case were forwarded by us to Washington (see Paper No. 1, appended hereto). It is to be hoped that the Indians can be reinstated in their homes. If the Pauma Ranch be purchased for Indian occupancy, as we recommend, it will, with the present reservation tracts of the Rincon, Pala, and La Jolla, make a sizable block of land, where the Indians will be comparatively free from white intrusion, and where they will have a good chance to support themselves by agriculture and stock-raising.

PAPER NO. 1, APPENDED TO EXHIBIT L.

Affidavit of the claims of Arthur Golsh, Gaetano Golsh, and others, to a certain piece of land in township of Pala.

Patricio Soberano and Felipe Joqua, being duly sworn by me through an interpreter, and the words hereof being interpreted to each and every one of them, each for himself deposes and says: I am an Indian belonging to that portion of the San Luisenos Indians under the captainship of José Antonio Sal, and belonging in the rancheria of Pala. I have occupied the land in question ever since my childhood, together with Geromino Lugo and Luis Ardillo, our wives and families numbering in all twenty-nine persons. I have resided on the land in question continuously until December, 1882. About five years ago one Arthur Golsh rented of Luis Ardillo a portion of said land for three months at a rental of $5 per month. After this, said Golsh claimed the property of Ardillo and of the three other Indians; ordered them to leave; used threats; on one occasion aimed a pistol at Patricio Soberano. He then proceeded to file on the land, and obtained a patent for the land, while these Indians were still residing upon it. The said Indians had upon the said land four houses, one of which is adobe, various enclosed fields, and a long ditch for bringing irrigation water to the said lands. In spite of the threats of Arthur Golsh and others, we continued to occupy the lands until December, 1882, when we were informed by Agent S. S. Lawson that if we did not leave voluntarily we would be put off by the sheriff.

Said affiants therefore pray that said land be returned to the said Indians by the United States Government.

Signed by Patricio Soberano and Felipe Joqua in presence of the justice of the peace, in Pala.

EXHIBIT M.

THE PACHANGA INDIANS.

This little band of Indians is worthy of a special mention. They are San Luisenos, and formerly lived in the Temecula Valley, where they had good adobe houses and a large tract of land under cultivation. The ruins of these houses are still standing there, also their walled graveyard full of graves. There had been a settlement of Indians in this Temecula Valley from time immemorial, and at the time of the secularization of the missions many of the neophytes of San Luis Rey returned thither to their old home. At the time of the outbreak of the Aqua Caliente Indians, in 1851, these Temecula Indians refused to join in it and moved their families and stock to Los Angeles for protection. Pablo, their chief at that time, was a man of some education, could read and write, and possessed large herds of cattle and horses. This Temecula Valley was a part of the tract given to the San Luisenos and Dieguinos by the treaty of January 3d, 1853, referred to in the body of this report. (See page 460.) In 1873 a decree of ejectment against these Indians was obtained in the San Francisco courts without the Indians' knowledge. The San Diego Union of September 23d, 1875, says on the subject:

"For forty years these Indians have been recognized as the most thrifty and industrious Indians in all California. For more than twenty years past these Indians have been yearly told by the United States commissioners and agents, both special and general, as well as by their legal counsel, that they could remain on these lands. Now, without any previous knowledge by them of any proceedings in court, they are ordered to leave their lands and homes. The order of ejectment has been served on them by the sheriff of San Diego County. He is not only commanded to remove these Indians, but to take of their property whatever may be required to pay the costs incurred in the suit."

Comment on the extracts would be superfluous. There is not often so much of history condensed in the same number of newspaper paragraphs. A portion of these Temecula Indians, wishing to remain as near their old homes and the graves of their dead as possible, went over in the Pachanga cañon, only three miles distant. It was a barren, dry spot; but the Indians sunk a well, built new houses, and went to work again. In the spring of 1882, when we first visited the place, there was a considerable amount of land in wheat and barley, and a little fencing had been done. In July, 1882, the tract was set off by Executive order as a reservation for these Indians. In the following May we visited the valley again. Our first thought on entering it was, Would that all persons who still hold to the belief that Indians will not work could see this valley. It would be hardly an extreme statement to say that the valley was one continuous field of grain. At least four times the amount of the previous year had been planted. Corrals had been built, fruit orchards started; one man had even so far followed white men's example as to fence in his orchard a piece of the road which passed his place. The whole expression of the place had changed; so great a stimulus had there been to the Indians in even the slight additional sense of security given by the Executive order setting off their valley as a reservation. And, strangely enough, as if Nature herself had conspired at once to help and to avenge these Indians in the Temecula Valley from which they had been driven out, the white men's grain crops were thin, poor, hardly worth cutting; while the Indians' fields were waving high and green—altogether the best wheat and barley we had seen in the county. It is fortunate that this little nook of cultivable land was set aside as a reservation. Had it not been it would have been "filed on" before now by the whites in the region, who already look with envy and chagrin on the crops the Indian exiles have wrested from land nobody thought worth taking up.

A Government school has been opened here within the past year, and the scholars have made good progress. We found, however, much unpleasant feeling among the Indians in regard to the teacher of this school, owing to his having a few years before driven off four Indian families from their lands at Pala, and patented the lands to himself. There were also other rumors seriously affecting his moral character which led us to make the suggestion in regard to the employment of female teachers in these Indian schools. (See report recommendation.) As one of the Indians forcibly said, to set such men as this over schools was like setting the wolf to take care of the lambs.

These Pachanga Indians had, before the setting aside of their tract as a reservation, taken steps towards the securing of their cañon, and the dividing it among themselves under the provisions of the Indian Homestead Act., They were counselled to this and assisted in it by Richard Eagan, of San Juan Capistrano, well known as a good friend of the Indians. They have expressed themselves as deeply regretting that they were persuaded to abandon this plan and have the tract set off as a reservation. They were told that they could in this way get their individual titles just as securely and without cost. Finding that they have no individual titles, and cannot get them, they are greatly disappointed. It would seem wise to allow them as soon as possible to carry out their original intention. They are quite ready and fit for it.

Exhibit N.

THE DESERT INDIANS.

The Indians known as the Desert Indians are chiefly of the Cahuilla tribe, and are all under the control of an aged chief named Cabezon, who is said to have more power and influence than any Indian now living in California. These Indians' settlements are literally in the desert; some of them being in that depressed basin, many feet below sea-level, which all travellers over the Southern Pacific Railroad will recollect. There is in this desert one reservation, called Aqua Caliente, of about 60,000 acres. From the best information that we can get this is all barren desert land, with only one spring in it. These Desert Indians are wretchedly poor, and need help perhaps more than any others in Southern California. We were unable to visit these Indians porsonally, but were so fortunate as to induce Capt. J. G. Stanley, a former Indian agent for the Mission Indians and a warm friend of theirs, to go out in our stead and report to us on their condition. His report is herewith given: —

Mrs. H. H. Jackson:

MADAM,—In compliance with your request I proceeded to the Cabezon Valley, and have endeavored, as far as was possible with the limited time at my command, to ascertain the present condition and actual necessities of these Indians that still inhabit that portion of the Colorado Basin known as the Cabezon Valley, that being also the name of the head chief, who, from the best information that can be obtained, is not less than ninety and probably one hundred years old, and who still has great influence with all the Indians in that region. I found it impracticable to visit all the rancherias, and accordingly sent out runners and called a council of all the Indians of all the villages, to be held at a point on the railroad known as Walter's Station, that being the most central point. The next day there were present in council about one hundred Indians, including the captains of all the ran-cherias and the old chief Cabezon. Having been special agent under the old superintendent system, and well acquainted with the Indians, I was received by them with the greatest cordiality. I read and interpreted your letter to Cabezon, and also explained that you were not able to visit them in person on account of ill health. The Indians, through their spokesman or interpreter, then stated their cause of complaint. First, that Mr. Lawson had never visited their villages nor taken any interest in their welfare ; that he had allowed his interpreter, Juan Morengo, to take the advantage of them ; that Juan Morengo had made a contract for them with a man in San Bernardino to cut wood on land claimed by the Indians for the railroad company, he taking the lion's share on the profits, and agreeing to pay them every Saturday in money; that Juan Morengo took some $200 belonging to the Indians and appropriated it to his own use; that the contractor did not pay as agreed, but wished the Indians to take poor flour and other articles at a great price. There may be some exaggeration of the causes of complaint, but it is evident that no one has looked after the rights of these Indians. The Indians have stopped cutting the wood, and they say the contractor tells them he will send others to cut wood if they will not do it. If I understand rightly this is Government land, and no one has a right to cut the timber. It is true, it is mesquite timber, and they profess to cut only the dry trees, but the mesquite is invaluable to the Indians. It not only makes their fires, but its fruit supplies them with a large amount of subsistence. The mesquite bean is used green and dry, and at the present time is their principal article of food. Moreover, without the mesquite tree the valley would be an absolute desert. The wood (the dead trees) could be made a source of employment and profitable revenue to the Indians if cut with proper regulations, but the present mode is destruction to the timber, and benefits but few of the Indians. I have extended my remarks on this subject, as I think it very important. If the wood is to be cut the Indians should be supplied with wagons and harness that they may do all the work of delivering the wood and get the profit of their labor. I would suggest that it is very important that a tract of country be segregated and set apart for these Indians. There is a vast amount of desert land in their country, but there are spots in it that have been occupied by them for hundreds of years where wheat, corn, melons, and other farm products can be grown. There is very little running water, but water is so near the surface that it can be easily developed. The Indians appear to know nothing of any lands being set apart for them, but claim the whole territory they have always occupied. I think that to avoid complications something should be done for these Indians immediately to protect their interests. At present there are eight villages or rancherias, each with its own captain, but all recognizing old Cabezon as head chief. I ascertained from each captain the number belonging to his village, and I found the aggregate to be 560 souls. These Indians are not what are called Christianized Indians. They never belonged to the missions and have never been received into any church. They believe in spirits and witchcraft. While I was among them I was told by a white man that the Indians intended to kill one of their number because he had bewitched a man and made him sick. I asked the interpreter about it. He acknowledged it to be true, but said they only intended to frighten him so that he would let the man alone. I told him it would be wrong to kill the Indian, and he said they would not do it. They are very anxious to have schools established amongst them, and are willing to all live in one village if a suitable place can be selected. I shall offer as my opinion that immediate steps should be taken to set apart lands for these Indians, that they be permitted to cut wood for sale only on the public lands in Cabezon Valley, that no one be permitted to cut any green timber in the valley, that two strong wagons and harness for twelve horses be furnished (or loaned) to the Indians for the purpose of hauling wood only, that lumber be furnished to make sheds for said wagons and harness. The Indians have horses of their own.

All of which is respectfully submitted.

J. G. STANLEY.

EXHIBIT O.

THE SAN GORGONIO RESERVATION.

This is the only reservation of any size or value in Southern California. It lies in the San Gorgonio Pass, between the San Bernardino and San Jacinto Mountains. The Southern Pacific Railroad passes throughout it. It is a large tract, including a considerable proportion of three townships. It is in an exposed situation, open to the desert winds, and very hot in summer. A small white settlement, called Banning, lies in this district. Most of the titles to these settlements are said to have been acquired before the reservation was set off. We received from the settlers in Banning the following letter:

To Mrs. Jackson and Mr. Kinney, Commissioners, &c.:

At a public meeting of all the residents on the lands reserved for Indian purposes, held at Banning, in San Gorgonio Pass, San Bernardino County, California, it was resolved that a delegation from our inhabitants be appointed to proceed to San Bernardino, and lay before the commissioners a statement of the existing status of the lands reserved for Indian purposes as affecting the citizens resident on those townships known as 2 and 3 S., R. 1 E., and 2 S., R. 2 E., in San Bernardino meridian. Believing that it is of the utmost importance that you should become conversant with facts affecting the condition and future well-being of the Indians whom it is designed to place upon these lands, we respectfully request a hearing. Among those facts as affecting the residents directly, and more remotely the Indians, are the following:

There is in San Gorgonio Township, of which these lands are a part, a population of two hundred and fifty souls. In township 3 S., R. 1 E., is the village of Banning, which is the business centre of the surrounding country, and has an immediately surrounding population numbering fifty souls. It has post and express offices, railroad depot, district school, church organization, general merchandise store, the flume of the San Gorgonio Fluming Company, two magistrates; and during the last year there was sold or shipped from this place alone fully 20,000 bushels of wheat and barley, over 200 tons of baled hay, a large amount of honey, butter, eggs, poultry, live stock, &c., besides 200 cords of wood. Although more than half of the area of this township is in the mountains and uninhabited, from the remaining portion which is surveyed land, there is at this time fully 1,200 acres in grain, and the value of the improved property is over $50,000, exclusive of railroad property. Vested interests have been acquired to all the water available for irrigation under the code of laws existing in this State. Wells have repeatedly been dug without success in this township. United States patents to lands were granted in this township long anterior to the Executive order reserving the lands for Indian purposes, and since then the population has not increased. No Indian has, within the memory of man, resided in this township. There are not over two entire sections of land in the entire area left available for cultivation; and on these, without abundance of water, no one could possibly succeed in earning a livelihood. One of these sections was occupied and was abandoned, the attempt to raise a cereal crop having failed. The extreme aridity of the climate renders the successful growth of cereals problematical, even when summer fallowing is pursued, and the amount of human casualty possessed by the average Indian does not usually embrace the period of two years. To intersperse Indians between white settlers who own the railroad land or odd sections and the remaining portions of the Government sections, where a "no fence" law exists, as here, would not be conducive to the well-being of the Indians, and would result in a depreciation of our property alike needless and disastrous. In township 2 S., R. 2 E., there are not over eighty acres available, — that in Weaver Creek cañon, where the water was acquired and utilized before the Executive order and the legal right well established. In township 2 S., R. 1 E., settlements were made many years before the issue of the order of reservation, especially on odd-numbered sections or railroad lands as then supposed to be, and these bona-fide settlers have acquired claims in equity to their improvements. On one ranch in this township,—that of Messrs. Smith & Stewart, who have cultivated and improved the mesa or bench lands,—there was produced several thousand sacks of grain; but this involved such an outlay of capital and knowledge, beside experience in grain-growing such as Indians do not possess. In this township, embracing the three mentioned, there are upward of forty voters; and these unanimously and respectfully ask you to grant us a hearing, when we can reply to any interrogatories you may be pleased to make. If you will kindly name the time when to you convenient, the undersigned will at once wait upon you.

> W. K. DUNLAP,
> BEN. W. SMITH,
> S. Z. MILLARD,
> WELWOOD MURRAY,
> GEO. C. EGAN,
> D. A. SCOTT,
> G. SCOTT.

There is upon this San Gorgonio Reservation a considerable amount of tillable land. There are also on it several small but good water-rights. One of these springs, with the adjacent land, is occupied by an Indian village, called the Potrero, numbering about sixty souls,—an industrious little community, with a good amount of land fenced and under cultivation. These Indians are in great trouble on account of their stock, the approaches to their stock-ranges having been by degrees all fenced off by white settlers, leaving the Indians no place where they can run their cattle without risk of being corralled and kept till fines are paid for their release. All the other springs except this one are held by white settlers, who with one exception, we were informed, have all come on within the past five years. They claim, however, to have bought the rights of former settlers. One of the largest blocks of this reservation lies upon the San Bernardino Mountain, and is a fair stock-range. It is now used for this purpose by a man named Hyler. The next largest available block of land on the reservation is now under tillage by the dry system by the firm of Smith & Stewart. There is also a bee-ranch on the reservation, belonging to Herron & Wilson. One of the springs and the land adjacent are held by a man named Jost. He is on unsurveyed land, but claims that by private survey he has ascertained that he is on an odd-numbered section, and has made application to the railroad for the same. He requested us to submit to the Department his estimate of the value of his improvements. It is appended to this exhibit. It seems plain from the above facts, and from the letter of the Banning gentleman, that a considerable number of Indians could be advantageously placed on this reservation if the whites were removed. It would be necessary to acquire whatever titles there may be to tracts included in the reservation; also to develop the water by the construction of reservoirs, &c., probably to purchase some small water-rights. Estimating roughly, we would say by an expenditure of from $30,000 to $40,000 this reservation could be rounded out and put into readiness for Indians. It ought to be most emphatically stated and distinctly understood that without some such preparation as this in the matter of water-rights and channels the Indians cannot be put there. It is hardly possible for one unfamiliar with the Southern California country to fully understand how necessary this is. Without irrigation the greater portion of the land is worthless, and all arrangements for developing, economizing, and distributing water are costly. This is an objection to the San Gorgonio Reservation. There are two others. The Indians for the most part have an exceeding dislike to the region, and will never go there voluntarily, — perhaps only by force. The alternative of railroad sections with the sections of the reservations will surely lead to troubles in the future between the white settlers and the Indians. These are serious objections; but it is the only large block of land the Government has left available for the purpose of Indian occupancy.

PAPER No. 1, APPENDED TO EXHIBIT O.

Claim of C. F. Jost and wife for improvements in San Gorgonio Reservation, Banning, San Bernardino County.

Settled on section 25, township 2 S., R. 1 E., S. B. M., San Bernardino County, in May, 1875. Bought out other white settlers. Hold railroad permission to settle on land; of date, November, 1875.

IMPROVEMENTS.

House	$300.00
Barn	150.00
Milk-house	50.00
Meat-house	50.00
Granary	50.00
Potato-house and cellar	50.00
Chicken-house	20.00
Two board flumes	50.00
Two water-dams	20.00
Honey-house	10.00
Wire fencing	300.00
Other fencing	200.00
One hundred and seventy fruit trees (mostly bearing this year)	400.00
Breaking up sod land and draining land	200.00
Amount paid to first white settler for claim (no improvements)	250.00
	$2,100.00

On the 1st of June I will have $50 worth of seed-potatoes in the ground, and labor, $100. It is necessary to plough the ground three times to properly prepare it for-potatoes. This crop in December of the same year is worth $500 to $600 in the markets. Have about seventy stands of bees, worth, say $300, which if I am moved will be a dead loss.

Exhibit P.

THE PAUMA RANCH.

The Pauma Ranch lies on the San Luis Rey River, between the Rincon and Pala Reservations. It contains three leagues of land, largely upland and mesa, good for pasturage and dry farming. It can be irrigated by bringing water from the San Luis Rey River. There is some timber on it; also some bottom-lands along the river and along the Pauma Creek. The ranch is the property of Bishop Mora, who made to us the following proposition for its sale:

For the sum of $31,000 in gold coin of the United States of North America, I am disposed to sell to the Government of the United States, for the benefit of the Mission Indians, the ranch called "Pauma Ranch, in the County of San Diego," containing three leagues of land, more or less, reserving to myself and to my assignees, 1st, two acres of land whereon the present Indian chapel stands; 2d, 320 acres on one half-section on the south side of the public road leading to Pala, whereon the frame house stands formerly belonging to Joaquin Amat. Terms, cash on delivery of deed of sale. This offer is made with the proviso that the transaction is to be concluded on or before the 31st day of October of the present year.

FRANCIS MORA,
Bishop of Monterey and Los Angeles.

Santa Ynez, Santa Barbara County, May 14th, 1883.

Upon being informed by us that this condition of time of sale would make it impossible for us to secure these lands for the Indians, the Bishop, in the following note, waived that condition: —

San Luis Obispo, May 21st, 1883.

Mrs. William S. Jackson:

DEAR MRS. JACKSON, — Your favor of the 17th instant has been received. I feel heartily thankful for the interest you take in behalf of our Indians, and do with pleasure waive the condition as regards to the time, and will let the offer stand until the proposed bill has been voted on by Congress; provided, however, that the purchase can be brought to a close during spring or summer of the year 1884, and subject to one year's lease, which will conclude December 31st, 1884, because I must try, *pendente transactione*, to get enough to pay taxes.

Hoping you will reach home in good health,

Yours, affectionately,

FRANCIS MORA,
Bishop of Monterey and Los Angeles.

It should be distinctly understood that Bishop Mora in making this offer, and generously allowing it to stand open for so long a time, is influenced by a warm desire for the welfare of the Indians.

EXHIBIT Q.

PROPOSITION FOR THE SALE OF THE SANTA YSABEL RANCH TO THE UNITED STATES GOVERNMENT.

Los Angeles, Cal., May 19th, 1883.

Mrs. Helen Hunt Jackson and Abbot Kinney, Esq.,
Special Commissioners to the Mission Indians:

Should the U. S. Government wish to purchase the Santa Ysabel rancho, in San Diego County, California, containing 4 leagues of land, or about 18,000 acres, we will sell said rancho for the sum of ninety-five thousand dollars ($95,000), gold coin.

Respectfully,

HARTSHORNE & WILCOX,
By E. F. SPENCE, Agent.

EXHIBIT R.

AN ACT for the government and protection of Indians, passed by the California State legislature April 22d, 1850.

SECTION 1. Justices of the peace shall have jurisdiction in all cases of complaints by, for, or against Indians in their respective townships in this State.

SEC. 2. Persons and proprietors of lands on which Indians are residing shall permit such Indians peaceably to reside on such lands unmolested in the pursuit of their usual avocations for the maintenance of themselves and their families; provided the white person or proprietor in possession of such lands may apply to a justice of the peace in the township where the Indians reside to set off to such Indians a certain amount of land, and on such application the justice shall set off a sufficient amount of land for the necessary wants of such Indians, including the site of their village or residence if they so prefer it, and in no case shall such selection be made to the prejudice of such Indians; nor shall they be forced to abandon their homes or villages where they have resided for a number of years; and either party feeling themselves aggrieved can appeal to the county court from the decision of the justice, and then, when divided, a record shall be made of the lands so set off in the court so dividing them; and the Indians shall be permitted to remain thereon until otherwise provided for.

This act has never been repealed, nor, so far as we could learn, complied with in a single instance. To-day it would be held as of no value in the California courts.